David Stevenson, a senior lecturer in Scottish history at the University of Aberdeen, is a graduate of Trinity College, Dublin, and the University of Glasgow. His publications include *The Scottish Revolution, 1637-44: the Triumph of the Covenanters* (winner of a Scottish Arts Council Book Award), *Revolution and Counter-Revolution in Scotland, 1644-51*, and *Alasdair MacColla and the Highland problem in the Seventeenth Century*.

Scottish Covenanters
and
Irish Confederates

Scottish-Irish Relations in the
mid-seventeenth Century

David Stevenson

Ulster Historical
Foundation

First published 1981
by Ulster Historical Foundation
12 College Square East, Belfast, BT1 6DD
www.ancestryireland.com
www.booksireland.org.uk

Reprinted 2004

© David Stevenson, 1981

ISBN 1 903688 46 9

Cover design by CheahDesign
Printed by Lightning Source

To Wendy

Scottish Covenanters and Irish Confederates

CONTENTS

Contents

PREFACE

The object of this book is to investigate the relations between Scotland and Ireland in the period of the 'war of the three kingdoms', of the Scottish, Irish and English revolutions of the mid-seventeenth century. The importance of Anglo-Scottish and of Anglo-Irish relations in these years is well known, but with a few exceptions Scottish-Irish relations have been strangely neglected. Yet for several years the Scottish Army in Ireland was the most formidable opponent of the Irish confederates, and Irish forces in Scotland provided the covenanters with the most serious challenge to their power before Cromwell's invasion. The fates of the revolutions of the confederates and the covenanters were closely inter-mingled, and their relations were also of great importance on occasion to the course of the English revolution.

At the heart of the book lies an extended study of the Scottish army in Ireland, the first ever made since the army has usually been ignored by historians of England and Scotland and neglected by historians of Ireland. This is preceded by analysis of the relations of Scotland and Ireland during the Bishops' Wars. The army's military activities, its diplomatic significance and its political and financial problems are considered; a complete history of the wars in Ulster is not attempted beyond what is necessary to elucidate the actions of the army; similarly the relations of the Ulster Scots with the Scots army and with Scotland are discussed but other aspects of their experiences in these years have been ignored. The origins and achievements of the Irish forces in Scotland have been analysed, but no detailed description of their part in Montrose's campaigns has been provided as I have attempted to describe their campaigns in *Alasdair MacColla and the Highland Problem in the Seventeenth Century* (Edinburgh, 1980).

David Stevenson
Department of History
University of Aberdeen

ACKNOWLEDGEMENTS

This book could not have been published without generous financial assistance from four bodies: The Court of the University of Aberdeen; The Carnegie Trust for the Universities of Scotland; The Institute of Irish Studies, The Queen's University of Belfast; and the Trustees of the Esme Mitchell Fund. This help I most gratefully acknowledge.

The late Dr J. G. Simms of Trinity College, Dublin, encouraged and guided my first attempts at research into Scottish-Irish relations when I was an undergraduate. At a later stage Professor J. C. Beckett provided much useful criticism of my text. Mr Brian Trainor (as administrator of the Ulster Historical Foundation), Dr A. P. W. Malcomson and Miss Ruth Dickson have worked hard over a period of several years to make the publication of this book possible. They all have my sincere thanks.

My thanks also to the Trustees of the National Library of Scotland, for permission to publish a transcript of NLS MS Adv 33.4.8, pp. 7-8 (see Appendix Two), and to Mr Ronald Black of the NLS for letting me use his xerox copies of the unpublished parts of the Black Book of Clanranald.

The following have kindly given permission for the reproduction of photographs of which they hold the copyright:

The British Library Board (pp. 94, 250, 303)

The Historic Monuments and Buildings Branch of the Archaeological Survey, Department of the Environment for Northern Ireland (pp. 7, 113, 243, 314)

Trustees of the National Library of Scotland (p. 81)

National Portrait Gallery (London) (pp. 164, 292)

Scottish National Portrait Gallery (pp. 42, 59, 283, 213)

The Earl of Haddington (p. 190)

CONVENTIONS AND ABBREVIATIONS

Date: Old Style dates (as used in contemporary Britain) are used throughout, New Style dates as used on the Continent (ten days ahead of the Old Style) being adjusted where necessary. The New Year is taken to begin on 1 January (the contemporary Scottish usage) not 25 March (the contemporary English and Irish usage).

Quotations: All abbreviations are extended, but otherwise the original spelling and punctuation are retained.

Money: The £ sterling was worth £12 Scots in the seventeenth century. The 'merk' is the Scots merk worth 13s.4d. Scots.

Irish Provincial Boundaries: In the text the modern boundaries have been assumed, though in the mid-seventeenth century Cavan was occasionally still regarded as being in Connaught, not Ulster. Similarly Louth was sometimes regarded as part of Ulster, and Longford as part of Connaught, though both are in modern Leinster.

Abbreviations in References: The following abbreviations have been used:

A.P.S.	*The Acts of the Parliaments of Scotland*, ed. T. Thomson and C. Innes (12 vols. 1814-75). The new edition (1870-2) of volumes V and VI has been used.
Carte MSS	Carte MSS, vols. 1-29, Correspondence of the first duke of Ormond, Bodleian Library, Oxford
C.J.	*Journals of the House of Commons*
C.S.P.D.	*Calendar of State Papers, Domestic*
C.S.P.I.	*Calendar of State Papers, Ireland*
C.S.P.V.	*Calendar of State Papers and Manuscripts, relating to English Affairs, existing in the Archives and Collections of Venice*
D.N.B.	*Dictionary of National Biography*
H.M.C.	Historical Manuscripts Commission. References to H.M.C. publications are in the form of serial number followed by the report number or collection title, as recommended in *Government Publications, Sectional List, No. 17*
I.H.S.	*Irish Historical Studies*

I.M.C.	Irish Manuscripts Commission
L.J.	*Journals of the House of Lords*
New History	T. W. Moody, F. X. Martin and F. J. Byrne, eds. *A New History of Ireland, III: Early Modern Ireland, 1534-1691* (Oxford, 1976)
N.L.S.	National Library of Scotland
N.M.A.S.	National Museum of Antiquities of Scotland
N.S.	New Series
P.R.O.L.	Public Record Office, London
R.M.S.	*Registrum Magni Sigilli Regum Scotorum. Register of the Great Seal of Scotland*
R.P.C.S.	*Register of the Privy Council of Scotland*
S.B.R.S.	Scottish Burgh Record Society
S.H.R.	*Scottish Historical Review*
S.H.S.	Scottish History Society
S.R.O.	Scottish Record Office
S.R.S.	Scottish Record Society
T.S.A.I.	Transactions of the Scottish Army in Ireland, N.L.S. MS Adv. 33.4.8.
U.J.A.	*Ulster Journal of Archaeology*

CHAPTER ONE

Scotland and Ireland in the Early Seventeenth Century

---

i. The Ulster Scots

The shortness of the sea crossing between Ulster on the one hand and Argyll and the western Lowlands of Scotland on the other has always ensured close contacts between the inhabitants of Ireland and Scotland. At the beginning of the sixth century the Scots, who had come from Ireland and settled in Argyll, created a new kingdom there, Dalriada; later they were to give Scotland both her ruling dynasty and her name. Christianity partly came to Scotland from Ireland, through the work of Columba (who landed on Iona in 563) and others.

In later centuries close links were maintained between the Celtic peoples of Scotland, especially those of the West Highlands and Isles, and Ireland. From the late thirteenth century onwards organized bodies of Highland mercenary soldiers are found in Ireland, first in the north but later spreading to the rest of the country. These were the 'galloglaigh', or 'foreign fighting men', a name anglicised as 'galloglasses'. The services of the galloglasses in Ireland coincided with the Irish revival of the fourteenth century—in which the invasion from Scotland of Edward Bruce (brother of King Robert I of Scotland) in 1315-18 played a notable part. Many galloglasses settled in Ireland, military service becoming hereditary in their families. Thus though few large bodies of galloglasses arrived from Scotland after 1425, they retained their identity and continued to play a significant part in Irish wars for many generations.[1]

---

1. G. A. Hayes-McCoy, *Scots Mercenary Forces in Ireland, 1565-1603* (Dublin, 1937), pp. 6-8, 15-76; A. McKerral, 'West Highland Mercenaries in Ireland', *S.H.R.*, XXX (1951), 1-14.

MAP 1 IRELAND AND SCOTLAND

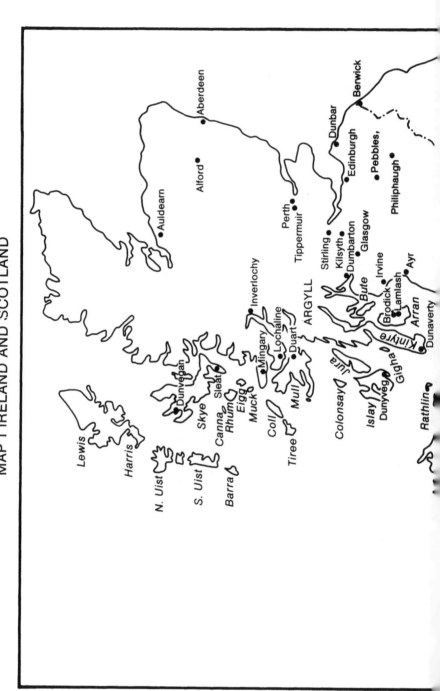

A second type of mercenary from Scotland became prominent in Ireland in the sixteenth century. These men, unlike the galloglasses, usually did not settle in Ireland, but returned to Scotland after a period of military service. They were often known as the 'redshanks', a name which was still widely used in the seventeenth century for Highland soldiers. The services of the redshanks in Ireland were connected on the one hand with unusually unsettled conditions in the Western Highlands, on the other with the opportunities for employment offered by Irish resistance to the Tudor conquest; their services came to an end with the final collapse of native Irish resistance in Ulster in 1603.[2]

Though the redshanks seldom settled in Ireland other Highlanders were doing so in the sixteenth century. In about 1399 a brother of the Lord of the Isles had married the heiress of the Glens of Antrim, which thus passed into the hands of the great Clan Donald. MacDonald settlement in Antrim was gradual at first, but was probably accelerated by the collapse of the Lordship of the Isles at the end of the fifteenth century.[3] The Clan Donald split into fragments and lost much of its territory in Scotland to the MacLeans, the MacLeods, and above all to the Campbells. Some branches of the clan, such as the MacDonalds of Keppoch, Glengarry, Sleat and Clanranald, survived; but the remnants of the Clan Ian Mor (or Clan Donald South) were in the end destroyed by the Scottish crown and the Campbells. Under their chief, the earl of Argyll, the Campbells seized Kintyre and Islay, the Clan Ian Mor's last major possessions in Scotland, in the first two decades of the seventeenth century; many MacDonalds fled to their kinsmen in Antrim.

The English and Irish governments of the later sixteenth century had at first been seriously worried by the flow of Catholic MacDonalds (or MacDonnells as they were usually known in Ireland) to Ulster. Rumours in 1568 that the earl of Argyll planned to invade Antrim raised fears that Ireland was to be drawn into a Scottish clan feud; but though plans were made to expel the MacDonnells nothing was done, and in

2. Hayes-McCoy, *Scots Mercenary Forces*, pp. 13-14, 77-341.
3. Ibid. pp. 9-14. See also C. Falls, *Elizabeth's Irish Wars* (London, 1950), pp. 76-85.

1586 their presence was finally accepted. Sorley Boy Mac-
Donnell received from Queen Elizabeth a grant of the lands
in north Antrim which his clansmen occupied.[4]

With the final collapse of the Clan Ian Mor Randal Mac-
Sorley MacDonnell (created earl of Antrim in 1620) assumed
leadership of the MacDonald cause. In 1635 the activities of
his son Randal, Viscount Dunluce, showed the continuing
interest of the MacDonnells of Antrim in their clan's former
lands in Scotland. The earl of Argyll had given Kintyre to one
of his younger sons, James (later created Lord Kintyre), and
Charles I had confirmed the grant on condition that Kintyre
should never be alienated to a MacDonald. In spite of this
Lord Kintyre arranged to transfer his lands to Lord Dunluce.
The Scottish privy council intervened and instead James
transferred Kintyre to his half brother, Archibald, Lord Lorne,
Argyll's heir.[5] Thus Dunluce's attempt to regain former clan
lands peacefully failed, but his ambitions in that direction had
been revealed; and on his father's death in 1636 he became
second earl of Antrim.

The position of the Campbells in resisting MacDonald
claims was weakened by the fact that the earl of Argyll had
left Scotland in 1617; he became a Catholic and eventually
settled in London, leaving the effective leadership of his clan
to his son, Lord Lorne. While his father still lived Lorne's
position was ambiguous, since any action he took might be
countermanded by his father. It was perhaps this weakness
which led the Campbells to allow the MacDonalds to retain
an outpost in the southern Hebrides. After the failure of the
MacDonald rising of 1614-15 Coll MacGillespie MacDonald
(nicknamed Coll Ciotach) had seized the island of Colonsay.
With Argyll an absentee and Lord Lorne at first a minor (he
was born in 1607) no attempt had been made to expel Coll,
and in 1633 Lord Lorne accepted his presence by giving him
a lease of Colonsay and Oronsay.[6] Coll was closely related to

4.   R. Dunlop, 'Sixteenth Century Schemes for the Plantation of Ulster',
S.H.R., XXII (1924-5), 55, 56-60, 115, 212; T. W. Moody, *The Londonderry
Plantation, 1609-41* (Belfast, 1939), pp. 53-6.
5.   A. Clarke, 'The Earl of Antrim and the First Bishops' War', *Irish Sword*, VI
(1963-4), 108.
6.   D. Stevenson, *The Scottish Revolution, 1637-44. The Triumph of the
Covenanters* (Newton Abbot, 1973), p. 296; J. de V. Loder, *Colonsay and Oronsay
in the Isles of Argyll* (Edinburgh, 1935), pp. 130-6, 219-20, 228, 229; G. Hill, *An
Historical Account of the Macdonnells of Antrim* (Belfast, 1873), p. 55.

the earl of Antrim, and also had other links with Ireland; his first wife is said to have been an O'Cahan.[7] Though when 'the troubles' began in Scotland in 1637 there had been no major conflict between the MacDonalds and the Campbells for twenty years, traditional enmities remained, and were to assume major importance.

A further link between Ireland and the MacDonalds (and many other clansmen of the Western Highlands) was provided by religion. After 1619 Irish Franciscan missionaries were active in the Western Isles and had a considerable amount of success, claiming thousands of converts—though, as a religious vacuum existed in many remoter Highland areas, in many instances these were not conversions from protestantism but rather the revival of Catholicism which had lapsed through lack of priests. Among the achievements of the missionaries was the reconciliation to Catholicism of many MacDonalds; most important among them were the entire population of Colonsay (Coll Ciotach himself already being a Catholic) and the captain (or chief) of Clanranald, whose zeal was such that in 1626 he begged Pope Urban VIII for help to enable him and other Highland chiefs to conquer Scotland for the true faith, a project to be undertaken in conjunction with a rising by native Irish chiefs.[8] The Franciscan missionaries established their headquarters in the old friary of Bonamargy, in north Antrim. By the 1630s hundreds were visiting Bonamargy each year to receive the sacraments, and a scheme for appointing a Catholic bishop of the Isles was discussed in Ireland and Rome.[9] This scheme had the support of the earl of Antrim, and it has been plausibly suggested that it was linked with his plans for reviving the power of the MacDonalds.[10] As Bonamargy Friary became the burial place of the family of the earls of Antrim in the 1620s[11] it seems likely that they were

7.   See R. Black, 'Colla Ciotach', *Transactions of the Gaelic Society of Inverness*, XLVIII (1972-4), 201-43.
8.   D. Mathew, *Scotland under Charles I* (London, 1955), p. 194; J. L. Campbell, 'The Letter sent by Iain Muideartach, Twelth Chief of Clanranald, to Pope Urban VIII, in 1626', *Innes Review*, IV (1953), 110-16.
9.   Mathew, *Scotland under Charles I*, pp. 193-6; C. Giblin, 'The Irish Mission to Scotland in the Seventeenth Century', *Franciscan College Annual* (Multyfarnham, 1952), pp. 7-21; C. Giblin, ed. *Irish Franciscan Mission to Scotland, 1619-1646* (Dublin, 1964), pp. x-xiii.
10.   Mathew, *Scotland under Charles I*, p. 196.
11.   Hill, *Macdonnells of Antrim*, p. 246.

Bonamargy Friary, County Antrim. Headquarters of the Irish Franciscan mission to Scotland and burial place of the earls of Antrim.

patrons of the Franciscan missionaries from the start.

It is a moot point whether one should call the MacDonnells of Antrim Scots or Irish. Irish governments tended to refer to them as Scots, while Scottish governments often called them (and other Highlanders) Irish. To the MacDonnells themselves the question was largely irrelevant; the political division that meant that MacDonnells were ruled from London through Dublin, MacDonalds from Edinburgh, was unfortunate and artificial. Wherever they lived, they had more in common with each other, and with the native Irish and Scots Highlanders with whom they shared a common Gaelic language and culture, than with those who ruled them. The Union of the Crowns of 1603 at least meant that Ireland and Scotland shared the same king. But though James VI and I confirmed the grant of lands in Antrim to the MacDonnells,[12] on the whole the union worked against their interests. Firstly, union enabled the Scottish and Irish governments to work together more closely than before in preventing breakers of the law in one country finding safe refuge in the other, and in breaking potentially dangerous links between the native Irish and Highlanders. The MacDonald rising in Islay and Kintyre in 1614-15 had close links with the plots of dissident Irish in Ulster, though a proposed Ulster rising failed to take place. It is, therefore, not surprising that English and Irish troops and ships were sent to help to subdue the MacDonalds.[13] Secondly, a serious threat to the MacDonnells arose in that union helped to open up Ulster to settlement by Lowland Scots and English protestants, who looked with suspicion on the Catholic Mac-Donnells, and greedily questioned their rights to their lands.[14]

The first Lowland Scots colonisation of Ulster was un-official, the work of Scots exploiting the fact that the accession of their king to the English and Irish thrones coincided with the end of Irish resistance in Ulster to English conquest. Hugh Montgomery of Braidstone, an Ayrshire laird, and James Hamilton, another Ayrshire man who had acted as James VI's agent in both Dublin and London, took advantage

12. M. Perceval-Maxwell, *The Scottish Migration to Ulster in the Reign of James I* (London, 1973), pp. 47-8.
13. W. R. Kermack, *The Scottish Highlands. A Short History* (Edinburgh, 1957), p. 85; Stevenson, *Alasdair MacColla*, pp. 38-9.
14. Perceval-Maxwell, *Scottish Migration*, pp. 60-5.

of the difficulties of a County Down landowner, Con O'Neill, to force him to grant them large areas of his estates in 1605. Soon they were leasing land to large numbers of Scots settlers, while other Scots sought and obtained grants of land in Down and (on a smaller scale) Antrim.[15] Thus 'within a generation a great part of both counties had been transformed, in population and way of life, into a sort of extension of the Scottish Lowlands.[16]

Large scale schemes to 'civilise' Ulster by bringing in English colonists had long been discussed,[17] but nothing could be done before the completion of conquest in 1603. Such plans were then revived, and an opportunity for implementing them occured in 1607; the earls of Tyrone and Tyrconnell fled abroad with many of their relatives. The earls, the former leaders of the resistance of the Ulster Irish to English rule, had grown increasingly frustrated at their treatment by the government, at what they saw as infringements of their rights, and it has been pointed out that Tyrone's main persecutor was George Montgomery, bishop of Derry, Raphoe and Clogher. He was the only Scot to hold an Irish bishopric at this time, and was a brother of Hugh Montgomery of Braidstone. George evidently shared his brother's ambitions for he had begun to encourage Lowland Scots settlements on his church estates even before the flight of the earls.[18]

After the earls had fled serious planning of a scheme for colonisation began. Sir Cahir O'Doherty's rebellion of 1608 added force to arguments that colonisation was the only way to bring peace to the area. It was agreed that Lowland Scots (though not Highlanders) should be encouraged to settle in Ulster along with Englishmen; they were already showing themselves successful planters in Antrim and Down, and the Scottish government had an interest in Ulster affairs in that any native Irish rising there caused fears in the western Lowlands and could stir up trouble in the Highlands. Scots troops were sent to help crush O'Doherty's rebellion, and in return

15. Ibid. pp. 49-67, 371; G. Hill, ed. *The Montgomery Manuscripts* (Belfast, 1869), pp. 21, 26-34.
16. J. C. Beckett, *The Making of Modern Ireland, 1603-1923* (London, 1966), p. 47.
17. Dunlop, op. cit. 116.
18. Perceval-Maxwell, *Scottish Migration*, pp. 68-74.

troops of the Irish army were kept ready to help Lord Ochiltree's expedition to the Western Isles.[19]

Six counties were eventually included in the 1610 plan for colonising Ulster—Tyrone, Fermanagh, Cavan, Armagh, Londonderry and Donegal. Partly through pressure from the king, partly from genuine interest, many leading Scots took part in the plantation. Nine of the chief undertakers were Scots. These included the king's cousin, the duke of Lennox, who had been involved in unsuccessful attempts to colonise Lewis after 1598, and Lord Ochiltree, who had acted as the king's agent in trying to establish order in the Western Isles;[20] interest in Highland affairs led naturally to involvement in Ulster. In the nine precincts in the six forfeited counties which were assigned to the Scottish chief undertakers, fifty Scots undertakers were granted lands.[21]

By no means all the Scots undertakers succeeded in their ventures in Ulster; some soon sold their lands, others never attracted many settlers. But on the whole the Scots colonists did better than the English, and the plantation might have failed without them; a survey of 1618-19 concluded that 'were it not that the Scottish colonists carried on arable farming in many places, the country would be liable to starvation'.[22] The explanation of the relative success of the Scots undertakers probably lies in the fact that, though they were often short of capital compared with their English counterparts, it was much easier to persuade Scots than English farmers and craftsmen to settle permanently in Ulster. Even in English precincts in some cases many of the settlers were Scots.[23] The reasons for this Scottish enthusiasm are not entirely clear; population growth and consequent land shortage in Scotland may have combined with the fact that the climate and farming conditions of Ulster were similar to those of many Lowland Scottish areas in persuading men to try their luck in Ulster. Moreover, at least for those from the western Lowlands, contact with their families and old homes could be maintained comparatively easily.

19. Ibid. pp. 77-80.
20. Ibid. pp. 12, 98-9, 323-30.
21. Ibid. pp. 101, 331-58.
22. Moody, *Londonderry Plantation*, p. 185.
23. K. S. Bottigheimer, *English Money and Irish Land. The Adventurers in the Cromwellian Settlement of Ireland* (Oxford, 1971), p. 23.

In 1625 there were at least 8,000 Scots in Ulster capable of bearing arms. By 1630 it has been estimated that there were 4-5,000 adult male Scots in Antrim and Down alone, representing well over 2,000 families, though this was more than the total number of Scots in the six counties of the official plantation.[24] Such figures suggest that if the total of 13,092 British (English and Scots) men in Ulster in 1633 aged between sixteen and sixty[25] is accurate, then well over half, perhaps two thirds, were Scots.

Most of this Scots migration to Ulster took place in the first two decades of the century; the 1620s and early 1630s saw little new Scots settlement. From about 1633 onwards immigration from Scotland may have risen sharply, perhaps as the result of bad harvests in Scotland,[26] but this presumably ceased soon after the start of the troubles in Scotland in 1637. How many Scots there then were in Ireland is impossible to estimate accurately. The figures given by the lord deputy of Ireland, Lord Wentworth, were gross exaggerations based on his growing fears of the Scots settlers rather than on their actual numbers. In August 1638 he accepted an estimate that there were over 40,000 Scots in Ulster able to bear arms. By January 1639 he was claiming that there were 60,000 Ulster Scots. In April and May he wrote wildly first of 150,000, then of 100,000 Scots. In fact a guess that there were about 10,000 adult male Scots in Ulster would have been much nearer the truth. Thus Scots settlement was substantial, but not massive.[27]

Like the MacDonnells, the Lowland Scots settlers maintained close links with their kinsmen in Scotland, and trade between Ulster and western Scottish ports thrived. Some English settlers also developed contacts with Scotland; at least two leading English planters, Sir Charles Coote and Hugh Clotworthy, sent their sons to Glasgow University.[28] This brings us to what had become one of the most important ties

24. Perceval-Maxwell, *Scottish Migration*, pp. 250-1, 311.
25. W. Knowler, ed. *The Earl of Strafford's Letters and Dispatches* (2 vols, London, 1739), I, 199. For the Ulster plantation as a whole, see *New History*, III, 196-205, 222-4.
26. Perceval-Maxwell, *Scottish Migration*, pp. 312-15.
27. Knowler, *Strafford's Letters*, II, 185, 195, 270; H.M.C. 23: *Cowper*, II, 230; M. Perceval-Maxwell, 'Strafford, the Ulster-Scots and the Covenanters', *I.H.S.* XVIII (1972-3), 549; *New History*, III, 175-7.
28. Mathew, *Scotland under Charles I*, p. 262.

between Scotland and Ulster; protestant religion. Both Coote and Clotworthy were men of puritan tendencies who believed that their children would get a sounder religious education in Scotland than in England. But royal control of the church of Scotland was growing steadily, bringing with it changes in church government, in worship and in theology. Many in Scotland were reluctant to accept the growing subordination of the presbyterian elements in the church to episcopalian ones. To such men the freer religious climate of Ulster seemed attractive. The discipline of the church of Ireland was weak, and as the main religious threat to the establishment in Ireland came from Catholicism, protestant settlement was at first encouraged without inquiring too closely into the exact religious views of the settlers. It is therefore likely that desire to escape from rather half-hearted persecution by the Scottish bishops helped persuade some Scots to migrate to Ulster. Once there, they found themselves free to worship in their own ways, and found ministers and even bishops to their own taste—and of their own nationality. In 1605-35 twelve Scotsmen held bishoprics in Ireland, seven of them in Ulster,[29] while the years 1603-25 saw at least sixty five (and probably many more) Scots ministers serving in the church of Ireland.[30]

Many of these ministers had no quarrel with royal religious policies in Scotland, but an important minority had. Several Ulster bishops favoured and granted benefices to Scots ministers who, because of their beliefs, could not get (or would not accept) parishes in Scotland. The most famous of such ministers were Robert Blair, who became minister of Bangor in 1627, and John Livingstone, minister of Killinchy in 1630. Both men, after settling in Ulster, made periodic forays into Scotland to preach and teach, retreating to safety before action could be taken against them. The complaints of the Scottish bishops at the freedom their enemies had in Ulster, and the realisation of the Irish authorities that non-conformity was growing fast in that province, led eventually to decisive action being taken. Blair, Livingstone and two other Scots ministers were deposed in 1632; a reprieve followed, but Blair

29. Perceval-Maxwell, *Scottish Migration*, pp. 255-67; J. M. Barkley, 'Some Scottish Bishops and Ministers in the Irish Church, 1605-35' in D. Shaw, ed. *Reformation and Revolution* (Edinburgh, 1967), p. 142.
30. Shaw, *Reformation and Revolution*,, pp. 142-56; Perceval-Maxwell, *Scottish Migration*, pp. 267-72, 363-5.

was again deposed in 1634, Livingstone in 1635, in spite of the support they received from several powerful Ulster Scots landlords. Other depositions followed, and a court of high commission was established in Dublin to deal with the problem of non-conformity—a problem primarily with the Scots in Antrim and Down.[31] By 1637 non-conformist ministers had nearly all been deposed, silenced, or driven out; Blair and Livingstone, after failing in an attempt to emigrate to New England with their supporters, returned to Scotland.[32]

The Scots bishops, as it turned out, would have been well advised to have put up with the irritation of their enemies having a base in Ulster, for stories of persecution of Scots settlers by bishops in Ireland contributed to the rising tension in Scotland caused by the king's religious innovations. And, in spite of the bishops, Scotland now became a refuge for those persecuted in Ulster, a reversal of the previous situation. Several persecuted ministers reached Scotland early in 1637, and some of their former parishioners came over either temporarily (to attend services) or permanently.[33] Blair and Livingstone were soon preaching widely throughout the Lowlands, and after the riots of July 1637 in Edinburgh against the imposition of a new prayer book they both took leading parts in organising the growing rebellion against the king.[34]

At the end of February 1638 the national covenant was drafted and signed as a bond of union among the king's opponents in Scotland. By this time effective control of the country was in the hands of the covenanters, and Charles I soon concluded that Scotland could only be reduced to obedience by force, by invasion from his other kingdoms to support the Scottish royalists. Both king and covenanters began to prepare for war. These events naturally had profound effects on Scottish-Irish relations. The Scots colonists in Ulster, originally seen as bulwarks of English authority in Ireland, now became regarded as the main threat to it.

Such an attitude was probably developing even before the

31. Perceval-Maxwell, 'Stafford', *I.H.S.* XVIII, 524-8; Stevenson, *Scottish Revolution*, pp. 24-5, 57; D. Stevenson, 'Conventicles in the Kirk, 1619-37: The Emergence of a Radical Party', *Records of the Scottish Church History Society*, XVIII (1972-4), 107-8.
32. Stevenson, op. cit. 108-11; Perceval-Maxwell, op. cit. 528.
33. J. Livingstone, 'Life', in W. K. Tweedie, ed. *Select Biographies* (2 vols, Wodrow Society, 1847), I, 157-8, 165.
34. Stevenson, op. cit. 111-12; Perceval-Maxwell, op. cit. 528-9.

troubles began in Scotland. Though the authority of the church of Ireland had been re-established in Ulster by early 1637, it is likely that the religious troubles in Antrim and Down had led the Dublin government to begin to rethink the policy of encouraging Scots settlement. Certainly the fact that presbyterian tendencies in Ulster were suppressed while Catholicism flourished with little official action being taken against it seems to indicate that presbyterianism was already seen as the most immediate threat to the *status quo*.[35]

The evidence of general anti-Scots sentiments (not confined to dislike of their religious tendencies) on the part of Lord Deputy Wentworth before the troubles began in July 1637 is strong. He supported and encouraged action against Scots non-conformists, though he had not initiated it,[36] and he consistently discouraged further Scots involvement in Ireland. In particular he resisted the marquis of Hamilton's attempts to gain property and influence in Ireland. Wentworth took for himself a monopoly of tobacco imports which Hamilton had sought, and he prevented a man whose patron was Hamilton from obtaining a lease of the alum farm.[37] He tried to dissuade Hamilton from seeking a grant of land in the projected plantation of Connaught, evidently being determined to exclude Scots from it.[38] And in May 1637 he showed himself hostile to the granting of Irish land to the earl of Mar.[39]

ii. The First Bishops' War, 1639

Not surprisingly, once resistance to the king in Scotland began, suspicion of the Scots grew fast in Ireland. In September 1637 Wentworth obstructed the attempts of the earl of Ancrum to obtain land in Ireland,[40] and in 1638 he strongly

35. A. Clarke, 'Ireland and the General Crisis', *Past and Present*, no. 48 (1970), 86, 94.
36. Perceval-Maxwell, op. cit. 525-6.
37. J. P. Cooper, 'The Fortune of Thomas Wentworth', *Economic History Review*, 2nd series, XI (1958-9), 236-40, 244; H. L. Rubinstein, *Captain Luckless. James, First Duke of Hamilton, 1606-1649* (Edinburgh and London, 1975), p. 125.
38. Knowler, *Strafford's Letters*, I, 472, II, 3-4, 195, 213. See A. Clarke, *The Old English in Ireland, 1625-42* (London, 1966), p. 107 and H. F. Kearney, *Strafford in Ireland, 1633-41. A Study in Absolutism* (Manchester, 1959), p. 101. For other attempts of Hamilton to gain Irish lands see below and *C.S.P.I. 1633-47*, pp. 152, 242, cited in Rubinstein, *Hamilton*, p. 46.
39. C. V. Wedgwood, *Thomas Wentworth, First Earl of Strafford, 1593-1641. A Revaluation* (London, 1961), pp. 248, 261n. 42.
40. Loc. cit.

opposed an offer by the marquis of Hamilton and other Scots to take over London's lands in County Londonderry. Wentworth denounced the scheme as likely to put all Ulster under Scots control, at a time when many of the Scots already there were showing their dislike of English laws, both civil and ecclesiastical.[41] In this he had the full support of William Laud, archbishop of Canterbury, who wrote to him denouncing the Scots and emphasising that it was 'no time to weed the English out of Londonderry to make room for more of that leaven'.[42] Ironically both Acrum and Hamilton were to prove supporters of the king in his struggle with the covenanters; Hamilton, indeed, was sent to Scotland as king's commissioner, Charles' personal representative, in mid-1638 to negotiate with the covenanters. By contrast Sir John Clotworthy, an English planter in Antrim, whose offer to take over the Londonderry lands Wentworth had preferred to Hamilton's,[43] was soon reported to be in Edinburgh 'to salute the Kirk', meeting (and evidently offering to supply intelligence to) leading covenanters.[44] English blood was no guarantee of loyalty.

Discouraging further settlement in Ireland prevented the threat posed to Wentworth by the Ulster Scots from increasing, but it did not reduce it. The success of the covenanters naturally raised the hopes of Scots settlers with presbyterian principles, and the persecution they had recently experienced inclined them to support the covenanting cause. The recently restored authority of the established church in Ulster collapsed as the Scots began again to defy the bishops, often crossing to Scotland to sign and swear the covenant,[45] while seditious pamphlets from Scotland were imported freely.[46] Scottish merchants when visiting Ulster boasted their support for the covenant and defied royal customs officials,[47] and the settlers stated confidently that events in Scotland would win them

41. Moody, *Londonderry Plantation*, pp. 394-5; T. Carte, *The Life of James Duke of Ormond* (3 vols, London, 1735-6), III, 19-20; Wedgwood, *Wentworth*, pp. 248, 249, 261; Perceval-Maxwell, op. cit. 530.
42. Kearney, *Strafford in Ireland*, p. 186; W. Laud, *Works*, ed. J. Bliss and W. Scott (7 vols, Oxford, 1847-60), VII, 439-40, 444.
43. Wedgwood, *Wentworth*, pp. 248-9.
44. Laud, *Works*, VII, 464; G. M. Paul, ed. *Diary of Sir Archibald Johnston of Wariston, 1632-1639* (S.H.S. 1911), p. 351, cited in Perceval-Maxwell, op. cit. 531.
45. Loc. cit.
46. Laud, *Works*, VII, 443-4.
47. Perceval-Maxwell, op. cit. 430, 531; Knowler, *Strafford's Letters*, II, 219.

liberty to set up their own church discipline.[48] In July it was rumoured in London that the covenanters had secretly sent to Ulster to prepare lists of Scots there able to bear arms;[49] whether this particular report was true or not, it was obvious that if armed conflict broke out between the king and the covenanters the Scots would appeal for the support of their compatriots in Ireland. Such a move by the covenanters would not be just an attempt to divert the king's attention from Scotland, for it was equally obvious that Ulster would be a good base from which to launch an invasion of Scotland—either of the western Lowlands or of the south west Highlands.

The problem of the Ulster Scots thus was no longer a problem for the Irish administration alone. In the circumstances it was decided that renewing religious persecution would probably exacerbate the situation. Laud pointed out that it would have been impossible to have kept Ulster quiet if earlier persecution had not driven out refractory Scottish ministers,[50] but (speaking for the king) he did not recommend immediate renewal of persecution when he wrote to Wentworth on 17 June 1638. Hamilton was in Scotland negotiating with the covenanters, and nothing was to be done which might make his task more difficult. If he persuaded the covenanters to submit, the Ulster Scots who had signed the covenant were to be left alone; only if he was forced to proclaim the covenanters traitors was Wentworth to act—'you must seize on their followers on that side'.[51] Wentworth accepted this policy, resolving that only if the covenanters proved stubborn would he send most of the Irish army to Ulster 'as well to amuse those upon that Side [in Scotland] as to continue their Countrymen amongst us in due Obediance'.[52]

The trouble with this policy was that it assumed that the covenanters would either submit, or be attacked by the king immediately. In the event the covenanters refused to submit but the king was not ready to invade Scotland. Consequently it was the king, not the covenanters, who was forced to make

48. Knowler, *Strafford's Letters*, II, 219.
49. Ibid. II, 185.
50. Laud, *Works*, VII, 464-5.
51. Ibid. VII, 444.
52. Knowler, *Strafford's Letters*, II, 192.

concessions, to try to restrain the covenanters until his military preparations were complete. This delighted the Ulster Scots; Bishop Henry Leslie of Down (himself a Scot) was told that a petition to the king was being circulated asking for similar concessions to be made in Ireland—'there is such insulting amongst them here, that they make me weary of my life'.[53] Clearly some action was necessary if control of Ulster was not to be lost through inaction on the part of the government, as Scotland had been lost. On 4 October Wentworth wrote that disobedience ought 'quickly and roundly to be corrected in the first Beginnings, lest dandled over long, the Humour grows more churlish and difficult to be directed and disposed to the Peace of Church and Commonwealth'; the names of non-conformists were to be collected and action taken against them.[54]

A month late (2 November) this policy received royal approval; the Ulster Scots were to be given no hope that concessions made in Scotland would be extended to them. They must, Laud told Wentworth on the king's orders, conform to the church of Ireland or 'return into Scotland, and leave honester Men to fill the Plantations'.[55] To help to reduce Ulster to obedience 500 men from the Irish army (which was about 3,000 strong) were sent to Ulster.[56] However, action against the Ulster Scots was hindered by the fact that the king had not yet broken completely with the covenanters. On 21 November a general assembly of the kirk met in Glasgow with Hamilton sitting in it as king's commissioner, and Wentworth was again instructed to do nothing which might provoke the covenanters.[57]

This restraint was soon removed; the general assembly refused to dissolve on Hamilton's orders in December, and proceeded to reform the kirk in defiance of the king, abolishing episcopacy and establishing presbyterian government. Wentworth was now free to implement his orders to force the Ulster Scots to conform or to return to Scotland.[58]

53. Ibid. II, 219, 227.
54. Ibid. II, 219-20.
55. Ibid. II, 231.
56. Perceval-Maxwell, op. cit. 534.
57. Perceval-Maxwell, op. cit. 535.
58. Loc. cit. argues that Wentworth was the originator of this policy, announcing it first in a letter of 5 January 1639. Laud's letter, quoted above, shows that the policy had its origins in orders from the king two months previously.

In January 1639 he ordered the trial of leading Scots non-conformists before the court of high commission, and a month later he began preparations to impose an oath on all Scots in Ireland whereby they would disassociate themselves from the treasonable activities of the covenanters. Taking such an oath might not change the loyalties of many Ulster Scots, but enforcing it would provide at least an outward show of obedience, those who refused it being severely punished or driven out of the country. Outside Ireland the oath would, it was hoped, demoralise the covenanters by depriving them of hope of support from Ireland; and the fact that the Ulster Scots seemingly denounced the covenant would discredit the covenanters abroad. To heighten the impression that the Ulster Scots genuinely supported the king, leading men among them were summoned to Dublin and forced to sign a petition requesting that an oath be imposed on them to enable them to demonstrate their loyalty. In response to this petition Wentworth then ordered the signing of what became known as the 'black oath' by the Scots. To exact obedience 1,500 soldiers were stationed in Ulster.[59]

Enforcement of the oath probably proved more difficult than Wentworth had anticipated. Many signed, but many others, especially in Antrim and Down but also in Tyrone and Londonderry, fled from their homes to avoid the oath. Large numbers crossed to Scotland, where many joined the covenanters' army. An English non-conformist who fled with them is said to have commanded a company composed of over 100 such refugees. When the Irish rebellion broke out two years later some covenanters noted with grim satisfaction that the religious people who had fled rather than take the black oath were safe in Scotland, whereas 'the bulk of the swearing and worldly people' who had submitted and remained in Ulster were killed, a true judgement of God.[60]

Resistance to the oath increased when news arrived that the king had signed a peace treaty with the covenanters on 18 June 1639, and after Wentworth left Ireland in September

59. The imposing of the oath is discussed fully in Perceval-Maxwell, op. cit. 536-40.
60. P. Adair, *A True Narrative of the rise and progress of the Presbyterian Church in Ireland*, ed. W. D. Killen (Belfast, 1866), pp. 50-1, 57, 59-60, 63; Livingstone, 'Life' in Tweedie, *Select Biographies*, I, 165; Perceval-Maxwell, op. cit. 542.

to advise the king in England imposition of the oath collapsed.[61] Far from showing the opposition of the Ulster Scots to the covenant, as had been intended, the oath had demonstrated and publicised the extend of support in Ulster for the covenanters, while the flight of men to Scotland had strengthened the covenanters' army. Instead of driving out a few fanatics the oath was seriously weakening the plantation, and orders had therefore to be issued in September 1639 forbidding any Scots to leave Ireland for Scotland without licence.[62]

The policy of giving Scots in Ireland the choice between conformity and flight had failed, and the black oath had increased hatred of Wentworth and distrust of the king among both the covenanters and the Ulster Scots. Far from being demoralised by the suppression of the Scots in Ulster, the covenanters were infuriated by it, and when in December 1640 the Scots commissioners in London were to publish charges against Wentworth they were to lay emphasis on his responsibility for the black oath.[63] Those who already suspected the king and Wentworth of Catholic sympathies could hardly avoid noting that the oath was imposed on protestant Ulster Scots but not on Catholics—not even Scots Catholics like the MacDonnells of Antrim[64]—and that while many protestants fled to Scotland to escape persecution, large numbers of Catholic Highlanders were flocking to Antrim since they could receive the sacraments there; over 700 were said to have come in 1639 alone.[65]

The arrival of a new wave of persecuted protestants from Ulster in 1639 helped to intensify support for the covenanters in Scotland, but some of the refugees soon posed problems for the covenanting kirk. Used to the free conditions of Ulster, and perhaps influenced by English puritans there, some of the refugees were reluctant to submit to the kirk's discipline in

61. Perceval-Maxwell, op. cit. 540-1.
62. Perceval-Maxwell, op. cit. 542-3.
63. Perceval-Maxwell, op. cit. 543; J. Spalding, *Memorialls of the Trubles*, ed. J. Stewart (2 vols, Spalding Club, 1850-1), I, 372.
64. Beckett, *The Making of Modern Ireland*, p. 75.
65. Giblin, 'Irish Mission to Scotland', *Franciscan College Annual*, p. 16. Wentworth had the previous year wisely rejected (with Laud's support) a suggestion by the queen, Henrietta Maria, that he should revive the great Catholic pilgrimage centre of St Patrick's Purgatory in County Donegal, on the grounds that this would offend Scots settlers in the area (Knowler, *Strafford's Letters*, II, 221, 257; Laud, *Works*, VII, 484-5, 511-12).

all things. In particular they sometimes refused to give up
the holding of conventicles or private prayer meetings, which
most of the kirk's ministers believed subversive to true
discipline, and they wished to abolish some traditional
practices in public worship. Their ideas had some support
within Scotland—conventicle-holding had evidently been quite
common in some areas before the troubles—but it was the
conduct of refugees from Ireland which brought disagreements on these matters into the open, especially the conduct
of Alexander Leckie of that Ilk. Leckie was a Stirlingshire
laird who had settled in Ulster. On his return to Scotland he
roused suspicion by holding private prayer meetings, but was
supported by other refugees like Robert Blair and John
Livingstone. For several years, in and after 1639, the kirk was
troubled by bitter disputes between the supporters of the so-
called 'Irish' innovations and the more conservative ministers
who denounced them for introducing corruptions into the
kirk.[66]

, While the kirk was absorbing the flood of refugees from
Ireland, the church of Ireland had to deal with a trickle of
clerical refugees moving in the opposite direction, victims of
persecution by the covenanters. One bishop and at least seven
ministers deposed in Scotland in 1638-40 fled directly to
Ireland or came later in search of employment.[67] They were
not always welcome. Bishop John Bramhall of Derry, a strong
supporter of the king, was bitterly opposed to giving Scots
bishops posts in Ireland; their failure in Scotland had proved
their incompetence, and anyway there were already too many
Scots clerics in Ireland.[68] From the opposite view-point
Archibald Adair, bishop of Killala, who had some sympathy
for the covenanters, denounced John Corbet (who had fled to
Ireland from his parish of Bonhill, Dunbartonshire) as 'an
impure corbie thrust out of God's ark' on being asked by
Wentworth to provide a living for him.[69] Corbet was found a
living elsewhere, and soon proved his worth by publishing two
works denouncing the covenanters which were to have

66. Stevenson, op. cit. 108, 113; D. Stevenson, 'The Radical Party in The Kirk,
1637-45', *Journal of Ecclesiastical History*, XXV (1974), 137, 143, 147, 148, 151.
67. H. Scott, ed. *Fasti Ecclesiae Scoticanae* (9 vols, Edinburgh, 1915-50), II, 407,
III, 163, 284, 331, 456, VI, 36-7, VII, 49, 355.
68. *C.S.P.I. 1633-47*, p. 221.
69. Loc. cit.; Scott, *Fasti*, III, 331.

considerable influence, *The Ungriding of the Scottish Armour* (Dublin, 1639), which was dedicated to Wentworth, and *The Epistle Congratulatorie of Lysimachus Nicanor* ([London ?], 1640).[70] Bishop Adair's refusal to help Corbet was turned to advantage by using it to provide a bishopric for John Maxwell, the deposed bishop of Ross, whom the king had asked Wentworth to provide with an Irish diocese; Adair was deposed and Maxwell put in his place.[71] Bishop Adair's deposition was probably connected with the fact that his nephew, Robert Adair of Kinhilt (in Wigtownshire), an Irish justice of the peace with an estate near Ballymena, had not only fled to Scotland and taken the covenant in 1638, but had acted as one of the covenanters' representatives in their negotiations with Hamilton. For this he was declared a traitor and his estate forfeited.[72]

As with the worldly settlers who had not fled to avoid the black oath, so it must have seemed to the covenanters that the Irish rebellion brought divine retribution on the episcopalian refugees in Ireland. Corbet was killed by the rebels, Bishop Maxwell beaten, stripped and left for dead by them, though he survived to continue his work as a leading anti-covenanter propagandist and to become archbishop of Tuam in 1645.[73]

It has been argued recently that not only did Wentworth's policies towards the Ulster Scots fail, but that he 'devised measures to meet a situation which did not exist'. In fearing a Scots rebellion in Ulster he was being unnecessarily alarmist; once part of his army was stationed there rebellion was almost impossible, since popular religious discontent lacked leadership. The most active non-conformist ministers had been driven out before the troubles began, and the landowners lacked the social and economic grievances which had led their counterparts in Scotland to revolt; and in any case they knew that they were dependent on English power to preserve their plantation against the native Irish.[74] There is much truth in this, though the supporters of the covenanters in Ulster did

70. Scott, *Fasti*, III, 331; Spalding, *Memorialls*, I, 372.
71. Knowler, *Strafford's Letters*, II, 369; Carte, *Ormond*, I, 95-7; R. Bagwell, *Ireland under the Stuarts* (3 vols, London, 1909), I, 233-4.
72. Bagwell, *Stuarts*, I, 238-9; Knowler, *Strafford's Letters*, II, 219. For Robert Adair's recovery of his Ulster lands see *C.S.P.I. 1633-47*, pp. 291-2 and J. Balfour, *Historical Works* (4 vols, London, 1825), III, 138-9.
73. Scott, *Fasti*, III, 331, VII, 355.
74. Perceval-Maxwell, op. cit. 543-50.

B

not see themselves as opposing English power in Ireland but government policies. However, the fact that the greater Ulster Scots landowners proved unwilling to defy Wentworth or resist the black oath hardly proved that the Ulster problem was not so serious as Wentworth thought, for leadership could come from outside Ulster as well as from within. Wentworth had to take seriously the possibility of an invasion of Ulster by the covenanters; if, in such an event, few Ulster landowners joined the invaders this would be little consolation if large numbers of lesser Scots settlers (especially in Antrim and Down) did so. This was a real danger. The covenanters threatened to send forces to Ireland, and the way in which royalist landowners in Scotland had found themselves powerless when their tenants took the covenant with enthusiasm demonstrated that securing the loyalty of landowners in Ulster was not enough. The black oath proved a failure, but it was an attempt to deal with a genuine threat—and indeed the very failure of the oath may be taken as an indication that the threat was greater than he had realised. In the event no invasion from Scotland took place, but Wentworth had good reason to think that the covenanters might be provoked into one, for Ireland was given a major part in the king's attempts to subdue Scotland.

The suggestion that Ireland should play a part in reducing the covenanters to obedience came first from the earl of Antrim, who hoped (by thus helping the king) to regain former MacDonald lands in the Highlands and Isles which had fallen into the hands of the Campbells. In June 1638 Archibald Mac-Donald of Sanda (an island off the Kintyre peninsula) received two letters, one addressed to himself, the other to be sent on to Coll Ciotach MacDonald, another of the most prominent surviving MacDonalds of the southern Hebrides. The letters were from the earl of Antrim's agent, Archibald Stewart of Ballintoy (a Scots Protestant settled in Antrim), and had been forwarded through his kinsman, Sir James Stewart, sheriff of Bute, an ardent royalist. MacDonald of Sanda was illiterate so sent for the local minister, Duncan Omey, to read his letter to him. In it Stewart of Ballintoy revealed that Antrim had spoken to the king, telling him that none of the MacDonalds had signed the covenant. Charles had then instructed Antrim to thank them for this, and to assure them that he would prevent Lord Lorne acting against them; 'when he comes next to court he will do no harm to you thereafter'. After the letter had been read Sanda told Omey that Antrim would bring an army of MacDonnells to Scotland as soon as war began there. All the MacDonalds would join them against the Campbells in seeking to recover 'their old patrimonie and what mair they might'. From this it appears that Antrim's plans, and his contacts with his kinsmen in Scotland, were well advanced by June 1638; and it was doubtless on his prompting that the marquis of Hamilton wrote to the king from Scotland (where he was negotiating with the covenanters on Charles' behalf) on the 15th of the same month proposing that use be made of the earl of Antrim. He was, Hamilton pointed out, beloved by many of his name in Scotland, had claims to lands in the Highlands, 'and uill no dout repare to Iyrland and bring shuch foors [forces] with him as uill put thoes countries in that disorder, and chiflie if the deputi [Wentworth] can spare ani of the armie ther to joyne with him, as I hoope that part of the countrie will dou us bot lytill hurtt'.[75] Antrim would thus command an invasion of the Western Highlands by part of the Irish army and his own MacDonald forces, which would prevent the covenanters from drawing forces from this area to the border to oppose invasion from England.

From a military point of view this plan was sound enough; but politically it was folly, damaging to the king's interests in both Scotland and Ireland. Any invasion led by Antrim would be bound to become primarily an attack on the Campbells, an attempt to regain Kintyre, Islay and other former MacDonald lands. But the Campbells as yet had played very little part in the covenanters' resistance to the king. Lord Lorne was known to sympathise with them, but he had not joined or aided them, and the fact that (though he was acting chief of the clan) his father, the earl of Argyll, lived on in London and supported the king greatly limited his freedom of action; if he joined the covenanters the king and his father might try to disinherit him, or his father might return to Scotland. But instead of trying to retain the admittedly dubious loyalty of the Campbells, the king drove them into rebellion by supporting the idea of an invasion of their lands by their hereditary

75. S.R.O., GD.14/19, Campbell of Stonefield Papers, pp. 135-7; S. R. Gardiner, ed. *The Hamilton Papers* (Camden Society, 1880), pp. 12-13.

enemies.[76] The covenanters had secret friends at court, and Charles' acceptance of the idea that Antrim should invade Scotland and be rewarded out of the lands of the Campbells[77] quickly became known in Scotland, while Duncan Omey's report to Lord Lorne on his meeting with MacDonald of Sanda provided more details of Antrim's plots. Lorne told Hamilton that he knew of Antrim's undertaking 'to come over upon his lands', and warned that 'if such oppression were offered' he would act to defend himself.[78] And it was not only Campbells who were turned against the king by news of the Antrim invasion plan; many other Scots were appalled that the king was ready to send an army of 'Irish' papists under a Catholic commander against good protestants.

For similar reasons the king's employment of Antrim endangered his regime in Ireland. It forced on the Dublin government 'the total reversal of that policy of absolute distrust [of the native Irish] which had never previously been questioned'.[79] The arming of the Catholic MacDonnells and their Irish allies horrified the king's own servants and supporters in Ireland, as well as the Ulster Scots. It was an action which might undermine the whole basis of English rule in Ireland.

The exact terms in which the king gave his backing to the plan for Antrim to invade Scotland are not clear. When Antrim wrote to Wentworth on 17 July 1638 he spoke only of defensive measures, relating that Hamilton had told him that Lorne (who possessed lands which had belonged to Antrim's predecessors) was raising men and arms as fast as he could to 'encounter' Antrim; 'This man is my Enemy, and what his Intentions are I do not know'. Therefore, for his own defence and the king's service, he had asked Charles to provide him with arms. Wentworth was requested to send arms to Coleraine for use in an emergency, since those stored at Carrickfergus would be too far away to be of use if the

76. Stevenson, *Scottish Revolution*, pp. 89, 99-100.
77. Wedgwood, *Wentworth*, p. 254.
78. R. Baillie, *Letters and Journals*, ed. D. Laing (3 vols, Bannatyne Club, 1841-2), I, 93. One of the covenanters' informants at court sent news to them of Hamilton's suggestion that Antrim should be made use of on 11 July, less than a month after Hamilton had first put forward the idea, D. Dalrymple, Lord Hailes, ed. *Memorials and Letters relating to the History of Britain in the Reign of Charles the First* (Glasgow, 1766), pp. 42-3.
79. Clarke, *Old English in Ireland*, p. 125.

Campbells invaded Antrim's estates.[80] Thus Antrim put the blame for reviving the Campbell-MacDonald feud on Lorne's shoulders, and tried to gain Wentworth's support by raising fears of a Scottish invasion. Lorne sent Wentworth a rather different version of events a few days later; some of the rebellious MacDonalds in Scotland 'who hes evir takine thair Adwantage of trowblesome Tymes to execute their Rebellionis' were in touch with many native Irish, both in Ireland and on the continent, especially the O'Neills and O'Donnells, and were plotting a general Irish rebellion if there was any 'sture' in the king's dominions. Lorne's source of information on this last point was Duncan Omey, who had told him that MacDonald of Sanda had said that the leaders of these two Irish families intended to land in Ireland with an army to regain their lands as soon as war broke out in Scotland.[81]

Wentworth needed no such warning of the untrustworthiness of the native Irish. He told the king that he was sure that the Irish council would never agree to send arms to Coleraine for Antrim—who, he pointed out, was a grandson of that great rebel the earl of Tyrone. Even if Antrim himself could be trusted, if arms were stored at Coleraine the Scots planters 'might chance to borrow those Weapons' and use them against the king. He agreed that the king needed more men in Ireland, but proposed that these should be provided by levying three or four thousand men to reinforce the existing standing army, not by indiscriminate arming of the Irish; as many as possible of the new soldiers should be men of English blood, for native Irish should not be given the opportunity to get military training. Ireland could help the king subdue the covenanters, not by providing a base for Antrim's invasion of Scotland, nor by sending men to join the king's forces in England, but by garrisoning most of the Irish standing army in Ulster. This would serve a double purpose; it would keep the Ulster Scots in order, and make the covenanters' fear that an invasion from Ireland was intended.[82]

In spite of Wentworth's advice the king continued to give support to Antrim's plans, which led Wentworth to try to change his mind by proposing a rival scheme; on 28 August

80. Knowler, *Strafford's Letters*, II, 184.
81. Ibid. II, 187; Carte, *Ormond*, III, 23, S.R.O., GD.14/19, pp. 135-7.
82. Knowler, *Strafford's Letters*, II, 187-8, 192.

1638 he recommended that the island of Arran (which belonged to Hamilton) and the castle of Dumbarton should be seized as bases for a blockade of Scottish west coast ports. Wentworth did not at this time specifically suggest using them as bases for an invasion from Ireland, but this was probably already his intention, for they were soon to have a central place in his invasion plans. Hopefully looking to the future, Wentworth recommended that once Scotland was conquered she should be ruled, like Ireland, by an English lord deputy, thus becoming a kingdom subordinate to England.[83] He continued to hope that Antrim's plans would be dropped, thus freeing Ireland of the dangers either of a Catholic rising or a Campbell invasion. In replying to Lorne's letter Wentworth went out of his way to emphasise his lack of sympathy for the Clan Donald—'I have Reason to believe them desperate and barbarous enough'. MacDonnells guilty of murder and rape had fled to Scotland and Lorne was asked to help to bring them to justice.[84] Fears that Lorne was going to invade Ulster were spreading rapidly, and were given plausibility by reports that he was building flat bottomed boats and making military preparations, but Wentworth refused to believe that he was planning offensive action; all Lorne was doing was preparing to defend himself, and this was Antrim's fault for indiscreetly boasting of his intention of attacking the Campbells.[85]

Wentworth's hopes of avoiding driving Lord Lorne into the hands of the covenanters failed. In October 1638 the old earl

83. Ibid. II, 235; Wedgwood, *Wentworth*, p. 251; Stevenson, *Scottish Revolution*, p. 100.
84. Knowler, *Strafford's Letters*, II, 210. For Lorne's reply see ibid. II, 220-1.
85. Ibid. II, 225-6; Carte, *Ormond*, III, 24. Bagwell, *Stuarts*, I, 238, states that an agent of Wentworth's who talked with leading covenanters at the end of 1638 reported that Alexander Leslie (soon to be the covenanters' commander in chief) said that in case of war the Scots would invade Ireland. In fact the agent, Ensign William Willoughby of the Irish army (son of Sir Francis Willoughby) merely reported that Leslie said that if the king attacked Scotland he would find 'enough to do in both his Kingdoms, especially in Ireland, o'er long' (Knowler, *Strafford's Letters*, II, 274)—which sounds more like a warning that the Ulster Scots would cause trouble than a threat of invasion. In any case the value of Willoughby's intelligence is doubtful; he claimed that he passed himself off as a Dutchman so that the covenanters would speak freely to him, but it is clear from his own report that the covenanters were well aware of his identity—not surprisingly as his sister, Antonia (with whom he stayed) was the wife of a Fife laird, Sir James Scott of Rossie. Thus the covenanters knew that whatever they told Willoughby would be passed on to Wentworth (ibid. II, 271, 274; H.M.C. 23: *Cowper*, II, 220-1; *R.M.S. 1634-51*, nos. 927, 1934.

of Argyll died;[86] Lorne, now eighth earl of Argyll, was at last freed from any restraints imposed by his father's hostility, and in December he openly declared his support for the covenanting cause. Though he did not actually sign the covenant for several months more he quickly became accepted as the leader of the movement, for the strength of his clan made him the most powerful noble in Scotland. He stepped up his military preparations; by March 1639 he had bought a fully armed frigate from Holland as well as other arms,[87] and it was said that he planned to expel all MacDonalds from Scotland.[88]

Antrim's plans, and the support of the king gave them, may have helped to drive the new earl of Argyll into rebellion (as Wentworth complained);[89] but once Argyll was in rebellion Antrim's plan became even more important for the king. A diversion in the Western Highlands would prevent Argyll supplying troops to the main covenanting army in the south. Yet Antrim's army never materialised, no invasion of Argyll's lands took place. Why? It has usually been argued that the scheme collapsed primarily because Antrim was utterly incompetent, his plans impractical.[90] While there is doubtless an element of truth in this, a more convincing explanation is that Antrim failed mainly because his plans required the full co-operation of the Irish administration, and in spite of the king's orders Wentworth systematically obstructed Antrim, and ridiculed and misrepresented his activities to the king.

The reasons for Wentworth's action were varied. Undoubtedly the most important was simple distrust of the Catholic Irish and MacDonnells, and reluctance to arm them; and in this, from the point of view of long term English interests in Ireland rather than the king's immediate needs, he was justified. But it seems clear that personal considerations and jealousies were also involved. Wentworth was hurt and indignant that when the king needed help from Ireland he had gone behind the back of the lord deputy to appeal to Antrim.

86. The exact date of his death is not known, but news of it had reached the new earl in Dunbartonshire before 4 October 1638, S.R.O. GD.112/39/744(a), Breadalbane Muniments.
87. Stevenson, *Scottish Revolution*, p. 128. Many papers relating to Argyll's military preparations are to be found in Inveraray Castle, Argyll MSS, Box V, 39.
88. Knowler, *Strafford's Letters*, II, 266.
89. Ibid. II, 325.
90. See A. Clarke, 'Antrim and the First Bishops' War, *Irish Sword*, VI (1963-4), 108-15.

Why should he provide Antrim with arms, men (from the standing army) and money, when instead he himself could use these resources to help the king more effectively (as he believed) and get credit for himself for doing so? A further reason for his distrusting Antrim probably lay in Antrim's association with Hamilton. Wentworth had tried on several occasions to prevent Hamilton gaining an interest in Irish affairs, and now he was again interfering in Ireland by sponsoring Antrim's plans; and in September 1638 Laud informed Wentworth that Antrim and Hamilton were 'grown into some nearness, and have had some treaties about Londonderry, but the conditions I know not'.[91] If Hamilton and Antrim played leading parts in bringing the king victory in Scotland, royal gratitude might bring them large estates in Londonderry, and Wentworth wanted neither Antrim's Scots-Irish Catholics nor Hamilton's Lowland Scots protestants in Ireland.

Judgement on the effectiveness of Antrim's preparations to carry out his promises is made difficult by the fact that almost all the information available about them is contained in Wentworth's hostile letters. Thus in March 1639 Wentworth listed the assistance Antrim had asked for, and his reasons for not giving it. The friends Antrim wished arms given to were 'as many Oe's and Macs as would startle a whole Council-Board on this side [in Ireland] to hear of'. He could not agree to the recruiting of a great many Irish, commanded by the heirs of former rebels, until his own army was well enough armed to defend Ireland against them. For Antrim to raise a Catholic army in Ulster might provoke the Ulster Scots (at least 80,000 strong!) into arming to defend themselves. Not all the land Antrim claimed in Scotland belonged to Argyll; some of the owners might be loyal subjects of the king. If Antrim's invasion failed Argyll might pursue him back to Ireland, where he would be supported by the Ulster Scots.[92]

By April 1639 Charles's plans for subduing Scotland were collapsing in confusion as the forces he hoped for failed to appear. Antrim was first instructed to invade Scotland that year; then ordered instead simply to make a pretence of being about to invade, so Argyll's forces would stay in the Highlands to oppose him; then Wentworth was told to commission

91. Laud, *Works*, VII, 484; *New History*, III, 266.
92. Knowler, *Strafford's Letters*, II, 300-6.

Antrim actually to carry out the invasion. In May, according to Wentworth, Antrim tried to take advantage of this confusion of orders to evade his responsibilities, and was finally driven to admit that he was incapable of invading Scotland; he had only agreed to do so to gain royal favour, and had counted on a settlement being reached before his bluff was called.[93] Antrim's conduct, Wentworth concluded with satisfaction, had freed the king of any obligations to him, though he had been ordered to continue building boats in the north so the covenanters would still fear Irish invasion; half the Irish standing army was sent north for the same purpose.[94]

There is some truth in Wentworth's account of his dealings with Antrim. Antrim probably did find it harder to raise an army than he had thought; but as the king was finding out exactly the same thing in England at the time, Antrim's difficulties do not necessarily indicate the gross incompetence Wentworth attributed to him. Wentworth's refusal to give him the help he expected put him in an impossible position, for (though the terms of his agreement with the king are unknown) in making promises to invade Scotland it seems certain that Antrim had been counting on official aid. Wentworth jusitified his obstructive conduct by arguing that the only advantage to the king of a scheme like Antrim's was that it might save the state expense; as soon as Antrim asked for state help his scheme became pointless.[95] It is true that the king may well have hoped that harnessing Antrim's clan feud with the Campbells would prove a cheap way of invading Scotland, but this was far from the only advantage to Charles of supporting Antrim. The main point of accepting his assistance was that it was hoped that many men in Ulster, MacDonnells and native Irish, would serve under him with enthusiasm, and that he would also get, as the champion of the MacDonalds, widespread support from the Highland enemies of the Campbells. Elsewhere Wentworth showed that he was well aware of this agrument in favour of Antrim, for he felt it necessary to stress that he had been told that Antrim's party in Scotland was not nearly so strong as Antrim had claimed—and that in any case the southern Hebrides were not

93. Ibid. II, 323, 334-6, 419-20; Clarke, op. cit. 113-14.
94. Knowler, *Strafford's Letters*, II, 323, 419-20.
95. Ibid. II, 296-7; Clarke, op. cit. 111-12.

worth conquering![96] In his prejudice against Antrim and Highlanders Wentworth closed his eyes to the strategic importance of the Isles; and anyway Antrim was not intending to land in the Isles but on the mainland, in Kintyre.

The evidence of the support that Antrim might have found had he landed is fragmentary, but it does suggest that his hopes of substantial support were more than figments of his imagination. In his letter of 15 June 1638 which had suggested employing Antrim, Hamilton had also announced that he was sending George Mackenzie, earl of Seaforth, home to the north west to try to gain support for the king, though Hamilton admitted that the Highlanders would not act out of any great affection for the king but 'becaus of ther splen to Lorne'; they would do the opposite to what the Campbells did. On 24 August Sir Donald MacDonald of Sleat (usually known as Donald Gorm) reported to Hamilton on his efforts to organise a royalist party in the Highlands. He had received two letters from Antrim, and had met with the captain of Clanranald, MacDonald of Glengarry and 'our haill name of Claine Donald'. They had sworn 'to doe and live with me in the Kingis service'.[97] If Antrim had landed and the MacDonalds had risen against the Campbells there is little doubt that other clans would have joined them, facing the covenanters with a major revolt in the western Highlands. But all depended on Antrim's help, and this failed to appear. In April he complained that his friends in Scotland, including Seaforth and Donald Gorm, had sent asking for the help they had been promised, warning that if it was not sent the Campbells would crush them. Archibald MacDonald of Sanda and his son were taken prisoner by Argyll's men; so were two of Antrim's agents who landed in Kintyre. It is notable that in this letter Antrim seems to assume that the delay in invading Scotland is Wentworth's fault, not his own.[98] In May, after the plan for an invasion of Scotland in 1639 had been abandoned, Antrim sent Archibald Stewart of Ballintoy to Donald Gorm, evidently to persuade him to come to Ireland on his way to meet the king in England; hardly surprisingly Antrim refused

96. Knowler, *Strafford's Lettters*, II, 357; H.M.C. 23: *Cowper*, II, 162, 233.
97. Stevenson, *Scottish Revolution*, p. 99; Gardiner, *Hamilton Papers*, p. 11; H.M.C. 21: *Hamilton*, II, 50.
98. Knowler, *Strafford's Letters*, II, 321; S.R.O. GD.112/39/57.

to explain the reason for this to Wentworth (since that would invite further obstruction).[99] Presumably Donald Gorm was sent to persuade the king to continue to support the MacDonald cause, and perhaps to get him to order Wentworth not to treat them with such hostility. About 300 MacDonald refugees (100 of whom Antrim described as gentlemen) arrived in Ireland at about the same time as Donald Gorm, driven out of Islay and Kintyre as Argyll tightened his grip. Antrim suggested that as they were suffering through their loyalty to the king they might be supported on the lands of friends of the covenanters in Ulster; Wentworth replied that, since it was Antrim's failure to send help to them in Scotland that had forced them to flee, he should support them himself.[100]

Though neither Antrim's plans to invade the Highlands nor Wentworth's to seize Arran and Dumbarton were put into effect, news of them did succeed to some extent in diverting the covenanters' attention from the main attacks planned by the king—the landing of 5,000 men at Aberdeen under Hamilton and an invasion across the Border led by the king. In late March 1639, when the covenanters' seized the remaining royalist strongholds in Scotland, Argyll was put in charge of action to prevent invasion from Ireland. He raised eight or nine hundred men, stationing five hundred in Kintyre and sending the rest further north 'to hold the islanders and these tod's-birds of Lochaber in some awe'. Argyll himself led a landing on Arran and captured Brodick Castle. The inhabitants were forced to swear to uphold the covenant and to send men to the Border and Kintyre when ordered to do so. Dumbarton Castle was also seized and a garrison of forty men under MacAulay of Ardincaple placed in it, with Argyll as governor.[101] In May, on further rumours of a pending invasion from Ireland, more men were raised in the Highlands. When the covenanters' army assembled on the Borders, Argyll remained behind to guard against rebellion or invasion.[102] News

99. Knowler, *Strafford's Letters*, II, 340, 357, 389; H.M.C. 23: *Cowper*, II, 162; Carte, *Ormond*, I, 92.
100. Knowler, *Strafford's Letters*, II, 340, 354.
101. Stevenson, *Scottish Revolution*, pp. 140-1; Baillie, *Letters*, I, 195-6; J. R. N. Macphail, ed. *Papers from the collection of Sir William Fraser* (S.H.S. 1924), pp. 237-8; S.R.O. GD.112/39/758; J. Gordon, *History of Scots Affairs* (3 vols, Spalding Club, 1841), II, 204-5.
102. Gordon, *History of Scots Affairs*, II, 252; C.S.P.D. *1639*, p. 226; S.R.O.

that the Irish army was gathering in Ulster and that Antrim was busy building boats 'put the people in the west shore in a continuall fray, and made them have little will to let any more men or armes be carried East to the Generall's campe'[103] — exactly the reaction which the king had hoped these moves would bring.

In fact, though the covenanters did not know it, all immediate danger from Ireland had passed. Antrim's scheme had been abandoned for the present, and since the beginning of April Wentworth had been urging the king to delay and attack on the Scots until 1640; military preparations in England were so backward that success could not be guaranteed in 1639.[104] Wentworth sent 500 men of the Irish army under Sir Francis Willoughby to garrison Carlisle, and is said to have sent the king £38,000 sterling;[105] and the earl of Barrymore was commissioned to raise 1,000 men in Ireland to be brought to England for use against the Scots.[106] But such limited aid from Ireland made little difference to the balance of poweron the Border. As has been seen, moving most of the Irish army north to Ulster on the king's orders to 'amuse' the covenanters and to land at Irvine, Ayr and the mouth of the Clyde if necessary[107] was effective in alarming the covenanters, but so far as Wentworth was concerned the army was needed in Ulster for defence, and could not be spared for offensive action.

The discovery in May of a plot (in which John Trueman, an English non-conformist minister, was involved) to betray Carrickfergus to the covenanters[108] emphasised the danger of the situation in the north, while the extent of opposition to the black oath made shipping the army to Scotland unthinkable. Charles urged Wentworth at least to send ships against

GD.112/41/1. Bundle of state papers c.1545-1639, letter of 15 May 1639; Perceval-Maxwell, 'Strafford', *I.H.S.* XVIII, 541.
103. Baillie, *Letters*, I, 206.
104. Wedgwood, *Wentworth*, pp. 257-8; Knowler, *Strafford's Letters*, II, 312-13.
105. Carte, *Ormond*, I, 89; *C.S.P.D. 1639*, pp. 12, 15, 37, 388; Bagwell, *Stuarts*, I, 288-9.
106. *C.S.P.D. 1638-9*, pp. 545-6.
107. Knowler, *Strafford's Letters*, II, 319, 323; Carte, *Ormond*, I, 89-90. The men sent north were not told that they might be sent to Scotland; an undated note concerning 500 men being sent to the north of Ireland has a marginal note 'They know no otherwise'. A postscript refers to a plan to seize an unnamed Scots town from the sea, though on landing the 500 men would need the help of 700 others, presumably Scots royalists, Knowler, *Strafford's Letters*, II, 290.
108. Perceval-Maxwell, op. cit. 538-9; Wedgwood, *Wentworth*, p. 258.

the covenanters, but Wentworth replied that the king's position was too weak even for such limited offensive action; at most royal ships should peacefully show the flag off the Scottish coast to encourage the king's friends.[109] On 16 May he did agree to send one ship to help Antrim's friends by supplying men, arms, ammunition and food, to preserve them 'or at least the principal of them, until a farther Occasion; and in the mean Time to countenance and encourage them'[110] (an indication, incidently, that Wentworth was aware of the potential value of Antrim's friends to the king, which he had earlier denied when aid to them was to have been channelled through Antrim). But early in June he was refusing to send ships as far north as Skye without direct orders from the king, for fear of leaving Antrim and Down open to pillage or invasion by the covenanters.[111]

iii.   The Second Bishops' War, 1640

The king's failure to invade Scotland forced him to make a peace with the covenanters, the treaty of Berwick, signed on 18 June 1639. Neither side expected lasting peace to follow; each agreed to the treaty to postpone a conflict until circumstances were more favourable to it, and Ireland continued to play a major part in Charles' plans for the eventual subjection of Scotland. Donald Gorm (at this time or soon afterwards) was apparently supplied with a ship and arms for 1,000 men;[112] and on 5 June (just before the start of negotiations with the covenanters) and 11 June (after negotiations had begun) Charles appointed Donald Gorm and Antrim to be his joint lieutenants and commissioners in the Highlands and Isles, to act against his enemies. In return Antrim was promised Kintyre, and Donald Gorm of Sleat was to have Ardnamurchan, Strathswordale in Skye, 'Punard' (evidently Sunart) and the islands of Rhum, Muck and Canna.[113] It was no doubt intended that Antrim should make use of his men in Ireland in

---

109. Knowler, *Strafford's Letters*, II, 313-14.
110. Ibid. II, 420.
111. Ibid. II, 359.
112. H.M.C. 23: *Cowper*, II, 233; Carte, *Ormond*, I, 92.
113. Hill, *Macdonnells of Antrim*, pp. 253-4, 441-6; A. J. and A. M. Macdonald, *The Clan Donald* (3 vols, Inverness, 1896-1904), II, 720, III, 56; A. Mackenzie, *History of the Macdonalds and Lords of the Isles* (Inverness, 1881), pp. 214-15; Stevenson, *Scottish Revolution*, pp. 151-2; N.L.S. MS 3784, Miscellaneous Documents, ff. 36-40.

attacking the king's enemies in Scotland but the commission made no mention of Ireland; probably Charles recognised that it was hopeless to try to get Wentworth and Antrim to work together, and therefore offered him no help from Dublin.

Certainly Wentworth's plans for using the resources of Ireland against Scotland in 1640 omitted Antrim, and he continued to denounce the seizure of Kintyre and the Isles as pointless.[114] He was summoned to England after the failure of the 1639 campaign and became Charles' most trusted adviser, being created earl of Strafford in January 1640. The needs of the king now overcame the new earl's fear of arming Irish Catholics; on his advice the Irish parliament met in March 1640 and voted the subsidies necessary to pay new forces, amid fervent professions of loyalty from the leaders of the Irish Catholics. The levying then began of a new Irish army, mainly Catholic, of 1,000 horse and 8,000 foot, to join the king's other forces in England and then invade Scotland.[115]

In the same month that Charles commissioned Antrim and Donald Gorm to be his lieutenants (June 1639) Argyll took further action against MacDonald interests, either not having heard of the negotiations with the king or ignoring them. Sir Donald Campbell and Colin Campbell with about 100 men from Islay landed on Colonsay and captured Coll Ciotach MacDonald and two of his sons and plundered the island. The Campbells thus destroyed the last MacDonald outpost in the southern Hebrides, to prevent it being used as a base by Antrim. Royalist ships (Antrim's or Wentworth's) were active in the area at this time—in June a landing party from one of them killed fifty cattle on Jura and captured three gentlemen on Islay—and it may have been thought they were being helped by the MacDonalds of Colonsay. But the Campbells' raid on Colonsay was not entirely successful; two of Coll Ciotach's sons escaped capture, one of them being Alasdair (or Alexander) MacColla or MacDonald, who was to emerge in the years to come as the most formidable Highland opponent of the Campbells. He and other exiles fled to Ireland, where they probably stayed with their kinsman, Archibald Stewart of Ballintoy.[116]

114. Knowler, *Strafford's Letters*, II, 422.
115. Clarke, *Old English in Ireland*, pp. 125-7.
116. Stevenson, *Scottish Revolution*, pp. 148, 296; Hill, *Macdonnells of Antrim*, pp. 57-8. 61, 240, 438; G. Hill, 'The Stewarts of Ballintoy', *U.J.A.* N.S. VI (1900),

The royalist ships on the west coast withdrew on hearing of the treaty of Berwick. Argyll then dismissed his 'host' in Kintyre and wrote to Wentworth asking for the release of the gentlemen captured on Islay. But he retained 200 men in arms, continued to hold Coll Ciotach and maintained his garrisons in most of the castles he had captured. MacDonald refugees, sent back to Kintyre by Antrim now that the war was over, were prevented from landing and had to return to Ireland. Antrim complained to the king of the continued dispossession of his Scots kinsmen, especially in Kintyre, but Charles' orders that their wrongs be redressed were ignored.[117]

The Campbells had good reason to continue to be suspicious of the MacDonalds; it was probably in the weeks after the treaty of Berwick was signed that Donald Gorm, as king's lieutenant, returned to Scotland to organise a secret alliance against the Campbells. In Edinburgh he met Sir James Lamont, Sir James Stewart (sheriff of Bute), Sir Archibald Stewart of Blackhall, John MacLeod of Dunvegan and Sir Lachlan Mac-Lean of Duart, and they agreed to attack Argyll in conjunction with an invasion of Kintyre by Antrim. Donald Gorm said the king intended to ruin Argyll and all who supported him, and his offices were to be granted to others; Seaforth would replace him as justice general of the Western Isles. If supplied with 1,000 sets of arms Donald Gorm would raise 2,000 men for the king.[118]

Thus in all three kingdoms the treaty of Berwick was used to provide a breathing space in which to prepare for a new war. The covenanters, while still fearing a Highland rising stirred up by Antrim and his friends, soon decided that the main threat to them from Ireland was that posed by Strafford's new army. As early as 17 March 1640 it was being said in Edinburgh that if Strafford brought his army to Scotland, Argyll would in

---

21, 23; S.R.O. GD.112/39/776; C. Innes, ed. *The Book of the Thanes of Cawdor* (Spalding Club, 1859), p. 299. The Campbell interest in Islay was led by the Campbells of Calder or Cawdor. Sir John Campbell of Calder had handed over the running of his estates to his eldest son John; but John was declared insane in 1639 and his brother, the Colin Campbell mentioned in the text, acted as his curator, ibid. pp. xxx, xxxi, xxxviii-xxxix.
117.   S.R.O. GD.112/39/777; Knowler, *Strafford's Letters*, II, 374, British Library, Add. MS 23, 112, ff. 96-v, 97v; H.M.C. 8: *9th Report*, II, 249, 250.
118.   Stevenson, *Scottish Revolution*, p. 148; H.M.C. 8: *9th Report*, II, 255; N. Lamont, ed. *Inventory of the Lamont Papers* (S.R.S. 1914), pp. 180-1; H. McKechnie, *The Lamont Clan, 1235-1935* (Edinburgh, 1938), pp. 155-6; Baillie, *Letters*, I, 193.

retaliation lead an army to Ireland (for which boats were already prepared), where supporters of the covenant would rise to join him.[119] Later Argyll was assigned responsibility for defending the west coast north of the Clyde from an Irish landing, while the earl of Eglinton defended the south.[120] It was a change in the king's plans that made these defensive measures necessary; instead of the whole of the new Irish army entering Scotland by way of England it had been decided that at least part of it should sail directly to Scotland. Dumbarton Castle had been handed back to the king after the treaty of Berwick and Strafford's idea of landing troops there had been revived, though he was worried by the presence of Argyll's frigate on the Clyde.[121] But, as with almost all royalist plans in 1639-40, Strafford's was ruined by delays. He had at first hoped to have his new army of 9,000 men at Carrickfergus in May, but in the event it was not fully assenbled until mid-July, and even then it probably still required training.[122]

The covenanters appear to have realised that the new Irish army was no more ready to invade Scotland than the king's army on the Border was, for they felt it safe to let Argyll and 4,000 of his Highlanders leave the coast opposite Ireland and, in June and July, carry out a long march through the Highlands to overawe any potential royalists.[123] It is likely that the covenanters had already resolved to force the king to fight by invading England, and were anxious to ensure that there was no Highland royalist rising behind their backs. The other main danger they foresaw if they invaded England was that Strafford would lead a diversionary raid from Ireland, or would send his army to help the king in England. Therefore before their army entered England on 20 August 1640 the covenanters commissioned Argyll to remain in Scotland and, if necessary, raise an army of 10,000 foot and as many horse as possible. If Strafford moved his army to England Argyll was instructed to invade Ireland; if Strafford landed in Scotland Argyll would lead forces against him. This commission to Argyll was undoubtedly partly intended to make the king think twice

119. *C.S.P.D. 1639-40*, p. 555.
120. Gordon, *History of Scots Affairs*, III, 163; S.R.O. GD.112/40/2, bundle letters 1640-9, Archibald Campbell of Glencarradale to Sir Colin Campbell of Glenorchy, 13 August 1640.
121. Knowler, *Strafford's Letters*, II, 405-7.
122. Clarke, *Old English in Ireland*, pp. 131-2; Bagwell, *Stuarts*, I, 289-92.
123. Stevenson, *Scottish Revolution*, pp. 197-200.

before using the Irish army against the covenanters; they wrote telling Hamilton of the commission, and obviously he would inform the king of it.[124] But those who thought the commission 'may be but a boast to hold the Irish army at home'[125] were wrong. In the event the covenanters did not send an army to Ireland, but their plans to do so if necessary were no idle boasting, a bluff which could safely have been called. The fact that at this very moment they were successfully invading England indicated that they lacked neither the daring nor the skill required for such an enterprise.

After returning from his march through the Highlands Argyll laid siege to Dumbarton Castle; it surrendered to him on 27 August,[126] thus at once depriving Strafford of a base in Scotland and giving Argyll a convenient headquarters for planning an invasion in the opposite direction. Two days later he wrote from Dumbarton to Eglinton; 'I doubt not bot your lordship hes heard of the resolution for ane outfit of ane armie to Irland, whairin your lordship hes speciall interest'. Eglinton was to gather boats and ships at Ayr secretly, without letting intelligence of it reach Ireland.[127] If Argyll's actions were entirely a bluff he was being remarkably thorough!

Argyll's army was not needed, for the resistance of the king's forces in England collapsed so quickly that the new Irish army could not be sent to help him in either England or Scotland. Newcastle surrendered to the covenanters on 30 August and Charles was forced to open negotiations with them. But the covenanters' forces remained in arms and Strafford continued to take seriously the threat that they would invade Ireland as well as England. In October he considered a plan 'to banish all the under Scots in Ulster', making a distinction between 'the under Scotts, who are soe numerous and so ready for insurrection; and such as have considerable estates in lands, to ingage and secure their fidelitie'. He believed he could get

---

124. *C.S.P.D. 1640*, p. 611; S.R.O. GD.112/40/2, bundle, letters 1640-9, Archibald Campbell of Glencarradale to Sir Colin Campbell of Glenorchy, 13 August 1640.
125. Baillie, *Letters*, I, 259.
126. Stevenson, *Scottish Revolution*, p. 208; Spalding, *Memorialls*, I, 336.
127. W. Fraser, *Memorials of the Montgomeries, Earls of Eglinton* (2 vols, Edinburgh, 1859), I, 298-9. The letter is dated 29 August; Fraser has wrongly suggested the year as 1651. The only year in which the letter makes any sense is 1640; and that this is the correct date is confirmed by the fact that 3 September was a Thursday in 1640, and is mentioned in the text of the letter as being a Thursday.

the Irish house of commons to agree to this by telling them of the dangers of invasion by Argyll's Highlanders and redshanks, eager to force religious reformation on Ireland, and that they would be joined by 40,000 able bodied Ulster Scots—and, probably, by many native Irish, whom the cunning covenanters would doubtless encourage to rise. If the under Scots were not banished, Wentworth claimed, the regime would face ruin if Argyll landed.[128]

Ironically, the only attack on the covenanters from Ireland which materialised in 1640 was probably inspired by Antrim. In November Alasdair MacColla MacDonald and his brother raided Islay with about eighty men, and tried to kidnap a son of Campbell of Calder,[129] presumably hoping to be able to exchange him for Coll Ciotach and his two sons whom Argyll still held prisoner. While not of any real military significance, the raid at least meant that Antrim could claim to have taken some action against the covenanters; Strafford's efforts to help the king against the Scots proved even more useless than those of Antrim, whose inefficiency he had denounced in 1639 with such enjoyment.

Of course in one respect Strafford had proved more efficient than Antrim; he had at least managed to raise in arms the number of men he had promised. So while it had been Strafford who had denounced as dangerous Antrim's plan to arm and train thousands of Catholics, it was Strafford himself who eventually did this, with disastrous consequences for English and protestant interests in Ireland. As soon as a cessation was signed between the king and the covenanters (at Ripon on 17 October) Strafford's new Irish army was transformed from an asset into a liability. The fact that it was largely Catholic meant that it roused deep suspicion in England, Scotland and Ireland; and the need for money to pay it forced the government to listen to the Irish parliament's demands for constitutional reform. In Ireland as in England discontent with the rule of Charles I was given 'an opportunity

128. T. D. Whitaker, *The Life and Original Correspondence of Sir George Radcliffe* (London, 1810), pp. 206-10. Wedgwood, *Wentworth*, p. 300 states that Strafford's plan 'reads like a paranoic fantasy'; but she exaggerates the scope of the plan by stating that he proposed to expel 'all the Scots in Ulster', whereas he only mentioned the under Scots, and she does not mention his reason for proposing expulsion—that invasion from Scotland was expected.
129. Stevenson, *Scottish Revolution*, p. 296; S.R.O. GD.112/39/823.

for political activity' by his failure to suppress the covenanters, which forced him to summon parliaments in both countries.[130]

The weakness of the crown, now powerless in Scotland and under attack in the English parliament, naturally encouraged the ambitions of various groups in Ireland. The 'Old English' (descendants of pre-Elizabethan English settlers who had remained Catholics) and protestant settlers combined in 1640-1 in an attack on Strafford and his policies.[131] Outside parliament Ulster protestant settlers of puritan or presbyterian outlook, mainly Scots, issued a remonstrance denouncing the Irish bishops for their sins—including their hostility to the covenanters.[132] In March and April 1641, during the trial of Strafford by the English parliament, there were mob attacks by protestant settlers (again mainly Scots) on conformist ministers in at least nine parishes in Antrim and Down, while 'the Scottismens frequent brags in the North, that General Leslie wold come over ere long, and make a general reformation' caused fear and unrest among the Irish.[133]

With both the civil and the ecclesiastical authorities under attack, the native Irish began to reconsider their position and prospects. On the one hand royal power was collapsing, which might provide them with opportunities to improve their position; on the other the bitter hatred of Catholics expressed by the covenanters and the English parliament seemed to indicate that they might well end up worse off than before. Strafford was executed in May 1641,[134] and the same month his new Irish army was disbanded, adding to the political instability in Ireland the presence of several

130. Clarke, *Old English in Ireland*, pp. 125, 132; Clarke, 'Ireland and the General Crisis', *Past and Present*, no. 48 (1970), 94.
131. Clarke, op. cit. 90, 94. See also 79-99 for discussion of the complexity of such terms as 'Old English' and 'native Irish'.
132. J. T. Gilbert, ed. *A Contemporary History of Affairs in Ireland* (3 vols, Dublin, 1879), I, 374-9; *New History*, III, 284-5.
133. Perceval-Maxwell, op. cit. 548-9; S. R. Lowry-Corry, 4th earl of Belmore, 'James Spottiswoode, Bishop of Clogher (1621-44)', *U.J.A.* 2nd series, Special Volume (1903), 125.
134. The marquis of Hamilton evidently had hopes of succeeding Strafford both as lord lieutenant of Ireland and in the Irish alum farm, but these hopes were disappointed, E. Hyde, earl of Clarendon, *History of the Rebellion and Civil Wars in England*, ed. W. D. Macray (6 vols, Oxford, 1888), I, 411n, cited in J. R. Mac-Cormack, 'The Irish Adventurers and the English Civil War', *I.H.S.* X (1956-7), 21; S. P. Cooper, 'The Fortune of Thomas Wentworth', *Economic History Review*, 2nd series, XI (1958-9), 244n.

thousand trained but leaderless Irish Catholic troops.

It was not just the collapse of royal power, and fear of how those who seized power from Charles would treat Catholics, which sparked off the Irish rebellion of 1641; the king's own incompetent plotting also made a major contribution. Finding himself unable to gather sufficient support in England to resist the English parliament, the king sought new allies in Scotland and Ireland in 1641. In Scotland he granted the covenanters all that they demanded, and heaped favours on their leaders, in the hope of persuading them to help him; in return he gained nothing, for they remained deeply suspicious of him.[135] In Ireland his plans were equally unsuccessful. He opened secret negotiations with the earl of Ormond, the most powerful protestant noble in the country, who had commanded Strafford's new army until its disbandment in May. In July, just before leaving for Scotland to try to win over the covenanters, Charles instructed Ormond and the earl of Antrim to try to re-assemble the new Irish army secretly, evidently with the intention that they should use it to seize Dublin in his name and declare against the English parliament. The conspirators also made contact with native Irish leaders to see if they would agree to serve the king.[136]

Did Charles I really expect to get the covenanters and a largely Catholic Irish army to work together against the English parliament? With his conviction of his own skill in producing political miracles it is certainly possible that he did; on the other hand the Irish plot does not seem to have been pursued by him with any great determination, and it may be that he intended it only as an expedient to fall back on if he failed to secure the help of the covenanters. But, as events proved, his rash tampering with an already dangerous situation in Ireland had results fatal to his reputation.

News that Charles was seeking help in Ireland naturally encouraged the Catholics of Ireland. Though they had joined in the prosecution of Strafford with enthusiasm, it was clear that the English parliament, the covenanters, and Strafford's

---

135. Stevenson, *Scottish Revolution*, pp. 223, 234, 237, 239.
136. Hill, *Macdonnells of Antrim*, pp. 448-51; Clarke, *Old English in Ireland*, p. 159; Beckett, *Making of Modern Ireland*, pp. 79-80. For Charles' plots see also S. R. Gardiner, *History of England* (10 vols, London, 1883-4), X, 7-8, 50-1; R. Dunlop, 'The Forged Commission of 1641', *English Historical Review*, II (1887), 527-9.

protestant opponents in Ireland were all much more violently anti-Catholic than the king had ever been. Fearing that their position would change for the worse, many native Irish leaders had begun conspiring early in 1641 with Irish exiles on the continent. By May an armed rising, to take place late in October, was being discussed. Then in August they, and the leaders of the Old English, heard through Antrim of his and Ormond's plan to secure Dublin for the king, and that the king was seeking Irish help. It seemed briefly that the royalist plot to help the king and the native Irish plots to protect themselves could be combined. The native Irish would help the king, and be rewarded and protected by the king for doing so. But in the end the native Irish, 'the fools' as Antrim later called them, decided to act on their own, without reference to the king, believing that once they rose in arms the king would support them. Like Ormond and Antrim, they planned to seize Dublin, hoping for a bloodless *coup d'etat*. This part of the plot was betrayed to the authorities on 22 October 1641, the day before it was to have been carried out. But a simultaneous rising in Ulster went ahead as planned. Sir Phelim O'Neill occupied the important strong-points of Charlemont and Dungannon, and within a few days virtually all Ulster except for the north of counties Down and Londonderry and County Antrim were in the hands of the Irish.[137] The main threat to Scottish interests in Ireland now came not from the regime in Dublin but from the Catholic Irish.

---

137. Clarke, *Old English in Ireland*, pp. 156-61; Bagwell, *Stuarts*, I, 315-58.

Alexander Leslie, earl of Leven. General of the Scottish army in Ireland. Anonymous portrait.

CHAPTER TWO

The Irish Rebellion and Scottish Intervention, 1641-1642

---

i. Reactions in Scotland and Treaty Negotiations in London

News of the Irish rebellion reached Edinburgh on 28 October, in letters to the king from Ulster. Though the extent of the rising was unknown, Charles immediately told the Scottish parliament of it, presenting it as 'a bussines of grate importance, and qwither it wes of more ore lesse importance, as zet he could not tell'. A letter from Lord Chichester was read to parliament 'showing the Irische had lepin out in Irland in opin rebellion, and that maney of the papists ther had ioynid to them'. If it was a small revolt there would be no need for Scottish help, but Charles expressed the hope that if it was a major one Scotland would aid him to prevent it spreading; 'if ther hoppes proceid from the papists of England, then he thought the bussines of a grater consequence, and of a more transcendent nature'. At his request parliament appointed a committee to discuss the matter with the general, Alexander Leslie (newly created earl of Leven).[1]

That an Irish Catholic rebellion, especially one centred in Ulster, was a potential threat to the covenanters and their countrymen in Ireland none could doubt, but in spite of this the covenanters' reaction could not be the simple one of immediately agreeing with the king's proposal that they help him suppress it. The political situation in Britain as a whole was too tense and confused for this to be possible. How quickly it became known in Scotland that the Irish claimed to be acting in the king's name is not clear, but even before this news arrived the covenanters had good reason to be suspicious of his attitude to the Irish. It was little more than

1. Balfour, *Historical Works*, III, 119-21; *A.P.S.* V, 376, 688.

a year since he had recruited a largely Catholic Irish army and threatened to invade Scotland with it; might further secret dealings by him with the Irish have led to the rebellion? It was, after all, well known that he had come to Scotland to seek the covenanters' aid against the English parliament, and that he had failed to get this; had he now turned in desperation to the Irish as allies? Moreover, even if the king could be trusted, how would the English parliament react to the news that not only were the Irish in rebellion but that the covenanters were gathering a new army at the king's request, ostensibly for use in Ireland. Many in the English parliament might well conclude that Charles had succeeded in gaining the support of the Scots, and that they were preparing a new invasion of England on his behalf. Even if the English accepted that the forces raised in Scotland were destined for Ireland, they could hardly fail to resent Scots intervention in an English dependency, undertaken on the king's orders without consultation with the English parliament.

Such considerations led the committee of the Scots parliament (which met on the afternoon of 28 October) to conclude that nothing should be done until further details of the rebellion were known, and that in any case 'the kingdome of Ireland being dependand wpoun ye Croune and kingdome of Ingland the Inglishe may conceave jelousies and mistake our forwardnes when they shall heir of our preparaciones without ther knowledge in this wherin they are first and most properlie concerned'. If the English parliament asked for help the Scots would send it, but they would not act without such an invitation. The Scottish parliament accepted this argument, and refused to take any immediate action except for ordering an investigation into how many boats were available on the west coast to carry men to Ireland if necessary.[2]

Charles indignantly urged that the situation was serious enough to warrant immediate action; parliament therefore conceded that consideration might be given to preparing men and supplies to be ready if the English parliament asked for them,[3] and the next day (2 November) a parliamentary committee advised that, if the English accepted the offer of

2.   *A.P.S.* V, 376, 377, 690; Balfour, *Historical Works*, III, 125-6.
3.   Balfour, *Historical Works*, III, 128-9, 132-3; *A.P.S.* V, 378.

help, eight regiments comprising 10,000 men, of whom 2,500 should be raised in Scotland.[4] This offer was reported to Westminster by commissioners of the English parliament who had accompanied the king to Edinburgh, and they urged acceptance of it. Men could be sent to Ireland from Scotland much more quickly and more cheaply than from England, and Highland troops would be especially useful; such redshanks were very 'proper to fight with the Irish in their own Kind and Country amongst Hills and Boggs'.[5]

The English parliament had first heard of the rebellion in Ireland on 1 November. Two days later, on learning of the Scots offer of help in suppressing it, the committee for Irish affairs was instructed to 'make us of the Friendship and Assistance of Scotland in this Business'. The committee duly resolved 'That an Assistance shall be desired of the Scotts, according to the Act of Pacification'.[6] Thus Scots intervention in Ireland would be the first action taken under the provision in the treaty between the two kingdoms which had ended the Bishops' Wars that each kingdom would help the other against rebels.[7]

But in England as in Scotland the matter proved to be less simple than it at first appeared, as suspicions emerged about the motives of the king and the Scots for making the offer. If the king was in league with the rebels, was he hoping to persuade the Scots to join them? If he was not, was he hoping to send the Scots (whom at heart he still regarded as rebels) to fight the Irish rebels so that he could concentrate on overthrowing the power of parliament in England without fear of intervention from Scotland?[8] On the whole, however, the arguments in favour of accepting the Scots offer outweighed those against it in the eyes of the king's opponents in the English parliament. Agreeing to send a Scots army to Ireland extricated them from an awkward dilemma. They wished to

4. Balfour, *Historical Works*, III, 135.
5. C. McNeill, ed. *Tanner Letters*, (I.M.C. 1943), p. 131; J. Nalson, ed. *An Impartial Collection of the Great Affairs of State* (2 vols, London, 1682-3), II, 612; *L.J.* IV, 427; S. D'Ewes, *The Journal of Sir Simonds D'Ewes from the first recess of the Long Parliament to the withdrawal of King Charles from London*, ed. W. H. Coates (New Haven, 1942), p. 103.
6. *C.J.* II, 304, 305; *L.J.* IV, 422; D'Ewes, *Journal*, pp. 77, 84-5, 86.
7. *A.P.S.* V, 342-3.
8. G. Burnet, *The Memoires of the Lives and Actions of James and William Dukes of Hamilton and Castlehearald* (London, 1677), p. 191.

MAP 2

Land Over 600 feet

- - - - County Boundaries   **—·—·—** Provincial Boundaries

crush the Irish rebels as quickly as possible, but levying forces in England to do this would have raised insurmountable difficulties. The king would insist on his right to organise and command such forces; if this was granted, he could hardly fail to be strongly tempted to use them to crush the English parliament before using them against the Irish. On the other hand if parliament (with or without royal consent) raised forces whose loyalty could be relied on, it would be folly for it to send them to Ireland, since this would weaken the parliamentary cause in England. In these circumstances a Scots army seemed the only hope of sending prompt help on a large scale to Ireland in a way agreeable to both king and parliament.

The fact that the king's opponents welcomed the Scots offer meant that his friends in parliament were suspicious of it, even though it had Charles' blessing. The king might argue that this was an excellent opportunity for getting rid of many of his Scottish enemies by embroiling them in Ireland, but many English royalists must have shared the doubts expressed by their Scottish counterparts; agreeing to the Scots sending forces to Ireland allowed them to keep an army on foot, and even in Ireland such an army would be a potential menace to the king's interests.[9]

On 4 November the committee of the Commons for Irish affairs voted to accept Scots help; but next day John Pym had to report to the Commons that the vote had been reversed at a thinly attended meeting on news that a Lords' committee had rejected the Scots offer. A long debate followed in the Commons, in which Sir John Hotham urged that accepting Scottish help in subduing Ireland, an English dependency, would be dishonourable. The argument was a popular one. Even many parliamentarians felt that the successful Scots invasion of England in 1640 had brought dishonour on the country—even though they had themselves benefited from it since it had forced the king to summon parliament. To have now to beg the Scots to restore English authority in Ireland for them would be an additional humiliation. The argument about dishonour was conveniently vague; it could unite men of very differing outlooks, from parliamentarians who favoured the covenanters to royalists who hated and distrusted

9.   Loc. cit.

them, in opposing Scottish intervention in Ireland. But in the end it failed to prevail. The majority opinion in the Commons was that delay might lead to all Ireland being lost, and that there could be no dishonour in the two nations acting together in accordance with their treaty.

The Commons therefore resolved to ask that, for the present, 1,000 Scots be sent to Carrickfergus. It was also resolved that England should offer to pay these men. The covenanters had probably assumed from the first that this would be the case, but the offer was partly made to undermine the arguments about dishonour; Sir John Hotham agreed that as it had been resolved to accept Scots forces they should be paid by England. But a further dispute now prolonged the debate; Pym proposed that sending help to Ireland should be made conditional on the king dismissing his evil counsellors and replacing them with ones approved by parliament. The proposal was rejected, but that it was made at all emphasises the extent to which, from the first, even those who supported Scots intervention in Ireland usually regarded the negotiations to bring this about as being of secondary importance to the great quarrel between king and parliament.[10] This was inevitable, especially in view of the king's alleged involvement in the Irish rebellion—the Commons was told as early as 6 November that the rebels expected Charles to cross from Scotland to Dunluce Castle to join them[11]—but the result was that the main advantage originally seen in sending Scots forces, that they could be sent quickly, was lost.

Instructions were approved by the English parliament on 10 November whereby the English commissioners in Edinburgh were to arrange for one Scots regiment of 1,000 men to land in Ireland as soon as possible,[12] but it was soon realised that this was inadequate; the next day both houses resolved that 10,000 Scots should be sent. But whereas the Commons now wanted to delay sending any Scots until a treaty had been negotiated, the Lords insisted on voting that

10. D'Ewes, *Journal*, pp. 90-5; *C.J.* II, 306; K. J. Lindley, 'The impact of the 1641 rebellion upon England and Wales, 1641-5', *I.H.S.* XVIII (1972-3), 163.
11. D'Ewes, *Journal*, p. 97; W. Bray, ed. *Diary and Correspondence of John Evelyn, F.R.S., to which is subjoined the Private Correspondence between King Charles I and Sir Edward Nicholas* (London, n.d.), p. 787.
12. J. Rushworth, ed. *Historical Collections* (8 vols, London, 1659-1701), III, i, 422-5; D'Ewes, *Journal*, p. 99.

1,000 be sent at once, a treaty for 9,000 more being arranged if this proved necessary. Compromise was reached on 13 November by both houses agreeing to ask for 5,000 Scots at once. Considerations of military necessity, which favoured a large army, had been modified by fear of the effect on Ireland of sending so many presbyterian Scots there,[13] and by the argument (doubtless fostered by those who themselves had little liking for the Scots) that the Irish had a special hatred for the Scots and would therefore be driven to desperation by Scots intervention.[14]

Meanwhile the king was fast concluding that he was wasting his time in Scotland. He had failed to win the support of the covenanters, and though they had agreed in principle to send an army to Ireland action was being delayed by squabbling at Westminster over how to react to the Scots' offer. He had clearly lost control of Scotland, and it was necessary that he hurry back to England to try to maintain his power there. On 11 November he told the Scottish parliament he would have to leave by 18 November 'for his staying went weill neire to losse him a kingdome, (he meind Irland)';[15] he might well have meant England too. The Scots parliament therefore agreed to dissolve on 17 November, without having taken any official action to send immediate help to Ireland. When a supplication by British (English and Scots) who had lands in Ireland asked that speedy action be taken and that arms be lent to volunteers who wished to fight in Ireland, parliament simply referred it to the king.[16] But parliament did appoint commissioners to negotiate with the English parliament on a number of subjects, the most urgent of these being the terms on which a Scottish army should serve in Ireland. The privy council was to supervise their work.[17]

Nearly a month had now passed since the outbreak of the rebellion and there was still no sign of the much talked-of Scottish army intervening, but in other ways the Protestants of Ireland were already receiving help from Scotland. Some of

13. D'Ewes, *Journal*, pp. 130-1, 137-8, 140; *C.J.* II, 306, 312, 313-14, 314-15; *L.J.* VI, 430-1, 435, 438; Nalson, *Imperial Collection*, II, 626, 642; Gardiner, *History of England*, X, 69-71.
14. *C.S.P.D. 1641-3*, pp. 167-8; Bray, *Evelyn*, p. 790.
15. Balfour, *Historical Works*, III, 143-4, 153.
16. *A.P.S.* V, 429, 706, 717.
17. Ibid. V, 404-5, 721.

the Ulster Scots and English who had fled to Scotland during the Bishops' Wars and served in the covenanters' armies were returning to Ireland when the rebellion began; the committee supervising the disbanding of the Scottish army had issued orders on 23 September for prompt payment to men who had come from Ireland of enough money to enable them to return there.[18] Once news of the rebellion reached Scotland many of those with estates, or relatives or friends with estates, in Ulster began to gather bodies of volunteers to be sent to Ireland. As the Scots army had just been disbanded there were doubtless many, uprooted from their former lives by military service, willing to try their fortunes in a new war. It is impossible to calculate how many Scots volunteers passed to Ulster in these first months of the rebellion, but their numbers ran into many hundreds. English pamphlets and letters are full of rumours of the exploits of the 'many Scots of quality who went as volunteers to help their countrymen',[19] of Scots who of their 'owne, free, and spontaneous will collect a number of themselves to goe voluntarily in Ireland to helpe and relieve the said poore Protestants'.[20] Accounts of their numbers and victories are often wildly exaggerated,[21] but clearly they were thought to be a significant element in the war.

In the work of sending immediate help from Scotland to Ireland the king played a leading part. Charles later claimed that this had been 'a great support to the northern parts of that kingdom'.[22] He persuaded the Scots parliament to agree to his buying arms and ammunition stored in Dumbarton Castle from their owners, to be sent to Carrickfergus.[23] On 16 November he signed commissions at Holyroodhouse to many of the leading Ulster Scots to raise and lead forces under the command of Ormond, whom he had just re-appointed lieutenant general of his army in Ireland. Lord Montgomery of the Ards was to have a foot regiment of 1,000 men and a horse regiment of five troops. His brother (Sir James

18. Ibid. V, 672.
19. H.M.C. 53: *Montagu*, pp. 144-5.
20. *A Glorious Victory obtained by the Scots against the Rebels in Ireland the last day of Decem. 1641* (London, 1641), pp. 2-3.
21. E.g. ibid. pp. 3-5; *More Happy Newes from Ireland of a battell fought betwixt the Scottish volunteers against the Irish Rebels* (London, 1641), pp. 4-5; *A Late and true relation from Ireland* (London, 1641); H.M.C. 23: *Cowper*, II, 303.
22. Hyde, *History of the Rebellion*, II, 492.
23. Balfour, *Historical Works*, III, 145-6.

Montgomery), Sir William Stewart and Sir Robert Stewart were each to have a foot regiment and a troop of horse, while two English settlers, Sir William Cole and Sir Ralph Gore, were to have regiments of 500 foot. Other planters received commissions from the lords justice in Dublin.[24] To help his new colonels raise their regiments Charles engaged as many officers as he could who had served in the covenanters' armies, and ordered them to regather as many of the men who had served under them as possible and transport them to Ireland. Arms and ammunition were sent with them; Sir Robert Stewart at Coleraine was offered the use of artillery from Dumbarton Castle if he needed it. In all Charles estimated that with the help of his cousin the duke of Lennox he had dispatched 1,500 fighting men to Ireland before he left Scotland.[25] The military survival of the Ulster protestants in these critical early months owed much more to the efforts of the king than to those of either the English or the Scottish parliaments.

Most of the men and supplies sent from Scotland naturally went to Scottish commanders in Ulster, but English settlers also received help. In December Lord Chichester and other English officers in County Down sent James Edmondstone to Scotland to obtain arms for about 1,500 foot and 500 horse, and three field guns. They complained that their requests for help from the king had not been answered and asked the Scottish privy council to help them buy arms on credit. The council agreed that the arms could be supplied from the public magazine, Edmondstone giving the committee for common burdens (which had been established to sort out the financial confusion arising from the Bishops' Wars) guarantees for eventual repayment. In January 1642 arms worth over £14,500 Scots were handed over to Edmondstone.[26] Scots settlers too sometimes had to pay (or promise to pay) for the

---

24. G. Hill, ed. *The Montgomery Manuscripts* (Belfast, 1869), pp. 157-60; J. Temple, *The Irish Rebellion* (6th ed. Dublin, 1724), p. 33; Carte MSS, 2 ff. 51, 53, 55; Bagwell, *Stuarts*, I, 327. In H.M.C. 23: *Cowper*, II, 298 the king's commissions are wrongly dated 19 November.
25. Carte, *Ormond*, I, 197, 198, 463; H.M.C. 23: *Cowper*, II, 298.
26. *R.P.C.S. 1638-43*, pp. 176, 177, 499-500, 605; J. S. Reid, *History of the Presbyterian Church in Ireland*, ed. W. D. Killen (3 vols, Edinburgh, 1867), I, 543-4; S.R.O. PA.14/1, Register of the Committee for Common Burdens, 1641-5, ff. 13v, 18v, 19v-21, 22v-23v. The arms still had not been paid for in 1647, S.R.O. PA.16/1/59/1; *A.P.S.* VI, i, 773-4.

arms they received from Scotland. Lord Claneboye probably had to pay for the 400 muskets he received out of the public magazine, and Lord Montgomery bought enough muskets in Scotland to arm his whole regiment.[27]

The need of the Ulster protestants for help was emphasised by the flood of refugees which soon reached Scotland. On 13 December the presbytery of Dunoon begged the privy council for help to support poor people from Ireland, over 500 of whom had landed on Bute alone.[28] From all along the western coast came similar reports—from Ayr, Irvine, Portpatrick and Stranraer. As a result on 1 February 1642 the privy council ordered a collection throughout the country, relating that parishes in the west had exhausted the contents of their poor boxes and that extra local collections had proved inadequate to support the refugees; 'by famine they will miserablie perish if they are not tymouslie supplied'.[29] The situation probably continued to grow worse for several months more, since many settlers who had at first remained in Ulster, hoping that a Scots army would soon restore them to their homes, had to be shipped to Scotland later as no army came, food ran short and the rebellion spread. In Londonderry in January 'All the shipping that hath bin here is imployed to carry people into Scotland, and if there were many more ships all were to little. The terror of the rebellion hath struck such a feare in the Brittish of these partes that their harts are gone, and, therefore, it is to little purpose to stay their bodyes'. In Coleraine men were retained to fight but the women and children were being shipped to Scotland.[30]

The special collections in Scotland for the refugees raised considerable sums. £1,000 Scots was distributed by John Livingstone (now minister of Stranraer), though he was upset that so few of the refugees were conscious that they deserved the punishments that God was inflicting on them. £4,000 Scots was set aside for the presbyteries of Ayr and Irvine, and the burgh of Glasgow raised over £1,000 Scots.[31]

27. S.R.O. PA.14/1, ff. 21v-22; Hill, *Montgomery Manuscripts*, p. 156n.
28. *R.P.C.S. 1638-43*, pp. 500-1.
29. Ibid. pp. 189-91, 208, 227, 231, 254-5.
30. J. Hogan, ed. *Letters and Papers relating to the Irish Rebellion, 1642-46* (I.M.C. 1936), pp. 3-4, 11.
31. Livingstone, 'Life', in Tweedie, *Select Biographies*, I, 166; *R.P.C.S. 1638-43*, pp. 209-10; J. D. Marwick, ed. *Extracts from the Records of the Burgh of Glasgow,*

C

But the money came in slowly and the total amount was inadequate. In April many refugees on Bute, including three ministers and their families and other persons of good quality, were still awaiting help, and in June about 4,000 refugees in the presbyteries of Ayr and Irvine were said to be in danger of starving.[32] These contemporary reports may well exaggerate the number of refugees but it is clear that a significant proportion of the protestant population of Ulster had fled to Scotland. Many others escaped to Dublin or England.

While most of the refugees found safety in Scotland a few found further tribulation. It was feared that the Irish rebels had links with Catholics in Britain and planned to spread the revolt. Consequently in Scotland as in England the few Catholics or native Irish among the refugees were treated with suspicion. A Captain Winter was imprisoned in Edinburgh Castle and interrogated on a charge of supplying intelligence to the Irish, but was eventually released. Six Irishmen arrested in Kirkcudbright were not so lucky; they were handed over to the English.[33]

In both Dublin and Ulster the failure to send an army from Scotland promptly provoked complaint. The lords justice warned that through the delay the whole kingdom would probably be lost.[34] Hugh Montgomery, who had been appointed lieutenant colonel of Lord Montgomery of the Ards' regiment, wrote on 17 December 1641 that 'except speidie assistance be sent from Scotland, be all outward appearance they will find but few of their cuntrie men to welcome them and verie evile landing heir, for we ar few and verie naket for want of armes to withstand them [the rebels]'. The Protestant forces were too weak to attack the rebels, 'yet it wer but a small matter if we had fyv thousand of such men and armes as wer at Newcastle [in 1640] to marche towards them and give battel to threttie thousand in the open feilds'. His colonel, Lord Montgomery of the Ards, made similar complaints about lack of help; the earl of Eglinton had sent him officers, but

1573-1642 (S.B.R.S. 1876), p. 436 and *1630-1662* (S.B.R.S. 1881), p. 51; Spalding, *Memorialls*, II, 107-8.
32. *R.P.C.S. 1638-43*, pp. 267, 546-7.
33. Ibid. pp. 175-6, 178, 203, 210, 221, 255, 260, 267-8. For refugees in England see Lindley, 'The impact of the 1641 rebellion', *I.H.S.* XVIII, 147-50.
34. H.M.C. 36: *Ormonde*, N.S. II, 30, 32, 36, 39, 41.

he had had to buy arms privately in Scotland.[35]

Such urgings from Ireland on the need for haste did little to speed the arrival of the Scots army, though the covenanters' actions indicate that they at least took them to heart. On 18 November, the day after the Scottish parliament had been dissolved, the Scottish privy council set up a committee to consider what instructions concerning Ireland should be given to the commissioners being sent to London. The next day the news arrived that the English parliament had accepted the Scots offer of 10,000 men, though it asked that only 5,000 be sent for the present.[36] As all the commissioners were not yet ready to leave for London it was decided on 22 November to send two of them, the earls of Lothian and Lindsay, ahead of the rest since the state of Ireland demanded haste.[37]

Lothian and Lindsay had reached London by 3 December, when the English parliament appointed commissioners to negotiate with them.[38] Difficulties soon appeared. The Scots had instructions to treat only for 'the full number of 10,000 men' and refused to treat for fewer, arguing that they would all be needed to defeat the rebels. The Commons accepted this, but the Lords, still suspicious of the Scots and fearing they had ambitions in Ireland, would only agree to negotiate for 10,000 men on the rather absurd condition that the Scots commissioners meanwhile sought permission to negotiate for fewer. Under pressure from the Commons the Lords eventually agreed that 10,000 Scots might be sent to Ireland—on condition that an equal number of English were also sent as a counter-balance. The Commons haughtily replied 'that they were not used to be capitulated withall' but the Lords stuck to their point. On 21 December they at last voted that 10,000 Scots might be sent, but they only did this after first voting

---

35. H.M.C. 10: *10th Report*, I, 48-51; Fraser, *Memorials of the Montgomeries, Earls of Eglinton*, I, 87, II, 293. This Hugh Montgomery who served as lieutenant colonel to Hugh, Lord Montgomery of the Ards, was probably Eglinton's eldest son, who confusingly was known by his courtesy title of Lord Montgomery. The regiment which this Lord Montgomery had commanded in the invasion of England in 1640 had been regarded as the best disciplined and most pious of the Scots army, Baillie, *Letters*, I, 201.
36. *R.P.C.S. 1638-43*, pp. 149, 150-3.
37. Ibid. pp. 155, 163, 485, 506-10; S.R.P. PA.13/2, Proceedings of the Scots Commissioners for concluding the articles of the Treaty, 1641-2, ff. lv-6.
38. *L.J.* IV, 459-61, 464; *C.J.* II, 331; Nalson, *Impartial Collection*, II, 711, 716-17, 720, 723.

that 10,000 English be sent.[39]

Luckily for the Protestants of Ireland the vote of the Lords was ignored in practice, for agreement on who should raise and command the English forces, king or parliament, would have been impossible. The Lords were not intending to obstruct the crushing of the Irish rebels but acted 'for the Honor, and it may be the Interest of England'.[40] The argument that acceptance of Scottish assistance would be dishonourable was being reinforced by a growing conviction that it might also be dangerous. Would 10,000 victorious Scots be willing to leave Ireland quietly once the war was over? Having been threatened with invasion from Ireland in 1639-40, would not the covenanters try to establish Scottish power there permanently to prevent the threat recurring? Many thought that the Scots 'meant to make their fortunes by a new conquest in Ireland, where they had a very great part of the province of Ulster planted by their own nation; so that, according to their rules of good husbandry, they might expect whatsoever they got from the rebels to keep for themselves'.[41]

Such fears were not entirely groundless, as the instructions given to Lothian and Lindsay make clear. They were to ask that all the major ports in Ulster be handed over to the Scots army as bases—Londonderry (with Culmore Fort), Coleraine and Carrickfergus. Moreover they were to request that 'our service and hazard may be rewarded with the like recompence as sall be granted to the English or Irish; which agrees with justice, seing that manie of our countriemen hes to thair great labour and expence made manie plantations there, and if we sall with hazard of our lyffes doe good service to his Majestie and Crowne of England, we aucht to be sharers of the fruits of our panes and recompence of our service with the English, being alwayes subject to his Majestie and the Crowne of Ingland as the English are and salbe'.[42] While neither entirely logical nor explicit, the underlying message here is clear. Presumably the defeat of the Irish rebels would be

39. *C.J.* II, 339-40, 341, 343-4, 349; *L.J.* IV, 471, 472, 478, 479, 481, 482, 483, 484-5, 486; D'Ewes, *Journal*, pp. 274-5, 291-4, 315, 325, 333, 351, 352-3; H.M.C. 45: *Buccleuch*, I, 289.
40. Nalson, *Impartial Collection*, II, 769.
41. Hyde, *History*, II, 382; *C.S.P.V. 1640-2*, pp. 265, 267; *C.S.P.D. 1641-3*, pp. 167-8.
42. *R.P.C.S. 1638-43*, pp. 508-9.

followed by widespread confiscation of their lands, and the Scots hoped to be rewarded for their services by grants of such lands, though they stressed they did not intend to undermine Ireland's dependence on England. In accordance with their instructions the Scots commissioners proceded (in a paper read in the Lords on 27 December) to demand equal privileges with the English in any new plantation.[43]

It was not only suspicion of the Scots that slowed down the progress of the treaty. Since the king's return from Scotland the constitutional disputes between him and parliament had become increasingly bitter. The Grand Remonstrance was presented to him on 1 December; on 3 January 1642 came his attempt to arrest five members of the Commons; on 5 March the Militia Ordinance, openly defying his authority, was passed. Negotiations with the Scots commissioners were naturally subordinated to debate on these great issues, making long delays inevitable. As early as 20 December the Scots commissioners complained of the lack of progress; they had been in London for twenty days but nothing had yet been agreed. The Scots privy council had expected to hear of a decision by 8 December; 2,500 men were still on foot of the Scots army, and could form the nucleus of an army for Ireland, but Scotland could not afford to pay them any longer. Unless England agreed to provide their pay (at Scots rates) from 8 December to their arrival in Ireland they would have to be disbanded. This complaint had the desired effect; the English agreed to pay the 2,500 Scots; it was the day after the complaint was made that the Lords finally agreed to 10,000 Scots for Ireland; and other decisions at last began to be taken.[44]

In the last ten days of December and in January the outlines of the eventual treaty were agreed upon,[45] though debate was to continue for months on details. The only major stumbling block proved to be the Scots demand for possession of Londonderry, Coleraine and Carrickfergus. Parliament granted them the latter two ports but, doubtless to avoid offending the city of London, refused them Londonderry.[46] Moreover,

43. *L.J.* IV, 492.
44. *C.J.* II, 341, 350, 354; *L.J.* IV, 482, 486; D'Ewes, *Journal*, pp. 336-7.
45. *C.J.* II, 363, 364, 376, 397, 398; *L.J.* IV, 489, 491-2; D'Ewes, *Journal*, pp. 368, 370-1; *R.P.C.S. 1638-43*, p. 179.
46. *C.J.* II, 363; *L.J.* IV, 491; D'Ewes, *Journal*, pp. 370-1.

it seemed that help for Ireland was to be delayed until all the details of the treaty were settled. On 5 January the earl of Loudoun, the chancellor of Scotland, wrote from Edinburgh in exasperation 'I belive if 5000 men had gone tymouslie to Ireland it might have keiped lyfe in the play and in many thousand of the britishe who hes lossed their lyfes for want of tymous assistance ... Ingland hes bein so slow as all Ireland wilbe in the Rebells hands befoir any armie can be sent over. I pray god gife the parliament wisdome and cowradge'.[47] The Scots privy council wrote in a similar vein; daily news from Ireland revealed the desperate state of affairs there, for 'The distractions in England hes lost the lives of manie thousands of the Brittish' and there would soon be nowhere left where a Scottish army could land safely. It was therefore urged that the English agree that the men already in arms in Scotland should cross to Ireland at once to secure landing places.[48]

The same solution to the delays had occured to the English two days before; on 22 January the Scots commissioners were asked to send 2,500 men to Ireland at once, before the Irish occupied all the ports. The commissioners could not give immediate consent, since they had no instructions on such a point, but they clearly favoured the idea, as did the earl of Leven—'It was to be wished that they had gone sooner there work had beene the lesse and thair danger also ... nothing is so prejudiciall for the managing of that warre as delayes'.[49] The king too gave his blessing to the plan, but agreement was delayed by yet another dispute. Charles agreed to all the proposed conditions on which the 2,500 men would be sent except for the handing over to them of Carrickfergus as a base, and the granting to them of power to give orders to other forces in Ulster, arguing that these terms were prejudicial to the crown of England. The Commons immediately reacted (27 January) by declaring that those who had advised Charles in this matter were enemies to the king and to England and Ireland. At this the king gave way and agreed to sign a commission granting the Scots the terms proposed; but this did not prevent the Commons naming his evil advisers and

47. N.L.S. Wodrow MSS, Folio LXVI, ff. 190-1.
48. S.R.O. PA.13/3, Register of Letters to and from the Scots Commissioners in London 1642, 1644-5, ff. 4-4v, 7¹-7².
49. Ibid. ff. 6, 10.

LORD of LAVDHN
1637

John Campbell, earl of Loudoun. Chancellor of Scotland, 1641-51. Late eighteenth century engraving after a lost portrait by George Jamesone of 1637.

denouncing them as incendiaries. Again negotiations for sending Scots to Ireland had become entangled in the struggle between king and parliament.[50]

Encouraged by the fact that agreement had been reached on sending 2,500 men the Scots turned back to completing the treaty for the full 10,000, urging the need for haste.[51] Having been granted Carrickfergus they renewed their demands for Londonderry as well, and revived claims that their services should be rewarded by grants of rebel lands. Both requests were refused, the former after protests against it from both the city of London and Londonderry itself. On 14 February the Commons resolved that as English troops going to Ireland were not being promised land the Scots had no right to expect any.[52] Three days before, it has been proposed in parliament that money should be raised for subduing Ireland with a promise of eventual repayment in rebel lands; this was the origin of the Adventurers' Act which received royal assent on 24 February.[53] Those to benefit from confiscations were thus to be those who provided money rather than those who actually served in Ireland. Nonetheless the Scots privy council continued to urge the commissioners in London to demand Londonderry and the right to rebel estates, since the Scots had been 'speceall advancers of the plantations there'. It was believed in Edinburgh that the proposal which led to the Adventurers' Act had only been made 'vpon ther hering that ye [the Scots commissioners] urged to have Londondarie and priviledge of plantation in recompence of our service'; many English seemed to be determined that the Scots should not benefit from their services in Ireland. However 'ther is latitude gifin to you to do whatsoever you shall judge most suitable to the Reputatione of your Cuntrie and most conducible to the good of the busines'.[54]

Taking advantage of this latitude the Scots commissioners

50. *C.J.* II, 392, 393, 399, 460-1; *L.J.* IV, 530, 532, 534, 546, 562-3; Burnet, *Hamilton*, p. 190; *R.P.C.S. 1638-43*, pp. 191-2, 202; Hyde, *History*, I, 559; R. Newrobe, *Delightful newes to all Loyall Subjects* (1642), pp. 2-3; *His Majesties Message to both Houses of Parliament, January 20* ... (London, 1641/2), pp. 17-24; S.R.O. PA.13/2, ff. 28v-30.
51. *L.J.* IV, 554-5.
52. S.R.O. PA.13/3, f. 10v; *C.J.* II, 429-30; Hogan, *Letters and Papers*, p. 47.
53. *C.J.* II, 425; K. S. Bottigheimer, *English Money and Irish Land* (Oxford, 1971), pp. 39-42.
54. S.R.O. PA.13/3, f. 13; N.L.S. Wodrow MSS, Folio LXVI, ff. 204-5.

abandoned their demands for Londonderry and reward for services in land, and asked instead that Scotsmen be allowed to subscribe money as adventurers equally with Englishmen, thus entitling themselves to repayment in grants of land. This the English parliament conceded,[55] but in the event the privilege proved of little interest to Scotsmen. The covenanters continued to urge in vague terms that they should be allowed to share in the success of the war in Ireland as well as in its dangers, but were not prepared to invest money in it.[56] Only two Scots can be identified among the 1,533 adventurers; but though both were major investors the fact that they were Scots has previously been overlooked. Thomas Cuningham, the conservator of Scottish privileges at Campvere in the Netherlands, subscribed £1,800 sterling as a sea adventurer; and the greatest of all the adventurers, the 'mysterious Lewis Dyke' said to have invested £5,200 sterling as a sea adventurer[57] was Lewis Dick, a younger son of the richest Scottish merchant of the age, Sir William Dick of Braid. Both Cuningham and Dick provided at least part of their contributions as sea adventurers in kind rather than cash. Cuningham had recently purchased for £7,000 Scots (£583.6.8 sterling) a frigate, the *Lorne*, from the Scottish government;[58] judging by its name this may well have been the frigate Argyll had bought in the Netherlands in 1639 for defence against invasion of his estates by the earl of Antrim. Cuningham fitted out his frigate for use against the Irish rebels, and Dick also captained his own frigate, the *Golden Lion*.[59]

The extent to which intervention in Ireland was necessary to the covenanters in their own interests was brought home to them in January 1642. News arrived from Ulster that two of Coll Ciotach's sons and many of the earl of Antrim's followers had joined the rebels. This naturally raised fears that the MacDonnells would receive Irish help in again seeking to regain their lands in Scotland. Argyll made immediate use of the

55. *C.J.* II, 456, 473-4.
56. N.L.S. Wodrow MSS, Folio LXVI, f. 213.
57. Bottigheimer, *English Money and Irish Land*, pp. 52, 73-4, 180; J. P. Prendergast, *The Cromwellian Settlement in Ireland* (3rd ed. Dublin, 1922), p. 448.
58. S.R.O. PA.14/1, ff. 5v, 22-v.
59. T. Cuningham, *The Journal of Thomas Cuningham of Campvere, 1640-54*, (S.H.S. 1928), pp. xxiv-xxv, 66, 68, 73-4, 101; J. S. Smith, *The Grange of St Giles, the Bass, and the other Baronial Homes of the Dick-Lauder Family* (Edinburgh, 1898), pp. 38, 50, 64.

news to get the privy council to approve of his maintaining fortifications he had built in Kintyre, and of his continuing to keep Coll Ciotach and his two other sons (captured in 1639) prisoner.[60] It was already feared that disaffected Highlanders 'who speak the same language the Irishe doe' might be helped by the rebels;[61] now it seemed Antrim's men might come to Scotland to join them.[62] In these circumstances it seemed unwise to send all the covenanters' forces to Ireland, and they therefore proposed that one regiment of 1,000 men should remain in Scotland to prevent 'turbulent spirits' breaking the peace—on English pay, since the threat to Scotland came from Ireland, an English dependency.[63]

The idea was soon dropped, but the marquis of Argyll decided that the threat to him from Antrim's followers was serious and could best be met by offensive action. He therefore proposed to the English parliament that he be commissioned to raise a regiment, as part of the 10,000 Scots, and to send it as soon as possible to help the protestant forces in Coleraine and the surrounding area. As Coleraine was the nearest important port to Antrim's estates the venture was clearly intended to be a Campbell attack on the MacDonnells, but parliament saw no harm in this. On 7 February it was agreed that Argyll should have a commission to transport 1,500 men to Ireland immediately, and that parliament would pay them from the time of their landing. Later it was also agreed that Argyll or his deputy should be governor of Rathlin Island.[64]

Thus even though the treaty was not yet complete provision had been made for sending 4,000 Scots (the 2,500 plus Argyll's 1,500) to Ireland. On 18 March Charles issued a commission to Argyll under the great seal of England; as his was the only one of the Scots regiments sent to Ireland to receive a royal commission it has been argued that the distinction proves that Charles intended the regiment to be 'a guard for his person'. However, it is obvious that the real reason that Argyll received

60. *R.P.C.S. 1638-43*, 185; *A.P.S.* VI, i, 367.
61. N.L.S. Wodrow MSS, Folio LXVI, ff. 199-200, quoted in Stevenson, *Scottish Revolution*, p. 243.
62. S.R.O. PA.13/2, f. 7[2].
63. N.L.S. Wodrow MSS, Folio LXVI, ff. 194, 201.
64. *L.J.* IV, 568, 591, 592, 604-6; *C.J.* II, 416, 417, 438; H.M.C. 53: *Montagu*, p. 147; Hill, *Macdonnells of Antrim*, pp. 74-5; Spalding, *Memorialls*, II, 133; N.L.S. Wodrow MSS, Folio LXVI, f. 213.

a royal commission was that since the treaty was incomplete some other warrant was necessary to authorise the regiment to land in Ireland; a similar commission had previously been signed by the king for the commander of the 2,500 men, for the same reason.[65]

It was proposed that Argyll should go to London to help in the treaty negotiations, since he had a personal interest in seeing the rebels defeated. As Antrim's men had risen, the Highlands, which 'dependis upon his [Argyll's] power and actioun', might be infected by rebellion. Later it was decided that Loudoun should go with him. But the English parliament asked that they remain in Scotland, on the grounds that they could best help to speed aid to Ireland from there (though the king agreed to Argyll's coming south). The underlying reason for this rebuff by parliament was the belief that the Scots were really sending their leaders to London to interfere in English affairs. Worried by the consequences for Scotland (and for her army in Ireland) of civil war in England, the covenanters were trying to mediate in the quarrel between king and parliament.[66] Loudoun went to the king in April to suggest Scots mediation, but Charles explicitly rejected the offer, as parliament had already done implicitly.[67] It was bad enough to have to accept Scots interference in Ireland; their meddling in purely English affairs as well was not acceptable.

Though the essentials of the treaty had now been agreed, sporadic negotiations over details dragged on endlessly. In April Johnston of Wariston carried copies of the articles agreed to the king (who had withdrawn to York) and to the Scots privy council,[68] But exasperating delays continued. The Scots commissioners complained that, as the affairs of England were taking up so much of parliament's time they had refrained from pressing demands for negotiations on any topic except the Irish treaty, which was too urgent to be delayed. But even this was neglected, for English affairs were becoming 'more rather than less pressing'. The complaint achieved nothing; it

65. *R.P.C.S. 1638-43*, pp. 203, 233; F. B. Maurice, *The History of the Scots Guards* (2 vols, London, 1934), I, 1-7; S.R.O. PA.13/2, ff. 28v-30; D. Stevenson, 'The Myth of the Founding of the Scots Guards in 1642', S.H.R. LVI (1977), 114-18.
66. *R.P.C.S. 1638-43*, pp. 198, 211, 217; S.R.O. PA.13/3, ff. 11, 16v; N.L.S. Wodrow MSS, Folio LXVI, ff. 199-200, 201; *C.J.* II, 449; *L.J.* IV, 602-3, 610.
67. Stevenson, *Scottish Revolution*, p. 248.
68. S.R.O. PA.13/3, ff. 30v, 31v-32, 38; *R.P.C.S. 1638-43*, p. 245.

was dated 6 April but was not read in the Lords until 18 April, and on 26 May the Scots were still urging that a conference of both houses be held to discuss it.[69]

The reason for this particular delay probably arose from the king's actions. In April he announced from York his intention of crossing to Ireland to suppress the rebellion, and urged the hastening over of the Scottish army to help him. Parliament immediately denounced the idea. There were fears that Charles intended to put himself at the head of the rebels instead of crushing them, or that he might take control of the Scottish army and other Protestant forces in Ireland for use in re-imposing his authority in England. To avert English suspicion that they might be involved in some plot with the king, the covenanters also demanded that he remain in England, threatening not to send troops to Ireland if he went there. Charles was forced to abandon his plan, but the episode inevitably heightened English suspicion of the Scots; parliament would be in no hurry to complete the treaty while there seemed any danger that the king would attempt to gain control of the Scots army for his own ends.[70]

On 7 July 1642, after further prompting from the Scots commissioners and over eight months after the idea of sending a Scots army to Ireland had first been put forward, the Lords and Commons approved the treaty.[71] It was then sent to the king, who requested several amendments; some of these parliament accepted, though only reaching agreement on them (on 6 August) under pressure from the Scots.[72] Even after this there was some further debate before, on 27 September, orders were given for sending the treaty to the king again,[73] and it was not to be until mid-1643 that the earl of Lindsay presented copies of the treaty to the Scottish privy council;[74] and not until July 1644 was it ratified by the Scottish parliament.[75] The king's assent to the treaty was never obtained; by

69. *L.J.* V, 3, 84.
70. *L.J.* IV, 709-10, 715, 719-20, 721, V, 3, 4, 12-14; *R.P.C.S. 1638-43*, pp. 241, 250-1; *C.S.P.V. 1642-3*, p. 54.
71. *L.J.* V, 188; McNeill, *Tanner Letters*, pp. 148-9.
72. *L.J.* V, 211, 220, 262, 269; *C.S.P.D. 1641-3*, pp. 360, 367.
73. *L.J.* V, 371, 374.
74. *R.P.C.S. 1638-43*, pp. 450, 578.
75. The copy of the treaty in W. Dugdale, *A Short View of the Late Troubles in England* (Oxford, 1681), pp. 910-15 is dated 6 August, but is identical with that in *A.P.S.* VI, i, 189-92 which is called the treaty as approved by the English parliament on 7 July.

September 1642 when it was sent to him the English civil war had already begun, and he had no wish to confirm the right of his enemies in the English parliament to employ and pay an army of 10,000 Scots, potential enemies, in Ireland.[76]

By the terms of the treaty the Scots agreed to send 6,000 musketeers and 4,000 pikemen, plus officers, to Ireland. Scotland was to pay the cost of levying the men and transporting them to Ireland. Their arms and ammunition were to be supplied out of Scottish magazines, but these would be replaced by arms sent later from England. England was also to provide artillery for the army. The officers and men were to be paid at English rates, which were considerably higher than Scots ones, from the time of their landing and for at least three months after 20 June 1642. In addition to the 10,000 footmen a lifeguard of 100 horsemen for the general was to be raised in Scotland, and England was to levy and equip ten troops of horse to join with the army to provide it with cavalry. The Scots were to serve in Ulster as a separate army, under their own general, but the army was to take orders from the lord lieutenant or other governors of Ireland. They could order the detachment of part of the army from the main body, or order the whole army out of Ulster into other provinces if necessary. Carrickfergus and Coleraine were to be handed over to the Scots as magazines and garrisons, and they were to have power to order the inhabitants of Ulster to help them. To protect the army while it was crossing to Ireland, and maintain its communications with Scotland once it had crossed, the English parliament was to provide two ships.[77]

ii.   The Recruiting and Organizing of the Army

At the time of the rebellion in Ireland about 2,500 men of the covenanters' army were still in arms; it had been thought prudent to keep up part of the army while the king was in Scotland to guard against a royalist *coup d'etat*. Pretexts for maintaining men in arms though a peace treaty had been

---

76. In both the Propositions of Uxbridge (November 1644) and the Propositions of Newcastle (July 1646) Charles was asked to ratify the Irish treaty of 6 August 1642, S. R. Gardiner, ed. *Constitutional Documents of the Puritan Revolution* (3rd ed. Oxford, 1906), pp. 278, 297.
77. For a summary of the Treaty see Appendix One. The Scots army included some archers, doubtless from the Highlands (Carte MSS, 3, f. 66v), though no provision for them is made in the treaty.

signed were provided first by the fact that not all the king's forces in England had disbanded, then by argument that they could not be disbanded without pay and that no money was available. The 2,500 men comprised three regiments of foot, those of Major General Robert Monro and Colonel John Cochrane at Edinburgh, and Lord Sinclair's at Aberdeen;[78] Cochrane was soon 'casheered for offering to be loyall', being involved in the obscure royalist plot known as 'the Incident', and was replaced by his lieutenant colonel, Robert Home, who had helped to thwart the plot.[79];

When the idea of sending an army to Ireland was suggested it was natural to look to these three regiments as a nucleus on which to build the new army. On 3 December the privy council ordered the earl of Leven to speak to the officers and men under Monro and Home to see if they were willing to serve in Ireland. Any who refused were to be replaced, and the two regiments were to be recruited to provide a total of 2,000 men. 3,000 more were to be levied in the shires; it was now known that the English had suggested that 5,000 men be sent to Ireland at once. Of the recruits as many as possible were to be men who had served in the Bishops' Wars. As for officers, the lieutenants were to be men who had served in the Thirty Years' War; so were the captains if this was possible, but they could be gentlemen without experience. Of the 3,000 recruits, 1,000 were to be Highlanders, thought to be especially suited to Irish conditions. Not all shires in the country were ordered to contribute to the levies. Kirkcudbrightshire in the south and all the north eastern and far northern shires were excluded. As the first two of these areas were ones in which there had been fighting in the Bishops' Wars, it looks as if the covenanters were reluctant to remove men they could trust from them for service in Ireland as royalist risings were still feared, and the same probably applies to the far north as well.[80] This seems

78. C. S. Terry, *The life and campaigns of Alexander Leslie, First Earl of Leven* (London, 1899), p. 157n; Spalding, *Memorialls*, II, 65, 86-7; J. Turner, *Memoirs of his own life and times* (Bannatyne Club, 1829), p. 17.
79. Turner, *Memoirs*, p. 18; Stevenson, *Scottish Revolution*, p. 238.
80. The omission of the tiny shires of Kinross and Clackmannan from the orders for levies has no real significance, *R.P.C.S. 1638-43*, pp. 170-1, 497-8. H. Hazlett, 'The Recruitment and Organisation of the Scottish Army in Ulster, 1642-9', in H. A. Cronne, T. W. Moody and D. B. Quinn, eds. *Essays in British and Irish History in honour of James Eadie Todd* (London, 1949), pp. 109-10 writes of two different plans for levies, but it seems clear that one is a draft version of the other. His list of shires which were to contribute to the levies erroneously omits five shires,

confirmed by the fact that Sinclair's regiment, based in the largest royalist burgh in the country (Aberdeen), was not at first ordered to prepare for transfer to Ireland. Orders were also given to provide shipping; Argyll was in Glasgow on 8 December arranging for boats to be held ready on forty-eight hours' notice.[81]

Little was done, however, to follow up this prompt action. There was evidently little enthusiasm for enlisting as common soldiers, and the delays of the English parliament over the treaty removed any sense of urgency. In the fast changing political circumstances of the day many must have thought it unlikely that the army would, in the end, ever be sent to Ireland. When, therefore, in January 1642 the English parliament agreed that the 2,500 men said to be already in arms in Scotland should cross to Ireland immediately, there were in reality fewer on foot—though the English parliament had provided nearly £6,000 sterling for pay for that number.[82]

A committee was established to consider what should be done to hasten levies. It concluded that from the shires 'nothing may be expected almost be anie thing that is yit done'. Lack of money and the fact that officers had not yet been appointed to command the men had made recruiting almost impossible.[83] On 3 February orders were again given to levy men to bring up the strength of Monro's and Home's regiments to 1,000 men each and a contract was made with Sir Mungo Campbell of Lawers to levy 500 men as part of a regiment.[84] It is possible that Lawers' men were to be levied to provide a force to remain in Scotland for defence after the 2,500 left for Ireland, but it is more likely that they were intended to replace Lord Sinclair's as part of the 2,500, for delay and neglect had led to Sinclair's regiment virtually disintegrating. When he arrived in Aberdeen in January to march it south after it had been decided that it should form part of the force being sent to Ireland he found that desertion had reduced its strength to about 260 men, and that those

and the total number of men to be levied was not Hazlett's 2,318 men, but 3,078.
81. *R.P.C.S. 1638-43*, pp. 171-2; Marwick, *Extracts from the Records of the Burgh of Glasgow, 1573-1642*, p. 435.
82. S.R.O. PA.13/2, ff. 23-24v; *C.J.* II, 410.
83. *R.P.C.S. 1638-43*, pp. 182, 501-2, 523-4.
84. Ibid. pp. 192, 197.

who were left spent their time (according to a royalist account) drinking, whoring, swearing and fighting. About sixty-six Aberdeen women were tried for their relations with 'this ribald regiment'; some accompanied it when it left Aberdeen.[85]

Morale in Monro's and Home's regiments was little higher. On news that they were about to leave for Ireland 'diverse of the souldiours ... have latelie disbandit', leading to the issue of proclamations against deserters.[86] Further demoralisation was probably caused by the news that the regiments would be paid at Scottish rates until they arrived in Ireland; they had evidently expected the higher English rates, and Monro refused to submit the accounts of his regiment calculated on any rates but the higher.[87]

In spite of such difficulties, however, detailed planning of the recruiting, supplying, arming and transporting of 2,500 men began early in February.[88] Finance proved an immediate problem; the committee for common burdens was ordered to make all payments necessary on the instructions of the privy council,[89] but the committee had little money at its disposal. The English parliament had fallen behind with the payments to Scotland of the Brotherly Assistance promised in the 1641 peace treaty, and it had been out of this that the covenanters had hoped to pay for the levy and transport of the army. A joint meeting of the council and the committee of 28 March therefore agreed to borrow £40,000 sterling.[90]

On 15 February the king's commission under the great seal of England appointing a commander for the 2,500 men and authorising him to wage war in Ireland and act as governor of Carrickfergus was produced before the privy council. The king had agreed to leave it blank, for the council to fill in the name of the commander, to avoid more time being wasted in consultations. The council inserted the name of Major General Robert Monro in the commission, and on 26 February issued instructions to him to cross to Carrickfergus with his men.[91]

By this time troops and shipping were gathering in the west.

85. Spalding, *Memorialls*, II, 99, 101-2.
86. *R.P.C.S. 1638-43*, pp. 200-1, 206-7.
87. S.R.O. PA.14/1, f. 32-v.
88. *R.P.C.S. 1638-43*, pp. 196-7, 203, 210, 223, 225-6, 228-9, 532-4.
89. Ibid. p. 218; S.R.O. PA.14/1, ff. 30, 32-v, 41v-42v, 64-v, 139v-140v.
90. S.R.O. PA.14/1, ff. 69-71; D. Stevenson, 'The Financing of the Cause of the Covenants, 1638-51', *S.H.R.* LI (1972), 96-7; *R.P.C.S. 1638-43*, pp. 232-3.
91. R.P.C.S. 1638-43, pp. 202, 203, 208-9, 211.

Monro's regiment embarked at Largs, Home's at Ayr, Sinclair's (though still much under strength) at Irvine. Adverse weather had delayed embarkation for two weeks, and the ships laden with men had to spend a further fortnight sheltering off Arran before a suitable wind allowed them to make the short crossing to Carrickfergus, where they landed on 3 April.[92]

Levying and organising the rest of the 10,000 men was by now well under way. The earl of Loudoun suggested that the privy council (in which, as chancellor, he presided) should have power to appoint the general officers, or that, if the king did the appointing, he should act on the council's advice. No general would be acceptable to Scotland except Leven, and the earl of Lothian should be lieutenant general; if he were not, then there should be no lieutenant general. This would both save money and 'avoyd contest about the persone' as nobles competed for the post. As to other officers Loudoun advised that the major general, the lieutenant colonels and the majors should all be trained soldiers, while the colonels and captains could be nobles or gentlemen. Similar limitations had been imposed on the covenanters' armies in the Bishops' Wars to ensure that among the officers enthusiastic amateurs were balanced by skilled professionals.[93]

Loudoun's advice was followed closely. The English parliament had already resolved to petition the king to appoint Leven to be general of the army, and the king agreed to this, to Lothian being lieutenant general and to Monro being major general. It was doubtless also on advice from Scotland that he appointed Sir Alexander Hamilton to be general of the artillery.[94]

Next came choice of the colonels. It was decided that there should be at least ten regiments, not for any military reason but simply to satisfy those who wished to be colonels. Loudoun remarked that it would be easier to find twenty colonels than to levy the men for ten regiments, and he hoped that Lothian would not insist on commanding a regiment so that one of the other applicants could be satisfied. To help provide places for the would-be colonels it was suggested that

92. Ibid. p. 235; Turner, *Memoirs*, p. 19; H.M.C. 36: *Ormonde*, II, 5.
93. N.L.S. Wodrow MSS, Folio LXVI, ff. 204-5, 206; Stevenson, *Scottish Revolution*, p. 129.
94. *L.J.* IV, 601; *C.J.* II, 436; *R.P.C.S. 1638-43*, pp. 211, 218-19, 221.

Argyll's regiment should not be regarded as part of the 10,000, and that another extra regiment above the 10,000 men should be raised for the general of artillery, but these ideas were dropped when it became clear the English were not interested in providing 'jobs for the boys'. In the end (on 11 March) it was agreed that the ten regiments should be commanded by Monro, Home, Sinclair, Argyll and Lawers (all of whom already had men in arms or had been commissioned to raise men), Leven, Eglinton, Glencairn, Lindsay and (if he insisted on having a regiment) Lothian. He did thus insist and was appointed a colonel on 28 March, though Loudoun had refused a regiment for himself to help, he claimed, to satisfy the other eager applicants.[95] Lord Montgomery, Eglinton's son, was at first appointed to command the regiment of horse which was to be attached to the army,[96] but the English parliament apparently claimed the right to select the colonel as it was to levy the regiment, and chose Sir William Balfour.[97]

In addition to the general officers mentioned above the Scots at first asked for a variety of general staff officers. Some of these the English refused to agree to pay—among them a secretary for the general, though the barely literate earl of Leven had earnestly urged the importance of such an officer since corresponding with the governments of all three kingdoms 'is not ane task fitt for everie ordinarie domine'.[98] However, the army was provided with a clerk to the council of war, a post later filled by David Anderson.[99] Since no muster of the general staff survives the names of all officers on it are not known. Patrick or Peter Leslie served as adjutant general as well as being a captain in Sinclair's regiment.[100] Dr Robert Cunningham (the son of an Ayrshire minister) was one of the general staff's two physicians, and quarrelled bitterly with one of the two apothecaries, Peter Primrose, in 1643. Andrew Brown was appointed one of the army's surgeons in 1644.[101]

95. *R.P.C.S. 1638-43*, pp. 218-19, 221, 223; S.R.O. PA.13/3, ff. 18v, 20, 21; N.L.S. Wodrow MSS, Folio LXVI, ff. 204-5, 214.
96. *R.P.C.S. 1638-43*, pp. 243-4.
97. *D.N.B.* under Sir William Balfour.
98. D. Laing, ed. *Correspondence of Sir Robert Kerr, first Earl of Ancram, and his son William, third earl of Lothian* (2 vols, Edinburgh, 1875), I, 132; Hazlett, op. cit. 114.
99. T.S.A.I. p. 47.
100. See Appendix Three.
101. T.S.A.I. pp. 45-6, 83; S.R.O. PA.14/1, ff. 98-v; G. E. Cokayne, *Complete Baronetage* (6 vols, Exeter, 1900-9), IV, 295.

At first no officers were appointed to supervise the paying and supplying of the army since the English were supposed to carry out these functions;[102] in the event such officials became necessary, for the English proved incapable of carrying out their promises. William Thomson had been involved in the army's finances since March 1642, and in November was appointed receiver general or commissary of the army, with John Campbell as receiver depute.[103] In 1644 Campbell took over from Thomson as receiver general and commissary, and Alexander Mure appears later in the same year as ordinary receiver and proviant master of the army.[104]

Once the senior officers had been appointed levying of the remainder to the army gathered speed. This at once raised problems; as the treaty had not yet been completed the men had no authority to land in Ireland; but who was to pay them if they remained in Scotland? Leven complained that the levies were very well advanced but that the men 'ly heavie' on the hands of the officers and gentlemen who had raised them, to 'thair infinit prejudice', for they had to borrow money to support the men.[105] As a result on 19 April the privy council of Scotland authorised Leven to send all companies that had been levied to Ireland at once;[106] it had been decided to ignore the incomplete state of the treaty and there had doubtless been indications that the English parliament would not object to this. It was not until 7 May that the king issued a commission to Leven to be commander in chief of the Scottish army in Ireland, and even after that there were doubts as to the adequacy of the commission. On 30 June three of the army's colonels (Argyll, Glencairn and Sinclair) and other members of the privy council protested at clauses which made the commission revokeable at the king's will; the privy council had been entrusted by the Scottish parliament with negotiating the terms on which the army would serve in Ireland so the commission should not be revokeable without the council's consent. Leven himself raised a different objection when his

102. Hazlett, op. cit. 114-15, 119-20.
103. *R.P.C.S. 1638-43*, pp. 232-3, 343-5; *A.P.S.* VI, i, 206. John Jossie sometimes acted as Thomson's deputy, e.g. *R.P.C.S. 1638-43*, p. 408.
104. *A.P.S.* VI, i, 206; S.R.O. PA.11/1, ff. 150-150¹; S.R.O. PA.11/3, f. 24; P.R.O.L. SP.46/106, f. 115; T.S.A.I. p. 83; S.R.O. PA.7/3/20.
105. Laing, *Correspondence*, I, 131-2.
106. *R.P.C.S. 1638-43*, pp. 244, 245.

commission was delivered to him on 12 July; by the commission he was bound to adhere to the articles of the treaty, but the treaty had not yet been finally agreed to.[107]

In spite of such technical difficulties, however, the build-up of the army in Ireland continued steadily in these months, as its muster rolls indicate. By the terms of the treaty the English parliament appointed a muster master to muster the Scots on their arrival in Ireland. But the man chosen, William Roberts, was 'a pernitious fellowe', unacceptable to the Scots; he had in 1640 been secretary to Sir Patrick Ruthven, Lord Ettrick, who had held Edinburgh Castle for the king against the covenanters.[108] The Scots therefore appointed their own muster master, Hew Kennedy, a burgess of Ayr.[109]

On 7 April Kennedy carried out his first muster in Ireland of the forces which had landed a few days before; 1,554 officers and men of Monro's own regiment, 856 of Home's and 486 of Sinclair's, a total of 2,896. Next to arrive was Lawers' regiment; 932 officers and men were mustered on 10 and 18 April. By 1 May Argyll's entire regiment, 1,099 strong, was in Ireland. Leven's Glencairn's, Eglinton's and Lindsay's all began to arrive in mid and late May, but it was early July before the first of Lothian's men reached Ireland. By 3 August virtually the entire army was in Ulster, 1,119 officers and 10,042 men. Subsequently twelve more officers and 102 more men joined Lothian's regiment.[110] Finally, probably in late August or September, the artillery train landed with ninety six officers and artificers.[111] According to the musters the covenanters had assembled over 10,000 men, exclusive of officers, in Ulster, as they had undertaken by the treaty. As the English parliament subsequently approved the musters, by accepting that the Scots should be paid according to them,[112]

107. Ibid. pp. 277, 287, 299; W. Fraser, ed. *The Melvilles earls of Melville, and the Leslies earls of Leven* (3 vols, Edinburgh, 1890), III, xlix, 168-70.
108. *C.J.* II, 416, III, 132; N.L.S. Wodrow MSS, Folio LXV, f. 198v.
109. S.R.O. PA.14/1, f. 45v; Bodleian Library, Tanner MSS, 62a, no. 145. Leven's order to Kennedy was dated February 1642, not 1643 as stated in McNeill, *Tanner Letters*, 162-3. From this and other instances it is clear that McNeill did not realise that the Scottish new year began on 1 January.
110. See Appendix Three.
111. Cambridge University Library, MS Ee.111.39(D), The Pay of the Scottish Army in Ireland; S.R.O. PA.14/1, f. 122; Spalding, *Memorialls*, II, 174; *R.P.C.S. 1638-43*, pp. 312-13, 214.
112. *L.J.* VI, 45-6, 289; McNeill, *Tanner Letters*, pp. 162-3, 164. When in December 1642 the earl of Lindsay complained of the lack of perfect muster rolls

it seems safe to assume that the rolls are substantially accurate. The point is worth stressing for there were later to be allegations, by those with political interests in minimising the part played by the Scots in Ulster, that the Scots never sent nearly so many men. Clarendon, for example, wrote merely of 'some soldiers' coming from Scotland,[113] while Cox argued that perhaps the Scots might have been 10,000 strong 'by the Muster, but not near that Number by the Poll'.[114] But there is no evidence that this really was the case, and the extent to which two sets of musters, by Kennedy and an Englishman, Thomas Clayton, coincide seems to argue against widespread falsification of the rolls. It is true that prevention of some fraud or error was almost impossible; it is quite possible that a few of the Scots soldiers were either Ulster Scot refugees who enlisted in Scotland, or were Ulster Scots recruited in Ireland, but this latter practice had been sanctioned by the Commons by a resolution of 13 May that if the Scots had difficulty in recruiting the full 10,000 men 'that if they will take those Forces of their own Nation, that ar already in actual Service in Ulster as Part of their Number' they would receive pay for them.[115] But there is no evidence that this actually happened on a significant scale; certainly none of the regiments already in arms in Ulster were incorporated into the Scots army.

In undertaking to pay this army the English parliament had assumed a major financial burden which proved impossible to bear once civil war began in England. The pay of the ten regiments and the lifeguards of horse and foot, as levied by Thomas Clayton in and after September 1642, plus the general staff and the artillery train, totalled approximately £16,900 sterling a month—with about £1,000 sterling a month more payable in wagon allowances.[116]

The only part of the Scottish army which did not reach Ireland in 1642 was the regiment of ten troops of horse which England had agreed to levy and attach to the army. The treaty

he probably meant that he had not received the rolls, rather than that he had but that they were inaccurate, *R.P.C.S. 1638-43*, p. 578.
113. Hyde, *History*, I, 438. See also Bagwell, *Stuarts*, II, 14.
114. R. Cox, *Hibernia Anglicana* (2 vols, London, 1689-90), II, 115.
115. *C.J.* II, 570.
116. These totals are calculated from the figures given in Appendices Two and Three.

had failed to specify where the troops were to be raised; in April 1642 Leven apparently thought they were to be levied in Scotland,[117] but in July the lords justice evidently expected them to come from England,[118] and this seems the more likely intention. Sir William Balfour, who was appointed to command the regiment, was a Scot who became naturalised in England in 1642. He had seen service in the Dutch army, and was governor of the Tower of London from 1630 to 1641. When the English parliament raised an army against the king late in 1642 Balfour became its lieutenant general of horse,[119] and it seems that, if he had levied any men for service in Ireland, they were incorporated into the parliamentary army in England. The only captains of troops appointed at first were Balfour himself and Sir Robert Adair of Kinhilt.[120] In July 1642 Leven complained of the failure of the English to supply his army with cavalry, and protested that he should be allowed to make use of horse troops already serving in Ulster, or to levy his own.[121] Cavalry was at first provided, as Leven had suggested, by assigning existing troops to the army. By September 1642 seven troops were thus assigned; Captain Arthur Chichester's, Lord Montgomery's, Lord Claneboye's, Sir James Montgomery's, Colonel Arthur Hill's, Sir William Cole's and Mr Upton's. In addition Sir Robert Adair's troop had been levied and was serving with the army.[122]

The earl of Leven finally joined his army in Ireland on 4 August, accompanied by two of his colonels, Eglinton and Sinclair, and Sir Alexander Hamilton soon followed with the artillery. But none of them stayed long. Leven returned to Scotland in November, Eglinton and Hamilton at about the same time. Sinclair stayed into 1643, only leaving when he

---

117. Laing, *Correspondence*, I, 132. Laing dates the letter February 1642 but it is clear from its contents that it was written in April—it refers to Wariston bringing the draft of the treaty to Scotland.
118. H.M.C. 36: *Ormonde*, N.S. II, 143.
119. *D.N.B.* under Sir William Balfour.
120. *C.J.* II, 416, 534, 570; H. Hazlett, 'A History of the Military Forces Operating in Ireland, 1641-9' (Ph.D. thesis, Queen's University, Belfast, 1938), I, 226-9. The army accounts in Cambridge University Library MS Ee.111.39(D) mention Balfour's troop but do not detail pay due to it, which probably means that it had not reached Ireland.
121. *R.P.C.S. 1638-43*, p. 299.
122. J. Hogan, ed. 'Rawlinson Manuscripts, Class A. 110', *Analecta Hibernica*, 4 (1932), 7-8, 88; Hogan, *Letters and Papers*, p. 186.

fell ill.[123] None of them ever returned to Ireland, but at least their record is better than that of Lothian and Lindsay, neither of whom ever set foot in Ireland. Glencairn only came to Ulster once, in 1645, and then he came not as a colonel but as a refugee. Argyll's sole visit to the army was to be in 1646, and he then acted as a representative of the Scottish government rather than as a colonel, but at least he provided an adequate substitute in his absence by (on 21 March 1642) virtually resigning command of his regiment to his lieutenant colonel, Sir Duncan Campbell of Auchinbreck, whom he appointed governor of Rathlin and chief commander of the regiment.[124]

Of the origins of the common soldiers of the army little is known; the scheme for raising set numbers of men in each shire having broken down, most of the men were probably recruited by the officers wherever they could find them.[125] In the case of regiments with noble colonels much of the recruiting was no doubt done on the estates of, or in the area dominated by, the noble concerned. Argyll's regiment was thus composed almost entirely of men from the west Highlands. But not all noble colonels recruited only in areas where they had influence; Major Borthwick was reported in May to be in Aberdeen recruiting for the earl of Lindsay's regiment and Captain George Gordon raised a company in Sutherland for Leven, though in general few men were raised in northern Scotland.[126] Many of the recruits had doubtless served in the Bishops' Wars and enlisted on finding it difficult to return to their old ways of life; special payments were offered to such trained men to tempt them.[127] But, as the problem of desertion from the regiments kept in arms and sent to Ireland indicates, not all who had served the covenanters in 1639-41 wished to prolong their military service. The crossing to Ireland made desertion more difficult but it remained enough of a problem for offenders to be threatened with death in a proclamation of 23 June 1642.[128] As to the general character of the common soldiers, a Protestant officer in Ulster described

123. Turner, *Memoirs*, pp. 23, 25, 29; Spalding, *Memorialls*, II, 174, 209; *R.P.C.S. 1638-43*, p. 314.
124. Inveraray Castle, Argyll Transcripts XII, 85.
125. Hazlett, op. cit. 111.
126. R. and G. Gordon, *A Genealogical History of the Earldom of Sutherland* (Edinburgh, 1813), pp. 509-10; Spalding, *Memorialls*, II, 140.
127. *R.P.C.S. 1638-43*, p. 228.
128. Ibid. pp. 280-1.

described them as 'but the scum' of Scotland;[129] and even if this was not a fair description of them when they arrived in Ulster, their hardships soon reduced them to a condition in which it seemed apt.

Like most armies of the day the Scottish army in Ireland was accompanied by large numbers of camp-followers; wives and families of soldiers, women of less regular status, men hoping for plunder. The latter raised difficulties about discipline since they were not members of the army. One of Argyll's captains complained that while his company from Islay was under strength the regiment was accompanied by 'volunteers' from that island of whom it was said 'ther is noe wrong done in Ireland bot onlie that quhilk is done by these men that comes out of Illa'. To prevent further freebooters of this sort troubling Ulster it was announced that any who came from Islay without passes would be prevented from returning home when they wished.[130]

The officer who described the Scottish soldiers as scum rather surprisingly noted that their officers were 'generally accomplished gentlemen, and indeed very musical and liberal'. Patrick Adair, a presbyterian minister, agreed that they were generally 'men of courage and conduct', but lamented that they were officers 'who had no inclination towards religion, except in so far as the times and State who employed them seemed to favour it' while most of the soldiers were even worse, 'haters of the purity and power of religion'.[131]

The officers were a mixture of professional soldiers, mainly trained as mercenaries on the continent, and nobles or lesser landowners and members of their families. Sometimes the two categories overlapped, for many of the professionals could claim some relationship with landed families. Thus the earl of Leven, though now himself newly ennobled and related (illegitimately) to noble families, was appointed general through the great reputation he had won in the Swedish service, where he had risen to the rank of field-marshal, and as the covenanters' commander in 1639-41. In spite of his new title he was still often referred to simply as General Leslie. On

129. E. Hogan, ed. *The history of the warr of Ireland from 1641 to 1646. By a British officer of the regiment of Sir John Clotworthy* (Dublin, 1873), p. 50.
130. Innes, *Book of the Thanes of Cawdor*, pp. 286-7.
131. Adair, *Narrative*, pp. 88-9, 124-5.

being offered the command of the army in Ireland he had claimed that he had hoped to be able to end his days in peace, though he accepted the offer.[132] It seems that it was expected that he would command the army in person; his failure to do so for more than a few weeks resulted from quarrels with his officers and increasing age—he had been born in about 1580. On the other hand it is probably true that no personal service was expected of the lieutenant general, the earl of Lothian, or of the other noble colonels. They were appointed primarily as leading figures in the covenanting regime in Scotland, the 'rigid lords' as a royalist called them,[133] and as great nobles whose rank entitled them to such positions. A partial exception was Glencairn, whose enthusiasm for the covenant was limited; he was appointed at the king's request. Instead of serving in the field the noble colonels played the part of patrons of the army, supporters of its interests in Scotland. They were especially useful in the initial recruiting of the army.

Of the non-noble colonels, Monro and Home had had the good fortune (along with Lord Sinclair) to command regiments already on foot when the new army was organised, and were allowed to retain them. Lawers doubtless owed his command to his brother, the earl of Loudoun; Loudoun's refusal of a regiment for himself was perhaps not so disinterested as he claimed, for there is no sign that he really wanted one and with his brother as a colonel the claims of friends and relatives for posts in the army could be satisfied. Many of the officers of the regiments turned out to be the kinsmen of the colonels. Argyll's lieutenant colonel, major and five of his captains were Campbells. The lieutenant colonel and three captains in Glencairn's regiment were Cunninghams. Lord Sinclair's lieutenant colonel was his brother.

Seven knights and baronets were atracted to serve in the army in Ireland; Colonel Sir Mungo Campbell of Lawers, Lieutenant Colonel Sir Duncan Campbell of Auchinbreck (Argyll's regiment), Captain Sir Charles Arnot (Home's) Captain Sir William Blair (Monro's)—who evidently lost interest in the army very quickly as he appears in the first of the 1642 musters but not the second—and three captains in Lothian's

132. S.R.O. PA.13/3, f. 19.
133. H. Guthry, *Memoirs of Henry Guthry: Late Bishop of Dunkeld* (2nd ed. Glasgow, 1747), p. 114.

regiment; Sir John Murray, Sir Walter Riddell and Sir James Lockhart (who was to be killed in Ireland in 1643). The stipulation that lieutenant colonels and majors should be experienced soldiers was at least partly adhered to. Thus Lieutenant Colonel George Monro (Leven's regiment), the major general's nephew and son in law, and Major James Turner (Sinclair's) had both served in the Swedish forces in Germany. Major James Bannatyne who commanded the life-guard of horse was a brother of the laird of Corehouse (Lanarkshire) and 'a souldier of great merite for conduct and valour'. He had led the covenanters' army across the Tyne at the battle of Newburn in 1640, and in Ireland he was to do 'notable executione upon the rebelles ... for without de-rogateing from the due praises of others, he was the sword of the Scots cavillrie'.[134] Many of the captains were close relatives of nobles or lairds, like William Drummond (Monro's), a son of Lord Maderty; Ensign (later Captain) John Gordon (Monro's), son of Sir Alexander Gordon of Navisdaill; George Gordon (Leven's), brother of the earl of Sutherland; and James Wallace (Monro's) of the Ayrshire family of Auchans.

Officers of fortune who had served the covenanters in 1639-41 were said to have been discontented at the lack of opportunities for them in the new army. They complained that most of the noble colonels insisted on also being captains of companies, 'suppose of small skill', to entitle themselves to extra pay, and that they chose as the other captains and as inferior officers their kinsmen and friends, excluding trained men eager to serve. Leven is said to have intervened to try to ensure that the army was adequately supplied with properly qualified officers, but with little success.[135] As a result some of the mercenary officers returned to the continent. Others found convenient opportunities for employment in the English civil war which was just starting, either on the king's side or on parliament's.[136] More were recruited in England to officer English forces being sent to Ireland, though this soon led to trouble. The absentee lord lieutenant of Ireland, the earl of Leicester, reported 'I finde a very great unwillingnes in

---

134. Turner, *Memoirs*, pp. 28-9; J. Somerville, Lord Somerville, *Memorie of the Somervilles*, [ed. Sir Walter Scott] (2 vols, Edinburgh, 1815), II, 202-4, 210.
135. Spalding, *Memorialls*, II, 140-1.
136. Ibid. II, 141; *C.S.P.D. 1641-3*, p. 367.

Sir James Turner. Major of Sinclair's regiment in the Scottish army in Ireland. Portrait from his volume of military essays *Pallas Armata* (Edinburgh, 1683).

the Captaines and other officers of our nation to be commanded by any but theyr oun countrymen, in so much as some have flatly refused to go, rather than they would be under Scottish commanders'. Efforts were being made to keep this quiet to avoid offending the Scots, and matters were further complicated by orders from the king that no English regiment sent to Ireland was to include Scottish officers.[137]

The man whose character and ability were to be of most importance to the Scottish army in Ireland in the years ahead was Major General Robert Monro, its effective commander except for the few weeks when Leven was in Ireland. Monro came from a family (said to be descended from the Irish family of O'Cahan)[138] which had greatly distinguished itself in the Swedish service. His cousin, the head of the family, Colonel Robert Monro of Foulis (known as the 'Black Baron') had been killed at Ulm in 1633. His eldest brother, Colonel John Monro of Obsdale, was killed in the same year. His nephew George (son of his brother John) had been present at the battle of Lutzen when King Gustavus Adolphus was killed.[139] Like his cousin and his brother, Robert Monro had first served in Sir Donald MacKay's regiment, rising to the rank of colonel. He had returned to Scotland in 1633 and devoted himself to trying to found a hospital for old soldiers and gain pensions for them, and to compiling a history of the regiment. This was published in London in 1637 under the title of *Monro his expedition with the worth Scots regiment (called MacKeyes Regiment) levied in August 1626. ... Collected and gathered together at spare hours by Col. Robert Monro ... for the use of all worthy Cavaliers favouring the laudable professing of arms. To which is annexed the Abridgement of Excercise, and divers practicall Observations, for the younger officer his consideration; ending with the souldiers Meditations going on service.*[140]

---

137. Carte MSS, 2, f. 266.
138. Gilbert, *Contemporary History*, I, 25, III, 379; A. Mackenzie, *History of the Monros of Fowlis* (Inverness, 1898), pp. 1-2.
139. Mackenzie, *Monros*, pp. 78-81, 169-77.
140. Ibid. pp. 210-32; *R.P.C.S. 1633-5*, pp. xxi-xxiii, 333-6, 349, 353-6, 615. Sales of the 1,500 copies of the book which were printed (*R.P.C.S. 1638-43*, pp. 423-4) were evidently disappointing, for in 1644 some were reissued with a new title page as *The Scottish Military Discipline learned from the valiant Swede ... collected ... by Major Generall Monro, Being now Generall of all the Scotch Forces against the Rebels in Ireland.* Copies of this rare second edition are to be

THE
Scotch Military Discipline
LEARND FROM THE VALIANT
SWEDE,

And collected for the use of all worthy Commanders
favouring the laudable profession of ARMES.

By Major Generall *Monro,*

Being novv Generall of all the Scotch Forces against the Rebels in
Ireland, communicates his Abridgement of Exercise, in divers Practicall
Observations for the younger Officers better instruction; ending with
the Souldiers Meditations going on in Service.

LONDON,
Printed for *William Ley* at Pauls-Chaine.
1644.

The Scotch Military Discipline. Title page of the work by Robert Monro, Major
General of the Scottish army in Ireland. No portrait of Monro exists.

On his return to Scotland in 1633 Monro had evidently regarded his career as a soldier as over; the date of his birth is unknown, but as he lived until 1675 he cannot have been born long before his father's death in 1589.[141] Thus in 1637, when the troubles in Scotland began, he must have been in his late forties or older. When war approached it is said that he first offered to serve the king but, getting no encouragement, turned to the covenanters instead. This indifference to which side he fought on in the Bishops' Wars he shared with many of the Scots mercenary officers who later became, like him, convinced covenanters.[142] Monro had served the covenanters well, on the Border in 1639 and as commander of their forces in the north east in 1640, moving back to the Border when the main Scots army invaded England. In these years no outstanding military genius was required of him, but he proved to have considerable ability in raising forces, holding them together and using them to crush royalist opposition. In view of the reputation for lack of energy which he was soon to acquire in Ireland it is worth stressing his active and decisive conduct in the Bishops' Wars—which included suppressing a mutiny by killing its leader with his own hands.[143]

Monro has been characterised as a 'rude soldier',[144] but his book gives a very different impression. 'Far from being the production of an illiterate soldier who despises learning, it is saturated in a mass of irrelevant erudition'.[145] Monro was at great pains to display his learning, stressing the importance of knowledge gained from books to the soldier. 'I dare be bould to affirme, that reading and discourse doth as much or rather more, to the furtherance of a perfect souldier, than a few years practice without reading'; 'as the Starres take light from the Sunne; even so from Histories, men draw knowledge and wisdome'.[146] Unfortunately all too often Monro showed a

found in the National Library of Scotland and in the J. T. Gilbert Collection in the Pearse Street Library, Dublin.
141. Mackenzie, *Monros*, pp. 169, 264.
142. Stevenson, *Scottish Revolution*, p. 131; Gordon, *History of Scots Affairs*, I, 49; P. Gordon, *A Short abridgement of Britane's Distemper*, ed. J. Dunn (Spalding Club, 1844), pp. 12-13.
143. Gordon, *History of Scots Affairs*, II, 204, III, 6, 159, 160, 166-9, 196-203, 210-14, 235-6, 251-5; Stevenson, *Scottish Revolution*, pp. 190, 197, 209.
144. S. R. Gardiner, *History of the Great Civil War* (4 vols, London, 1893-4), I, 115.
145. J. H. Burton, *The Scot Abroad* (2 vols, Edinburgh and London, 1864), II, 135, quoted in Hill, *Montgomery Manuscripts*, p. 213n.
146. *Monro his expedition*, To the Reader.

lack of ability to discriminate between the useful and the useless, the profound and the obvious. While many of the
'observations' which follow sections of confused narrative in
his book are sound enough, many are trite, sometimes to the
point of absurdity—though it is a relief to find that the worst
of all ('When cannons are roaring, and bullets flying, he that
would have honour must not feare dying')[147] is plagiarised
from a military song.[148]

The picture that emerges from Monro's book is one of a
conscientious and thoughtful man, skilled in his trade but
pedantic and over serious. That in later life he was prone to
melancholy comes as no surprise,[149] though any natural
tendancy in this direction must have been exacerbated by the
tribulations he was to experience in Ireland.

iii.   The Attitude of the Irish Rebels to the Scots

That the attitude of the Irish who rebelled in 1641 to the
king was ambiguous is well known; on the one hand they
rebelled to force concessions from him, on the other they
claimed to be fighting for him against his enemies. Less well
known but even more remarkable is the ambiguity of their
attitudes to the Scots settlers in Ulster and to the covenanters
in Scotland. The Ulster Scots had played a leading part in the
plantation of Ulster which the rebels wished to undo, and the
rebels claimed that they were driven to rebellion by a threat to
send a Scots army to Ireland to extirpate Catholicism. Yet at
first the rebels spared the lives and property of the Scots
settlers, and they spread the word that they were acting in
alliance with the covenanting regime in Scotland. These two
sets of ambiguities, towards the king and towards the Scots,
were connected by the rebels' claim that it was the king who
had ordered them to spare the Scots.

These seemingly bewildering ambiguities can be explained
at two levels. The first and simplest is that of the exigencies
of propaganda; different claims were made by the rebels to
different groups to try to justify their actions and win support.
The second, underlying this, was a genuine ambiguity in the

147.   Ibid. part 1, p. 65.
148.   P. Young & W. Emberton, *The Cavalier Army. Its Organisation and Every-
day Life* (London, 1974), pp. 85-6.
149.   Hill, *Montgomery Manuscripts*, p. 213.

minds of many of the rebels which led them to make statements which conflicted with each other.

The ambiguity towards the king is the easiest to understand. His and his father's governments had deprived many of the Ulster Irish of their lands and threatened the position of Catholic landowners throughout the country, Old English as well as Irish. Revolt against him to force him to make concessions was therefore logical, and 1641, when his authority was crumbling in all three kingdoms, was clearly an opportune moment for action. On the other hand, the very fact that the king's power was collapsing meant that he posed no immediate threat to Irish interests. The real threat came from those who were seizing power from him—the covenanters in Scotland, parliament in England, and the lords justice (who tended to favour the English parliament) in Dublin. These new regimes and movements were all much more strongly anti-Catholic and anti-Irish than the king had been. Thus the Catholics of Ireland now had at least a negative interest in common with Charles, that of opposing those who were destroying his power in the three kingdoms. That a basis for an alliance between them existed had been implicitly admitted by the king when he had undertaken the abortive negotiations with Antrim and Ormond to provide Irish forces to seize Dublin for him; and of course these negotiations had played a part in bringing about the rebellion.

It seems certain that the claim of the rebels, and of Sir Phelim O'Neill in particular, to be acting on a commission from Charles under the great seal of Scotland (or, according to a few early reports, of England) was false. It is impossible to believe that Charles, for all his political ineptitude, would have acted in a way which would so obviously damage his own interests and, in Britain as a whole, be certain to make him more enemies than friends. At a more practical level, it seems very unlikely that he had free access to the great seal of Scotland on 1 October 1641 (the date of the supposed commission); it is most improbable that he would have addressed such a commission to Sir Phelim O'Neill rather than to Antrim or Ormond; and the commission, if genuine, would almost certainly have been dated from Holyroodhouse, not Edinburgh.[150]

150. Clarke, *Old English in Ireland*, pp. 165-7; R. Dunlop, 'The Forged Commi-

It has, therefore, come to be generally accepted that Sir Pehlim and his colleagues forged the commission to win support, and, further, that they appended to it an impression of the great seal of Scotland taken from the papers of Lord Caulfield captured at Charlemont at the beginning of the rebellion. Though there is some later evidence to support this argument[151] the fact that the register of the great seal of Scotland contains no grants by Charles I to Lord Caulfield or his predecessors weakens it.[152] Indeed the refusal of Sir Phelim ever to show anyone the king's commission which he claimed to have, and the weakness of the evidence that (as is usually said) he had it proclaimed at Newry, gives force to the argument that though O'Neill certainly claimed that he had a commission, he never actually forged (or had forged for him) such a document. Why go to the trouble of manufacturing a forged commission with seal attached if it was never to be produced publicly? According to this argument it was the enemies of both the king and the Irish who forged the actual text of the commission of which copies survive, in order to add substance to Sir Phelim's convenient claim that the king was involved in the rebellion, and thus help to discredit Charles.[153] Acceptance of this solution neatly disposes of many problems, but it creates others. In particular, there is the reference in the commission to the Ulster Scots; 'all Catholic subjects within the Kingdom of Ireland' were to seize the goods, estates and persons of all English Protestants in Ireland, but not those of 'Our loyal and loving Subjects the Scots'.[154] It seems wildly unlikely that any enemy of the king, forging the text of a commission in order to implicate him in the rebellion, would have included such a clause. Since the forgery would presumably have been designed to unite all Protestants, in England, Scotland and Ireland, against the king it would have been counter-productive to have singled out the Scottish settlers to be spared; this might well have been taken to imply that the Scots as well as the Irish were in

ssion of 1641', *English Historical Review*, II (1887), 529-31; Carte, *Ormond*, I, 179-81; Gardiner, *History of England*, X, 91-3.

151.   Dunlop, op. cit. 532-3; Clarke, *Old English in Ireland*, pp. 167-8; Nalson, *Impartial Collection*, II, 529.

152.   *R.M.S. 1620-33* and *1634-51, passim.*

153.   T. Fitzpatrick, 'Sir Phelim's Commission', *New Irish Review*, XXI (1904), 333-48; T. Fitzpatrick, 'The Ulster Civil War', *U.J.A.* N.S. XIII (1907), 133-4.

154.   Dunlop, op. cit. 529-30.

D

league with the king. The provision that the Scots be spared on the other hand, also undermines the argument that the commission was genuine and showed the king turning to the Irish since he had failed to win the support of the covenanters.[155]

But the order to spare the Scots does fit in well with the attitude of the rebels to the covenanters, and this puts responsibility for forging the text of the commission back in their hands. It seems most likely therefore that Sir Phelim did at least have a forged text of a commission, but that he probably did not actually possess a carefully forged document which purported to be the original commission and had an impression of the Scots great seal attached to it. The evidence that a full forgery in this sense did actually exist is weak; to claim that it did but that it was never produced for fear that the forgery be detected[156] brings us back to the point that surely the only reason for a full forgery of an 'original' commission would be so that it could be produced.

The attitude of the Irish to the Scots also helps to explain another problem raised by the 'commission'. Assuming that it was forged by the rebels, why did they claim that it was under the great seal of Scotland? The point has often been overlooked, it being tacitly assumed that this was simply because Charles was in Scotland at the time when he was supposed to have issued the commission. But the exact date assigned to the forged commission can have been of little significance to the Irish, and a commission to them under the great seal of Scotland would, one would have thought, have carried much less weight than one under an English seal, since Ireland was an English dependency. This has been developed into an argument in favour of the genuineness of the commission; if the Irish had forged it surely they would have claimed to be acting by authority of the great seal of England, for to suppose that in preparing the forgery they could only find an impression of the Scottish seal and not the English one would be 'one of the strangest [accidents] that ever happened'.[157] Since, as argued above, the forgery probably never got to the stage where an actual seal had to be appended to it, the real question

155. Dunlop, op. cit. 529.
156. Dunlop, op. cit. 532.
157. J. H. Burton, *History of Scotland* (8 vols, Edinburgh, 1876), VI, 344-6, quoted in Gardiner, *History of England*, X, 92n.

is why the rebels should have claimed that it had the Scottish rather than the English seal. The answer is simple; the legality in Ireland of a commission under a Scottish seal might be dubious, but in other respects use of a Scottish seal added plausibility to the commission. It was well known that Charles had gone to Scotland in the hope of winning Scottish help against the English parliament. The Irish, by claiming to be acting in alliance with the Scots as well as with the king, implied that Charles had won the Scots support he sought. In these circumstances was it not logical that Charles would use the Scottish seal in authorising the Irish to act against the English in Ireland while sparing the Scots? The two propaganda arguments of the Irish, that they were allied to the Scots and that they were acting in the king's name, were thus plausibily combined.

The success of the Scots in the Bishops' Wars had simultaneously inspired the Irish to revolt, created circumstances in which they could hope revolt would be successful, and made their revolt necessary.

The covenanters' victories had shown the Irish what determined and united action could achieve. This was realised in England; 'the Scots' successes animated other subjects to their illegal pretences and impious actions'.[158] Lord Maguire stressed the importance to the Irish of the king's military weakness as revealed by his defeat by the covenanters in 1640,[159] and Robert Maxwell, the Scottish rector of Tynan (County Armagh) reported that the Scottish seizure of Newcastle in August 1640 was greeted with joy by Sir Phelim O'Neill and his popish neighbours.[160] The subsequent diplomatic triumphs of the Scots in winning concessions from the king in politics and religion also inspired the Irish. They 'doubted not but by taking the like method, they should fare no worse than the Scots, in the redress of their grievances'; 'the Scots have taught us our ABC'. Not only had the Scots won themselves pardon and concessions, the king had actually agreed to pay them for having invaded England! If the king

---

158. B. Whitelock, *Memorials of the English Affairs* (4 vols, Oxford, 1853), I, 137.
159. E. W. Hamilton, *The Irish Rebellion of 1641* (London, 1920), p. 130; Gilbert, *Contemporary History*, I, 501, 502, 509.
160. M. A. Hickson, *Ireland in the Seventeenth Century* (2 vols, London, 1884), I, 326.

had allowed the Scots a new religion, why should he not allow the Irish their old one?[161] The Scots had, by insurrection, won themselves liberty of conscience ('such as their conscience is'), and the Irish were more powerful than the Scots.[162] Why should the king not let the Irish have a parliament independent of the English one, 'as that of Scotland is'?[163] Hugh MacMahon wanted to rebel to overthrow tyrannical government 'and to imitate Scotland, who got a Privilege by that Course'; the rebels wanted to procure 'more liberty for their Country, as did (say they) of late Scotland'.[164] In their first printed statement of their aims the rebels confirmed that they were following the example of the Scots.[165]

But if the Irish admired the Scots, they also feared them and realised that the interests of the two nations conflicted. The Scots had taken a major share in the Ulster plantation, and were now powerful enough to do further harm to the Irish.[166] The specific form Irish fear of the Scots usually took was belief that the covenanters would join with the English parliament to extirpate Catholicism in Ireland. This fear was stupidly spread by these Ulster Scots who boasted that General Leslie would land with a Scottish army to carry out a reformation.[167] The general remonstrance issued by the rebels on their first rising stressed the 'threat to send over the Scottish army with the sword and Bible in hand against us' to wipe out Catholicism.[168] All Irish Catholics would be put to the sword and Catholicism suppressed in all three kingdoms; the Scottish army, 'soe much in reputation for great attempts', would not disband until this had been done.[169]

161. J. Tuchet, earl of Castlehaven, *The Earl of Castlehaven's Review, or his Memoirs* (Dublin, 1815), pp. 5, 7-8; [J. Howell], *Mercurius Hibernicus: or a Discourse of the late Insurrection in Ireland* (Bristol, 1644), p. 3; Bagwell, *Stuarts*, I, 339.
162. H.M.C. 65: *Franciscan*, p. 138.
163. Ibid. p. 108.
164. Nalson, *Impartial Collection*, II, 521, 522; Gilbert, *Contemporary History*, I, 509.
165. J. T. Gilbert, ed. *History of the Irish Confederation and the War in Ireland, 1641-9* (7 vols, Dublin, 1882-91), I, 236-9, cited in J. C. Beckett, 'The confederation of Killkenny reviewed', *Historical Studies*, II (1959), 33.
166. [Howell], *Mercurius Hibernicus*, p. 3.
167. Lowry-Corry, earl of Belmore, 'James Spottiswoode', *U.J.A.* 2nd series, Special Volume (1903), 125.
168. Nalson, *Impartial Collection*, II, 555-6; Gilbert, *Contemporary History*, I, 360.
169. Gilbert, *Contemporary History*, I, 450, 454, 504, III, 196-7; Gilbert, *Irish Confederation*, I, 18; Nalson, *Impartial Collection*, II, 54.

However, unless the Irish leaders were remarkably out of touch with events in Scotland, fear of imminent invasion by the Scottish army cannot really have been a major influence in persuading them to rebel on 23 October (as was claimed), for the Scottish army (except for three regiments) had been disbanded at Leith on 27 August.[170] The threat posed by the Scots doubtless had influenced the early planning of the rising—the covenanters had after all talked in 1640 of invading Ulster—but by the time the final decision to rise on 22 October was taken, on 5 October,[171] the fact that the dreaded Scots army had been disbanded must surely have been known. But the argument that there was an immediate threat from Scotland was too powerful a one for persuading the Catholics of Ireland that they must rebel to defend themselves to be abandoned. Moreover, the news that the Scots had disbanded must have been a great relief to the leaders of the proposed rebellion, since it removed the only formidable standing army in Britain which could have been sent against them promptly. The decision of 5 October is much less likely to have been influenced by fear of the Scots army than by the removal of that fear.

Nonetheless, though the covenanters' army was no more, Irish fears of the military prowess of the Scots remained. While the Irish saw their quarrel as being essentially with the English, the large numbers of Scots in Ulster and the anti-Catholic attitudes of the covenanters obviously made it likely that Scotland would help England against the Irish. To try to prevent, or at least delay, this the Irish leaders boldly decided to claim friendship with, and even alliance with, the Scots. Such a claim had a number of other advantages. Men would be encouraged to join the rebellion, for the prospects of defeating the English alone, whose military incompetence had just been displayed in the Bishops' Wars, were clearly far better than those of defeating the English and Scots combined. In the end the claim of alliance with the Scots was bound to be proved false, but it might well sow discord between the English and the Scots. The English in Ireland would be demoralised to find themselves singled out for attack, and might be provoked into hostility to, or at least suspicion of,

170. Terry, *Alexander Leslie*, pp. 155-7; *A.P.S.* V, 333, 335 643-4.
171. Clarke, *Old English in Ireland*, p. 160; Nalson, *Impartial Collection*, II, 551.

the Scots. Scots settlers would be confused and, finding themselves spared by the Irish, might well at least delay joining in action against the rebels until the extraordinary claim that they had an alliance with the covenanting regime in Scotland was investigated. By the time it was proved false, the rebels hoped they would have had time to crush the resistance of the English in Ireland and would therefore be ready to turn on the Scots.

In retrospect the idea of the covenanters and the Irish making an alliance might seem preposterous, but the Irish were to some extent right to think that they and the Scots had something in common. Both complained of rule from England, and the dislike of the Ulster Scots of rule from England through Dublin was also clear. There was logic in the idea that the two lesser kingdoms of the three should unite against the greater to prevent it dominating them. It was perhaps inevitable that many Irish should see the covenanting movement as anti-English, though in reality the covenanters had triumphed partly by seeking and getting English support against the king. There had been rumours during the Bishops' Wars that the covenanters were plotting with the native Irish to stir up trouble in Ireland. Lord Maguire recounted that it had been said in 1640 that if the covenanters were menaced by Strafford's forces from Ireland, Argyll 'would kindle such a fire in Ireland as would hardly or never be quenched'. John O'Neill, the titular earl of Tyrone and leader of the native Irish exiles on the continent, was said to have asked for Argyll's help in Ireland, and there was talk of his marrying Argyll's daughter or sister. These were no more than rumours, but they seemed plausible to some; Argyll's Highlanders or redshanks had much in common in race, language and culture with the native Irish.[172] It thus seems that, though the claim to have Scots support was primarily a propaganda gambit, some Irish leaders really did believe that there was at least a chance that the Scots actually would join them or remain neutral. Lord Maguire made it clear that the Scots were spared mainly because they were feared; to avoid danger from them 'it was resolved on, not to meddle with them, or any thing belonging to them, and to demean themselves towards them, as if they

172. Nalson, *Impartial Collection,* II, 552-3; Gilbert, *Contemporary History*, I, 510.

were of themselves, which they thought would pacifie them from any opposition'. But he seems to have thought that the Scots really might welcome the Irish offer—only 'if the Scots would not accept of that offer of amity, but would oppose them' would the rebels act against them. George Creighton, vicar of Lurgan (County Cavan) reported that the native Irish seemed genuinely surprised and dismayed that the Scots did not join them.[173]

However, few can have had any hope that a permanent alliance of Irish and Scots could emerge; how could it if the Irish were going to undo the Ulster plantation? The Irish leader who said he hoped that before long the Scots would be driven out of Ireland[174] summed up the rebels' basic attitude to the Scots. Moreover any plan for an alliance would have broken down on the religious issue; the covenanters had, admittedly, tried during the Bishops' Wars to get help from Catholic France through Cardinal Richelieu, but that had been when outside help seemed vital if they were to survive. Now that they were victorious they would not contemplate alliance with Catholics. An Irish cleric who regretted that the Scots had joined the English against the Irish and stated that the reason was that 'our people avowed that the war was one of religion' was right,[175] but the Irish could hardly have done otherwise. It is very doubtful whether even if they had tried to play down the religious issue they would have won Scots support, and even if they had the gain would have been outweighed by the fact that popular support in Ireland largely depended on emphasising the religious nature of the conflict.

Such calculations can have entered the heads of few of the rebel leaders, for most accepted from the start that the Scots were their enemies. They were spared at first 'since they were both numerous and powerful' and to have taken them on at the same time as the English 'would make the matter more difficult'.[176]

When the rebellion began the Ulster Scots certainly showed no signs of welcoming it as a rising against the English, though

173. Gilbert, *Contemporary History*, I, 510, 528; Nalson, *Impartial Collection*, II, 552.
174. Nalson, *Impartial Collection*, II, 604-5.
175. H.M.C. 65: *Franciscan*, p. 110; D. O'Connell and B. O'Ferrall, *Commentarius Rinuccinianus*, ed. S. Kavanagh (6 vols, I.M.C. 1932-49), I, 331, VI, 66.
176. Clarke, *Old English in Ireland*, p. 160.

they seem at first to have confined themselves to defence. While English settlers were driven out, plundered, imprisoned, and in some cases brutally treated or killed (though there was no general massacre)[177] the Scots on the whole remained passive observers, 'lookers on'.[178] Some, however, were plundered, ill treated or murdered through error or indiscipline on the part of the rebels, or resisted them and were killed fighting. Especially unlucky was the Catholic laird of Forsyth, who had left Scotland to escape persecution and was now driven from his house in County Cavan by his Irish co-religionists.[179] The leading Scots Catholic in Ulster, Lady Strabane (a sister of the marquis of Huntly, the Scottish royalist leader) fared better. She handed Strabane Castle over to Sir Phelim O'Neill after only token resistance, whereupon he offered to marry her! She refused, but they were to be married some years later.[180]

The Irish leaders usually managed to enforce the policy of not harming the Scots. The Irish were said to have been warned by proclamation that the penalty for molesting them would be death. Scots settlers, or so it was claimed, were instructed to 'write over the Lyntals of their doores, that they were Scotch men, and so destruction might passe over their families'.[181]

As well as being spared the Scots settlers were subjected to propaganda aimed at convincing them that they should help the Irish. Two Irish colonels addressed a letter to 'our Honourable Friends, the Gentlemen of the never conquered Scotch Nation' emphasising the common origins of the people of both kingdoms.[182] Sir Phelim O'Neill stressed in a letter to Sir William Stewart that 'The intention of these troubles is nothing against your nation'.[183] While four other O'Neills

177. See W. D. Love, 'Civil War in Ireland: appearances in three centuries of historical writing', *Emory University Quarterly*, XXII (1966), 57-72 and J. M. Read, 'Atrocity Propaganda and the Irish Rebellion', *Public Opinion Quarterly*, II, (1938), 229-44.
178. McNeill, *Tanner Letters*, p. 133.
179. E. S. Shuckburgh, ed. *Two Biographies of William Bedell, Bishop of Kilmore* (Cambridge, 1902), p. 173; W. E. H. Lecky, *A History of Ireland in the Eighteenth Century* (5 vols, London, 1892), I, 59n.
180. T. O'Mellan, 'A Narrative of the Wars of 1641', in R. M. Young, ed. *Historical Notices of Old Belfast* (Belfast, 1896), p. 210; Gilbert, *Contemporary History*, I, 372, III, xxxii, xxxix; J. B. Paul, *The Scots Peerage* (9 vols, Edinburgh, 1904-14), I, 50, IV, 545.
181. Gilbert, *Contemporary History*, I, 466; A Mervyn, *An Exact Relation* (1642), p. 3.
182. Mervyn, *Exact Relation*, pp. 3-4; Gilbert, *Contemporary History*, I, 466-7.
183. *C.S.P.I. 1647-60*, p. 253.

assured Stewart that the Irish knew that the Scots 'are a nation that never wished the decay of this kingdom, but ever have been ready to further the happiness and prosperity of this nation'; they apologised for the fact that some of his tenants had been plundered.[184]

Along with such general assertions of friendship went specific statements that the rebels were allied to the co-venanters in Scotland. Sir Phelim O'Neill is alleged to have stated that he acted through powers given to him not only by the Irish and the king but by letters from Argyll.[185] Depositions taken in Dublin from refugees tell of Irish boasts that 'the Scottish nation was joined with them in a covenant for extirpation of the English', and that the king had approved of it; the new covenant had been signed by Argyll and the prime nobility of Scotland.[186]

It seems unlikely that any Scots settlers were taken in by this propaganda; some of the rank and file Irish rebels may have been, since their own leaders assured them that the new covenant existed. But from the first it must have been hard to reconcile this with the argument that they had rebelled to resist potential Scots aggression—or actual aggression, for some rebels had risen in the belief that large numbers of armed Scots had landed.[187] Protestants in general, whether in England or Ireland, jumped immediately to the correct conclusion that the sparing of the Scots was a politic ruse, and that the Irish would turn on them later. When the Irish told Sir James Craig that on the king's orders the English were being attacked and the Scots spared, he replied that he would as soon believe that 'the king will command his left hand to cut off his right'.[188] The Scots thus 'resolutely scorned' Irish favour.[189] Their immunity seems to have lasted about a month in most areas; some of the Irish then claimed that the king had sent fresh orders that the Scots as well as the English were to be

184.   Ibid. p. 252. See also Gilbert, *Contemporary History*, I, 529.
185.   Hickson, *Ireland in the Seventeenth Century*, I, 193.
186.   Fitzpatrick, 'The Ulster Civil War', *U.J.A.* N.S. XIII (1907), 136, 139, XIV (1908), 170, 171; Carte, *Ormond*, I, 179; Whitelock, *Memorials*, I, 141.
187.   Hickson, *Ireland in the Seventeenth Century*, I, 212. There was also a rumour that 500 of Argyll's men were marching on Dunluce Castle, ibid, I, 251.
188.   Shuckburgh, *Two Biographies*, p. 171; Temple, *Irish Rebellion*, pp. 37-8; Whitelock, *Memorials*, I, 141; F. Warner, *History of the Rebellion and Civil War in Ireland* (2 vols, London, 1768), p. 75.
189.   Mervyn, *Exact Relation*, p. 4; Gilbert, *Contemporary History*, I, 467.

Sir Phelim O'Neill. Commander in chief of the Irish in the early stages of the 1641 rising. Contemporary engraving in British Library, reproduced in Gilbert, *Contemporary History*.

attacked.[190] Irish sources usually attribute the change in their policy to the refusal of the Scots to join them,[191] but as most of the leaders had never expected this to happen the change presumably came because the old policy had served its purpose. The rebels were now strong enough to attack the Scots as well as the English. On 28 November they attacked and burnt Lisburn in what was interpreted as a first move towards over-running the Scots of Counties Down and Antrim, but were then forced to retreat by forces made up mainly of English settlers.[192] Only the day before this attack Turlough O'Neill had written from Armagh 'I protest that no Scotsman should be touched by any of the gentry, and what hurt others should do them should be repaired to the utter most of our powers',[193] and even a month later the rebels gave Lady Forbes a protection since 'it is gevin out that you ar not to meddle with anie of the Scotishe natioune except they give cause, the which this good ladie will never give'.[194] George Creighton remained among the rebels for nearly a year without being pillaged, 'because he was a Scotchman'.[195]

The favour at first shown to the Scots can hardly have failed to arouse some resentment and suspicion of them among English settlers. There were allegations that English refugees seeking help from Scots neighbours were handed back to the Irish, who killed many of them.[196] Though the story is doubtless exaggerated it may well be that some Scots, fearing to provoke the Irish who had so far miraculously spared them, refused help to English refugees. Another rumour spoke of the Scots, exaggeratedly said to number 40,000 well armed men in Ulster, cynically standing aside though they could have crushed the rebels.[197] But on the whole the Irish failed to provoke discord between the English and the Scots in Ireland. Indeed it seems likely that many Scots never realised that they

190. Shuckburgh, *Two Biographies*, p. 172; Hickson, *Ireland in the Seventeenth Century*, I, 212, 362.
191. O'Connell and O'Ferrall, *Commentarius Rinnuccinianus*, I, 331, VI, 66; Gilbert, *Irish Confederation*, I, 23.
192. Gilbert, *Irish Confederation*, I, 23, 49; Temple, *Irish Rebellion*, p. 40; Bagwell, *Stuarts*, I, 348-9.
193. D. Coffrey, *O'Neill and Ormonde: a Chapter in Irish History* (Dublin and London, 1914), p. 48.
194. Gilbert, *Contemporary History*, I, 372-3.
195. Fitzpatrick, 'The Ulster Civil War', *U.J.A.* N.S. XV (1909), 13.
196. T. Fitzpatrick, *The Bloody Bridge and other papers relating to the insurrection of 1641* (Dublin, 1903), p. 213.
197. Carte, *Ormond*, III, 77-8.

were being purposely spared by the Irish; many fled on the rebels' approach, others attributed the rebels' mercy to divine providence. It is certainly remarkable that there appear to be no references whatever in Scottish sources to the Irish policy of sparing Scots settlers and claiming alliance with them, which would seem to indicate that it never became widely known in Scotland that this was happening.

The gradual disappearance of the story of an alliance with the covenanters still left the Scots with a major place in Irish propaganda. The much more convincing story that the revolt had been necessary because of Scottish plans to extirpate Catholicism in Ireland came into its own. Now that the revolt had begun a new dimension was added to the story; support for the rebellion was necessary from all Catholics in Ireland because the Dublin government would use the revolt as an excuse to bring over a Scottish army which would crush all Catholics, not just those actually in rebellion. News that a treaty was being negotiated in London for sending a Scottish army to Ireland made this seem credible. Some of the Old English became convinced that the lords justice had purposely let the rebellion spread by inaction and were now trying to provoke them into joining it, so that the Old English as well as the native Irish could be punished when order was restored. This belief, that they would be over-run by an invading army of fanatically anti-Catholic covenanters whether or not they rebelled, was influential in persuading many of the Old English to join the rebels in December 1641.[198]

Even while claiming to have the support of the covenanters Sir Phelim O'Neill had secretly been seeking a very different sort of ally from Scotland. On 30 October, just a week after the outbreak of the rebellion, he had written to Father Patrick Hegarty, the head of the Irish Franciscan mission to Scotland based at Bonamargy Friary and the earl of Antrim's candidate for a revived Catholic bishopric of the Isles. 'Send word to Scotland to Donald Gorm. ... And to the people of Rathline. ... And everie place in Scotland where you haue freindes, and let them cum hither and we will use them weill'.[199]   Sir Phelim

---

198. Clarke, *Old English in Ireland*, pp. 224-5; Gilbert, *Irish Confederation*, I, 28.
199. The letter only survives in a badly damaged copy, S.R.O. PA.7/23/2/9. It is addressed merely to 'Father Patrick', but the circumstantial evidence that this was Hegarty is very strong—see D. Stevenson, 'The Irish Franciscan Mission to Scotland and the Irish Rebellion of 1641', *Innes Review*, XXX (1979), 54-61. I have

was apparently thinking only of getting Highlanders to come to Ireland to reinforce his army, but according to Lord Maguire the Irish were also prepared to use the Highlanders in another way if necessary. If the covenanters took action against the Irish, the rebels 'were in good hope to cause a stir in Scotland that might divert them from them'; the Highlanders were Irish in blood, language and manners and could be persuaded to rebel against the covenanters.[200]

At this stage, however, the appeals of the Irish rebels to the Highlanders had little effect. The earl of Antrim had not joined the rebellion and without his influence there was little hope of winning the co-operation of any prominent Mac-Donalds. Even if Donald Gorm MacDonald of Sleat could have been persuaded that the Irish were, as they claimed, fighting for Charles I this would not have won them his support, for he was reported to have resolved to help the king no more since Charles had betrayed his supporters and heaped favours on their enemies, the covenanters.[201] A few individual Highlanders seeking adventure probably crossed to Ireland to join the rebels, but their numbers were not significant.

On news of the rising of the Irish on 23 October leading English and Scottish settlers in Ulster alike had usually withdrawn with their tenants to whatever houses, castles, forts or towns were available as places of refuge, and prepared to defend themselves. As the leading Scots assumed from the first that the rebellion was aimed at them as much as the English the rebels gained little military advantage from their policy of sparing the Scots. The slowness of many Scots in turning to offensive action against the Irish is attributable primarily (like the similar slowness of many of the English) to the fact that the rising came as a complete surprise, and that time was needed to organise resistance, not to any willingness to trust rebel promises of immunity. In retrospect it seems clear that the Irish could have saved themselves much trouble in the years ahead if they had undertaken an attack on the Scots simultaneously with that on the English. They would then have been able to capture or destroy at least some of the

assumed that the Donald Gorm of the letter was MacDonald of Sleat, but this is not certain.
200. Nalson, *Impartial Collection*, II, 552-3.
201. Guthry, *Memoirs*, p. 109.

Scots settlers who were soon to emerge as military leaders of Protestant forces, and to drive out the lesser settlers who were to form the rank and file of these forces. As it was, the Scots were given a breathing space in which to organise their defences, so when the Irish did eventually turn on them they were not taken by surprise, and the Irish had little success in dealing with them.

Nonetheless, though in military terms a failure, the sparing of the Scots brought the Irish some gains; recruiting men to join in the rising must have been made much easier when it was explained that only a minority of Ulster Protestants, the English, were to be attacked. Moreover, the rebels simply did not have the resources to seize all Ulster simultaneously; attacking only the English in the first instance was partly a case of trying to make a virture out of necessity.

The rising brought the rebels control, within a few days of all Ulster except County Antrim, northern Down and Londonderry, and isolated castles and forts scattered throughout the western part of the province—in Counties Donegal, Tyrone, Londonderry and Fermanagh. Refugees, Scots and English, fled to these Protestant-held enclaves, and the organising of resistance began; the training of men, the supplying of food, arms and ammunition. In the west what was soon to be called the 'Lagan army', dominated by the Scots but including many English settlers, emerged; among its leaders were the Scots Sir Robert Stewart, Sir William Stewart and Sir Frederick Hamilton. In Antrim and Down the leading Scots commanders were Lord Montgomery of the Ards, his brother Sir James Montgomery, and Lord Claneboye. After the first few weeks of confusion the situation in Ulster became fairly static. The rebels made few further gains; the rising lost its initial impetus as the rebels found it impossible to overcome their remaining enemies. Equally, while the Protestants found it possible to defend themselves successfully, they had not the resources necessary to turn to offensive action on any significant scale. At first time seemed on their side; they just needed to hold out, with the help of some arms and men sent from Scotland, until the Scottish army arrived to relieve them. But as the months passed and no army came it began to look as if they would be starved out by lack of supplies, or even driven out, for the rebellion gradually spread to other parts of

Ireland. It seemed now that only lack of organisation among the Irish, and the winter weather which made a large-scale offensive by the Irish virtually impossible, was saving the Ulster Protestants.

In January 1642 their position was further weakened by the spread of the rebellion to County Antrim. Antrim and north Down had at first escaped any violence of a significant scale; it was not the case that rebellion failed in these areas but that it was not attempted. This is explicable in terms of the Irish leaders believing the Scots settler population was too dense for a rising to have any hope of success. But the fact that all Antrim, including areas occupied by Catholic MacDonnells and native Irish, remained quiet is interesting. First of all it adds weight to the earl of Antrim's protestations that he was not in league with the rebels, though few Protestants believed them at the time. But why did the Irish not attempt a rising without him? It may be that they simply thought that a rising without Antrim to lead it would fail; but it may be suggested that the way in which the rebel leaders ignored County Antrim indicates that they had hopes of persuading the earl to join them, for if this was the case it would be better to wait for him to lead a rising there than to risk alienating him by undertaking a rising in the area he dominated without his co-operation—especially as the MacDonnells at least might not have risen without him. It is certainly quite possible that the rebels were convinced that Antrim would join them. He had been involved in Charles' plot to seize Dublin, a plot which had helped inspire the rebels to action. The Irish believed that Ormond was likely to join them if they claimed to be fighting for the king.[202] so it would be surprising if they did not have similar hopes of Antrim— especially as, unlike Ormond, he was a Catholic.

In the event Antrim refused either to join the rebellion or to help to suppress it. Like many others he was probably at first doubtful as to the king's true attitude to the rising, and determined to try to remain neutral. As a Catholic he was suspect to the government in Dublin. If he returned home to Dunluce Castle it would be impossible for him to avoid having to declare his position clearly. He therefore tried to sit on the

---

202. Clarke, *Old English in Ireland*, p. 229.

fence by occupying himself with visits to friends and relatives; but as these were in rebel held areas many concluded that it was only a matter of time until he joined the rebels.[203]

What orders, if any, Antrim sent to his followers, are unknown, but his agent, Archibald Stewart of Ballintoy, raised a regiment (without a commission from Dublin)[204] from Antrim's lands to oppose the rebels. The regiment included many Catholics; among them was Alasdair MacColla, Coll Ciotach's son. Alasdair had evidently been arrested at the start of the rebellion by Colonel Arthur Chichester, the governor of Carrickfergus, on suspicion of planning to seize the town. Stewart had got him released and made him a captain in his regiment with a company made up mainly of Highlanders, many of them no doubt (like Alasdair himself) refugees driven out of Scotland during the Bishops' Wars. There was one other Catholic captain in the regiment, Tirlough Og O'Cahan, but the majority of the officers and men were Protestant.[205]

Not surprisingly it proved impossible to hold the regiment together, for the rebellion intensified the fears, hatreds and suspicions between races and religions. The Catholic captains therefore decided to change sides with their companies. Their motives are not entirely clear; they may have cynically judged that the rebels were most likely to be victorious, or they may simply have decided that there was no future for them, as Catholics, in the forces opposing the rebels. To stay might lead to imprisonment or death at the hands of the Protestants as bitterness grew. Such fears would have been heightened by news that an army of covenanters was coming to Ulster, for Argyll of course still held Alasdair MacColla's father and two of his brothers prisoner. James MacDonnell, another Catholic officer, afterwards claimed that there had been a plot among Stewart's Protestant officers—'those captains of yours whom you may call rather cowboyes'—to massacre them and their families. Whatever their motives, on 2 January 1642 Alasdair MacColla and O'Cahan led their companies in an attack on Protestant companies of the regi-

203. Hill, *Macdonnells of Antrim*, pp. 256-7; H.M.C. 65: *Franciscan*, p. 116. The report in ibid. p. 134 that Antrim had joined the rebels is false.
204. H.M.C. 3: *4th Report*, p. 108; *L.J.* IV, 478.
205. Hill, *Macdonnells of Antrim*, p. 62; G. Hill, 'The Stewarts of Ballintoy', *U.J.A.* N.S. VI (1900), 23; Hickson, *Ireland in the Seventeenth Century*, I, 145-6.

ment which were guarding the crossing of the River Bann at Portnaw, killing about sixty of them. They then joined up with rebel forces from across the Bann in County London-derry and tried unsuccessfully to persuade Dunluce Castle to surrender to them. James MacDonnell seized and garrisoned Oldstone (now Clough) Castle between Ballymena and Ballycastle.[206] They proceeded to demand that Archibald Stewart, their kinsman and former commander, surrender Coleraine to them, urging that virtually all Ireland except Dublin was in rebel hands; all the garrisons between Oldstone and Carrickfergus had fled. Stewart was offered boats to 'send all the people away into Scotland' before Sir Phelim O'Neill arrived to besiege the town, after which flight would be impossible. They claimed the rebels were not opposing the king; all they asked was 'to have their religion setled and every one his owne ancient inheritance'.[207] Obviously this would involve overthrowing the Ulster plantation; when said by a MacDonnell it may also have implied the restoration of MacDonald lands in the Highlands.

Stewart refused to surrender Coleraine and was therefore besieged by Alasdair MacColla. On 11 February he led a sally in search of food but was ambushed by Alasdair near Bally-money. In the battle of the Laney (or of Bendooragh) which followed several hundred of Stewart's men were killed, and the battle has additional significance in that it is the first occasion on which the devasting tactic later known as the 'Highland charge' is known to have been used; after firing one volley Alasdair's men threw down their muskets and immediately charged with sword and targe (shield) to engage

206. Hickson, *Ireland in the Seventeenth Century*, I, 148-9, 234-49, 252-5; Hogan, *Letters and Papers*, pp. 6-7; Hill, op. cit. 23, 78, 80-9; Fitzpatrick, *The Bloody Bridge*, pp. xxiv-xxv; Hill, *Macdonnells of Antrim*, pp. 62-3, 75. Some accounts state that James MacDonnell was, like Alasdair, a captain in Stewart's regiment, but on balance it seems more likely that he served in Alasdair's company. The fact that both James and Alasdair had fathers called Coll (and were therefore referred to as 'Maccoll' on occasion) led to them being assumed to be brothers; on at least one occasion James appears erroneously as 'MacColl Ciotach Mac-donnell', Hickson, *Ireland in the Seventeenth Century*, I, 145-6.
207. Hogan, *Letters and Papers*, pp. 6-7. Hill, *Macdonnells of Antrim*, pp. 64-8 states that the author of this letter was Sir James MacDonnell (a first cousin of James MacColl MacDonnell), but all accounts (with one exception) of these events refer simply to James MacDonnell. The exception (cited in Hill, o. cit. 79) refers to 'Sir James MacColl MacDonnell', which erroneously conflates the two cousins. Thus, the author of the letter was probably James MacColl, who was a prisoner in Carrickfergus in 1642 (Hickson, *Ireland in the Seventeenth Century*, I, 254) and was evidently

the enemy in hand to hand fighting. But in spite of this 'Black Friday' Stewart managed to hold Coleraine, and by this time Protestant hopes were beginning to revive as it became known that it would only be a matter of weeks before the Scots army began to land to reinforce them. The rebels had failed to take full advantage of the long delays in sending large-scale help to the Ulster Protestants; the initiative in the war was now to pass to the Scots army.[208]

later executed.
208. Hill, *Macdonnells of Antrim*, pp. 69-70, 75-6; Fitzpatrick, *The Bloody Bridge*, p. 222; Shuckburgh, *Tow Biographies*, pp. 173-4; Gilbert, *Contemporary History*, I, 33.

CHAPTER THREE

The New Scots in Ireland, 1642-1644

---

i. The Campaign of 1642

When Robert Monro landed in Ulster on 3 April 1642 his actions were dictated by orders from the privy council of Scotland. These instructed him to garrison Carrickfergus, consult with local nobles and gentry about the state of the country, and in general do all he could to suppress the rebels; 'and be carefull that no prejudices nor jealousies aryse betuix the English and these of our nation thair, since yow are to have equal respect to both'.[1] These instructions were clear so far as they went, but much remained obscure. Who was Monro to receive further orders from? His commission was from the king, his instructions were from the Scottish council, his paymaster was the English parliament. The general of the whole army was Leven, and the treaty laid down that the army was only to receive orders through him—but it failed to say who he was to get them from, beyond specifying that the Dublin government could order him to do certain things. Apart from this, and stating that the army could only be recalled by the king and English parliament, the treaty did not define the relative powers over the army of king, parliament and Scottish government. In the circumstances this is understandable. One of the advantages of sending a Scottish rather than an English army to Ireland had been that this would make it possible to avoid dispute between king and parliament over control of forces sent against the rebels. The English parliament certainly saw the army as its own instrument; since it paid it, it expected to be able to control it. But it was recognised that the Scottish government, since it was providing the men (and

1. *R.P.C.S. 1638-43*, p. 209.

levy and transport money) had some rights over the army; the reason for not defining these rights was probably that to have done so would have involved the explicit granting to Scotland of the right to interfere in Irish affairs, and this would have aroused opposition in England.

Such ambiguities as to control of the army were to cause much trouble, but in April 1642 Monro's immediate objectives were clear. Having garrisoned Carrickfergus he turned to driving back the rebels, to establish secure quarters for his men and the rest of the army which was to follow. He had the alternatives of moving north to clear Antrim of rebels, and then west to relieve the British forces (as the regiments raised by the English and Scots settlers in Ulster were called) in Londonderry, Tyrone and Donegal, or of marching south through Down. He decided on the latter, probably because it was from the south that the danger of a major attack from the rebels seemed greatest, and because a move south would be most likely to relieve rebel pressure on Dublin as the rebels would fear that he intended to march into the heart of Ireland. The Irish forces in County Londonderry were fully occupied in resisting the British forces there, and the Irish and MacDonnells in Antrim must have known by this time that Argyll was preparing to land his regiment on the north coast of Antrim; fearing such an attack from the north they would be unlikely to move south to attack the New Scots (as the men of the Scottish army in Ireland became called to distinguish them from the Old Scots, the Scottish settlers in Ulster). Moreover the New Scots were probably in no mood to hurry to the relief of Londonderry as the city had opposed being handed over to them as a base.[2]

On 27 April Monro marched out of Carrickfergus, leaving a garrison to hold it, with about 1,600 New Scots foot.[3] He camped near Belfast, and was joined next day by British

2. Gilbert, *Contemporary History*, I, 419.
3. The main sources for this expedition are Monro's letters to Leven in *A True Relation of the proceedings of the Scottish Armie now in Ireland, by three letters* (London, 1642), which is reprinted in Gilbert, *Contemporary History*, I, 419-23; R. Pike, *A True Relation of the Proceedings of the Scots and English forces in the North of Ireland* (London, 1642); Turner, *Memoirs*, pp. 19-23. Extracts from these three sources are to be found in W. Pinkerton, 'Proceedings of the Scottish and English Forces in the North of Ireland, A.D. 1642', *U.J.A.* VIII (1860), 77-87. See also H.M.C. 36: *Ormonde*, N.S. II, 124, 131; R. M. Young, ed. *Historical Notices of Old Belfast* (Belfast, 1896), p. 211; Carte, *Ormond*, I, 309-10; Bagwell, *Stuarts*, II, 15-16.

forces—1,000 or 2,000 foot and five troops of horse under Lord Conway and Colonel Arthur Chichester. The joint force then marched south, but lack of baggage horses forced Monro to leave behind some of his supplies—even though he had only managed to gather supplies for ten days. He therefore ordered a ship to carry ammunition and food to Carlingford Lough to await his arrival. It had already been decided that the main objective of the expedition should be to take Newry and the ship would also serve to prevent the Irish sending help to their garrison in Newry by sea. At Lisburn Monro was joined by further British forces, 800 foot and two troops of horse under Lord Montgomery and Lord Claneboye. The army was then divided into two divisions, the British under Lord Conway and the New Scots under Monro. Each took the position of honour, the vanguard, in turn, and Monro and Conway similarily gave orders to the army on alternate days. This was a common if awkward expedient for preventing disputes over command; Monro would have liked the undisputed command for himself but Conway would not allow this, insisting on his rights as marshal of the army of Ireland. It was hardly surprising that he proved touchy in co-operating with the New Scots, for less than two years before he had commanded the king's forces which had been routed by the Scots at the battle of Newburn in the Second Bishops' War.

After leaving Lisburn the first contact was made with rebel forces. Monro's route lay through Kilwarlin Wood, an area of shrubby marshes and low hills partly covered with trees,[4] an excellent terrain for ambushing and splitting up a large force, which would find it hard to manoeuvre under such conditions. If Monro knew anything of the Irish wars of the late sixteenth century he must have known that the favourite (and most successful) tactic of the Irish was the ambush of armies lured into constricting woods, bogs or passes.[5] However, though the Irish were said to have had 2,500 foot and sixty horse in the wood under Arthur Magennis, Lord Iveagh, Monro succeeded in driving them back in a series of sharp skirmishes, killing about 150 for the loss of only two of his own men. The rebel dead included prisoners, who were all shot; after what the

4.   E. McCracken, *The Irish Woods since Tudor times. Distribution and Exploitation* (Newton Abbot, 1971), p. 40.
5.   G. A. Hayes-McCoy, 'Strategy and Tactics in Irish Warfare, 1593-1601', *I.H.S.* II (1940-1), 267, 274-7.

British had suffered during the winter, and the wide circulation of wildly exaggerated atrocity stories about the rebels' conduct, there was no inclination to show them mercy. Even Lieutenant Colonel James Turner (Sinclair's regiment), who was later to denounce the killing of prisoners as inexpedient (since it would in turn encourage the Irish to kill their captives) evidently saw nothing morally wrong with such murders.

The night was spent camped in the woods, and on 30 April Monro advanced out of them, driving the rebels before him and hanging all prisoners. He passed the next night at Lough-brickland where 'there lay a wicked garrison in a fast place environed within a loch'. It refused to surrender and was stormed the following day, 'the whole sixty therein' being 'put to the sword'. Brutal as this was it at least had some justification in contemporary military custom, whereby a garrison which refused to surrender on terms could expect no mercy if subsequently stormed. Monro then moved on to Newry. The town was easily captured but many of the townsmen fled to join the garrison in the castle which, hoping for help from Sir Phelim O'Neill, refused to surrender. The subsequent attack on the castle was called off for fear of endangering the lives of British prisoners in it; and a new offer of terms made. This time the Irish agreed to surrender, and the garrison was allowed to march out unharmed. But the townsmen of Newry were detained 'till trial should be had of their behaviour' in the alleged atrocities. On 5 May 'we entered in examination of the townsmen, if all were Papists; and the indifferent being severed from the bad whereof 60 with two priests were shot and hanged, the indifferent are banished'. Many of those left alive were pressganged into the British forces. These summary trials and executions were mainly the work of Lord Conway and the embittered British forces, but there is no sign that Monro made any attempt to stop them. All that can be said for him is that when soldiers proceeded without orders to throw Irish women into the river and shoot at them in the water he and Lieutenant Colonel Turner put a stop to it—though they were too late to save some of the women.

A garrison of 400 men was left in Newry, half from Sinclair's regiment, half Old Scots who were to leave when the rest of Sinclair's men arrived. Monro was now established on the south eastern border of Ulster, but though he had met with little resistance he had no intention of advancing further south. He sent a small force to Dundalk to bring its commander, Sir Henry Tichbourne, to consult with him at Newry, but this was only to gain intelligence of enemy movements. Monro's refusal to advance seems at first sight over cautious, but there were good reasons behind it. It seems likely that he had orders from Scotland not to leave Ulster or risk any major engagement with the enemy; his job was simply to clear a safe base for the rest of the Scots army, and if he moved too far south he would leave Carrickfergus open to Irish attack. The further south he went the greater his already pressing supply problems would become. Moreover, if he moved south to relieve Dundalk his route would lie through the Fews, a dangerous country of hills and narrow passes.[6] Even if he escaped ambush on his way through it, he would risk being cut off from the rest of the army now landing at Carrickfergus. Monro therefore contented himself with sending raiding parties into the Fews which killed many Irish, men, women and children, and drove off their cattle.[7]

The treaty had laid down that the Scots army was to prosecute the war in Ulster in the first instance, though the Dublin government could order it to move into other provinces. No such orders had come from the lords justice, for as the treaty was not yet complete they had no idea what powers they were supposed to have over the New Scots. Since, however, they believed that Monro was best occupied in Ulster at this time, they did not encourage him to come south,[8] to the annoyance of Tichbourne who had held onto Dundalk in spite of orders from Dublin to abandon it[9] and who now urged that the New Scots be ordered to leave Ulster.[10]

Instead Monro turned to consolidating his hold on south east Ulster. The rebel garrison at Carlingford had fled when Monro's ship had arrived from Carrickfergus, and Tichbourne sent some of his men there to replace it; a few weeks later 500 of Sinclair's regiment were able to land there on their way to Newry. To clear the country to the north and west Monro

6. Hayes-McCoy, op. cit. 267.
7. Fitzpatrick, *The Bloody Bridge*, p. xiii.
8. Gilbert, *Irish Confederation*, II, 30; H.M.C. 36: *Ormonde*, N.S. II, 124, 131-2.
9. R. Colles, *The History of Ulster* (4 vols, London, n.d.), III, 41.
10. Carte MSS, 3, f. 176.

decided to march towards Armagh, but as soon as he sent out an advance party of cavalry the demoralised Irish fled, thinking his whole army was approaching. Sir Phelim O'Neill burnt and abandoned Armagh, killing many British prisoners before leaving;[11] the brutality of Monro's army towards Irish prisoners probably was, as intended, terrifying the Irish, but it was also provoking them into retaliation in kind. The Irish retired into Tyrone, leaving a garrison in Charlemont and Monro 'being scarce of victuals and our body weakned, our souldiers burthened with unnecessary trash of baggage' (their loot gathered during the campaign) decided not to follow them but instead to return to Carrickfergus, suppressing on the way the only 'considerable enemy in the countrey of Down', the rebels in the Mountains of Mourne and Maccartan's Wood to the north. While most of the army marched to the north of the mountains, Monro and 800 men moved through them to drive out the Irish and to 'rob them of their cattell, which we did'. The army reunited near Dundrum, and there divided into several columns which moved slowly north, skirmishing with small parties of Irish and rounding up thousands of cattle. At Drumbo, near Lisburn, the army split up to return to its quarters and the captured cattle were divided, or at least such cattle 'as remained unstolen by the horsemen and plunderers, being an infinite number of poor contemptible countrey-men, which could not be reduced to order'. This explanation of the disappearance of most of the cattle was not accepted by the English part of the British forces, which alleged that the Scots had made off with the cattle and complained that because of this they would be reluctant to act jointly with the Scots in future.[12] Whatever the truth of the matter, large numbers of the cattle taken from the Irish were soon being exported to Scotland; in June the lords justice complained that the Scots and their camp followers 'do export cattle in mighty numbers'.[13]

Monro and his men returned to Carrickfergus on 11 or 12 May. His fortnight's campaign had been, superficially, a

11. Loc. cit; Gilbert, *Contemporary History*, I, 421.
12. Pike, *A True Relation*, p. 6. When a report to this effect was published in London the Commons had the pamphlet burnt and the publishers imprisoned, *C.J.* II, 613; Carte, *Ormond*, I, 309-10.
13. H.M.C. 36: *Ormonde*, N.S. II, 144-5.

complete success. Down had been cleared of organised rebel forces. Land communications, though rather tenuous ones, with Dublin had been established. The garrison at Newry provided a firm base for further advances, and Monro recommended that a third of the whole army be quartered there as it was near rebel strongholds in southern Ulster. He had learnt several valuable lessons from the expedition. The difficulties of transport and communications in Ulster tended to exhaust the men before they got to grips with the enemy, so secure bases should be set up close to enemy positions. No guns bigger that field pieces were of any use; on the Newry expedition even field guns had proved difficult to move, five of their carriages breaking. Scarcity of baggage horses limited the amount of supplies that could be carried, and the horses were so weak that most heavy carriages had to be drawn by oxen. Even cavalry was often a hindrance rather than a help to the infantry in the many parts of the province where bog and forest predominated.

Monro was puzzled by the Irish as an enemy; 'it will be a war in my judgement very strange, for in the whole march I had never any alarme given us being quartered in the fields untrenched'.[14] The Irish had made no attempt to attack him, and when they had been attacked they had not stood and fought. Thus though Monro had met with no reverses, he had won no major victory; the number of men lost by the Irish had been fairly insignificant. The enemy scattered before him, but their main army retreated intact and bands of Irish tended to reassemble after he had passed, threatening any small outposts he had established—according to one report while he was at Newry small parties of rebels had put to flight two detachments of his men, one at Malone, the other only six miles from Carrickfergus.[15] In the wilder areas it was virtually impossible to clear the Irish from the bogs and woods; even if it was done, they tended to filter back almost immediately. The problem facing the Scottish army in Ireland was thus partly the classic one of how, with a regular army, to defeat guerilla forces which will not stand and fight to retain any particular position, which melt away before the concentrated power of an organised army, only to reappear once it has

14. Gilbert, *Contemporary History*, I, 421, 423.
15. Pike, *A True Relation*, pp. 6-7.

passed. According to James Turner the refusal of the Irish to fight made Monro under-estimate them; 'the rebells not dareing face him, which made him conceave, because they did not then, that there after they neither could nor would'. Turner believed it was such over-confidence which was to lead Monro to disaster at Benburb in 1646.[16]

Monro's first expedition of 1642 was typical of many of the years ahead—and of many anti-guerilla campaigns in other wars—in that the best way of attacking the elusive enemy proved to be to attack its food supplies, a tactic made doubly useful by the perennial shortage of food in the British and New Scots quarters. One of the reasons that the Ulster Irish took so easily to guerilla warfare was that many of them were semi-nomadic, without permanent houses, spending their lives driving their cattle, the main form of wealth, from pasture to pasture, living in temporary huts. A herd or group of herds which travelled together, along with their herdsmen, guards and their families, made up a creaght. In time of war, as in the 1640s, the forces of the Ulster Irish were accompanied by their creaghts.[17] As Monro quickly discovered, while the nimble Irish might escape when attacked, the slow moving creaghts were much more vulnerable. They could often be overtaken, the herdsmen and guards killed, and the cattle driven off; cattle were a very convenient form of booty in that they provided their own motive power back to quarters! Grain supplies taken from the Irish, on the other hand, often had to be destroyed if they could not be consumed on the spot, through lack of baggage horses. Growing crops were burnt if it seemed that the Irish might return to harvest them when ripe, while settled Irish peasants who engaged in such arable agriculture were killed or driven out to prevent them supplying the rebels in the future. As so often in this type of war, it seemed that those who had most suffering inflicted on them were the herdsmen and peasants, not the soldiers.

On his return to Carrickfergus Monro found letters awaiting him from Argyll, asking for advice on where to land his regiment in County Antrim, and from the earl of Antrim. Antrim's letter, it seemed to Monro, was intended 'rather to intrap me

---

16. Turner, *Memoirs*, p. 23.
17. J. P. Prendergast, 'The Ulster Creaghts', *Journal of the Royal Society of Antiquaries of Ireland*, III (1855), 420-30; G. A. Hayes-McCoy, 'Gaelic Society in Ireland in the Late Sixteenth Century', *Historical Studies*, IV (1963), 57-8.

then to approve himselfe a loyall subject' for 'my Lord Antrum is joyned strong with the rebels, making a pretext of laying downe armes, in the meane time doth what he can to cut our throats'.[18] This interpretation of Antrim's conduct was false but understandable. It was not long since he had been threatening to invade Scotland, and since the start of the rebellion in Ireland he had lived in rebel held areas. Though in fact he had not joined the rebels many of his followers had, and his own behaviour had done little to dispel suspicion. But he still believed it would be possible to clear himself and thus prevent Argyll's regiment occupying his estates. He had, therefore, hurried north, reaching Dunluce Castle on 28 April. Desperate to prove his loyalty he tried to get Alasdair MacColla to abandon his siege of Coleraine; he was unsuccessful, but did manage to send supplies to the British garrison.[19]

On 30 April he wrote to Monro, welcoming him on his safe arrival in Ireland and suggesting that they meet in Glenarm to agree on 'the quieting of my countrey'. Meanwhile he promised to try to help Coleraine, and expressed sorrow that in his absence 'my people were so unfortunate as to doe any hostile act, though in their own defence'.[20] Antrim can have had little real hope that Monro would treat him with anything but deep suspicion, yet he seemed the only possible protector against Argyll and the Campbells. But Monro sent no answer and imprisoned the messenger who had brought Antrim's letter. Approaches to British commanders met with a similar lack of success; as Lord Conway wrote to Ormond, Antrim's actions had been very odd for one who claimed to be a loyal subject.[21]

Monro had hoped to move north into Antrim as soon as he returned from Newry, to help Argyll's regiment land and drive the rebels over the Bann, but supply problems made this impossible. Instead of, as he hoped, a magazine of foodstuffs having been built up in his absence, he found there was not enough food for the men he already had and that more men were landing all the time from Scotland without food for themselves, let alone for the rest of the army.[22]

18. Gilbert, *Contemporary History*, I, 422, 423.
19. Ibid., I, 33; Hogan, *Warr of Ireland*, p. 23; Hill, *Macdonnells of Antrim*, pp. 69-70, 75-6, 257-8, 261.
20. Gilbert, *Contemporary History*, I, 425.
21. Carte MSS, 3, f. 214.
22. Gilbert, *Contemporary History*, I, 423.

In spite of such difficulties, Monro left Carrickfergus on 24 or 25 May, dividing his army into columns to drive back the Irish.[23] Boats had been stationed on the Bann and Lough Beg (north of Lough Neagh) to cut off rebels trying to escape from the Route and the Glens (north-western and eastern Antrim) into County Londonderry, and Monro himself marched down the Bann for the same reason. The operation was only partly successful; an attempt to surround a large body of Irish failed and most of them fled across the river, though thirty or forty were 'cutt downe, withe sume wyves and chyldrene for I promis ... such gallants gotis but small mercie if they come in your comone sogeris handis, tho the officeris doe stryve to represse it' as Patrick (or Peter) Leslie, the New Scots adjutant general reported. On 29 May Monro reached Dunluce Castle and summoned Antrim to surrender. In a final attempt to disarm suspicion Antrim welcomed Monro to a 'mighty feast' prepared for him. According to an account written by Sir John Clotworthy eight months later, citing Monro as his informant, Antrim said 'that he himselfe had done now what he could not answer with his head, for sayd the Earle, the King wreat to me I should not give up the castle to any of you, and offered to send me a commissione to become Generall of the Catholique army of Ulster'. It is possible that Clotworthy made up this story, to discredit the king by implicating him in the Irish rebellion; by the time he told the story civil war had begun in England and Clotworthy was supporting the parliamentarians. But he stated confidently that Monro would vouch for the story, and on balance it seems likely that the story was true. Clotworthy himself expressed doubts as to the truth of what Antrim said, and it seems probable that Antrim was trying to prove his own innocence by proving the king's guilt. The moral of the tale was supposed to be not only that Antrim had not joined the rebels, but that he had refused a direct order from the king to do so.

23.   The main sources for the expedition to Antrim are, *A true and exact relation of divers principall actions of a late expedition in the North of Ireland* (London, 1642), pp. 1-5; J. A. Fairley, 'Lord Sinclair, Covenanter and Royalist', *Transactions of the Buchan Field Club*, VIII (1904-5), 179-80 (this is a letter to Lord Sinclair without a signature; but a seal on it bears the initials P.L. and the arms of the Leslie family. Its writer was almost certainly Patrick (or Peter) Leslie, adjutant general of the army and a captain in Sinclair's regiment); Innes, *Thanes of Cawdor*, pp. 286-8; Hogan, *Warr of Ireland*, pp. 25, 27; Carte MSS, 3, ff. 239-40; Carte, *Ormond*, I, 310; *L.J.* V, 146; H.M.C. 21: *Hamilton*, II, 68.

Dunluce Castle. Main residence of the 'Scots-Irish' earls of Antrim. Garrisoned by the Scottish army in Ireland, 1642-8. On the left is the late sixteenth or early seventeenth century gatehouse, Scottish in style.

Antrim's stories did him no good. Monro at once made him a prisoner pending trial for compliance with the rebels. Dunluce Castle was plundered and a garrison from Leven's regiment placed in it under Monro's nephew, Lieutenant Colonel George Monro.[24] George, 'a surly Mercenarie', was also given command of Coleraine; his garrison was to remain there for six years, mainly on free quarters, 'to the utter depauperatinge' of the inhabitants.[25]   Antrim was said to have been arrested 'by the instigation of old Argyle, then in Scotland the only Man in those days',[26] but in some respects it soon turned out that Monro had acted to forestall Argyll's regiment rather than to help it, for though he soon handed over all Antrim's other houses to the Campbells, at first he refused them Dunluce, to their indignation 'for they think all that is their to be their owne propertie'. In refusing the Campbells Dunluce Monro was probably demonstrating that he intended to keep some direct control over the area and not simply hand it over to them, but he was also probably influenced by the fact that at first Antrim remained in Dunluce as a prisoner; he may well have feared for the earl's safety if he placed him in the hands of the Campbells. After some weeks Antrim was transferred to Carrickfergus by sea, 'hearing behind him the rocks and hills covered with the lamentation of his poor followers' as he embarked, and held in Lord Chichester's house there. Dunluce Castle was then handed over to Lieutenant Colonel Sir Duncan Campbell of Auchinbreck, 'a main adversary of his'.[27]

On 30 May Monro marched east along the coast from Dunluce. 150 Irish women and children who surrendered were allowed to go free, but about 100 men were killed. Antrim's mother, Alice, daughter of the great earl of Tyrone, fled from Ballycastle on hearing that Monro was approaching from one side while from the sea she was threatened by 'MacCailim's army'; MacCailin Mor was Argyll's Gaelic title, and his regiment was now gathering on Rathlin Island.[28]

At Ballycastle Munro waited some days while Argyll's men landed and were settled in garrison. He then set off south

24. Carte MSS, 3, ff. 239-40; H.M.C. 21: *Hamilton*, II, 68-9; Hill, *Macdonnells of Antrim*, pp. 72-3, 76, 261; Gilbert, *Contemporary History*, I, 33.
25. Fitzpatrick, *The Bloody Bridge*, p. 263.
26. Hogan, *Warr of Ireland*, p. 25.
27. Fairley, op. cit. 180; Carte, *Ormond*, i, 310; N.M.A.S. MCR 40, Black Book of Clanranald, ff. 165-8.
28. Hickson, *Ireland in the Seventeenth Century*, I, 279-80.

through the Glens of Antrim to drive out the Irish. On his return to Carrickfergus it was claimed that all Antrim had now been subdued.[29] As on his Newry expedition he had met with little resistance, thousands of cattle had been captured, and many of the Irish killed had been herdsmen.[30] But though most of the Irish had fled, many remained, in small parties, in the Glens, the wildest part of the county. Monro's worries about these remaining rebels were deepened by the attitude of Argyll's regiment, which persisted in trying to act as if it was an independent army. He wrote to Argyll asking that Auchin-breck be given orders to obey him, expressing fears that the regiment, through lack of experience, would prove an easy target for the Irish. It refused to obey his orders about quartering, and opposed Monro's plans to take further action against the rebels in the Glens for fear that he would drive off the enemy cattle which the regiment hoped to capture for it-self. Even Monro's tactful suggestion that only the other regiment led by a Campbell, Lawers', should join it in scouring the Glens was rejected.[31]

A more serious threat to Protestant interests in Ulster than the rebels who remained in the Glens was those who had escaped over the Bann to join the Irish already in County Londonderry. It was at first rumoured that Alasdair MacColla had stayed in the Glens, but it was soon established that he and his Highlanders, the 'clan' of Coll Ciotach, had fled west to join Sir Phelim O'Neill's forces.[32] Thus while Monro's first two expeditions had been of great service to the British of Antrim and Down, those in Ulster west of Lough Neagh found that his activities were making their plight worse. Sir Robert Stewart, one of the leaders of the Lagan army, com-plained that as the Irish were unable to resist Monro they had turned against the 'small and weake Brittish force in this remote part of this province of Ulster'. Whatever the city of Londonderry might think, it was clear that the great majority of the British forces in the area regretted that part of Monro's army had not landed at that port.[33]

29. *A true and exact relation of divers principall actions*, p. 5.
30. Carte MSS, 3, ff. 239-40.
31. N.L.S. MS 3368, no. 1.
32. Carte MSS, 3, ff. 239-40; Young, *Historical Notices*, p. 212; Hill, *Macdonnells of Antrim*, p. 74.
33. Hogan, *Letters and Papers*, p. 47; Gilbert, *Contemporary History*, I, 424-5.

The British of western Ulster were saved by the inadequacies of Sir Phelim O'Neill as a general. Long before the New Scots had landed he had lost the iniative in Ulster by failing to organise decisive action against the centres of resistance to the rebels which had survived the first Irish onslaught. Once that first impetus of the rebellion waned he proved incapable of holding the rebel forces together, or of organising the mass of enthusiastic native Irish into an effective army. He had failed to offer any real resistance to Monro but now, reinforced by the Irish from Antrim, he was persuaded to attack Sir Robert Stewart's forces. In doing this it was said he relied on the judgement and valour of Alasdair MacColla.[34] On 16 June at Glenmaquin Alasdair and his brother Ranald led their Highlanders in a fierce charge on Stewart's forces, but they were driven back after bitter fighting and the whole Irish army then retreated. Alasdair was injured but carried to safety.[35] Thus for the time being the pressure on the Lagan army was reduced.

The most outstanding result of Monro's Antrim campaign had been the capture of the earl of Antrim, but custody of such an important prisoner was an embarrassment. Monro was soon appealing for instructions as to what to do with him.[36] The king ordered that he be sent to York, or to Dublin, but Monro refused.[37] The English parliament first ordered that Antrim be retained in Ireland, then (in July) that he be sent to England. In September this order too was revoked, but another change of mind led parliament to give instructions on 7 October that he be sent to London![38] Parliament was just too late; on 6 October Antrim escaped from Carrickfergus. On 4 October he had got out of Lord Chichester's house disguised as a servant, intending to board an Isle of Man boat which had been secretly hired for him. But the boat could not sail because of contrary winds, so Antrim calmly returned to captivity until the wind changed two days later. His disuise was then used to fool the guards again, and he made good his

---

34. H.M.C. 23: *Cowper*, II, 300-1.
35. Hogan, *Warr of Ireland*, pp. 23-4; Hogan, *Letters and Papers*, pp. 46, 49-51; Innes, *Thanes of Cawdor*, pp. 287-8.
36. N.L.S. MS 3368, no. 1.
37. Fraser, *The Melvilles*, II, 22; Hill, *Macdonnells of Antrim*, p. 261; Carte, *Ormond*, III, 165; *R.P.C.S. 1638-43*, p. 278.
38. *C.J.* II, 631, 665, 763, 764, 793, 797; *L.J.* V, 146, 351, 391; S.R.O. PA.7/23/2/8.

escape to England, joining the royalists at York.[39]

On his return from Dunluce, as on his return from Newry, Monro had hoped to be able to set out immediately on another expedition, but again lack of supplies delayed him.[40] By 16 June such problems had been partly overcome and he marched south; while he had been in northern Antrim British forces in southern Down had been forced to retreat by the rebels[41] so Monro probably thought it necessary to reassert his power there. He took with him over 2,000 of his own men, four troops of British horse and over 1,100 British foot. The British marched through Killultagh Wood (which lay roughly between Lisburn and Lough Neagh),[42] the New Scots through Dromore, rejoining on the upper Bann River. There it was learnt that the Irish had fled deep into Tyrone, beyond Dungannon. The British were eager to pursue them, but Monro refused to co-operate, claiming that he had not sufficient supplies for such a march. Instead he insisted on moving south to inspect the garrison at Newry, then returning to Carrickfergus by way of the Mourne Mountains and Maccartan's Wood, where the rebels were still troublesome. The British refused to follow him; they crossed the Bann, occupied Armagh briefly, established garrisons at Dungannon and Mountjoy, and summoned Charlemont to surrender. But when it refused lack of food and equipment prevented them undertaking a siege and they were forced to retreat.[43]

The British blamed Monro for this failure, but in reality he was no better equipped for a siege than they were. Arguments about the relative powers of Monro and Lord Conway flared up again. On 7 July Conway complained that the Scots pretended 'that they onely are to make the warre in Ulster'. Monro had refused to allow a march into Tyrone, claiming that orders had reached him from Scotland that no one was to besiege any place or establish any garrison in Ulster without

39. Carte MSS, 3, f. 579; Baillie, *Letters*, II, 73; N.M.A.S. MCR 40, Black Book of Clanranald, ff. 168v-171.
40. N.L.S. MS 3368, no. 1.
41. Fairley, op. cit. 180.
42. McCracken, *Irish Woods*, p. 35.
43. G. Benn, *History of the Town of Belfast* (2 vols, Belfast, 1877-80), I, 686-90; Carte MSS, 3, f. 302; Carte, *Ormond*, I, 310; Turner, *Memoirs*, p. 23; Bagwell, *Stuarts*, II, 23-5; *A True Relation of the taking of Mountjoy in the County of Tyrone ...* (London, 1642), pp. 3-5.

E

his permission.[44]

It was not just questions of military command and strategy that were causing tension between the British (especially the English) commanders in Ulster, led by Lord Conway and Sir John Clotworthy, and the Scots army 'or Party as they call it'.[45] It was becoming clear that the New Scots saw themselves as being concerned with more than just defeating the rebels; they also undertook the creation of a 'party' in Ulster, the establishment of Scottish influence there permanently, so that Scotland could never again be threatened (as she had been in 1640) with invasion from Ulster organised by the Dublin government. The main instrument in this work on the civil (as opposed to the military) side was religion; presbyterianism was to be so deeply rooted in Ulster that it could not be suppressed, as had happened in the 1630s. 10 June 1642 saw the first meeting of a presbytery ever held in Ireland. Its membership was confined to chaplains and elders from four New Scots regiments, but the meeting (at Carrickfergus) resolved not only that the other six regiments should be urged to join but that Old Scots regiments and local parishes should be invited to apply to become part of the presbytery. Soon fifteen parishes in Antrim and Down had made such applications, electing elders and asking to be supplied with preachers.[46]

The great shortage of ministers could only partly be met by the efforts of the New Scots chaplains, so the 'most part of the Scottish Nation in the North of Ireland' petitioned the Scottish general assembly to send them ministers.[47] For the next six years the assembly and the commission of the kirk dispatched groups of ministers to spend a few months at a time in Ulster, preaching to Scots and English settlers. Shortage of ministers in Scotland was given as the reason for not sending men to settle permanently in Ulster, but it may also have been calculated that it would be much easier for the Scottish assembly, which had no jurisdiction in Ireland, to retain control of the growing presbyterian church in Ulster

44. Carte MSS, 3, ff. 302, 325-7; Carte, *Ormond*, I, 311; Warner, *History*, pp. 224-5.
45. Carte MSS, 3, ff. 325-7; N.L.S. Wodrow MSS, Folio LXV, ff. 198-201.
46. Reid, *History of the Presbyterian Church*, I, 372-4; Adair, *True Narrative*, pp. 92-5.
47. A. Peterkin, ed. *Records of the Kirk of Scotland* (Edinburgh, 1838), pp. 330-1.

if many of those ministering in that church remained Scottish parish ministers as well.[48]

Major General Monro proved 'very instrumental for promoting presbyterial government',[49] and, after persecution under Strafford and the Irish rebellion, violently anti-Catholic presbyterianism proved popular in Ulster, spreading especially among settlers of Scottish origin but to some extent among the English as well. It faced little competition, for the organisation of the church of Ireland had collapsed in many areas. In these circumstances it was hardly surprising that many English commanders should come to be suspicious of the New Scots and fear that they intended to bring Ulster under Scots domination both in military affairs and religion.

Partly to satisfy the discontented British, Monro undertook a second march towards Charlemont soon after his return from the first, but its results were equally disappointing. According to Conway Charlemont could easily have been captured, but Monro first occupied himself in sweeping the country for cattle and then insisted on retreating to Newry; all his supplies were coming from there and intelligence reports indicated that the Irish intended to cut this supply route. In these circumstances Monro's withdrawal was probably wise; even Conway admitted that Monro's men had had nothing to eat for 'a day or two' and this seems a pretty good reason for retreating. Monro's military experience was much greater than Conway's and he must have feared that lack of food would soon cause his army to disintegrate. Once camped near Newry Monro sent out parties to raid Irish creaghts; many cattle were captured, many Irish killed while his own losses were light except among the camp-followers seeking loot 'heere called Plunderers, an ill race of people and very hurtfull to an Army', who could well be spared.[50]

The British denounced Monro as preferring to plunder Antrim and Down (causing more damage than the rebels had done) and to export great numbers of cattle to Scotland than

48. See ibid. 331-2, 345-6, 354-5, 396-7, 406, 432, 452, 453, 480, 481, 517, 518; A. F. Mitchell and J. Christie, eds. *Records of the Commissions of the General Assemblies of the Church of Scotland* (3 vols, S.H.S. 1892-1909), I, 33-4, 145, 201, 402, 513; D. C. Mactavish, ed. *Minutes of the Synod of Argyll, 1639-51* (S.H.S. 1943), I, 43, 86, 91, 95, 118, 203; Adair, *True Narrative*, pp. 95-151; Blair, *Life*, pp. 166-8; Livingstone, 'Life', in Tweedie, *Select Biographies*, I, 166-8.
49. Adair, *True Narrative*, p. 150.
50. Carte MSS, 3, ff. 325-7; Turner, *Memoirs*, p. 23; Gilbert, *Contemporary History*, I, 519, III, 198; Carte, *Ormond*, I, 310-11.

to face the enemy,[51] but this was hardly fair. He had not defeated the Irish in open battle but his expeditions had contributed greatly to the completely demoralised state that they were now in. On 18 July (while Monro was at Newry)[52] the Ulster Irish were meeting twenty-five miles away at Glaslough in County Monaghan. They decided despondently, it is said, that they should disband their forces and flee abroad since their rebellion had failed. It seemed that Monro's restraint was to be vindicated, that constant minor reverses were leading to the collapse of the rebellion. But with dramatic timing, just as all seemed lost, news was brought to the Ulster Irish that Owen Roe O'Neill had landed at Doe Castle in northern Donegal. Owen Roe, nephew of the great earl of Tyrone and cousin of Sir Phelim, was by far the best known Irish soldier of the day, having served for over thirty years with the Spanish army. He had been in close touch with the Ulster Irish both before and since the start of the rebellion, and had now at last reached Ireland in spite of diplomatic efforts by the English to prevent him leaving the Spanish Netherlands.[53] Through both his reputation as a soldier and his ancestry the landing of Owen Roe raised Irish morale. Sir Phelim sent men to meet him and on 13 August he arrived at Charlemont. At the end of the month an assembly of Irish leaders elected him lord general, with Sir Phelim as lord president of Ulster. With the help of two or three hundred veteran soldiers he had brought with him, Owen Roe was soon hard at work trying to turn the confused mass of Irish which Sir Phelim had commanded into an efficient, trained army, preferring a relatively small and disciplined force to a large undisciplined one.[54]

The arrival of Owen Roe and Irish reactions to it converted what had very nearly been complete success for Monro in his 1642 expeditions into a very limited victory. In retrospect it seems obvious that a little more effort and determination on his part might have broken the back of the rebellion before Owen Roe arrived. But Monro could not have known this,

51. Carte, *Ormond*, I, 311.
52. Carte MSS, 3, ff. 325-7.
53. Gilbert, *Contemporary History*, III, 198; J. J. O'Connell, *The Irish Wars* (Dublin, n.d.), p. 106; J. I. Casway, 'Owen Roe O'Neill's Return to Ireland in 1642: The Diplomatic Background', *Studia Hibernica*, IX (1969), 48-61.
54. Casway, op. cit. 62-4.

and in any case he probably saw his function in these months as not being to press on to final victory, but to create conditions under which the New Scots army could build up to its full strength in safety, and to clear the way for a full-scale assault on the rebels by the whole army when Leven arrived to lead it. The fact that Leven did not land in Ireland until 4 August,[55] just as the army reached full strength, strongly suggests that no all-out action against the rebels had been contemplated before then.[56] It seems likely that Monro had specific orders, either from Leven or the Scots privy council, limiting his freedom of action, perhaps by forbidding him to send any large force over the Bann, either north or south of Lough Neagh; certainly, as will be seen, some such limitation was in force in 1643. It would be hardly surprising if there was reluctance to let Monro, a highly competent officer but one with little experience of independent command of an army, act freely and thus perhaps put the army at risk when the great Alexander Leslie, who had just added the successful invasion of England to the renown he had won in Germany, was soon to take over the command from him.

By the time Leven landed, however, the opportunity for quick victory in Ireland had passed. Not only had Owen Roe begun to revive Irish morale but civil war between king and parliament in England was imminent. This naturally was a matter of great concern to the covenanters, for victory for the king in England would undoubtedly lead to attempts to overthrow their regime in Scotland, either by invasion or royalist rebellion. In this situation the Scottish army in Ireland, the only Scottish army in existence, became of central importance to the Scottish government. It was rumoured in England that the Scots had only sent an army to Ireland so as to have it ready to invade England to help the English parliament.[57] This was not true, but even though the army was not intended for this purpose it obviously could be diverted to it. The covenanters had sent an army to Ireland because they believed Ulster in hostile hands would pose a threat to them;

55. C. S. Terry, *The Life and Campaigns of Alexander Leslie, First Earl of Leven* (London, 1899), p. 167.
56. The allegation that Monro and the British were preparing a great attack on the Irish but withdrew on news of Owen Roe's landing (Gilbert, *Contemporary History*, III, 198; Casway, op. cit. 62) seems to be without foundation, an invention designed to heighten the drama of the latter's arrival.
57. *C.S.P.V. 1642-3*, p. 148.

but for England to be in hostile hands would be even more dangerous. Therefore, though the complete defeat of the Irish rebels remained desirable, it no longer had priority; if trying to achieve it meant taking risks with the New Scots army, or involving it so deeply in Ireland that it could not quickly be withdrawn, then it was too dangerous an objective for the moment. A major campaign in Ireland might leave Scotland temporarily without an army with which to intervene in England or suppress rebellion in Scotland, and Leven was probably given strict orders to ensure that this did not happen. The common opinion that the Irish rebels 'would be quickly subdued if all things were right in England.[58] referred primarily to the fact that the approach of civil war prevented English help being sent to Ireland, but the situation in England also diverted Scottish attention from Ireland.

Moreover, the approach of civil war had led to the complete collapse of the English parliament's efforts to supply the New Scots; even if the political situation had allowed Leven to undertake a determined drive against the rebels, lack of food and equipment would have held him back. This contributed to a further difficulty which faced him on his arrival in Ireland. Failure to supply and pay the army as promised had contributed to the fast growth in it of a strong sense of identity; though it had only been in Ireland for a few months many of its officers felt closely bound together not by a sense of common purpose but by common grievances. Though the army was always to deny that it was a mercenary force the influence of the many former mercenary officers in it was strong, and by their code no loyalty was due to employers who did not keep promises about pay. This combined with another influence, that of the national covenant, which had shown how much could be achieved by men with common interests taking a sworn oath to stand together. The officers had, under these influences, sworn such an agreement, angry at how they were being treated and (so rumour had it) disillusioned by Monro as a commander.[59]

Information about the officers' agreement comes from only one source, the memoirs of Major James Turner. 'The officers ... finding themselves ill payd, and which was worse, not

---

58. Gilbert, *Contemporary History*, I, 519.
59. H.M.C. 65: *Franciscan*, p. 188.

knowing in the time of the civill warr who sould be their paymaster, and reflecting on the successful issue of the National Covenant of Scotland, bethought themselves of making one also; but they were wise enough to give it ane other name, and therefore christened it a Mutual Assurance; whereby ... they made themselves independent of any except these who wold be their actuall and reall paymasters'. Turner was writing many years later, and he may well exaggerate the extent to which the mutinous mood of the army had developed by the autumn of 1642, but clearly the situation was serious if, as he alleges, Leven 'was very dissatisfied with this bond of union, as he had reason; and at first he spoke hie language of strikeing heads of; bot the officers sticking close one to another, made these threates evanish in smoake'. Unable to divide the officers and persuade them that they were guilty of 'blacke mutinie' Leven returned to Scotland 'and so gave an everlasting adieu to Ireland'—followed by accusations from the officers that he had appropriated for his own use £2,500 sterling supplied by the English parliament to buy wagons for the army;[60] in reality he used the money to buy food for the army,[61] but the officers still felt cheated.

However, Leven did undertake two expeditions before deserting his army. In September he crossed the Bann into Londonderry. He had written to Owen Roe O'Neill expressing surprise that a man with such a reputation should have joined a rebellion; in reply Owen Roe pointed out that he had only come to help his country, whereas Leven and the covenanters, not content with seizing control of Scotland, had invaded England as well. He also inquired who Leven was serving in Ireland, the king or the English parliament? Finding he was getting into deeper water in this polemical correspondence than he had expected, Leven abandoned it and turned to military action.[62] From County Londonderry his forces marched south through Tyrone to Dungannon; but he then returned to Carrickfergus 'without doing anything of note'. There had been some skirmishing with Owen Roe O'Neill's forces but they had fallen back before the Scots to avoid a major engagement, and Leven probably lacked the supplies

---

60. Turner, *Memoirs*, pp. 24-5; Terry, *Alexander Leslie*, pp. 167-8.
61. T.S.A.I. pp. 23, 35, 82.
62. Carte, *Ormond*, I, 349; Terry, *Alexander Leslie*, p. 167; Gilbert, *Contemporary History*, I, 45, III, 198.

necessary to follow them further.[63]

Leven's second expedition was an attempt to besiege Charlemont and relieve the garrison left in Dungannon. The main artillery train had now arrived from Scotland, and some of its guns and one Henry Jardine, described as 'the great engineer', accompanied him. The new Scots rendezvoused with British forces at Lisburn on 26 September, but the combined force had only provisions for fourteen days, there were not enough baggage and carriage animals for all the cannon and ammunition, and 'it rained so extreamely for two nights and a daye that it made the wayes extreameldy bad and the rivers very high'. In spite of these difficulties Leven reached Tranderagee in Armagh, but he had to abandon the planned attack on Charlemont; he marched instead to Newry, from whence parties were sent to try yet again to clear the Mourne Mountains and Maccartan's Wood of the Irish who remained there. No attempt was made by the New Scots to relieve Dungannon. Lord Conway tried to keep it supplied across Lough Neagh but soon it was forced to surrender, the garrison withdrawing to Mountjoy which continued to hold out. Leven's expedition had achieved almost nothing—except increasing the exasperation of the British at what they saw as the excessive caution of the New Scots—and in November he returned to Scotland.[64]

Thus the great Alexander Leslie's long-awaited offensive in Ireland failed. Political circumstances, lack of supplies and consequent indiscipline had combined to defeat him. He was probably past his prime as a soldier, as Lord Moore indicated by his remark that 'the Earle of Levens actions' did not make 'such a noyse in the world as these of Generall Lesley'.[65] Leven appears, if it is true that on leaving he told Monro that Owen Roe O'Neill would defeat the New Scots if he assembled an army,[66] to have lost confidence in his army. His subsequent neglect of it suggests that he allowed his indignation at its

63. T. W. Moody and J. G. Simms, eds *The Bishopric of Derry and the Irish Society of London, 1602-1705*, I (I.M.C. 1968), p. 244; Young, *Historical Notices*, p. 216; Carte, *Ormond*, I, 349; [D. Newark], *A true relation of the last great battall fought in Ireland* (London, 1642), pp. 1-5.

64. Moody and Simms, *The Bishopric of Londonderry*, I, 244; Turner, *Memoirs*, p. 24. The main source for this expedition is the narrative printed in Young, *Historical Notices*, pp. 49-52, which is erroneously headed 'Monro's Raid on Newry, 1643'.

65. Turner, *Memoirs*, p. 25.

66. Gilbert, *Contemporary History*, III, 198.

indiscipline to overcome considerations of its great importance to his country. His disillusionment was probably partly due to the fact that he had not only met with mutiny from the New Scots but suspicion from the British. Lord Conway had heard at last from England that the British forces were not entirely under the command of the New Scots; he had therefore made no attempt to meet Leven when he landed. Instead in August he undertook plundering raids into Tyrone, though he found it hard to get men to campaign at harvest time.[67] In western Ulster the Lagan army was weakened by its own disputes over command. At first all its colonels commanded in turn, though Sir Robert Stewart seems to have predominated. But early in September the lords justice in Dublin appointed Sir William Stewart commander. Sir Robert and the other colonels protested violently, and in December the old joint command was restored.[68] It is thus hardly surprising that Leven only got half hearted support from the British for his expeditions. Resentful of Scottish attempts to dominate them, even worse supplied than the New Scots, anxious about political developments in England, the British neither co-operated fully with Leven nor achieved much by themselves—in spite of continuing allegations that they were defeating the rebels while the New Scots did nothing.[69] On top of all the other circumstances that prevented effective action being taken against the rebels, British and New Scots alike had suffered from the unseasonable weather; on 24 September Lord Conway complained that the British at the 'end of a wet summer are entring into winter without hay for our horses, without howses for the men, it rains continually, every one is sicke, few cloathes, little money, ill meate, worse drinke'.[70]

However, though Leven had won no victories in Ireland, he had again demonstrated the ability of the Scots army to march freely over much of Ulster, and this in itself was demoralising for the Irish. One sign of this was that a number of rebels agreed to submit and were, along with their followers, 'received into protection' by Leven. Most prominent among them were Alasdair MacColla and his brother Ranald. They

67. Carte MSS, 3, f. 457.
68. Carte, *Ormond*, I, 365-6.
69. E.g. E. Borlase, *The History of the Exerable Irish Rebellion* (London, 1680), p. 101.
70. H.M.C. 29: *Portland*, III, 99, 101.

had joined the Irish because they feared attack by the British and because, with the rebels carrying all before them, this seemed the course that would be most likely to win them powerful enough support to persuade Argyll to free their father and brothers. But now the rebel cause seemed to be collapsing and Argyll's regiment had occupied the earl of Antrim's lands, where the brothers had found a refuge after being driven out of Scotland. They therefore decided to change sides. On 19 September, between Leven's two expeditions, they negotiated terms with him. The two brothers and their followers (presumably mainly MacDonnells from Antrim and MacDonald refugees from Scotland) would receive a full pardon for their actions. Their father and brothers would be released by Argyll, who would also restore the family and its followers to the lands and possessions they had enjoyed before the troubles. If the brothers could raise companies of men willing to fight the Irish these men would receive pay equally with the Scottish army. But in order to gain these concessions Alasdair and Ranald were first to prove their good faith by doing service against the Irish, both in shedding their blood and despoiling them of their goods and cattle.[71] Alasdair kept his word at least in part; on 7 October it was reported from Londonderry that 'Col Kitto and divers rebels have submitted and brought in many cows for pledges'[72] (Alasdair was frequently confused with his father Coll Ciotach). His conduct satisfied Leven, for on 11 November he issued orders from Carrickfergus that Alasdair and Ranald were to choose 300 men from those who had submitted with them, who were to be enrolled for service. Alasdair was to lead some of them against the rebels, but Ranald and others were to remain behind, presumably as pledges that Alasdair would return. The former rebels were to receive maintainance from Archibald Stewart, the earl of Antrim's agent and Alasdair's former commander.[73]

This agreement soon collapsed, however, probably because Argyll was not willing to free Alasdair's father and brothers.[74] Whatever the reason, Alasdair and his men were soon back

71. Hickson, *Ireland in the Seventeenth Century*, I, 244; Young, *Historical Notices*, p. 49; Carte MSS, 4, f. 230, printed in D. Stevenson, 'The Desertion of the Irish by Coll Keitach's Sons, 1642', *I.H.S.* XXI (1978-9), 82-3.
72. Moody and Simms, *The Bishopric of Londonderry*, I, 245.
73. Carte MSS, 4, f. 32, printed in Stevenson, op. cit. 83-4.
74. Stevenson, op. cit. 82-3 citing Carte MSS, 4, f. 231.

with the rebels. Nothing more is heard of them for a year; having unsuccessfully tried to change sides they can hardly have received a very warm welcome from the Irish. At the time the failure to win over Alasdair MacColla from the rebels must have seemed of minor importance; but his later activities as the commander of Irish troops in Scotland was to give the failure great significance.

In all its campaigns in 1642 the Scottish army had failed to live up to expectations; so much had been expected of it that it was bound to be a disappointment. Yet its achievements had been considerable. With the help of the British it had temporarily broken the morale of the Irish. Down, Antrim, Londonderry and much of Tyrone had been cleared of organised rebel forces. Southern Tyrone, parts of Donegal, northern Monaghan and northern Fermanagh remained largely no men's lands, but they contained no major Irish garrisons. This meant that the rebels had almost been driven south of the line from Ballyshannon in the west to Newry in the east which separated Ulster proper from the rest of Ireland. It had been largely the strength of this relatively easily defended line stretching from coast to coast which had enabled the native Irish of Ulster to hold out against English conquest half a century before. Half the length of this frontier was constituted by the River Erne, Lough Erne and Upper Lough Erne; the only practical crossing points for large forces were near Ballyshannon on the west coast and the less important route through Enniskillen (which was held by a British garrison) between the Loughs. On the east coast the main route in or out of Ulster lay through the narrow Moyry Pass between Dundalk and Newry, with the mountainous country of the Fews stretching inland through southern Armagh. Between the Fews and Upper Lough Erne lay equally difficult country for armies, the wooded hills interlaced with bogs and loughs of Monaghan and Cavan.[75]

Once driven south of this line, it would have been hard for the Irish to break back through it again—as hard as it had been for the English under Elizabeth, or even harder as a British garrison now held Dundalk which commanded the southern approaches to the Moyry Pass. But the New Scots and British

75. Hayes-McCoy, 'Strategy and Tactics', *I.H.S.* II, 264-7; Prendergast, op. cit. 421; R. D. Edwards, *An Atlas of Irish History* (London, 1973), pp. 59, 61.

had not quite driven the Irish back this far; the Irish managed to hold on to Charlemont on the Blackwater, and could use it as a secure assembly point for forces infiltrating from the south through Monaghan and Cavan. While the Irish retained Charlemont the New Scots could never feel that it would be safe for them to march out of Ulster, and they never did succeed in capturing the fort and thus gaining complete control of the area to the south of Lough Neagh, a land of rivers, loughs, boggy woods and low hills[76] in which campaigning was difficult. Moreover, if Ulster's natural defences made the province hard to break in to, they made it equally difficult to break out of. The six year stay of the New Scots in Ireland was to see a prolonged strategic deadlock in Ulster, with the position reached by the end of 1642 never being seriously altered.

It was not only geographical and military considerations which made it hard for the New Scots to advance out of Ulster; political considerations made them doubt whether it would be wise to do so even if they could. The Scottish government was determined that the New Scots should remain a separate force, and should remain in or near Ulster, ready to intervene in England or Scotland if necessary. But the treaty had laid down that the Dublin government could give orders to the army, and could order it to leave Ulster. Orders from Dublin were easy to ignore while the army remained in Ulster; communications were difficult and the army had little contact with forces controlled directly from Dublin. If the army marched out of Ulster it would be increasingly difficult for it to keep closely in touch with Scotland, and pressures on it to be obedient to orders from Dublin would increase. If it joined with Ormond's army, it might be in danger of losing its separate identity. Ulster was what mattered to Scotland's security, and the New Scots army was too important an asset to the Scottish government to be risked elsewhere in Ireland.

Naturally things looked different from London and Dublin. The New Scots army was the largest organised army in Ireland; once it had scattered the rebels in Ulster it seemed obvious that it should send help to other parts of Ireland, as the treaty provided. Thus as early as 16 July 1642 the English house of commons resolved that 2,500 New Scots and three of the

76. McCracken, *Irish Woods*, p. 40.

troops of horse attached to them (together with one troop and 3,500 foot from the British forces) should march south by way of Dundalk to join the Leinster forces centred on Dublin in a campaign against the rebels in Munster. A month later parliament ordered that all the New Scots move into Munster as the rebels were concentrating their forces there.[77] The Dublin government still did not know whether by the treaty it could give orders to the New Scots, but on 1 August it was resolved to ask Monro and Lord Conway to bring forces to clear rebels from Longford and Westmeath, as the estimated 20,000 men of the New Scots and British in Ulster were more than enough to deal with the rebels in that province.[78] But the New Scots did nothing and even Lord Conway thought up reasons for remaining in Ulster.[79]

The New Scots made no attempt to keep Dublin informed about their activities. On 13 September the lords justice and the council complained that 'we know not how far their numbers are lessened by the sword, sickness or otherwise, or how they are stored with armes, municion, victualls, or other provisions, nor do we know what agreement was contracted on that side with the Scotch nation concerneing those forces, nor how farr they are to be governed by any commands from us'. Yet Ulster had more men in arms to oppose the rebels than the other three provinces of Ireland put together. If anything was to be done to stop the rebels building up their armies in Munster unmolested, help would have to come from Ulster.[80] But the New Scots continued to ignore pleas for help. In September Leven refused to send to Dublin match, powder, spades and pickaxes from the magazine at Carrickfergus which had been there when the New Scots landed. A request for the loan of some gunpowder was also refused.[81] The lords justice complained at the concentration of all the New Scots and many of the British in quarters in Antrim and Down, which left the rest of Ulster open to enemy attack since it was so sparsely garrisoned,[82] but the New Scots made no attempt to leave the area closest to Scotland. In November the lords

77. *C.J.* III, 677; *L.J.* V, 294.
78. Hogan, *Letters and Papers*, p. 99.
79. Carte MSS, 3, f. 457.
80. Hogan, *Letters and Papers*, pp. 127-33; Gilbert, *Irish Confederation*, II, 60-5; H.M.C. 36: *Ormonde*, N.S. II, 191-5.
81. Carte, *Ormond*, I, 349; H.M.C. 36: *Ormonde*, N.S. II, 208.
82. H.M.C. 36: *Ormonde*, N.S. II, 218.

justice tried to call 2,500 New Scots out of Ulster but Monro refused to obey.[83]

Understandable as the refusal of the New Scots to leave Ulster was, its consequences were far reaching. Only they could possibly have put an end to the rebellion in 1642. Their failure to attempt this gave the Irish time to recover from the defeats inflicted on them earlier in the year, time to establish both political and military organisation. In May and June a supreme council had been set up by the Irish as a provisional government, and in October the first general assembly of the confederate Irish met at Kilkenny, which was to become their permanent headquarters. Four generals were appointed to lead provincial armies, Owen Roe being given command of the Ulster army.[84] After Leven left Ireland in November 1642 Monro made no attempt to act against the Irish until the following spring.[85] By that time the civil and military organisation of the Irish, for all its weaknesses, was sufficiently strong to ensure that the rebel cause did not collapse in the face of his attacks. It was impossible for an army which refused to leave Ulster to defeat the rebels completely and thus place Ulster securely in hands friendly to Scotland. Thus even if the Scottish government was only interested in Ulster, failure to let the New Scots march into other provinces was a fatal mistake.

ii. The Campaign of 1643

1643 saw little change in the military situation in Ulster. Neither New Scots nor Irish were strong enough to upset the stalemate. Monro's army was constantly hindered by lack of supplies. In February Captain Thomas Dalyell (Monro's regiment) reported that, unless more care was taken of the army, neither 'tempist nor ane thing elis vill lock us ane loinger in ignorens and necessate'; the army would have to leave Ireland. Six men of Leven's regiment had stolen a boat in a despairing attempt to get back to Scotland, even though none of them

83. Ibid. II, 235-6.
84. D. F. Cregan, 'The Confederation of Kilkenny', in B. Farrell, ed. *The Irish Parliamentary Tradition* (Dublin, 1973), pp. 103-4; J. C. Beckett, 'The Confederation of Kilkenny reviewed', *Historical Studies*, II (1959), 27-41; Bagwell, *Stuarts*, II, 25-7. Beckett, op. cit. 32, compares the confederation, as an alliance of individuals bound together by oath, to the national covenant.
85. Carte, *Ormond*, I, 350.

could row; they had been captured and some were to be executed. Monro intended to march shortly in search of food, but lack of baggage horses to carry provisions meant that he could not take provisions for more than eight days with him.[86] The British forces were no better off. In April Lord Montgomery urged that he be allowed to march his regiment to Dublin; if he did not it might be forced to disband.[87] In addition to supply difficulties, the actions of Monro's army were again limited by orders from Scotland. Unlike the previous year, there is now definite evidence for this; in August it was feared that there would be complaints from Scotland that the army had gone 'beyond their limits' on an expedition, but its representatives in Edinburgh assured it that no one was displeased—except perhaps Leven, who wanted nothing done in his absence![88]

On 12 May Monro, having just returned from one expedition, rendezvoused at Drumbo with 2,000 foot and 300 horse, each supplied with half a pound of meal per day for ten days, for an expedition towards Armagh. His objectives were 'to find and tutch the enemies pulse ther' and to place himself between enemy forces and garrisons which the Irish had established (presumably during the winter) at Greencastle and Newcastle, so that these garrisons could be attacked in safety. On 13 May Monro reached Tanderagee, driving out an enemy garrison, while Colonel Home with 600 men marched towards Newcastle, where he was joined by boats from Carrickfergus carrying cannon and more men. Having been reinforced from Newry Monro advanced on Armagh, clearing the countryside of Irish. Hearing that Owen Roe was at Charlemont he resolved to try to surprise him; intelligence reports indicated that General Thomas Preston (the Irish commander in Leinster) was coming north to help Owen Roe, and that Sir Phelim O'Neill was bringing further Irish forces from Dungannon, and Monro hoped to defeat Owen Roe before these other forces joined him. Surprise was nearly achieved; it was Owen Roe himself, out hunting, who saw the advancing Scots and hastened back to defend Charlemont. His men managed to stop the Scots in a series of hard fought engagements—at one point Monro himself fought on foot with a pike, furiously

86. H.M.C. 10: *10th Report*, I, 78-9.
87. Carte MSS, 5, f. 49.
88. T.S.A.I. p. 24.

shouting to his men as they gave ground 'Fay fay, run awa frae awheen rebels'. Short of food, ammunition and other equipment, Monro could not undertake a siege and therefore retired to Newry. From there he marched to Newcastle.

Colonel Home had already stormed the castle's outer defences, and on Monro's arrival the garrison agreed to negotiate a surrender on terms. While talks were in progress, and fighting had therefore ceased, a ship appeared and sent a man ashore who was promptly captured. He proved to be a servant and foster brother of the earl of Antrim, James Stewart, sent to see if it was safe for his master to land. On being threatened with immediate execution he signalled to Antrim that all was well by waving his hat over his head. The earl was thus lured ashore, where he was greeted by some of Monro's soldiers, who claimed they had been sent by Owen Roe O'Neill to meet him. When he found himself a prisoner he offered Monro £5,000 sterling to release him, but without success; he was sent guarded by a horse troop to Carrickfergus, where he was placed in close confinement in the castle. A few days later one of his servants, Thomas Nandicke, was executed for having aided his previous escape.

The recapture of Antrim was at least partial compensation to Monro for the lack of military success of his expedition. He attributed his failure to take Charlemont to lack of supplies; through food shortages 'we ar all of vs civillie dead' as he oddly put it. Far from terrifying the Irish the New Scots were 'being now derided by them'. To add to Monro's difficulties Leven, his commanding officer, was still sulking, refusing to have anything to do with the army and not even answering Monro's letters. 'If your Excellency be resolued to returne no answere to my former letteres, I resolue by letteres not to be more troublesome vnto your Excellency, my patience being so exhausted'.[89]

The capture of Antrim, however, soon proved to be an event of major political significance. Monro's wish to capture Newcastle and Greencastle had resulted in part from suspicion that they were being used in communications between the

89. For this expedition and the capture of Antrim see Fraser, *Melvilles*, II, 93-5; Turner, *Memoirs*, pp. 26-9; *A letter of great consequence: sent by the Honourable, Robert Lord Monro, out of the Kingdom of Ireland* (1643), pp. 3-6; Gilbert, *Contemporary History*, III, 199; Young, *Historical Notices*, pp. 219, 221; Carte, *Ormond*, I, 432; Carte MSS, 5, ff. 323-4; N.M.A.S. MCR 40, Black Book of Clanranald, ff. 180-188v.

Irish rebels and English Catholics and royalists. Antrim's capture proved such suspicions justified, for letters found on him, and subsequent interrogation of him and his servants, proved that he was deeply involved in plots to obtain help for the king in the English civil war from the Irish rebels and from Scottish Catholics and royalists. Antrim had been sent to negotiate with the Irish for an army, to be provided partly by the Irish, partly by the royalist government in Dublin, to help the king in England. Attempts were to be made to get the New Scots to co-operate by offering Monro £5,000 sterling and a senior command in the army. If this was refused, Dublin and the Irish were to be persuaded to act jointly to destroy Monro's army. Antrim had also been negotiating with Scots royalists—the marquis of Huntly, the earls of Montrose and Nithsdale and Lord Aboyne—to raise men in Scotland to fight for the king in England. This Antrim admitted, though he denied an allegation by one of his servants that he had also intended to do all the mischief he could against Scotland. As it emerged that Antrim's brother Alexander MacDonnell was already in Ireland trying to reach an agreement with Alasdair and Ranald MacColla, Coll Ciotach's sons, whose main interests lay in Scotland, his denials were not very convincing. It seems clear that he was planning renewed action in Scotland on behalf of the MacDonalds.

The propaganda impact of the revelation of Antrim's plots (often greatly exaggerated) on Protestant opinion in all three kingdoms was immense. It was a major influence in persuading many in Scotland that they would have to help the English parliament to defeat the king, since he seemed determined to destroy the regime in Scotland. In fact though Queen Henrietta Maria was deeply involved in Antrim's plots the king was not; but few believed this. The king's enemies could not have asked for better propaganda than that supplied through the Scottish Army in Ireland's capture of Antrim.[90]

As in 1642, however, Antrim was a diplomatically embarrassing prisoner. The king demanded that he be sent to Dublin, and Archibald Stewart worked to the same end, while the Scottish covention of estates and Leven ordered that he

90. Stevenson, *Scottish Revolution*, pp. 270, 273; S. R. Gardiner, *History of the Great Civil War* (4 vols, London, 1893-4), I, 176-8; Baillie, *Letters*, II, 73-4, 80; *A.P.S.* VI, i, 7; Spalding, *Memorialls*, II, 244, 247-50; H.M.C. 29: *Portland*, I, 120-2; *R.P.C.S. 1638-43*, pp. 436, 442-4.

MAP 3 PLACES MUSTER OF TH
According to Thomas Clayto

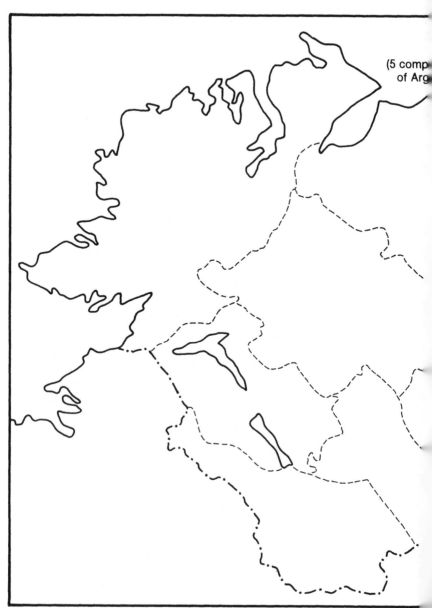

(5 comp
of Arg

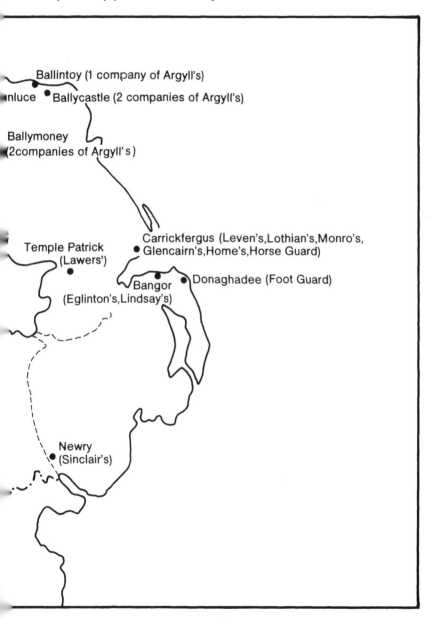

Ballintoy (1 company of Argyll's)

nluce ● Ballycastle (2 companies of Argyll's)

Ballymoney
(2companies of Argyll's)

Carrickfergus (Leven's,Lothian's,Monro's,
● Glencairn's,Home's,Horse Guard)

Temple Patrick
(Lawers')

Bangor ● Donaghadee (Foot Guard)
(Eglinton's,Lindsay's)

Newry
(Sinclair's)

be handed over to the English parliament.[91] Again, Antrim solved the problem of what to do with him by escaping. After several months of close confinement he had been given freedom to walk within the castle walls (though only when accompanied by a guard). He suborned one of the Scots officers, Lieutenant John Gordon (Monro's regiment), who 'craftellie convoyit wp vnespyit in his breikes' a rope. Early in October Antrim managed to use the rope to escape over the walls—falling in the sea in the process—and made his way to the 'Irish quarter' of the town. On his way he passed a soldier who remarked 'that if the Earle were not in the castle he would sweare that was he that past then by him'! He had sent a message to Phelim O'Neill to send horses and guides to meet him, but these failed to appear. Nonetheless, he managed in spite of an intensive search for him by the New Scots to reach Charlemont. From there he went to Dublin and then on to the king at Oxford.[92]

On returning to Carrickfergus after capturing Antrim, Monro prepared for 'the whole Armies outgoing' as soon as sufficient food arrived.[93] It never did, so Monro and the British had to content themselves with relatively short and small scale raids, with limited objectives. These proved surprisingly effective. Though the Irish retained Charlemont they withdrew most of their Ulster forces into Connaught, Leitrim and Longford in June; Owen Roe O'Neill and some of the Irish were surprised on the march at Clones by Sir Robert Stewart and the Lagan army, and were heavily defeated. On 7 July Dungannon surrendered to a combined British and New Scots army under Monro. Raiding parties plundered Owen Roe's

91. Carte, *Ormond*, III, 165; Fraser, *Melvilles*, II, 22; *A.P.S.* VI, i, 17, 19; *R.P.C.S. 1638-43*, p. 556; Carte MSS, 6, ff. 440, 541; S.R.O. PA.11/1, Register of the Committee of Estates, 1643-4, f. 33v; T.S.A.I. p. 34.

92. N.M.A.S. MCR 40, Black Book of Clanranald, ff. 189v-198v; Spalding, *Memorialls*, II, 291-2; Gordon, *Genealogical History*, p. 513. Lieutenant John Gordon was the second son of Sir Alexander Gordon, a brother of the twelfth earl of Sutherland; he is presumably the Ensign John Gordon who appears in the 1642 muster rolls in Monro's regiment. His father was a Catholic who had lived in Ireland in the 1630s to escape persecution, and his elder brother was killed fighting for the king at Edgehill in 1642, so it is understandable he should have some sympathy for Antrim—Paul, *The Scots Peerage*, VII, 346; W. Fraser, *The Sutherland Book* (3 vols, Edinburgh, 1893), I, 206-8. Hill, *Macdonnells of Antrim*, pp. 76-7n wrongly identifies Antrim's helper as Captain George Gordon (Leven's regiment), the 14th earl of Sutherland's brother, who had married Antrim's sister early in 1643.

93. Carte MSS, 5, ff. 323-4.

creaghts in Monaghan and Cavan.[94] 'Ulster in a maner is quite cleered, as is sayd most of the inhabitants have left that province and goe away with there caittaile into Conaght'.[95]

In Dublin it again seemed that Ulster could spare forces to attack the rebels in other provinces; and the very success of the New Scots and British made this more necessary, for the Irish driven from Ulster proceeded to attack Ormond's garrisons in Leinster.[96] The lords justice therefore resolved in July that 2,200 foot (500 of them New Scots) and 360 horse (120 of them from the troops attached to the New Scots) should attack the rebels in Connaught. Monro refused help even on this small scale, giving as an excuse the difficult position of his 'discontented Army'. It was almost destitute of supplies, and with civil war in England it did not know who its paymaster was, the treaty 'being frustrat altogether'. It had sent to Scotland demanding that it be either paid or disbanded. Monro added that Antrim's plots had given rise to fears that the English in Ireland would join the Irish in attacking the Scots, and that rumours that the Dublin government was negotiating a truce or cessation with the Irish gave credibility to such an idea. Ormond and the lords justice denounced the story that they would join with the Irish against the Scots as rebel propaganda, but they admitted that, on the king's orders, they were treating with the rebels for a cessation. They argued that the fact that Monro would not help them left them in such a weak position that they would be forced to conclude a cessation, but Monro still would not send men out of Ulster.[97]

Monro wrote to the committee of estates (which had replaced the privy council as the main executive body in Scotland) asking for instructions as to what to do if Dublin and the Irish did sign a cessation, but a reply was delayed while the English parliament was consulted.[98] Meanwhile Monro continued his campaign. In August he was at last in a position to begin a formal siege of Charlemont; it was now harvest time and food could be supplied by reaping crops that the Irish

94. Carte, *Ormond*, I, 432-3; Gilbert, *Contemporary History*, III, 199; Young, *Historical Notices*, pp. 223-4; P. B. O Mordha, 'The Battle of Clones', *Clogher Record*, IV, 3 (1962), 148-54.
95. Gilbert, *Irish Confederation*, II, liii.
96. O'Connell, *Irish Wars*, pp. 108-10.
97. Carte, *Ormond*, I, 449, 450; H.M.C. 36: *Ormonde*, N.S. II, 307-8; Carte MSS, 6, ff. 118-19, 194-5; Gilbert, *Irish Confederation*, II, xcix-c.
98. Carte MSS, 6, ff. 327, 328; S.R.O. PA.11/1, ff. 12-13, 13v.

had sown. The New Scots and British constructed a fortified camp near Armagh, from which fresh men could be sent each week to blockade Charlemont. Scots forces raided as far as Virginia in Cavan. This further increased rebel pressure on the Dublin forces and the lords justice urged Monro to undertake a joint attack with Ormond on the Irish forces and cattle which had been driven into Meath. Monro himself at first favoured the idea, but his council of war advised against the plan, preferring to concentrate on taking Charlemont. He admitted to the lords justice on 9 September that if he had tried to help Ormond he would have had to have gone alone, for his officers would not have followed him. They were deeply suspicious of Ormond, who was taking a leading part in the negotiations with the Irish, and demanded that no cessation should be made prejudicial to the interests of the New Scots.

The suspicions of the New Scots officers were justified. On 15 September a cessation was signed, and they first heard of it in letters from Owen Roe demanding that Monro cease hostilities. The chances of taking Charlemont had never seemed better, but Monro concluded that he had no choice but to abandon the siege. Whether or not he was eventually instructed to observe the cessation, he could not risk remaining before Charlemont now the Irish were free to concentrate all their forces against him. The New Scots and British therefore retreated, leaving garrisons in Dungannon and Mountjoy.[99] They did not retire peacefully, however; Owen Roe complained that Monro 'in all hostile and warlike manner, rather like a madd bull in fury, then any human creature, fell upon all the poore labourers, women and children' who were harvesting, killing them and destroying their crops and houses.[100] He doubtless exaggerated, for he was trying to persuade Ormond to join him in military action against Monro as a breaker of the cessation. The supreme council at Kilkenny formally demanded this in October, but before anything could be done Monro reluctantly agreed to observe the cessation until he received orders. It was, however,

99. Turner, *Memoirs*, p. 29; Hogan, *Warr of Ireland*, pp. 34-5; *C.S.P.I. 1633-47*, p. 386; Young, *Historical Notices*, p. 227; Gilbert, *Irish Confederation*, II, cvii, cviii; Carte MSS, 6, ff. 384, 395, 442-3, 458, 571, 7, ff. 383-4.
100. Gilbert, *Contemporary History*, I, 550-1.

clear that the New Scots were not reconciled to such an end to the war in Ireland.[101]

iii.   Financial and Political Problems, 1642-1644

If the Scottish army in Ireland broke the treaty under which it served by refusing orders from Dublin, it at least had the excuse that the English parliament had broken the treaty first by failing to pay and supply the army as promised. As early as 7 June 1642 the Scots commissioners in London complained that though 8,000 Scots had reached Ireland by that time only one month's pay for 2,500 men had been supplied by parliament.[102] As the result of such complaints money was soon sent; in July £10,000 sterling was ready to be transported to Ulster,[103] and on 19 September £15,000 sterling (which probably included the previous £10,000) was delivered to Leven in Ulster.[104] On 6 October £3,500 sterling more was ready for dispatch from London, being half of the £2,000 allowed in the treaty for the army's 'incident charges' and all the £2,500 allowed for buying baggage horses.[105] In addition, instead of paying the Scottish army and then letting it buy food, parliament supplied it directly with food. In February 1642 it had appointed John Davies, a Carrickfergus merchant, commissary for Ulster. By 1 December 1642 he had supplied the New Scots with foodstuffs worth over £9,000 sterling.[106]

These payments and supplies sent by the English parliament were substantial but, though it is not possible to calculate the total paid, it is clear that they never amounted to anything like the full pay due to the army, which was of the order of £16,000 sterling a month. No complete accounts of pay due to the army have survived, but draft accounts dealing with the period from the landing of the army to 1 February 1643 exist. These are in two parts, corresponding to the two sets of muster rolls. The first part covers the officers and men of the ten regiments, and the horse and foot lifeguards, from their

101.   Gilbert, *Irish Confederation*, III, 30.
102.   McNeill, *Tanner Letters*, pp. 148-9.
103.   S.R.O. PA.7/23/2/2-3.
104.   S.R.O. PA.7/23/2/4-6; T. Birch, ed. *A Collection of State Papers of John Thurloe*, I (London, 1642), pp. 16-17.
105.   S.R.O. PA.7/23/2/7.
106.   *C.J.* II, 453; *C.S.P.D. 1625-49*, pp. 638, 644, 686; J. Hogan, ed. 'Rawlinson

first musters by Hew Kennedy to their second in September 1642 by Thomas Clayton. In this period £67,390:17:8 sterling was payable including baggage allowances. The second part covers the period from Clayton's musters to 1 February 1643; in addition to the regiments and guards it includes the pay and wagon allowances of the general staff and the artillery train, the total due being approximately £79,270 sterling.[107]

Thus by early 1643 about £146,650 sterling should have been paid to the New Scots; and by the end of the year it was said £312,000 sterling was due. Only a tiny part of this was ever received. When in December 1642 the Scots commissioners urged how disgraceful it would be if the army starved while in the English parliament's service, parliament expressed regret at its suffering, which it blamed on the civil war preventing supplies being sent, and promised to do all it could in future to keep the treaty.[108] But with parliament fighting for its life against the king its repeated promises, resolutions and orders in favour of the New Scots proved to have little value. The army therefore had to look elsewhere for support. Ireland itself could supply substantial quantities of food. The army raised contributions from the inhabitants of its quarters; in May 1643 Lord Montgomery complained of the burden imposed on his lands by the 'sessing' of a New Scots regiment quartered on them.[109] Large amounts of grain and huge numbers of cattle were captured from the enemy. Food could be bought from merchants; in March 1643 Lieutenant Patrick Gray (Sinclair's regiment) was in Dublin buying malt, beer, salt, French wine, cloth and other goods for the Newry garrison.[110] But the army soon found it impossible to buy further food on credit, as it could not pay for previous purchases.[111]

Moreover, in spite of such sources of supply, the army could not have survived without help from Scotland. On 18 August 1642 the Scottish privy council resolved that if the troubles in England prevented parliament paying the army, Scotland

Manuscripts, Class A.110', *Analecta Hibernica*, 4 (1932), 28, 29, 30; P.R.O.L. SP.28/139/13-14.
107. Cambridge University Library, MS Ee.111,39(D).
108. *A.P.S.* VI.ii.23; *L.J.* V, 524; *R.P.C.S. 1638-43*, pp. 373-4.
109. Carte MSS, 5, f. 238.
110. Fairley, op. cit. 117.
111. *A.P.S.* VI, i, 15.

would take over responsibility for supplying it.[112] The continued existence of the army and the clearing of Ulster of rebels were too vital to Scotland's interests for the army to be disbanded simply because parliament could not pay it, though efforts to get money for it from England continued. Arrangements were made for immediate dispatch to Ulster from Scotland of 10,000 bolls of oatmeal, contracts being signed with Edinburgh and Aberdeen merchants. Other such contracts soon followed, and at Leven's request food exported to the army was freed from customs duties.[113] These exports were on a large enough scale to have considerable effects on food prices in Scotland. John Spalding, writing in Aberdeen, recorded that they led to high prices in 1642 and 'to the breiding of gryt dearth heir' in 1643.[114] Payment for foodstuffs sent to Ireland under such contracts was made (or promised) in Scotland; merchants soon stopped shipping food to Ulster to be paid for by the army itself since on some occasions the starving and penniless soldiers siezed food by force without paying for it.[115]

To raise money to pay for supplies sent to the army the privy council decided in February 1643 to raise a loan of £20,000 sterling, or more if it was offered, by 1 May (later extended to 1 July), to be repaid out of whatever money the English parliament sent for the army. Of the colonels of regiments in the army Argyll lent £1,000 sterling, Leven, Lothian, Lindsay, Eglinton and Glencairn £500 each, but the loan was not a success. In the end it seems that only about £13,700 sterling was raised.[116]

By early 1643 it was becoming increasingly likely that the covenanters would intervene in the English civil war, since they feared that the king would otherwise be victorious and that he would then seek to destroy their regime in Scotland. It seems to have been taken for granted at first that if the

112. *R.P.C.S. 1638-43*, p. 315; H. Hazlett, 'The Financing of the British Armies in Ireland, 1641-9', *I.H.S.* I (1938-9), 38.
113. *R.P.C.S. 1638-43*, pp. 315, 321-2, 356, 364-6; *A.P.S.* VI, i, 24-6. One boll of oats was approximately 13,000 cubic inches, J. M. Henderson, *Scottish reckonings of time, money, weights and measures* (Edinburgh, 1926), p. 14.
114. Spalding, *Memorialls*, II, 133, 237.
115. *A.P.S.* VI, i, 15.
116. *R.P.C.S. 1638-43*, pp. 366, 400, 403, 407-9, 412-13, 417-18, 421, 422, 423-4, 425-6, 639-41, *1544-1660*, pp. 83-92; D. Stevenson, 'The Financing of the Cause of the Covenants, 1638-51', *S.H.R.* LI (1972), 97-8. Hazlett, op. cit. 38-9 misunderstands the account; his total of money raised is nearly twice the true figure.

Scots did intervene they would do so by transferring their army from Ireland rather than by raising a new one. The importance of the New Scots army was thus greatly increased. The king, though he had not assented to the treaty which had sent the army to Ireland, suddenly began to express an interest in its welfare, since he hoped that if it remained in Ireland the Scots would not be able to intervene in England. On 21 April 1643 he instructed the marquis of Hamilton and other royalists to work to keep the New Scots in Ireland if it seemed likely that they would leave and that this would damage his interests; they were even to offer pay to the army out of his own Scottish revenues.[117] On the same day Hamilton reported that he had already got a promise from Leven that the king should not be harmed by the New Scots, though lack of pay would make it hard to keep them in Ireland.[118]

The English parliament too was taking a new interest in the army. In May the Scottish commissioners in London threatened that the army might have to be withdrawn if it was not paid; parliament replied that it could neither pay the army its wages nor even pay for its withdrawal. But orders were given to raise £30,000 sterling for the army out of sequestrations of royalist property, and parliament offered to send commissioners to Scotland to negotiate about the army's future.[119] There was little doubt that in fact such commissioners would be mainly concerned with persuading the Scots to help them in England, by levying a new army or transferring the army in Ireland. A similar deception was being carried out almost simultaneously in Scotland. On 10 May Argyll proposed to the privy council that it meet jointly with the committee for common burdens and the conservators of the peace 'that by joynt advyce some course may be tane concerning the Scottish armie in Ireland'. Two days later the joint meeting voted to summon a convention of estates (a body identical in membership to parliament but with more limited powers) to decide on the best way to supply the army.[120] The

---

117. Stevenson, *Scottish Revolution*, p. 265; Burnet, *Hamilton*, p. 220.
118. Burnet, *Hamilton*, pp. 215, 217.
119. *C.J.* III, 83, 132; *L.J.* VI, 45-6, 59-60, 63.
120. *R.P.C.S. 1638-43*, p. 425; S.R.O. PA.14/1, Register of the Committee for Common Burdens, ff. 224-6; S.R.O. PA.14/2, Proceedings of the Scots Commissioners for Conserving the Articles of the Treaty, pp. 60-3; Stevenson, *Scottish Revolution*, pp. 266-7.

real issue was that raised by the English civil war, and the fate of the army in Ireland was only part of that problem—as the king obviously realised, for he agreed that the convention might meet to discuss supplies for the army, but he forbade it to remove the army from Ireland or to raise men in Scotland.[121]

The convention ignored the king's limitations. Just before it met in June came the revelation of Antrim's plots, and this was of great importance in swinging many of its members behind Argyll and the more extreme covenanters. On 28 June a commission for furnishing the army in Ireland was appointed, and this proceeded to arrange for the sending of food to Ireland and for action to be taken against Dunkirk pirates and Irish frigates which were preying on the supply ships crossing to Ulster.[122] No English commissioners had yet appeared for the convention to negotiate with, so renewed demands were sent to London that the army be paid or disbanded and that other breaches of the treaty be rectified; there were no ships permanently guarding the crossing to Ulster: officers and equipment had not been provided for the horse troops attending the army. Moreover the treaty itself had proved inadequate in that it did not settle the question of command in Ulster clearly, and it was now demanded that the commander of the New Scots be commander of all forces in Ulster.[123]

Most of these demands originated from the army itself. In June three officers had arrived in Edinburgh as its representatives, Lieutenant Colonel Walter Scot (Lothian's regiment), Captain John Moncrieff (Lawers') and Captain George Gordon (Leven's), the earl of Sutherland's brother. From the instructions given to them by the army it is clear that it was known in Ulster that there was talk of sending the army to England, for the officers were ordered to assure the convention that if the army's arrears were paid and satisfactory arrangements were made for its pay in future, the army would be willing that part of itself should be sent to defend the religion, laws and liberties of Scotland—which was the recognised euphemism for intervention in England.[124] The voluntary loan raised

121. Stevenson, *Scottish Revolution*, p. 269; Burnet, *Hamilton*, p. 232.
122. *A.P.S.* VI, i, 7, 9, 11-12, 18, 19, 20.
123. Ibid. VI, i, 13, 15-17.
124. Stevenson, *Scottish Revolution*, p. 281; T.S.A.I. pp. 9-16; *A.P.S.* VI, i, 15-16.

earlier in the year having failed to provide much help for the army, the convention agreed to impose a forced loan of £800,000 Scots (£66,666:13:4 sterling) on Scotland for the army.[125] This failed to satisfy the officers; it was obvious that the loan was really intended to finance intervention in England. They demanded payment of four months' arrears of pay as soon as possible. If the rest of the arrears could not be paid in money, the army would accept grants of land in Ulster. In addition they asked that officers who did not serve in Ireland, or who left the army, should not be paid, their wages being given to the subordinates who had to act for them. If they did not return to Ireland they should be replaced. Unless these and other demands were met, the English parliament was to be warned that 'we will doe our vtmost for recovering our owne Interest any way best we can',[126] which sounds like a threat to refuse to serve parliament or even to join its enemies.

By this time English commissioners had arrived in Scotland, and negotiations for Scots intervention in England had begun. Parliament had already invited Leven to command any Scottish army sent to England,[127] and it was assumed that such an army would include the army from Ireland. That army was offered payment of its arrears 'either in the Confiscate Lands in Ireland, by way of Adventure' at the same rates as English adventurers, or in money paid in instalments once peace was restored, or in clothes and food. For the future it was declared that the English parliament could not pay the army. It should therefore be withdrawn, though it could leave garrisons in Carrickfergus and Coleraine until its arrears were paid off if it wished.[128] In reply the committee of estates (sitting during an adjournment of the convention) demanded immediate payment of at least £60,000 sterling to the army, this being roughly equivalent to the four months' arrears the army had asked for, and denounced the proposal to withdraw the army without full payment of arrears as contrary to the treaty.[129] But in spite of such complaints the convention

125. *A.P.S.* VI.i.26-39. Hazlett, op. cit. 39 wrongly gives the sterling equivalent of £800,000 Scots as £75,000 sterling.
126. *T.S.A.I.* pp. 16-23.
127. *L.J.*, VI, 139; Terry, *Alexander Leslie*, pp. 175-6.
128. *L.J.* VI, 140-1; *A.P.S.* VI, i, 38, 39-40; Stevenson, *Scottish Revolution*, pp. 281-2.
129. *S.R.O.* PA.11/1, ff. 6-7. The version in *T.S.A.I.* pp. 26-8 is wrongly titled an act of the convention.

still favoured withdrawing the army; when it sent the English proposals to the army it posed the alternatives open as complete removal, or removal of the great majority, small garrisons being left behind.[130]

The three officers who had been sent to Edinburgh took the proposals to the army. Not surprisingly, a meeting of officers (at Armagh on 18 September) rejected them as unsatisfactory; what was the point in paying their arrears in land in Ulster if they were then to leave Ireland, abandoning these lands to the rebels? The most the officers were willing to accept was that half the army should return to Scotland—provided some arrears were paid, lands were assigned to the army, and it was properly supplied for the future.[131] Believing their forces were urgently needed for an invasion of England, the officers felt they could insist on receiving satisfaction. But though the covenanters had reached agreement with the English commissioners to send an army of 21,000 men into England and impose the newly-drafted solemn league and covenant there, the stubbornness of the army in Ireland, the way it seemed to regard itself as a separate power able to negotiate with the governments of England and Scotland, aroused such resentment in Scotland[132] that it was decided that the whole army to be sent to England should be levied in Scotland.

There were also other reasons for this decision; news of the cessation in Ireland, and the reactions of the British to talk of withdrawing the New Scots. The English parliament had wished to transfer the New Scots to England since their first priority was defeating the king there. But the king was also hoping for help from Ireland; he had negotiated the cessation so that he could transfer much of Ormond's army to England for use against parliament. He also hoped for help from the confederate Irish, who might be persuaded by concessions to ally themselves to him. Even though the rebels distrusted Charles it was easy to predict that victory for the anti-Catholic English parliament would place them in much greater danger than victory for the king. If the English parliament withdrew the New Scots from Ireland the Irish would be free to

130. *A.P.S.* VI, i, 49-50; T.S.A.I. pp. 24-6, 28-9.
131. T.S.A.I. pp. 30-5; M. Perceval-Maxwell, 'The adoption of the Solemn League and Covenant by the Scots in Ulster', *Scotia, American-Canadian Journal of Scottish Studies*, II (1978), 4.
132. Carte MSS, 9, ff. 199-200.

concentrate all their forces against any of the British in Ulster who might refuse to accept the cessation. All Ireland would probably fall into the hands of the royalist Dublin government and the king's potential allies, the Irish. There would then be nothing to stop the Irish sending military help on a large scale to the king in England. Even if the New Scots remained in Ireland, the Irish might destroy them now they no longer had to fight Ormond as well. Certainly one of the reasons the Irish had agreed to a cessation was so that they could concentrate on defeating the Scots,[133] and the Dublin government had found that the Scottish successes in southern Ulster in August and early September had been decisive in persuading the rebels to make the concessions that made the cessation possible; the rebels 'are growen soe kinde as to offer that which they have hetherto refused'.[134] But even if the New Scots were conquered by the Irish, this would take time, providing parliament with a breathing space before Irish troops were sent to help the king in England. On balance, therefore, it seemed to the English parliament that the New Scots might be more use in Ireland, hindering the king there, than in England.

Moreover, the king continued to believe until well into 1644 that the New Scots would be used against him in England. This increased his determination that he too should get help from Ireland,[135] and he urged Ormond to do all he could to ensure that the New Scots remained in Ireland. On 19 October 1643 he instructed Ormond to incite the Scots secretly to break the cessation. Once they did this, he was to turn to the Irish and urge them to attack the Scots as breakers of the cessation. In this way Monro's army would become so heavily engaged in Ireland that with luck, it would be destroyed, or at least would find it hard to leave. If in spite of this the New Scots tried to leave Ireland bribes were to be offered to prevent them going, and the Old Scots settlers were to be stirred up to beg them to stay by rumours that the Irish intended to extirpate the Ulster Protestants if the New Scots left. If they did leave, the Irish were to attack the Ulster Scots to try to draw Monro back to protect his compatriots.[136]

133. Gilbert, *Irish Confederation*, I, 163, II, 321; J. Lowe, 'The Negotiations between Charles I and the Confederation of Kilkenny' (Ph.D. thesis, University of London, 1960), pp. 97-8.
134. Gilbert, *Irish Confederation*, II, 362.
135. Carte, *Ormond*, III, 172-3, 174.
136. Gardiner, *Civil War*, I, 248-9.

In the event these complicated intrigues proved unnecessary. The English parliament denounced the cessation,[137] and the committee of estates decided that, in the changed circumstances that the cessation created, the continued presence of the New Scots in Ireland was necessary, though it still at first maintained that 'It will be necessary that some of your number be employed in this expedition', the invasion of England.[138] It had been possible to contemplate abandoning Ulster previously because it had been believed the British there could continue to hold the Irish at bay. The cessation not only made this less likely, it made it seem probable that if the New Scots left the great majority of the British forces in Ulster would obey the Dublin government, thus coming under royalist control, and accept the cessation. Scotland might again be faced with the threat of royalist invasion from Ulster.

Having previously been trying to persuade the New Scots to leave Ulster and invade England, the Scottish government now turned to trying to persuade them to stay there, and to urging action on the English parliament; if it did not pay the army it would be very difficult to prevent it deserting Ireland, thus 'exposing that kingdome wholly to the will of the cruel and bloody rebells'.[139] Parliament, now equally convinced of the usefulness of the New Scots in Ulster, had in fact already voted that they be paid £60,000 sterling (including the £30,000 previously voted from sequestrations) and sent 10,000 suits of clothes.[140]

In mid-November Captain Gideon Murray (Lothian's regiment) arrived in Edinburgh to represent the army; the demands he was to make had only been agreed upon by the officers after long and heated debates since 'some are set upon going, others upon staying'.[141] The army had decided to agree to leave Ireland; whether it did this because it thought that this was still what the Scottish government and the English parliament wanted, or because it had heard that it was now expected to stay in Ireland and believed that the best way to get

137.   *C.J.* III, 294; *L.J.* VI, 275-6; S.R.O. PA.11/1, ff. 14v-15, 31, 32v-33v, 34-35, 35v-36; Hogan, op. cit. 82-7.
138.   S.R.O. PA.11/1, ff. 32v-33v.
139.   Ibid. f. 40v; H.M.C. 29: *Portland*, I, 136-7.
140.   *C.J.* III, 248; McNeill, *Tanner Letters*, pp. 163-4.
141.   H.M.C. 36: *Ormonde*, N.S. I, 67. Perceval-Maxwell, op. cit. 4 states that at this point the New Scots were refusing to swear the solemn league and covenant, but in fact they had not yet been ordered to swear it.

concessions was to threaten to do the opposite of what it was asked, is unknown. Whatever the reason, the army now declared that it would only stay in Ireland if stringent demands were met. The £60,000 and 10,000 suits parliament had promised must reach it by 15 December, and 50,000 bolls of meal were to be provided by 30 April 1644. Agreement was to be reached on payment of arrears 'out of the landis of the rebellis or in moneyis'. One general was to command New Scots and British alike, and he was to be obliged (unlike Leven) to reside in Ulster. Confusion over where he should obey orders from (Dublin, London, Edinburgh, or even the king!) should be removed. Unless these conditions were met the army would be unable to continue in Ireland.[142]

On 28 November the English commissioners in Edinburgh and the committee of estates reached agreement on an answer to these demands. The English parliament undertook to send £10,000 sterling, 10,000 suits and 10,000 bolls of meal to the army as soon as possible, together with arms and ammunition. A further £50,000 would follow by 1 February 1644. If it did not arrive, then the New Scots would be transported to England, and serve with the Scottish army there. If they remained in Ireland a united command would be established as they asked.[143]

These terms were sent to the New Scots and accepted by them,[144] and the agreement was subsequently ratified by the English parliament—though only after prolonged debates which prevented the supplies promised from being sent by 1 February. Some parliamentarians wished virtually to abandon Ireland until the war in England was won. Others urged that the British could withstand the Irish without the help of the New Scots. Sir John Clotworthy, who had developed something approaching hatred for the New Scots through their increasing domination of Ulster, argued that the British were much stronger than the New Scots. But the adventurers, those who had invested money in the conquest of Ireland, strongly opposed any withdrawal of troops, and argued that it was necessary to maintain both the British and

142. S.R.O. PA.7/23/2/14; other copies of the demands are in T.S.A.I. pp. 36-9 and N.L.S., Wodrow MSS, Folio LXV, f. 196.
143. McNeill, *Tanner Letters*, p. 165; S.R.O. PA.11/1, ff. 81-2, 85v; *C.J.* III, 338-9, 349-50, T.S.A.I. pp. 39-42.
144. T.S.A.I. pp. 42-3.

the New Scots so as to retain a foothold in Ireland to provide a base for eventual reconquest, and to divert the Irish from invading England and Scotland. Parliament eventually accepted such arguments, but there was also disagreement over a united command for Ireland. The Scots naturally urged that Monro should be commander in chief, claiming he would have strong support from the Old Scots. But many in England, including Clotworthy, were unwilling to accept a Scot and instead supported the claims of Lord Lisle (son of the earl of Leicester, the nominal lord lieutenant), arguing that an Englishman would be most likely to win the support of the British forces of Ulster, and perhaps even of some of Ormond's forces, for parliament. In the end, however, it was agreed that the commander of the New Scots should command the British as well.[145]

The decision to keep the New Scots in Ulster came as a great relief to the British; news that they might leave had caused panic. The officers of Sir James Montgomery's regiment offered, without consulting their colonel, to incorporate themselves and their men in the New Scots army,[146] evidently hoping thus to ensure that they too would be transported to England. Londonderry, in spite of its past suspicions of the New Scots, now joined the leaders of the Lagan army in begging the chancellor of Scotland to prevent their withdrawal.[147] A petition in name of the inhabitants of the north of Ireland to the nobility and estates of Scotland urged that removing the New Scots would be dishonourable to God and would bring victory to his enemies. Moreover, after the Irish had overrun Ulster 'are they not ready to sett upon you' by invading Scotland?[148]

The cessation made the British anxious that the New Scots should remain in Ireland, but another, almost simultaneous, development was to strain relations between many of the British leaders and the New Scots almost to breaking point. This was the solemn league and covenant. Until late in 1643

145. McNeill, *Tanner Letters*, pp. 169-71; *C.J.* III, 349-50; *L.J.* VI, 460-1, 512-13; Carte, *Ormond*, III, 197; N.L.S. Wodrow MSS, Folio LXV, ff. 198-201 and Folio LXVII, f. 39; K. S. Bottigheimer, *English Money and Irish Land* (Oxford, 1971), p. 187; J. R. MacCormack, *Revolutionary Politics in the Long Parliament* (Cambridge, Mass. 1973), p. 18.
146. Hill, *Montgomery Manuscripts*, pp. 325-6.
147. H.M.C. 29: *Portland*, I, 149-50.
148. Carte MSS, i, f. 252.

F

most of the British had managed to evade declaring either for or against the king in the English civil war; it had been possible to insist that the war in Ireland was a separate war, fought over different issues. Now, however, the Dublin government and Ormond had come out strongly in support of the king, and the Scottish government, which effectively controlled the New Scots, had allied itself with the English parliament and imposed a new covenant as a symbol of this alliance. Neutrality was no longer possible. The British found themselves under increasing pressure to take sides. Ormond urged them to accept the cessation, as the king had ordered, and reject the covenant. Many of the British were reluctant to defy the king, but soon concluded that they had no real choice. Neither the king nor the Dublin government could send them the supplies on which their survival depended; their only hope lay in parliament. Moreover to declare in favour of the king would probably involve them in war with the New Scots. Thus though on 2 January 1644 many of the British commanders (including Lord Montgomery, Sir James Montgomery, Sir Robert Stewart and Sir William Stewart) met in Belfast and agreed in principle to refuse the covenant and obey Ormond, they did not make their decision public for fear of jeopardising their chances of supply from parliament. Ormond's efforts to make them declare openly for the king were hindered by the fact that at the same time he continued to instruct them to do all they could to keep the New Scots in Ireland (so they would not be sent against the king in England);[149] for the New Scots would probably crush any royalist party which emerged in Ulster.

As the New Scots stayed in Ireland, the Scots army to invade England had to be recruited in Scotland. One consequence of this was that the New Scots benefited little from the £800,000 Scots loan imposed by the convention to pay them, for the loan had only been imposed on the understanding that they would be transported to England. Most of the loan was diverted to financing the levy of a new army. Only about £122,000 Scots was eventually devoted to the army in Ireland and even this provided no extra pay or food for the army as it was used to pay for supplies already sent to it.[150]

149. Hogan, op. cit. 92-4; *C.J.* III, 298; Carte, *Ormond*, I, 485-8, iii, 217-18, 221-2; H.M.C. 36: *Ormonde*, N.S. II, 339-40; Carte MSS, 8, ff. 55, 72, 114-15; Bagwell, *Stuarts*, II, 57. Perceval-Maxwell, op. cit. 6-7.
150. S.R.O. PA.16/3/2/5; S.R.O. PA.11/1, f. 150; Stevenson, op. cit. 100, 102-3.

The army which invaded England did in the end receive some help from Ulster. In December 1643 Leven was authorised to remove his lifeguard of horse and Sir Robert Adair of Kinhilt's horse troop from Ireland, and much of the artillery train (including six heavy guns) was also withdrawn, having proved useless for the type of warfare being waged in Ulster.[151] In addition Ulster provided many recruits for the new army; the New Scots officers complained that the men and horses crossing to Scotland would weaken the British forces and make it harder to find recruits for their own regiments.[152] The numbers who thus left Ulster, despairing of adequate food and pay there, to take part in the invasion of England was probably considerable. The most notable figure among them was Sir Frederick Hamilton, sent to Scotland from Londonderry to tell of the miserable state of the British there. He eventually obtained command of a regiment sent to reinforce the army in England. Colonel Lawrence Crawford who had been serving in Ormond's forces did even better; having taken the covenant he was invited to Scotland and promoted to major general. Many of the colonels of the New Scots regiments also became colonels of the army in England. Leven and Sir Alexander Hamilton served as general and general of the artillery respectively in both armies.[153]

If the army in Ireland had been neglected in the past, it now seemed that its situation would get worse, for Scotland's primary interest now lay in her new army which entered England in January 1644. The New Scots were no longer the only, or even the biggest, Scots army, and many of their senior officers were now seeking fame and fortune in England, having failed to find them in Ireland. In spite of all promises, there was no sign of the £50,000 sterling promised by 1 February, and the covention of estates in Edinburgh became reconciled to abandoning Ireland in order to reduce the financial burdens on Scotland. On 11 January it gave Monro and his officers permission to leave Ireland if the money promised had not arrived by 2 February. When they reached Scotland they would be supplied equally with the army that had entered

151. S.R.O. PA.11/1, ff. 89, 95-v, 103.
152. T.S.A.I. p. 44; H.M.C. 36: *Ormonde*, N.S. I. 71.
153. Carte MSS, 7, ff. 606, 635, 8, ff. 55, 9, f. 348; *A.P.S.* VI, i, 75; C. S. Terry, ed. *Papers relating to the Army of the Solemn League and Covenant* (2 vols, S.H.S. 1917), I, xxiv-lxxii; Perceval-Maxwell, op. cit. 8.

England.[154] A few days before the convention had imposed excise duties on Scotland to help pay its armies. This had led to a serious riot in Edinburgh, and the fears this aroused probably contributed to the convention's decision; bringing the New Scots from Ireland would both reduce the need for extra taxes in Scotland and would provide a force to over-awe any burghs which resisted the excise.[155] The convention had the full support of the committee of estates (presided over by Argyll) which accompanied the Scots army in England; it urged the transport of the New Scots to Cumberland to help defeat the king.[156]

Not all were content to abandon Ireland, however. Most influential was the chancellor, Loudoun. On 6 February he wrote to Monro regretting that England could not supply the army but pointing out that Scotland was doing all she could; 10,000 bolls of meal and £10,000 sterling were being raised for it.[157] Monro himself wanted to remain in Ireland. Doubtless he wished to retain his command, but he was also worried about the fate of the British if his army left Ireland. Moreover he had personal ties in Ulster; his first wife had died early in 1642 and he was now planning to marry the widow of the second Lord Montgomery (who had died in November 1642). Though the marriage was against the wishes of her son (the third Lord Montgomery) and his friends, Monro was reluctant to desert her relations—and, perhaps more important, her lands.[158] In their efforts to keep the army in Ireland Loudoun and Monro were helped by Ormond, who was still busy persuading the British to insist that the New Scots stay, so that they could not serve against the king in England. But Ormond had come to believe that this policy was no longer in the king's best interests, since the Irish confederates would not send help to Charles until the New Scots left.[159]

A meeting of the officers of the army in Ireland was held at Carrickfergus on 13 February 1644. In spite of opposition from Monro and others it was decided that the army should

154. *A.P.S.* VI, i, 72-3; Perceval-Maxwell, op. cit. 7.
155. Carte MSS, 9, ff. 287-90; Stevenson, op. cit. 103-4.
156. S.R.O. PA.11/2, Register of the Committee of Estates (Army), 1643-4, ff. 14v-15, 18-19v.
157. T.S.A.I. pp. 54-6; Perceval-Maxwell, op. cit. 8-9.
158. Spalding, *Memorialls*, II, 122; Carte, *Ormond*, I, 486, III, 227; Carte MSS, 4, ff. 38, 42, 7, f. 262.
159. Carte, *Ormond*, III, 227.

leave Ireland immediately. Monro had lost control of his officers, who since their successful defiance of Leven in 1642 had taken an increasingly large part in running the army and negotiating with Edinburgh and London. It was resolved that all officers should swear an oath not to disband or lay down their arms in Scotland until all arrears due to them were paid. The order in which the regiments should depart was agreed. Sinclair's would go first, followed by Lothian's and Lawers'. Monro's would be last, since he was still unwilling to leave.[160] Monro wrote gloomily (evidently to Loudoun) that the officers were very eager to leave, 'all of them striveing who should first embarke'. He warned of the serious consequences if the army withdrew; 'now Irishe Papist rebels and English Conformists in this kingdome are like to cast their pactes together for banisheing the Scotyish, and the true Religion out of Ireland'. The Ulster Scots would have to flee to Scotland, probably bringing famine and disease with them, 'And it is to be feared the rebels will follow'. To desert the Ulster Scots would be dishonourable, and Scotland 'by all appearance shall never attaine to such a plantation heir againe as at this present'.[161] Other reports confirmed Monro's argument; if the New Scots left many of the British forces would do the same; so would most of the country people, at least of Antrim and Down, leaving the country waste and unable to support whatever forces remained.[162] Terrified Protestants begged the New Scots to stay until they could escape with their families and goods to Scotland.[163]

In spite of this, preparations for withdrawal continued. Monro withdrew his garrisons from Dungannon and Mount-joy.[164] Newry was abandoned by Sinclair's regiment without orders from Monro. As an isolated outpost the garrison had probably suffered even more than the rest of the army. Major Turner stated that it had had to survive largely by cattle raiding, and that from April 1642 to February 1644 it only received three months' pay. As early as 3 December 1643 it was said that the garrison had offered to sell Newry to the

160. T.S.A.I. pp. 50-7, 69-70; Carte MSS, 9, 199-200, 287-90; Perceval-Maxwell, op. cit. 7.
161. S.R.O. PA.7/23/2/17.
162. Carte MSS, 9, ff. 199-200, 207, 209-10, 217-18, 252.
163. Ibid. 9, ff, 287-90.
164. Ibid. 9, ff. 205, 208; Young, *Historical Notices*, p. 228.

Irish for 140 cows. Certainly three days later Lieutenant Colonel Henry Sinclair was offering to sell it to Ormond for £80 sterling to reimburse him and Major Turner for money they had spent on fortifications, though he denied any intention of surrendering the town to the Irish. The money was apparently paid, for on 17 February men from Colonel Arthur Chichester's British regiment (sent from Belfast) took over Newry; they had already garrisoned Mountjoy and Dungannon.[165]

At this point Monro recieved Loudoun's letter of 6 February which promised supplies and made no mention of the army leaving Ireland. Seizing on this as a pretext he ordered that the preparations for leaving be halted. The officers had evidently expected Monro to raise difficulties, for they had appointed a small group of officers to supervise the removal of the army. On 19 February this group summoned a general meeting of officers and denounced Monro's decision. Loudoun's letter was dismissed as a private letter with no authority. It made no mention of the convention's order that the army leave Ireland, so could not be held to cancel that order, and its promises about supplies were similar to ones which had often been broken in the past.[166] No record of the decision of the general meeting of officers survives, but what followed indicates that it resolved to defy Monro.

Meanwhile in Scotland those who wished the army to remain in Ireland were working hard to get the convention's decision reversed. On 13 February the committee of estates decided that the 'bringing away of that armie is a mater of so publict concernement as makes us sparing be our selves to determine in that bussines'. The convention, conveniently, had been adjourned, so a joint meeting of the committee and the privy council was summoned for 20 February to make a decision[167] —to the annoyance of the army in England which continued to demand that the New Scots be sent to Cumberland.[168]

The joint meeting decided unanimously that it would be

165. Turner, *Memoirs*, pp. 24-5, 29-30; Carte MSS, 8, ff. 44, 55, 57, 59, 61, 62, 9, ff. 17, 213; Carte, *Ormond*, I, 486; Young, *Historical Notices*, p. 228; Perceval-Maxwell, op. cit. 7-8.
166. T.S.A.I. pp. 57-8; Carte MSS, 9, ff. 287-90.
167. S.R.O. PA.11/1, ff. 125-126v.
168. S.R.O. PA.11/2, ff. 23, 27v-28v; Turner, *Memoirs*, pp. 30-1.

most expedient to retain the New Scots in Ireland if possible; supplies were promised but if adequate arrangements had not been made by the end of March the army could then leave.[169] This resolution came almost too late. On 26 February news reached Edinburgh that Sinclair's regiment had already landed in Scotland,[170] whereupon Sir Mungo Campbell of Lawers and Sir Frederick Hamilton were hastily sent to the army with £10,000 sterling to beg it to remain in Ireland to protect the British, uphold religion and defeat the rebels. If the army still insisted on leaving all efforts were to be made to see that it came in an orderly fashion; there were fears it would disband on reaching Scotland, whereas it was hoped to keep it together as a fighting force for use in England. It was specified that Argyll's regiment should not be allowed to land in Argyll, presumably for fear the soldiers would disperse to their homes.[171] Two more regiments, Lothian's and Lawers', landed in Scotland before anything could be done to stop them, and rumour spoke of 40,000 Ulster Protestants following them. But on 14 March the officers of the regiments left in Ireland reluctantly agreed to delay their departure until 1 April, to give a last chance for satisfactory terms to be offered to them.[172] This was a triumph for Monro; it was said he and Colonel Home were resolved to stay in Ireland even if the rest of the army left.[173]

One of the reasons which had persuaded the Scottish government to order the army to remain in Ireland may well have been fear of it. It was known that the army believed that it had been treated unjustly, and it had sworn to remain in arms in Scotland until it obtained satisfaction. Rumour claimed that it had also resolved to quarter itself on the estates of leading covenanters, and to join the royalist cause if attempts were made to use force against it.[174] The arrival of the three regiments that did cross to Scotland caused panic, through fear that they intended to plunder the country. On

169. S.R.O. PA.11/1, ff. 135v-136, 137-8; Reid, *History of the Presbyterian Church*, I, 545-6; Turner, *Memoirs*, p. 33.
170. S.R.O. PA.11/1, f. 138v.
171. Reid, *History of the Presbyterian Church*, I, 546-50; S.R.O. PA.11/1, ff. 139-140v, 148v-149; 150²v; McNeill, *Tanner Letters*, p. 181.
172. T.S.A.I. pp. 65-70; H.M.C. 29: *Portland*, I, 173; S.R.O. PA.11/1, ff. 177-8; Bodleian Library, Tanner MSS, 62B, f. 625v; Turner, *Memoirs*, pp. 33-4; Carte, *Ormond*, I, 488-90.
173. Carte MSS, 9, f. 560.
174. Carte, *Ormond*, I, 488, III, 256.

reports that Sinclair's and Lothian's regiments were marching on Paisley local lairds raised forces and garrisoned the burgh against them; after hard bargaining it was agreed that the men from Ireland should be split up into relatively small parties and quartered in Paisley and other western burghs. News of the landing of Lawers' men caused a fresh alarm. The burgh of Dumbarton at first refused to let some of Lothian's men in. But eventually the committee of estates arranged quarters and supplies for the regiments and order was restored.[175]

At first there was hesitation over what to do with the three regiments; to order their return to Ireland would have provoked mutiny. Late in March, however, news arrived of a royalist rising in the north-east led by the marquis of Huntly, and there were fears of a royalist invasion from Carlisle led by Montrose. This turned the three regiments into a welcome reinforcement for the covenanters. Huntly's rising soon collapsed, and though Montrose reached Dumfries he was forced to retreat back into England, so the regiments were not called upon to fight. This was just as well, for some of the officers of Lothian's and Sinclair's regiments had resolved to join Montrose; messages were sent to him, and Sinclair's officers held meetings with his relatives and associates.[176] Montrose's retreat back into England made joining him impossible, and the three regiments, whatever their bitterness at the broken promises of the Scottish government and the English parliament, soon reconciled themselves to continuing in their service. All eventually joined the Scottish army in England, though men from Lothian's and Lawers' were first sent to police the north-east of Scotland— where at one point they threatened to plunder Aberdeen unless they were paid.[177]

That the other seven regiments would remain in Ireland was no foregone conclusion, but it seems likely that many of the officers who had been most insistent on leaving had been in the three regiments which had left, so that those who wished to stay now found it easier to dominate the army. To gain

175. H.M.C. 10: *10th Report*, I, 52-3; Fraser, *Montgomeries*, I, 265-6; F. Roberts and I. M. M. Macphail, eds. *Dumbarton Common Good Accounts, 1614-60* (Dumbarton, 1972), pp. 133-4; Turner, *Memoirs*, pp. 33-4; Guthry, *Memoirs*, pp. 149-50. S.R.O. PA.11/1, ff. 138v, 144v, 145, 148v, 151-151v, 154v, 156v-157, 157v, 158v, 159v, 160, 183, 183v, 188v-189; *A.P.S.* VI, i, 84, 86, 87.
176. Turner, *Memoirs*, pp. 35-8; S.R.O. PA.11/1, f. 159.
177. Spalding, *Memorialls*, II, 354, 355-6, 368, 372, 375-6.

further time the committee of estates urged the army to remain in Ireland until 24 April so that the convention of estates, due to meet on 10 April, would have time to consider its desires. As a sop to those bitter about absentee officers Monro was instructed to promote Eglinton's lieutenant colonel, James Montgomery to colonel of the regiment. On 2 April the officers of the seven regiments duly voted to remain in Ireland until the 24th, and sent commissioners to Edinburgh to represent them, Lieutenant Colonel George Monro (Leven's regiment), Lieutenant Colonel John Hamilton (Lindsay's) and Captain James Wallace (Monro's). As well as making the usual demands for pay and supplies they were to complain of the lack of 'great officers', insist that the three regiments in Scotland still be treated as part of the army, and get agreement that even if the army was withdrawn Monro and a garrison should remain in Carrickfergus.[178]

The officers also agreed by a majority vote to break the assurance or oath that the officers of all ten regiments had taken. Once part of the army decided to stay in Ireland the oath had become an embarrassment. It had required the regiments which first landed in Scotland to remain near their landing-places until the rest of the army joined them, so that the army could remain together to demand justice. But the committee of estates had insisted on its right to use the army to suppress royalists. The officers of the three regiments had therefore to choose between breaking the oath or defying the state; the cancellation of the oath freed them from their dilemma.[179] In agreeing to abandon the oath the officers in Ireland had probably also been influenced by the fact that the presbytery in Ulster had denounced it as 'ambiguous, scandalous, contrary to the Covenant, and a devisive motion'.[180]

News that part of the Scottish army had left Ireland, that the rest might follow, and that the British forces probably would submit to the cessation or flee the country had at last stirred the English parliament into action. On 9 March an ordinance confirmed that the commander of the New Scots

178. S.R.O. PA.11/1, ff. 164v-165v, 169v-172, 172v; T.S.A.I. pp. 66-7, 70-8; H.M.C. 29: *Portland*, I, 173-6.
179. S.R.O. PA.11/1, ff. 169v-171; T.S.A.I. pp. 66-8, 75, 79-80; [W. Muir], *Memoir of Rev. William Guthrie* (Edinburgh, [1827]), p. 22.
180. Adair, *True Narrative*, p. 102.

should be commander in chief in Ireland; the war was to be prosecuted by him with the advice of the committee of both kingdoms (England and Scotland) in London. £10,000 sterling and 10,000 suits were to be dispatched to the army immediately.[181] Further resolutions of both houses on 11 April promised (yet again) speedy payment of £60,000 sterling. For the future parliament promised to pay £4,000 sterling a month to the New Scots and the same to the British forces. This offer was hardly generous—full pay even for the seven regiments left in Ireland amount to something of the order of £11,000 monthly—but at least it sounded more relistic than previous promises; better this paid regularly than promises of much more which came to nothing. Leven was to appoint a commander in chief (of all Scots and British forces in Ireland) under him to reside in Ireland—it was taken for granted that this would be Monro—and the war in Ireland was to be run by Scottish and English commissioners who would form a committee of both kingdoms such as already accompanied the Scottish army in England.[182] More determined efforts were to be made than in the past to see that promises were fulfilled; it was admitted that the £30,000 sterling promised in May 1643 had been raised but then diverted to other purposes; orders were given that this should not happen to the £60,000.[183] £30,000 was ready for dispatch to Leith by mid-June 1644, but the other half of the sum promised was delayed; the last £16,000 or it was still unpaid in March 1645.[184] Even the money that was sent did not always benefit

---

181. *L.J.* VI, 460-1; McNeill, *Tanner Letters*, pp. 172-3; Birch, *State Papers*, I, 32-3.
182. Birch, *State Papers*, I, 33-4. *L.J.* VI, 512-13, *C.J.* III, 456; Hogan, op. cit. 95-7; *C.S.P.D. 1644* pp. 79-80; H. W. Meikle, ed. *Correspondence of the Scots Commissioners in London, 1644-6* (Roxburghe Club, 1917), p. 18. The precise extent of Leven's (or his deputy's) authority as commander in chief was left ambiguous; the impression was given (doubtless to please the Scots) that he was to command all parliament's forces in Ireland, but only the Scots and British of Ulster were specifically mentioned. At the time the importance of this discrepancy was purely theoretical as the Scots and British were parliament's only forces in Ireland. But later Inchiquin's Munster army was to declare for parliament, and parliamentary forces were to occupy Dublin. As the Scots never appear to have claimed that these forces should come under Leven's command it seems that in practice that they accepted that they had only been given command of the Ulster forces, in spite of much talk of them being given command of all Ireland.
183. *C.S.P.D. 1644*, pp. 119, 123, 133.
184. *C.S.P.D. 1644*, pp. 170, 189, 197, *1644-5*, p. 333; Meikle, *Correspondence*, pp. 31, 32; Cuningham, *Journal*, pp. 90-1; *A.P.S.* VI, i, 161; Balfour, *Historical Works*, III, 201; *C.J.* IV, 77, 78.

the army directly; the committee of estates insisted that the money be sent by way of Scotland so that it could be used to repay the large sums Scotland had advanced to the army.[185]

To the promises of the English parliament were added concessions by the committee of estates. It reached agreement with the army's representatives that George Monro should command the ten troops of horse attached to the army (since Sir William Balfour had never gone to Ulster) and that lieutenant colonels in the army should receive the pay of any colonels who were absentees. The committee also agreed to do all it could to uphold the army's interests and get its arrears paid. Even if it was withdrawn Monro was to remain in Carrickfergus until arrears were paid.[186] The army's three representatives in Edinburgh recommended the terms agreed to the army; as one of them, George Monro, was promoted to colonel by the agreement and another, Captain Wallace, had just been offered the command of Stirling Castle by the committee of estates,[187] this was hardly surprising. But the settlement also proved acceptable to the army in Ireland, as it indicated on 4 May. The only remaining disagreement was over the three regiments that had crossed to Scotland. The army asked that they be sent back to Ireland but the committee of estates insisted that they remain in England or Scotland until the English civil war was over.[188]

After six months of confusion, it had at last been agreed that the New Scots should remain in Ireland. But the position of the army was precarious. The Irish, taking advantage of the cessation, were preparing to crush it. Ormond had taken credit for persuading the British 'urged and fomented by such as I set on' to petition the army to stay in Ireland, but at the same time he was trying to unite the British in obedience to the king. This was proving difficult, because it was emerging that though on the whole the senior officers favoured the king, the soldiers and common people did not, and their resistance would be difficult to overcome while the New Scots remained in Ulster. It was therefore a relief to Ormond to receive instructions in March that he was only to work to keep them

---

185. Meikle, *Correspondence*, p. 26.
186. Ibid. p. 33; *A.P.S.* VI, i, 84, 92; S.R.O. PA.7/3/20; S.R.O. PA.11/1, ff. 196v-197, 198-200v; T.S.A.I. pp. 80-4.
187. S.R.O. PA.11/1, ff. 192-192v, 195v.
188. Ibid. ff. 196-196v, 226-7.

in Ulster for one month more—to give Montrose's plan for invading Scotland from Carlisle a chance to succeed. The king had at last decided that it was not in his interests that the New Scots remain; the policy had been intended to prevent the Scots from invading England, but they had proved able to invade without Monro's help. The New Scots were now damaging the king by making the Irish reluctant to send help to him in England.[189]

The change of policy came too late; there was no longer much chance of Ormond being able to persuade the New Scots to leave, and their activities soon showed how damaging to the king's interests their presence was. Once it became likely that he could get his army to remain in Ireland Monro, now with new authority as commander in chief, began the work of imposing the solemn league and covenant and securing obedience in Ulster to the English parliament. Tension between the New Scots and the British had been growing for months—and was exacerbated when Monro seized for the use of his army charitable supplies raised in the Netherlands for the relief of the poor distressed Protestants of Ulster, arguing that none were more distressed than his own men![190] The tensions came to a head when four Scottish ministers arrived to impose the covenant. On 4 April Monro and his officers signed at Carrickfergus; only one refused, Major Thomas Dalyell of Monro's own regiment.[191] The covenant was then offered to the British forces. Though no order had come from the English parliament for them to sign many did so eagerly, officers as well as common soldiers. Nearly all the colonels opposed it, but they were unable to prevent their subordinates and the country people from signing. Some tried to enforce orders from Dublin denouncing the covenant, but with little success.[192] Ormond began to fear that once Monro had imposed the covenant in Ulster he would advance on Dublin. Money and supplies were hurriedly sent to Colonel Arthur Chichester in Belfast to enable him to hold the town against

189. Carte, *Ormond*, III, 243, 255-6, 257.
190. Ibid. I, 490; Carte MSS, 10, ff. 115-16, 153, 429; Meikle, *Correspondence*, p. 15; Cuningham, *Journal*, pp. 86-7.
191. Carte MSS, 10, f. 153; Carte, *Ormond*, I, 490; Adair, *True Narrative*, p. 102; Perceval-Maxwell, op. cit. 9. In the 1642 muster rolls Dalyell appears as a captain.
192. Adair, *True Narrative*, pp. 102-3; Carte MSS, 10, ff. 201, 207, 227, 292, 331-2; Carte, *Ormond*, I, 490-1; Perceval-Maxwell, op. cit. 13-14.

Monro if necessary, to hinder such a march.[193]

At this point Sir James Montgomery summoned a meeting of British colonels in Belfast on 13 May to discuss whether to accept Monro as commander in chief. There had previously been New Scots garrisoned in Belfast as well as Chichester's men, though there had been ill feeling between them,[194] but the New Scots had been withdrawn when it had seemed they were going to leave Ireland. Monro's officers had demanded that they be replaced, since they did not trust Chichester to hold the town in their interests. But Chichester had refused to agree to this, had begun to fortify Belfast, and was now using the town for a meeting which might decide to reject Monro's authority. There was also a rumour that Ormond was sending a force to help Chichester hold Belfast for him.

In these circumstances Monro felt obliged to act; if he had not, his officers threatened to act on their own. A force was therefore sent from Carrickfergus which seized Belfast without bloodshed on the morning of 14 May. This was possible since many of the British soldiers in the town supported him; scouts, sent out by Chichester to investigate a rumour that Monro was approaching, treacherously reported that there was no sign of him, and the guards at the town gates opened them and welcomed the New Scots. Chichester's garrison was expelled, though he was offered the chance of retaining possession of the castle, and replaced by New Scots. His men were offered quarters in the country near by, but Chichester himself went to England to complain to parliament, some of his men fled to Dublin, and part of his regiment under Lieutenant Colonel Edmund Mathews withdrew to strengthen Chichester's garrison at Newry. The supporters of the covenant in one company burnt their colours in the market place in Belfast and then disbanded. After occupying Belfast Monro marched on to Lisburn, intending to establish a garrison there too, but the British commander Sir Theophilus Jones showed that he was prepared to resist. Unwilling to start a new civil war Monro withdrew to Belfast.[195]

193. Carte, *Ormond*, III, 286; Carte MSS, 10, f. 509.
194. Carte MSS, 8, f. 11; Perceval-Maxwell, op. cit. 9-10.
195. Carte MSS, 10, ff. 642, 662, 665-6, 765-6, 11, ff. 18-19; Gilbert, *Contemporary History*, I, 586-7; Reid, *History of the Presbyterian Church*, I, 561-2; Benn, *History of Belfast*, I, 103-10; *C.S.P.I. 1633-47*, pp. 393-4; Carte, *Ormond*, I, 493-4; III, 311-13; H.M.C. 36: *Ormonde*, N.S. I, 76-7.

Monro's sudden expulsion of the British from Belfast was justified by him on the grounds that Chichester had accepted the cessation, denounced the covenant, and was preparing to hold Belfast against him. While undoubtedly Monro had acted ruthlessly he must have felt he had had to act to assert his authority as commander in chief if it was to mean anything. It was well known that the Irish were preparing a major attack on his army, and his chances of withstanding this would be slight if he could not rely on the British to support him. It had looked as if Ulster might drift into civil war between supporters of the king and of parliament, which would have made the task of the Irish easy. Moreover he had good reasons for believing that a sharp assertion of his power would lead to the collapse of British resistance to him. Though many British officers were anxious to help the king, many of their men had shown support for the new covenant and hatred of the cessation. Many of the countrymen and townsmen soon displayed similar attitudes. After Monro occupied Belfast the commons all 'except a very few' took the covenant. They further defied the town's superior, Chichester, by demanding changes in their constitution—that all have votes in electing burgesses, and that all burgesses swear the covenant. This was evidently allowed, for the sovereign (major) of Belfast fled to Dublin to complain about it. In Antrim and Down it was said that 16,000 people had taken the covenant by 25 May.[196] Monro's action and the enthusiasm for the covenant persuaded nearly all the British officers to submit to him, and he showed some generosity in return for their support. In some cases provided they undertook to continue the fight against the Irish he agreed to supply them equally with his own men and not to force the covenant on them.[197]

In the Lagan army as well as in Atnrim and Down most colonels soon found themselves forced to sign the covenant, not so much by pressure from Monro as by the attitudes of their own men. Had they not signed they would have lost control of their regiments—and all hope of receiving supplies from parliament or Scotland would have been lost.[198]

196. Benn, *History of Belfast*, I, 110; Reid, *History of the Presbyterian Church*, I, 465-7.
197. Carte MSS, 10, ff. 684-5; Carte, *Ormond*, I, 495.
198. Carte, *Ormond*, I, 490-3, 495; H.M.C. 36: *Ormonde*, I, 90-1; Adair, *True Narrative*, pp. 106-17; Perceval-Maxwell, op. cit. 10-13. See also ibid, 15, 'The

Ormond believed the attack on Belfast presaged an attack on Dublin; the fact that Monro answered his protests about what had happened in Belfast politely did not reassure him; 'the civility ... I am told (by those that know him) is a probable sign that he hath some design upon us'. He therefore appealed to the Irish for supplies to enable him to withstand an attack from the New Scots. But there is no evidence that Monro had any such design. His intention was to secure control of Ulster so he could face the Irish with confidence without fear of treachery behind his back. This meant that he did (as was soon to be seen) have designs on the British in Lisburn and Newry, who continued to obey Ormond rather than him. The garrison of Lisburn appealed for and received supplies from Owen Roe O'Neill, which, if Monro knew of this, must have increased his distrust of it.[199]

royalists lost the Protestant part of Ulster because they could furnish no supplies; the Scots won it because they could and because they were willing to continue the war against the Irish'.
199.   Carte MSS, 10, ff. 674-5; H.M.C. 5: *6th Report*, p. 13; Carte, *Ormond*, III, 301, 314; Gilbert, *Contemporary History*, III, 202.

James Butler, duke of Ormond. Lord Lieutenant of Ireland 1643-7, 1649-50.
Portrait after Sir Peter Lely.

CHAPTER FOUR

The Irish in Scotland, 1644-1647

The covenanters had sent an army to Ireland in 1642 primarily to protect Scotland from any threat by the Irish rebels. In 1643 they agreed to send an army to England to prevent a royalist victory there, since they believed that that would lead the king to attempt to overthrow their revolution in Scotland. Both armies were thus intended to increase Scotland's security. Instead they provoked invasion of Scotland by the Irish, organised and inspired by royalists.

That this might happen had been realised, and in the 1643 treaty under which a Scots army entered England provision was made for preventing or suppressing such an invasion. England undertook to provide eight ships (including the two specified in the 1642 treaty for sending an army to Ireland) to guard Scotland's coasts, especially those opposite Ireland, and if Scotland was invaded the English parliament promised to send military help to Scotland.[1] These treaty provisions proved largely ineffectual. The English parliament ignored requests for aid in suppressing Irish invaders, and it is doubtful whether there were ever eight ships guarding Scotland's coasts. Often there were none, and even when a few were present they did little to interfere with communications between Ireland and the Highlands.[2]

Within three months of agreeing to intervene in England the covenanters had to deal with forces which had landed from Ireland. On 24 November 1643 the privy council and the committee of estates commissioned Argyll to act as King's

1. *A.P.S.* VI, i, 49; Stevenson, *Scottish Revolution*, p. 287. The deeds of the Irish in Scotland under Alasdair MacColla in 1644-7 are narrated and analysed in detail in Stevenson, *Alasdair MacColla.*
2. E.g. Balfour, *Historical Works*, III, 253; *C.S.P.D. 1644-5*, pp. 161, 412; Meikle, *Correspondence*, pp. 61-2, 66; *The Lord Marques of Argyle's speech ... and a letter from General Major Monro* (London, 1646), p. 11.

lieutenant against rebels in the Western Isles. Reports had arrived that Alasdair MacColla had landed with 300 men and that his brother Ranald was following with more ships and men; particular indignation was expressed that they should invade Scotland after having submitted to Leven in Ireland a year previously. The invasion was not considered serious enough for Argyll to take the field against it in person. Instead he appointed James Campbell of Ardkinglas to act as his deputy. Beginning in December 1643 Ardkinglas and 600 men spend several months driving the rebels from island to island until most fled back to Ireland. They left a garrison on Rathlin, but in May or June 1644 Ardkinglas occupied the island. By July Argyll could report that all rebels had been driven out or killed, except for thirteen who had fled to the Outer Hebrides. In all 115 had been killed, or captured and then executed.[3]

The origins of this abortive foray into the Hebrides by Alasdair MacColla are obscure. As Antrim only escaped from Carrickfergus in October 1643 and Alasdair had landed in the Isles by mid-November, it seems very unlikely that Antrim organised the raid himself. But one of his servants had stated in May 1643 that his brother Alexander MacDonnell had already reached Ireland to make contact with Coll Ciotach's sons, and it seems likely that Alexander was responsible for organising the raid—though it may have been delayed until Antrim escaped to avoid enraging his captors against him.

Even before the raid failed Antrim was busy with new plans for sending Irish forces to Scotland (and to England) to fight for the king. Invading Scotland would help the king, advance Antrim's own claims to former MacDonald lands, and perhaps restore him to his Irish estates by forcing the New Scots to withdraw from Ulster. He had been in contact with Montrose before he was captured in May 1643 and had probably given him hopes of help from Ireland; certainly in November 1643 Montrose thought it worth sending a messenger to Ormond to tell him of the condition of the king's affairs in Scotland.[4]

After his escape from the New Scots in October 1643

3.. S.R.O. PA.11/1, ff. 64-6; Balfour, *Historical Works*, III, 198-9; H.M.C. 3: *4th Report*, p. 490; *A.P.S.* VI, i, 61, 167; Inveraray Castle, Argyll Transcripts, XII, 125, 134; Innes, *Thanes of Cawdor*, p. 302; Carte, *Ormond*, III, 300; McNeill, *Tanner Letters*, pp. 165-6, 168-9; Stevenson, *Scottish Revolution*, pp. 295-6.
4.   Carte MSS, 7, f. 684.

Antrim was invited to join the confederate Irish but refused. Nonetheless he managed to win the confidence of some of the Irish, partly through the influence of his wife, the duchess of Buckingham. As the widow of the king's favourite she had considerable influence at court, and as she was a Catholic resident in Ireland the Irish hoped she would help them in negotiations with the king. What Antrim wanted from the Irish at this point was some public recognition that would make the king take seriously his plans to get Irish help for the royalist cause. In this he was only partly successful; he was granted the title of lieutenant general of the confederate forces, but not given any powers. However, Antrim ignored this limitation and, once he reached the royal court at Oxford, claimed a much more important position. He informed the king that he was in effect commander in chief of the con-federate armies and asked Charles to legitimise his position by granting him a royal commission to command the Irish. This piece of sleight of hand failed; his claim to be commander in chief of the Irish was not believed. But in spite of this his other proposals were much too attractive for the king to ignore. Antrim undertook to provide 10,000 Irish soldiers to fight for the king in England, and 3,000 for use in Scotland.[5] The king and his advisers might doubt whether he could carry out these promises, but he was still worth encouraging on the off chance that he could.

But two major changes were made in Antrim's proposals before they were accepted. Firstly, he had to give up the idea of being commissioned to command the Irish confederates. For the king to give him (or anyone else) such a commission to command men whom he still regarded as rebels and with whom he had only signed a temporary cessation would be a very odd proceeding, and would seem to give royal approval to the actions of the Irish. Secondly, Antrim hoped his expedi-tion to Scotland would lead the New Scots to leave Ireland. To achieve this he proposed to encourage them with bribes. But Lord Digby concluded that this 'must be lookt upon as a ruinous and disruptive thing, it being our worke for the present to keepe the Scots there'. Royalists still believed that if the New Scots stayed in Ireland the covenanters would be unable

5.   J. Lowe, 'The Earl of Antrim and Irish Aid to Montrose in 1644', *Irish Sword*, IV (1959-60), 191-3; Gilbert, *Irish Confederation*, III, 4-5.

to invade England, or at least would have great difficulty in doing so. Antrim was therefore instructed to bribe the New Scots not to go but to stay in Ireland 'by fit instruments and apt temptations'—it was said Monro and some of his officers were 'as most of that Nation, gainable by interest'.[6]

With these alterations Antrim's proposals were accepted. On 20 January 1644 Charles instructed him to negotiate with the Irish. His first task was to be to persuade them to send 10,000 men to England 'whereby we may be the better enabled to resist the Scotch invasion'. They were also to be asked to send 2,000 men under Antrim or his brother to the Highlands, to fall on Argyll's lands with the help of the earl of Seaforth, who was to act as joint justiciary of the Highlands with Antrim, and Sir James MacDonald of Sleat. In this work Antrim was to correspond with Montrose, who was to be lieutenant general of the king's forces in Scotland. As to the New Scots 'You are ... to treat with Monro, and to see whether you can draw him over, with the forces under his command, unto our service; in which case, we shall make good unto him What you in your discretion shall agree with him for, so far forth as to make the said Monro an Earl of Scotland, and to grant him a pension of £2,000 sterling per annum'.[7]

Eight days later Antrim signed an agreement with Montrose dealing with the Scottish side of his plans; Antrim now described himself as the king's general of the Isles and Highlands of Scotland. Montrose and the Scots royalists undertook to rise in arms on the Borders and in the north-east of Scotland by 1 April 1644 to assert the king's rights 'and for the opposing of any attempt that the rebellious party of that Kingdom shall make upon the Kingdom of Ireland'. Antrim on his part promised to do his utmost to raise forces in the Isles 'as also what forces he can for that purpose, within the Kingdome of Ireland', invading Argyll's country by 1 April.[8]

By this agreement Antrim set himself an impossibly tight schedule—just over two months to return to Ireland, persuade the Irish (and Ormond, who distrusted him) to support him,

6. Carte, *Ormond*, III, 214.
7. Gilbert, *Irish Confederation*, III, 88-90; R. Scrope and T. Monkhouse, eds, *State Papers Collected by Edward, earl of Clarendon* (3 vols, Oxford, 1767-86), II, 165.
8. Hill, *Macdonnells of Antrim*, pp. 266-7. Lowe, op. cit. 195 states that the king made Antrim a Marquis before he left Oxford. In fact this did not happen until 6 January 1645.

raise and equip the men required, and transport them to Scotland. But at first he made good progress with the Scottish side of his plans. He arrived in Kilkenny late in February and within a few days the supreme council had agreed to aid an expedition to Scotland. Provided Antrim himself supplied the men, the Irish would supply arms, ammunition and food, though they would not promise to complete their side of the bargain until 1 May. Nor would they agree to send troops to England, the dispatch of which the king had made Antrim's first priority. The reasons for the Irish reacting so differently to the requests to send troops to Scotland and to England are easy to see. Sending 2,000 men to Scotland would not seriously weaken their armies; sending 10,000 men to England would. Dispatching men to England would not bring any direct benefit to the Irish; they therefore calculated that it would not be worth their while to do it unless in return the king would make major concessions to them, especially in religious matters. As these concessions were not made, no troops were ever sent to England.[9] Intervening in Scotland on the other hand, even if only on a fairly small scale, might benefit the Irish by leading to the withdrawal of the Scottish army from Ireland, thus removing the greatest remaining obstacle to the complete domination of Ireland by the confederates. Intervention in Scotland would also demonstrate to the king that the Irish really were willing to send troops to help Charles, and that they were capable of doing this effectively.

One major difficulty seemed for a time likely to frustrate the plan to send men to Scotland. The Irish could not resist asking for one important concession in return for their support. They insisted that Ormond (whom the king had appointed lord lieutenant of Ireland in November 1643) hand over to them a convenient port in Ulster, on the pretext that this was necessary to ensure that the supplies they were providing could be assembled and shipped safely. The port the Irish wanted was Carlingford (County Louth), and they also asked for Greencastle, on the other side of Carlingford Lough in County Down. The Irish had sought possession of these ports for some time; in January 1644 Ormond had instructed Lord Moore, his governor of Drogheda, to take

9. J. Lowe, 'The Negotiations between Charles I and the Confederation of Kilkenny, 1642-9' (Ph.D. thesis, University of London, 1960), p. 272.

particular care of the garrisons in them.[10]

The strategic importance of these ports was great. Possession of them would enable the Irish to supply forces operating against the New Scots by sea, instead of overland with great difficulty. This in itself Ormond would not have minded, but he feared that the Irish would also use the ports for action against the British of Ulster, whose support he was trying to win. Even if he decided that the ports should be handed over to the Irish, he doubted whether their garrisons would obey such orders from him.[11] For the Irish to hold Carlingford would greatly strengthen their hold on the south-eastern borders of Ulster. If war again broke out between them and Ormond, they would be in a position to cut off contact between his Leinster forces and the British and New Scots of Ulster, thus isolating from each other the two main centres of Protestant resistance in Ireland.

Thus though Ormond, on the king's instructions, proved ready to help Antrim and to provide shipping for his men, the one thing he would not do was grant the Irish Carlingford.[12] In this he received support from England. Lord Digby agreed that he was right to be suspicious of the motives of the Irish, and raised a new fear. Was Antrim perhaps, under pretence of serving the king, simply raising men to help him regain the ancient possessions of his clan? This fear referred primarily to Antrim's ambitions in Scotland, but it was also well known that, not unnaturally, he wished to drive the New Scots and British from his estates in County Antrim. He had asked that Ormond be instructed to help him do this, and demanded that he be appointed governor of both Coleraine and Londonderry. It was therefore feared that if Antrim was allowed to assemble his 2,000 men at Carlingford on the Ulster border he would use them first in regaining his estates; if the New Scots left Ireland (as was still believed likely) such a venture would seem very attractive to Antrim. But for the Catholic Antrim to raise Catholic forces under a royal commission and then use them against the British in Ulster would greatly damage the

10. Gilbert, *Irish Confederation*, III, 113; Gilbert, *Contemporary History*, I, 570-1; Carte, *Ormond*, III, 250-1; Carte MSS, 9, f. 62. Lowe, 'The Earl of Antrim', *Irish Sword*, IV, 195-6, implies that Ormond was unduly suspicious in believing the Irish were trying to gain possession of Carlingford; but there is no doubt that they were.
11. Carte, *Ormond*, III, 261.
12. Ibid. III, 235, 262; Gilbert, *Irish Confederation*, III, 125.

king's interests. Ormond was therefore urged to do all he could to ensure that Antrim's men sailed from some other part of Ireland.[13]

Ormond was thus left in the awkward position of being told to help Antrim but not to trust him. On 22 April he wrote to Daniel O'Neill (a royalist agent who had accompanied Antrim to Kilkenny) urging him to prevent the Irish insisting on possession of a port. He was prepared to let the men be shipped from Carlingford, but only on condition that his garrison still held the port and that Antrim's men were not armed until after they had boarded ship. He also insisted that the men be assembled on the south side of Carlingford Lough, not on the Greencastle side in County Down; ostensibly this was so they would be safe from attack by Protestant forces in Ulster, but the real reason was doubtless to try to prevent Antrim using them in Ulster to recover his estates. In spite of all doubts and difficulties, however, Ormond was enthusiastic about the expedition to Scotland. Reports had arrived of Huntly's rising in north-east Scotland, diverting Argyll's attention from the West Highlands. 'Now or never is the tyme to compleat the distraction of that fatall kingdom, and to return into their bosome their own mischeefe'. But there was still no sign of the arms promised by the Irish.[14]

Daniel O'Neill shared Ormond's satisfaction that the war was to be spread to Scotland—'from the lord to the jockie, I beeleeve them all false-loones'—and he was able to send news that progress was being made. Antrim himself had suggested that the Irish shipped the arms and provisions promised to him from Waterford and Wexford, though he still hoped to ship the men from Carlingford. Moreover 'My Lord's friends in the Isles incourage him much to attempt something ther, whyl those partes are disgusted with the present government off their country'.[15]

This at least went some way towards removing difficulties over Carlingford, but a further point was now beginning to worry Ormond; 'I feare the person to comand these men was not seasonably, nor sufficiently, thought of'.[16] Antrim himself

13. Carte, *Ormond*, III, 273-4.
14. Ibid. III, 281; Gilbert, *Irish Confederation*, III, 157, 158; Gilbert, *Contemporary History*, I, 582.
15. Gilbert, *Contemporary History*, I, 583; Carte, *Ormond*, III, 284.
16. Gilbert, *Contemporary History*, I, 582.

could not command the expedition, for he was still negotiating with the Irish about their sending men to England. In any case he had probably intended from the first that Alasdair MacColla should lead the men. His experience in the previous few years, the fact that he was well known in the West Highlands, and his burning desire for revenge on the Campbells all made him suitable. Yet Antrim apparently had not yet revealed his intention that Alasdair should command, perhaps both through fear that the Irish would distrust him after his flirtation with Leven in 1642, and because there may have been doubts about whether he would return to Ireland from his previous raid to the Isles in time. In the event he was back in Ireland by mid-March 1644—if, as seems very likely, he was the 'Collakitagh's Son' reported to be at Portumna, County Galway, with '800 Scotch Irish'. Significantly Antrim was nearby, at Loughrea, at the same time.[17]

Antrim had little difficulty in raising the men he had promised, but delays were caused by the slowness of the Irish in performing their side of the agreement. On 16 May he claimed (probably with some exaggeration) that he had maintained 2,000 men for three months, but would be forced to disband them, withdraw the men still holding Rathlin Island, and leave Alasdair to fend for himself if supplies were not provided promptly.[18] However, the Irish did in the end agree to abandon their insistence on being given an Ulster port, agreeing that Antrim could ship the men from Passage and Ballahack, both near Waterford. Ships were provided by Patrick Archer, a Kilkenny merchant, on Ormond's orders; of the three ships one was Irish, two from the Spanish Netherlands.[19]

At last, at the end of June, the expedition set sail from Passage. According to Antrim he sent 'hard upon 1600' men, having had to disband seven or eight hundred more for lack of shipping. But three weeks later Ormond referred to Antrim having sent 2,500 men to Scotland, and in November Antrim informed Ormond that he had sent 2,030 men plus officers.[20] From these figures it seems likely that Antrim had managed

17. Carte, *Ormond*, III, 268-9.
18. Ibid. III, 300.
19. Gilbert, *Contemporary History*, I, 584-5, 586; Gilbert, *Irish Confederation*, V, 1, 224-6; Lowe, op. cit. 196-7.
20. Hill, *Macdonnells of Antrim*, p. 80; Carte, *Ormond*, III, 318-19, 328.

to dispatch a few hundred more men after the first 1,600, making a total of something over 2,000. The men were divided into three regiments under Alasdair MacColla, who held the rank of major general. Judging by the names of the officers the force was composed mainly of native Irish from the northern parts of Antrim and Londonderry, plus the 'Scots Irish' MacDonnells of Antrim. Some officers came from other parts of Ulster, some from Leinster, and a few were probably Highlanders who had fled from Scotland during the Bishops' Wars. Most had doubtless had considerable military experience through fighting for the Irish; some probably had been with Alasdair in the Isles in 1643-4.[21]

It had been known in Scotland since at least mid-April that invasion from Ireland was imminent, and the English parliament had been urged to send ships to prevent it. But the Irish had the good fortune to sail just after Liverpool had fallen to the royalists, disrupting parliament's naval activities in the Irish Sea.[22] Far from themselves being captured, the ships managed to capture a ship carrying two Scots ministers home from Ulster, where they had been imposing the solemn league and covenant; one was to die a prisoner, but the other was freed in an exchange of prisoners in 1645.[23] Early in July the Irish expedition reached the Sound of Mull, and the castles of Kinlochaline and Mingary were soon captured. But in spite of this initial success Alasdair quickly found that the widespread support Antrim had hoped for from Highland royalists did not exist. With the collapse of Huntly's rising and of Montrose's attempted invasion from England, few believed that a successful royalist rising was possible. Neither the earl of Seaforth nor Sir James MacDonald of Sleat, the two men whose help was particularly expected, were willing to commit themselves to what seemed a hopeless venture. In these circumstances it seemed likely that all the Irish would be able to achieve would be a repeat on a larger scale of Alasdair's raid on the Isles of November 1644, gradually withdrawing to Ireland when forces were concentrated against them. When news of his

21. C. O'Danachair, 'Montrose's Irish Regiments', *Irish Sword*, IV (1959-60), 61-7; L. Duggan, 'The Irish Brigade with Montrose', *Irish Ecclesiastical Record*, LXXXIX (1958), 179-81; Gilbert, *Irish Confederation*, IV, 54-6.
22. *C.S.P.D. 1644*, p. 111; Meikle, *Correspondence*, p. 18; Hill, *Macdonnells of Antrim*, p. 80.
23. Reid, *History of the Presbyterian Church*, I, 555-9; Guthry, *Memoirs*, p. 161; S.R.O. PA.11/3. Register of the Committee of Estates, 1644-5, ff. 85, 89-90.

landing reached Edinburgh Argyll's commission as king's lieutenant was renewed, but no forces were assigned to him; it was assumed he would be able to crush the rebels with his own resources, though Major General Monro was ordered to send men from Ireland to help him if this proved necessary.[24]

However, it soon became clear that Alasdair had no intention of trying to escape. Nor did he intend to wait passively on the coast until Argyll was ready to advance to attack him. Instead he marched inland, eventually meeting Montrose in Atholl.[25] This meeting saved both the Irish and Montrose from failure. Montrose had failed to raise men according to his promise to Antrim, and though Antrim had sent men they were months late and had been unable to persuade a significant number of Scots to join them. But now the Irish provided Montrose with an army, though a small one, while he as a Scots noble provided them with respectibility, at least in the eyes of some royalists, and with leadership; though his previous military experience was limited he soon proved to be a brilliant organiser of large scale guerilla warfare.

Montrose and the Irish now embarked on a year of unbroken victories, the six major battles being Tippermuir (1 September 1644), Aberdeen (13 September), Inverlochy (2 February 1645), Auldearn (9 May), Alford (2 July) and Kilsyth (15 August). In all but two of these (Alford and Kilsyth) the majority of Montrose's men were Irish;[26] they were the most permanent part of his army, to which were added whatever Highland and other Scots royalists had for the moment joined him. The Highlanders proved difficult for Montrose to control, for they often insisted on leaving him to protect their homes, carry their loot to safety and pursue clan feuds, without regard to the interests of the king for whom they were nominally fighting. Even the Irish, usually Montrose's most reliable troops, had a tendency to go their own way when it suited them; their commander Alasdair MacColla saw himself as being concerned primarily with a feud with the

24. Balfour, *Historical Works*, III, 208-9, 215, 217; S.R.O. PA.11/3, f. 10.
25. A. Macbain and J. Kennedy, eds, *Reliquiae Celticae. Texts, Papers and Studies in Gaelic Literature and Philology left by the late Rev. Alexander Cameron* (2 vols, Inverness, 1892-4), II, 177-8; Gordon, *Britane's Distemper*, pp. 64-70; G. Wishart, *The Memoirs of James Marquis of Montrose*, ed. A.D. Murdoch and H.F.M. Simpson (London, 1893), pp. 48-56; Gilbert, *Irish Confederation*, III, 256, 257, 258-9, V, 224-6.
26. O'Danachair, op. cit. 61.

Campbells, and such a feud tended to prove more attractive to the Irish than service to a distant king who had recently been at war with them. Montrose was thus frequently weakened by the divergences between his own objectives and those of his Highland and Irish troops.

This of course is a conclusion arrived at through seeing the campaigns from Montrose's standpoint; for Alasdair it was Montrose who was obstructive, whose ambitions to conquer Scotland and lead an army into England to help the king interfered with his and Antrim's more limited plans to destroy the Campbells and regain former MacDonald lands—which would of course in itself be of some benefit to the king. It was Montrose's insistence on breaking out into the southern Lowlands after Kilsyth which led to his prompt defeat a month later at Philiphaugh (13 September 1645). Montrose's supporters blamed Alasdair for having, after Kilsyth, returned to Argyllshire with the Highlanders and some of the Irish, and they attributed the disaster at Philiphaugh to his action. But Alasdair could congratulate himself on having avoided involvement in the debacle into which Montrose had been led by his overweening ambition.

Looked at from the standpoint of the confederate Irish, Montrose's ambitions corresponded more closely with their objectives in sending men to Scotland than Alasdair's did. Carrying the war into the Lowlands would be more likely to persuade the covenanters to withdraw the New Scots from Ulster than confining it to the Highlands. Yet it would be wrong to suggest that Montrose and the Irish would have been better off without Alasdair. It was he who inspired and led the great charges of Irish and Highlanders which contributed so much to most of Montrose's victories; he was a superb fighting man who inspired his men in a way no one else could have done. Moreover his contribution to the tactics and strategy of these campaigns was much greater than has usually been allowed.[27] Montrose needed him as much as he needed Montrose. This Montrose went some way towards acknowledging when he knighted Alasdair after the battle of Kilsyth; it was the only knighthood he ever bestowed.

To historians the campaigns fought in Scotland in 1644-5

---

27. For a reassessment of the career of Alasdair MacColla see D. Stevenson, *Alasdair MacColla.*

have always been known as Montrose's campaigns, and this is obviously justified by the quality of his leadership; it was this above all else which brought the forces opposing the covenanters success. But too much concentration on Montrose and his Highland and other Scottish troops has often led to the contribution of the Irish being played down.[28] Yet, especially at first, accounts of his victories often attributed them mainly to the Irish. There were many references in depositions about rebel movements to 'the Irish rebells and their associatts', or some similar phrase; sometimes Montrose is not mentioned, sometimes he appears merely as one of the associates of the Irish.[29] Only gradually did his reputation outgrow that of the Irish. Of course it is true that this was, no doubt, often simply the result of misunderstanding, the importance of Montrose's role not being recognised at first by his enemies. It was also partly the result of the covenanters' propaganda; they found it convenient to denounce their enemies simply as 'Irish', with all the word's associations (for most Scots) of barbarity, popery and treachery. Thus when in September 1644 the covenanters offered £20,000 Scots for Montrose or Alasdair dead or alive, Montrose was described as having 'now joyned with ane Band of Irish Rebels, and Masse-Priests, who haue thir two years by-gane, bathed themselves in the bloud of God's People in Ireland', while Alasdair was denounced for having committed many murders in Ireland.[30] Montrose replied to such attempts to discredit him by associating him with Alasdair and the Irish by pointing out that Leven had tried to ally himself to Alasdair in Ireland in 1642. If they were fit allies for Leven, surely they were fit for him too.[31]

But it is not only in covenanting sources that the part of the Irish is emphasised. In Highland sources such as the Book of Clanranald Alasdair MacColla rather than Montrose is the real hero, and clan conflict is the real war.[32] It is notable that an early account of the defeat of Argyll at Inverlochy which

28. John Buchan even indicated at one point that all the men who came from Ireland were Scots exiles, *Montrose* (London, 1931), p. 180.
29. M. Napier, ed. *Memorials of Montrose and his Times* (2 vols, Maitland Club, 1848-50), II, 167 and 127-92 *passim*.
30. R. Steele, ed. *A Bibliography of Royal Proclamations of the Tudor and Stuart Sovereigns* (2 vols, Oxford, 1910), II, 325-6.
31. Napier, *Memorials of Montrose*, I, appendix li.
32. Macbain and Kennedy, *Reliquiae Celticae*, II, 177-203.

circulated in Ireland attributed the victory entirely to Alasdair, specifically (though of course wrongly) stating that Montrose and his men had been in a different part of Scotland at the time.[33] Many Scots royalists regarded Montrose's campaigns as largely 'Irish' ones, and refused to join him to avoid alliance with such men.

Thus the campaigns in Scotland have many aspects. They are usually seen as a war of Scottish royalists against covenanters, but they were also part of a war of Irish against the Scottish allies of the English parliament, of Gael (Irish or Highlander) against non-Gael (English or Lowlander), of Catholic against Protestant, and, most narrowly of all, a Gaelic civil war of MacDonnell and MacDonald against Campbell.

The campaigns were conducted with little mercy on either side. Montrose's men took few prisoners, for they would have been a major hindrance to an army constantly on the move; in his victories it was usually the case that few covenanters were killed in the actual fighting, but many hundreds were cut down in the long pursuits which followed. Throughout Argyllshire and the north-east of Scotland Montrose and his men burnt and plundered widely. His allowing his men to plunder Aberdeen and kill over a hundred of its inhabitants was a major disservice to the royalist cause. The Aberdeen royalist John Spalding was particularly horrified by the cold blooded way in which the Irish forced well dressed men to undress before killing them, to avoid damaging their clothes.[34] Patrick Gordon, another royalist, observed that the Irish 'did ordinarily kill all they could be maister of, without any motion of pitie, or any consideration of humanitie'. They killed 'with the same carelesse neglect that they kill ane henne or capone for their supper'.[35] Irish stragglers who broke away from Montrose's army to steal and pillage were a constant problem to him.[36] As Lowlanders still sometimes described Highlanders as 'Irish', some of the misconduct attributed to the Irish was no doubt the work of Highlanders. But certainly it was the men from Ireland who congratulated themselves in August 1644 on having marched through Argyll's lands for forty miles

33. Carte MSS, 14, f. 121.
34. Spalding, *Memorialls*, II, 407, 410-12.
35. Gordon, *Britane's Distemper*, p. 161.
36. Spalding, *Memorialls*, II, 457-8; Napier, *Memorials of Montrose*, II, 205-6, 236.

'burning, pillaging, killing, and spoyling all the way'.[37] The winter campaign of 1644-5 against the Campbells in Argyll was especially bitter. The book of Clanranald speaks proudly of 895 men killed in cold blood, without any battle or skirmish. An Irish officer boasted with, no doubt, some exaggeration, that no house in Argyll had been left unburnt, and that all the cattle and corn had been carried off.[38]

The conduct of the covenanters was equally brutal. Few prisoners received any mercy. Irish in particular were executed automatically. Irish women camp followers straggling behind Montrose's army in July 1645 were rounded up and killed,[39] though again these are perhaps as likely to have been Highland as Irish. The real opportunities for revenge by the covenanters occured once the tide turned in their favour. At Philiphaugh about 500 Irish formed the main part of the small army which remained to Montrose. The majority were killed in the fighting but the rest surrendered on promise of quarter. On the quibble that the quarter only applied to the officer who had negotiated it, the Irish were all then killed. So too were many Irish women, and many of the Irish who escaped were rounded up and shot in the days that followed. Colonel Manus O'Cahan and Major Lachlan (the Sergeant Major Thomas Laghtnan mentioned in Antrim's list of officers sent to Scotland in 1644) were at first spared, but by order of the committee of estates they were hanged without trial in Edinburgh on 20 October 1645.[40]

How successful were Montrose's campaigns from the points of view of the different parties which contributed to them? As the king had hoped, victories by Montrose led to the removal of regiment after regiment of the Scottish army in England. Among these were two of the regiments which had returned to Scotland from Ulster in February 1644, Lothian's and Lawers'. Both were present at the battle of Auldearn, where they were 'for the most pairt cut af, fighting to the death most valiantlie'. Lawers' regiment suffered most, almost

37. Gilbert, *Contemporary History*, I, 795-6.
38. Macbain and Kennedy, *Reliquiae Celticae*, II, 183; T. Carte, ed. *A Collection of Original Letters and Papers* (2 vols, London, 1739), I, 75.
39. Wishart, *Memoirs*, p. 117.
40. Ibid. p. 144; Guthry, *Memoirs*, pp. 200, 203-4; Gordon, *Britane's Distemper*, pp. 160-1; *Three Great Victories* (London, 1645), p. 6; O'Danachair, op. cit. 64; S.R.O. PA12/1, Warrants of the Committee of Estates, 1640-6, minute of 16 October 1645.

ceasing to exist, its colonel, Sir Mungo Campbell, being killed.[41] But though the withdrawal of regiments to oppose Montrose gravely weakened the Scottish army in England, the army did remain there, and in any case the king benefited little from its weakness. Montrose's activities did not prevent or even significantly delay Charles' defeat in England. All they did was greatly reduce the part played by his Scottish enemies in that defeat.

The Irish confederates probably benefited more than the king from Montrose's victories in Scotland. Fear of Montrose and his Irish forces prevented the New Scots taking any decisive action in Ireland in 1645; the army had to be kept in a position where it could return to Scotland quickly if it was needed. Parts of it were soon recalled. First to leave was Sir Duncan Campbell of Auchinbreck 'and divers other commanders of his name' from Argyll's regiment, summoned to Scotland at the beginning of 1645 after Montrose had invaded Argyll-shire.[42] Probably all or nearly all the regiment was present at the battle of Inverlochy in February. Sir Duncan was killed commanding the covenanters' army there, but not all his regiment fought on the same side; one of his captains, Ewen MacLean of Treshnish, had deserted to Montrose with his followers on returning to Scotland. After the battle the Scottish parliament ordered Monro to send 1,000 men to Scotland. After negotiations 1,400 New Scots reached Scotland by early April 1645, under Colonel Robert Home. There were also plans to transfer some of the British forces in Ulster to Scotland, but these came to nothing.[43]

In August, after the battle of Alford, Monro himself was sent for, to command an army against Montrose. He was ordered to bring 1,000 men with him from Ireland,[44] but before anything could be done Montrose won his final and greatest victory at Kilsyth. For some weeks thereafter there was no army in Scotland to oppose him. Some leading

41. Spalding, *Memorialls*, II, 414, 416, 424, 431, 451, 473, 474; Wishart, *Memoirs of Montrose*, p. 101; *A.P.S.* VI, i, 356, 449-50, 467-8, 491.
42. Guthry, *Memoirs*, p. 175; Macbain and Kennedy, *Reliquiae Celticae*, II, 183; Rushworth, *Historical Collections*, IV, i, 399.
43. *A.P.S.* VI, i, 357, 363-4; S.R.O. PA.11/4, ff. 4-5, 41, 41v-42, 43, 43v, 50; Guthry, *Memoirs*, pp. 183-4; Carte, *Ormond*, III, 403; Meikle, *Correspondence*, p. 66; [J.C. Sinclair], *Historical and Genealogical Account of the Clan Maclean ... By a Senachie* (London, 1838), pp. 124-6, 285; J. P. Maclean, *History of the Clan Maclean* (Cincinnati, 1889), p. 276.
44. *A.P.S.* VI, i, 450-1; Balfour, *Historical Works*, III, 301.

covenanters fled to England, others (including Glencairn) to Ireland. As Montrose tried to reduce south-west Scotland to obedience many lesser men and their families also sought refuge in Ireland, and—unlike the noble refugees—many settled permanently in Ulster 'and added to the new Plantation here'.[45] Leading covenanters who had fled to Berwick sent the earl of Cassillis to Ireland to recall Monro's whole army to help its native country.[46] But again there was no time for the orders to be carried out before another change of fortune altered the situation completely; on 13 September Scots forces recalled from England defeated Montrose at Philiphaugh and he fled back to the Highlands without an army.

In spite of this, however, the covenanters decided that they still needed reinforcements from Ireland. Monro was asked to send 2,500 men to Scotland. But the New Scots proved reluctant to obey, and though negotiations dragged on until April 1646 no further troops were sent to Scotland. By that time it had become clear that Montrose was no longer a serious threat to the covenanters so men from Ireland were not needed.[47]

Thus, in the end, sending over 2,000 Irish troops to Scotland only led to the withdrawal of about 1,400 New Scots, plus Argyll's regiment (perhaps 1,000 more), from Ireland, so the primary objective of the Irish confederates in supporting Antrim's expedition to Scotland had not been achieved. The successes of the Irish in Scotland had forced the New Scots to remain on the defensive, but most of them still remained in Ireland. Consequently the Irish refused to respond to pleas from Antrim, Ormond and the king for further help for the Irish in Scotland; they had decided that it would be better to employ the resources at their disposal in Ireland rather than in Scotland. Ormond's arguments that further intervention in Scotland would lead the New Scots to leave Ireland were ignored. The supreme council explained that sending 2,000 men to Scotland in 1644 'hath taught us the chardge and difficulties interposed in such enterprises'. Only if Ormond was willing to make concessions in return for help

45. Guthry, *Memoirs*, p. 194; Wishart, *Memoirs of Montrose*, p. 134; Reid, *History of the Presbyterian Church*, II, 14.
46. H.M.C. 10: *10th Report*, I, 55.
47. T.S.A.I. pp. 97-107; S.R.O. PA.11/4, Register of the Committee of Estates, 1645-6, f. 107v; Meikle, *Correspondence*, pp. 138-9; Balfour, *Historical Works*, III, 336; *A.P.S.* VI, i, 596.

would the Irish consider providing it. Since Montrose was now emerging as one of the great hopes of the royalists in all three kingdoms it seemed to the Irish reasonable to expect that Ormond and the king would be willing to make concessions to get help for him. In February 1645 the Irish again demanded Carlingford, and that Ormond join them in action against the New Scots; only on these conditions would they aid Montrose. Ormond refused to give way; he would provide ships at Carlingford and guarantee the safety of men and supplies sent there by the Irish, but he would not hand over the port, and argued that sending aid to Scotland could be more easily done from Waterford and Wexford. Desperate as the king was to get help to Montrose he evidently decided that the Irish were asking too high a price. Possession of Carlingford would greatly strengthen their position if war between them and Ormond broke out again.[48]

No further Irish help ever reached Montrose. Through his victory at Kilsyth he almost succeeded in forcing the removal of all the New Scots from Ireland, but defeat at Philiphaugh prevented this. After the defeat it must have seemed that the Irish would be even less likely than before to consider further intervention in Scotland. But in fact it was in the months after Philiphaugh that the Irish changed their minds. The main reason for this appears to have been the arrival in Ireland of Rinuccini, the papal nuncio, in October 1645. He soon gained great influence among the confederates, and Pope Innocent X had instructed him to take care to maintain the army in Scotland since its achievements 'were of the greatest advantage to Ulster ... and also to the Crown'.[49] Another influence was probably the realisation that the king was now facing complete defeat in both England and Scotland; the two kingdoms would then be free to turn their attention to subduing Ireland. In such circumstances it would be worth while to try to maintain an 'Irish' cause in Scotland, even if Ormond did not make the concessions formerly demanded.

Since Philiphaugh the Irish and the royalist causes in

48. Carte, *Ormond*, I, 529-30, II, 380-1, 386, III, 358-9, 364, 384, 389-90, 395, 399, 405; Scrope and Monkhouse, *Clarendon State Papers*, II, 186; Gilbert, *Irish Confederation*, IV, 138-9,154; Carte MSS, 14, f. 259; McNeill, *Tanner Letters*, pp. 177-8.
49. G. Aiazza, ed. *The Embassy in Ireland of Monsignor G. B. Rinuccini* (Dublin, 1873), p. liv.

G

Scotland had become separated. Alasdair MacColla, having moved to Argyllshire before the battle, had ignored Montrose's orders to rejoin him after it, and Montrose showed no intention of joining Alasdair. Montrose occupied himself in the central and eastern Highlands in trying to rebuild a royalist army while Alasdair, his Highlanders and the remaining Irish acted independently in Argyll. Alasdair had achieved one of his main objectives in Scotland in May 1645; his father, Coll Ciotach, and two brothers had been freed by Argyll in an exchange of prisoners,[50] and he was now busy trying to clear his clan's former lands of Campbells, failing to recognise that a permanent MacDonald victory in the Highlands was impossible without a wider royalist victory in Scotland—and, indeed, in Britain as a whole.

Nonetheless, the separation of the Irish and royalist causes in Scotland after Philiphaugh may have contributed to persuading the confederates to send help to Alasdair. It must have been very galling to the Irish in 1644-5 to find victories won in Scotland largely by Irish troops, sent from Ireland with arms and supplies, appropriated by royalists and hailed as great royalist triumphs. Now that Alasdair was acting independently of Montrose perhaps Irish troops would be given the credit due to their achievements.

For whatever reasons, in February 1646 the general assembly of the confederates at Kilkenny resolved, with the approval of Rinuccini, to attempt to divert the attention of the New Scots from Ulster by sending reinforcements to Scotland. Antrim had again offered to provide the men, 2,000 of them, from the former inhabitants of County Antrim driven out by the wars, and the confederates promised him a loan of £3,000 sterling to raise, equip and transport them. Alexander MacDonnell, Antrim's brother, was to command them if he wished. In the event Antrim himself led the reinforcements to Scotland. Like Owen Roe O'Neill and the Nuncio he opposed the secret 'Ormond Peace' that the confederates had signed with Ormond, and it may have been hoped that he could persuade Alasdair MacColla to help to overthrow the supporters of the peace, by force if necessary.[51]

50. *A.P.S.* VI, i, 324, 328, 367; Spalding, *Memorialls*, II, 478.
51. Hill, *Macdonnells of Antrim*, pp. 331, 446-8; Aiazza, *Embassy*, pp. 149-50; Gilbert, *Irish Confederation*, VI, 334.

Archibald Campbell, marquis of Argyll. Colonel of a regiment of the Scottish army in Ireland. Portrait by David Scougal.

Antrim landed in Kintyre in May or early June 1646; how many men he brought with him is uncertain, but he may have brought Alasdair the full 2,000 promised.[52] They had left Ireland just in time, for changing political circumstances soon caused the Irish to reconsider yet again their attitude towards intervention in Scotland. In May 1646 the king, faced by military defeat in England, fled to the Scottish army in England. Differences between the Scots and the English parliament over the conduct of the war and the nature of an eventual peace settlement had led to growing tension between them, and Charles hoped to be able to play off the allies against each other, to persuade the Scots (by granting them concessions) to restore him to power in England. If the king and the Scots were now allies, as was rumoured, what was their attitude to the Irish? To send men or supplies to Scotland, ostensibly on the king's behalf, for use against the covenanters, who were now the king's allies, would be absurd. In June the confederates therefore turned down a plea from Montrose for aid.[53]

The king had at first hoped, absurdly, that the covenanters would accept Montrose and other Scots royalists as allies. But they insisted that he order all royalists to lay down their arms. Montrose obeyed and went into exile; a few Irish who had remained with him marched west to join Highland allies or return to Ireland.[54] The king's orders met with a different reception, however, from Antrim and Alasdair MacColla. Antrim at first refused to disband as the terms offered did not give sufficient protection to Highlanders who had joined him, but on a second message from the king, containing a promise that he would be given Kintyre as soon as the king could overcome the marquis of Argyll, he obeyed. But when he ordered his men to lay down their arms they 'did mutiny highly to leave the Marquiss of Arguiles country, he being then possessed of a great deal of the said Marquiss of Antrims Estate in Ireland'. Antrim himself therefore returned to Ireland in September

52. H. Cary, ed. *Memorials of the Great Civil War* (2 vols, London, 1842), I, 40; D. O'Connell and B. O'Ferrall, *Commentarius Rinuccinianus* (6 vols, I.M.C. 1932-49), II, 163-4. It was rumoured in London in June 1646 that the royalist Lord Digby was soon to go to Ireland to raise 10,000 men to join Montrose in Scotland, C. L. Hamilton, 'Scotland, Ireland and the English Civil War', *Albion*, VII (1975), 127, n. 32.
53. Gilbert, *Irish Confederation*, V, 222, 311-12, 353.
54. Guthry, *Memoirs*, p. 223; H.M.C. 21: *Hamilton*, I, 113.

1646, but left Alasdair and the Irish still in arms; as the Ormond Peace had by this time been overthrown by Owen Roe O'Neill there was no need for the services of these men in Ireland to oppose the the Peace, and Antrim was probably content with this outcome whereby he obeyed the king yet still maintained a MacDonald party in arms in Scotland.[55]

Though Alasdair MacColla thus stayed in Scotland there is no evidence that he had any military plans except to try to hang on to as much of Argyll as possible. By the end of 1646 the Campbells had driven him into Kintyre, his last foothold on the mainland. In February 1647 the Scottish army in England returned to Scotland, leaving the king to fall into the hands of the English parliament as he had failed to make the concessions the covenanters demanded. The withdrawal from England freed troops for a determined attempt to crush the remaining resistance to the covenanters in Scotland. In March 1647 Lieutenant General David Leslie led an army to the north east and quickly captured the few remaining royalist castles. Scots in their garrisons were usually spared but all Irish were executed.[56]

Next Leslie turned towards Argyll, spurred on to make haste by rumours that the Irish were sending 3,000 more men to Scotland.[57] The rumours were substantially true. Now that the king's attempts to form an alliance with the covenanters had collapsed, the confederates thought it was in their interests to send further aid to Alasdair MacColla. When the decision was taken is uncertain, but by 3 May 1647 Rinuccini could write that 'The interests of the kingdoms of Ireland and Scotland are so closely united, that if the Supreme Council has means of supplying the wants of both, the progress of the cause of religion and of the King of Great Britain would be twofold'. On 11 May the supreme council ordered supplies to be provided for an expedition to Scotland; a further order issued in June reveals that the plan was to raise and transport

55. Hill, *Macdonnells of Antrim*, pp. 273, 306, 331; Inveraray Castle, Argyll Transcripts, XII, 149; Gilbert, *Irish Confederation*, V, 1-2; MacBain and Kennedy, *Reliquiae Celticae*, II, 203; H.M.C. 21: *Hamilton*, I, 111-13; Scrope and Monkhouse, *Clarendon State Papers*, II, 237-8, 242.
56. Birch, *State Papers*, I, 89-90; S.R.O. PA.11/5, Register of the Committee of Estates 1647-8, ff. 6v-7, 16, 17v-18.
57. J. G. Fotheringham, ed. *The Diplomatic Correspondence of Jean de Montereul* (2 vols, S.H.S. 1898-9), II, 83; *C.S.P.V.* 1643-7, p. 313; *A.P.S.* VI, i, 765; Rushworth, *Historical Collections*, IV, i, 448.

5,000 men to Scotland jointly with Antrim, who was to be paid £5,000 sterling.[58]

This new scheme came too late, for by the end of June there was no longer an Irish force in Scotland for the reinforcemenrs to join. Alasdair MacColla had wintered in Kintyre. He is said to have refused to co-operate with the royalist Huntly, who still held out in the north, stating bluntly that he did not pretend to be fighting for the king; he was seeking to recover his lands and revenge himself on his enemies.[59] The MacDonald cause was his primary interest, and his best hope of help lay in Antrim and the Irish, not in the king. It seems likely that he was considering a temporary withdrawal to Ireland before David Leslie's superior forces, hoping to return within months with the new expeditionary force being raised by the Irish. But, whatever his intentions, he allowed his forces to be surprised and scattered by Leslie on 24 May. That night he and most of the Irish and MacDonalds fled to the island of Gigha and then to Islay. Many of his Highland allies were abandoned in Kintyre; after a short siege they surrendered Dunaverty Castle to Leslie and most of them, two or three hundred men, were massacred.

On reaching Islay Alasdair established a garrison in Dunyveg Castle under the command of Coll Ciotach before fleeing to Ireland with most of the Irish and many Highlanders. Coll Ciotach's ideas of the accepted conventions of warfare did not accord with those of the covenanters, for he ventured out of the castle without a safe-conduct to negotiate with Leslie's forces and procure whisky. Surprisingly, the first time he was allowed to return to his garrison, but the second time he appeared, on 1 July, he was made a prisoner. The garrison then surrendered, but for once the Irish were spared, being allowed to leave the country. These unusually generous terms resulted from the fact that Leslie lacked the equipment necessary for a long siege or an assault.[60]

Having subdued Islay Leslie moved on to Mull. Sir Lachlan Maclean of Duart agreed to submit and to hand over all the

58. Aiazza, *Embassy*, p. 286; *C.S.P.I.1633-47*, pp. 666, 723.
59. Fotheringham, *Correspondence*, II, 83, 120.
60. D. Stevenson, 'The Massacre at Dunaverty, 1647', *Scottish Studies*, XIX (1975), 27-37; S.R.O. PA.7/23/2/49, 50, 52, 54; A. McKerral, *Kintyre in the Seventeenth Century* (Edinburgh, 1948), pp. 53-72; Turner, *Memoirs*, pp. 45-8, S.R.O. PA.12/2, Warrants of the Committee of Estates, 1647-8, letter of 23 June 1647; Birch, *State Papers*, I, 91; Guthry, *Memoirs*, p. 243.

Irish with his forces to Leslie; they were all, 'fourteene very prettie Irishmen', hung.[61] As to Coll Ciotach, Argyll saw to it that he and his son Ranald (who had also been captured) were executed.[62]

Thus ended the three year career of the Irish forces in Scotland, though a few scattered Irish remained to be dealt with. Mercy was shown in one instance; orders were given in July to free some Irishmen from the thieves' hole in Edinburgh tolbooth and send them back to Ireland. But in general policy towards the Irish remained harsh. In December 1647 the committee of estates approved the resolution of Major General John Middleton, who was engaged in suppressing Huntly, to hang all his Irish prisoners.[63] In April 1648 forces were sent to suppress the MacDonalds of Clanranald and some Irish who were causing trouble in Skye and the Outer Hebrides.[64] Some Irish took part in Sir Thomas MacKenzie of Pluscardine's rising in 1649; after it had been crushed order was given that the Irish prisoners 'bee putt to present execution, to be done upon them be there associat rebells of the Clankenzie'[65] to make any co-operation between Irish and the MacKenzies impossible in the future. As late as 1649 Antrim and Montrose were seeking help from the pope to renew the war in Scotland,[66] but nothing came of their plans.

The Irish in Scotland had achieved a remarkable series of victories under Montrose in 1644-5. Without him in 1645-7 those who had survived achieved little. Similarly, he achieved nothing without them in the brief campaign in 1650 which led to his capture and execution. The Irish and Highlanders who fled to Ireland as David Leslie advanced in 1647 proved equally unfortunate.

Alasdair MacColla reached Ireland in June with seven or eight hundred men; they landed in the Lecale (County Down) and managed to make their way safely to confederate-held

61. S.R.O. PA.7/23/2/54; Turner, *Memoirs*, p. 49. According to another account Maclean only surrendered on a promise that the Irish, 'eight Irish gentlemen', would be spared, but the covenanters then shot seven of them, Hill, *Macdonnells of Antrim*, pp. 112-13.
62. W. Cobbet, ed. *State Trials* (34 vols, London, 1809-28), V. 1391-2, 1396, 1411, 1462-3; Guthry, *Memoirs*, p. 246.
63. S.R.O. PA.11/5, ff. 44, 161v.
64. *A.P.S.* VI, ii, 21-2.
65. S.R.O. PA.11/8, Register of the Committee of Estates, 1649, f. 74.
66. O'Connell and O'Ferrall, *Commentarius Rinuccinianus*, IV, 274-5; Aiazza, *Embassy*, pp. 367, 368, 369.

areas.[67] Others followed from Scotland in small groups. Alasdair intended to join the Ulster army under Owen Roe O'Neill, but Antrim was on bad terms with O'Neill and refused to allow this. Instead Alasdair was appointed governor of Clonmel and lieutenant general of Lord Taaffe's Munster army, while another regiment of 'redshanks' under Angus MacDonald of Glengarry was attached to General Thomas Preston's Leinster army.[68] Soon most of the men who had come from Scotland were dead. On 8 August 1747 Preston's army was destroyed at the battle of Dungan Hill by Michael Jones, who now commanded Protestant forces based on Dublin for the English parliament. Glengarry's men fought bravely but the majority were killed; one account puts their numbers at 400, another at 800 of whom less than 100 escaped.[69]

Alasdair had at first better luck, successfully defending Clonmel from Protestant forces under Lord Inchiquin.[70] But on 13 November 1647 he commanded the right wing of Taaffe's army against Inchiquin in the battle of Knocknanuss. Alasdair had perhaps 1,500 'redshanks' with him, Highlanders and Ulster Irish who had fought in Scotland, and he led one of the irresistible charges which had so often brought victory to Montrose. But though he routed Inchiquin's left wing the rest of Taaffe's army failed to support him adequately, and soon fled. Alasdair and his men were surrounded, and most of them died fighting. He himself, 'as stout and strong a Man as ever carried a Broad Sword and Targett of late days, and so Vigorous in Fight, that had his conduct been equivalent to his Valour, he had been one of the best Generalls in Europe', either died in fair fight or (by some accounts) was killed after surrendering on offer of quarter.[71]

In spite of these disasters other Highlanders soon came to Ireland, leaving the Highlands as the covenanters tightened their hold on them. In 1648 the captain of Clanranald, sent his son Donald MacDonald 'and all those who remained with

67. H.M.C. 63: *Egmont*, I, ii, 414-15; Rushworth, *Historical Collections*, IV, i, 561-2.
68. Gilbert, *Contemporary History*, I, 151, 153.
69. Bagwell, *Stuarts*, II, 148-9; Aiazza, *Embassy*, pp. 306-7; Gilbert, *Contemporary History*, I, 155-6; Rushworth, *Historical Collections*, IV, ii, 779-80.
70. Gilbert, *Contemporary History*, I, 159; Carte, *Ormond*, II, 7.
71. Bagwell, *Stuarts*, II, 157-8; Hogan, *Warr of Ireland*, pp. 71, 73-4; Aiazza, *Embassy*, pp. 335-7; McNeill, *Tanner Letters*, pp. 275-6; Gilbert, *Irish Confederation*, VII, 35; Gilbert, *Contemporary History*, I, 173-5; Macbain and Kennedy, *Reliquiae Celticae*, II, 205.

him of the men of Ireland, and some of his Scottish gentlemen along with them'. They sailed from Uist with about 300 soldiers. On arriving in Ireland they were attached to Preston's army where 'those who lived of the Scots and Irish of the Mac Donnells and their friends' who had come to Ireland the previous year, including Glengarry, were still serving under Colonel Alexander MacDonnell, Antrim's brother; the regiment was 1,500 strong and Donald MacDonald became its lieutenant colonel. But the luck of the Highlanders in Ireland remained bad. The Irish confederation was now collapsing through internal feuds between the supreme council on the one hand and Rinuccini and his party on the other. Antrim declared in favour of the nuncio and withdrew the Highlanders from Preston's army. He tried to assemble one or two thousand of the 'Scotch Irish' at Wexford, but they were attacked and scattered by confederate forces, about sixty being killed. Donald MacDonald, Glengarry and others were captured and sent to Kilkenny. Antrim soon secured their release, but most of the Highlanders had had enough of Ireland; Glengarry went to the continent to join royalists there, Donald MacDonald and many others returned to Scotland. Some, however, may have remained, for in June 1650 there is a record of one 'Neal Mac Colkittagh', perhaps one of Coll Ciotach's sons, being killed in Ireland by the English.[72]

The Highlanders in Ireland in 1647-8 had won neither fame nor fortune, but their involvement in the fighting in Ireland is of some interest; this was the last occasion on which the native Irish received military help from their fellow Gaels, the semi autonomous chiefs of the western Highlands and Isles. The Highlanders who fought at Dungan Hill and Knocknanuss were the last of the redshanks.

72. Macbain and Kennedy, *Reliquiae Celticae*, II, 205-7; Bagwell, *Stuarts*, II, 172-3; A. J. and A. M. Macdonald, *The Clan Donald* (3 vols, Inverness, 1896-1904), II, 337-8, 426; Aiazza, *Embassy*, pp. 419, 423, 441; Gilbert, *Irish Confederation*, VII, 114-16, 277; Gilbert, *Contemporary History*, II, 150, 167.

Sir Alexander Hamilton. General of the Artillery of the Scottish army in Ireland.
Portrait by George Jamesone in Tyninghame House.

CHAPTER FIVE

The New Scots in Ireland, 1644-1646

i. The Campaign of 1644

Early in 1644 the prospects of the New Scots looked bleak. They had been weakened by the transport of three regiments back to Scotland. Ormond's signing of a cessation with the Irish had deprived them of an ally, and his encouraging of the British to accept the cessation while the New Scots rejected it had nearly caused civil war in Ulster between those who supported the king and those who obeyed parliament. Monro's seizure of Belfast and the submission of most of the British to him had demonstrated that the New Scots were still the dominant force in Ulster, but it remained to be seen to what extent the British would support and obey him in a campaign.

Not only was Monro's position in some ways weaker than the previous year, it was known that the enemies he would have to face would be stronger. The cessation freed the Irish to concentrate their attention on subduing Ulster. In November 1643 a general assembly of the confederates met at Waterford to elect agents to negotiate with the king and to organise the war against the Scots.[1] In the assembly Owen Roe O'Neill demanded the help of the other three provinces for his Ulster army, emphasising the strength of the New Scots and the British, and threatening to retreat into the other provinces (as he had been partly forced to do in 1643) unless he was reinforced. He undertook to provide 4,000 foot and 400 horse himself, and the assembly agreed that the rest of the country would contribute 6,000 foot and 600 horse. But as usual the confederates were much divided among themselves by political differences and personal jealousies. There was much argument

1.   D. F. Cregan, 'The Confederation of Kilkenny; its organisation, personnel and history' (Ph.D. thesis, University College, Dublin, 1947), pp. 75-6.

over who should command the expedition into Ulster. Eventually the earl of Castlehaven was chosen as general of the whole force, as a fairly inoffensive compromise candidate; but inevitably the appointment offended Owen Roe, who was expected to continue in command of the Ulster army under Castlehaven.[2]

A further complication was the position of the earl of Antrim. His plan to invade Scotland was welcomed by the confederates as it would threaten the New Scots from the rear, but his determination to make the courtesy title granted to him by the confederates of lieutenant general an office with real power caused trouble. He wished to take a leading part in the conquest of Ulster, and early in March it was said that the army Castlehaven was assembling would be commanded by Antrim as soon as it crossed into Ulster. Antrim's attempts to get command of the Ulster campaign made plausible Ormond's suspicions that he intended to divert to Ulster the men he was ostensibly raising for the invasion of Scotland, but it seems that Antrim's interest in Ulster may itself have been a deception; it is possible that from the first Antrim's attempts to get authority over Castlehaven's army were motivated by the hope that once he got command of it he could divert it to England to help the king there. This is certainly what some of the Irish came to believe, and probably what led to his being excluded from any command in the confederate armies.[3]

To add further to the confusion there was the position of Ormond in relation to the New Scots and their British allies. The Irish repeatedly demanded that Ormond join in action against them as breakers of the cessation. Ormond's protests that some of the British of Ulster were still obedient to him and the king were dismissed as evasions. As early as the beginning of March 1644 Daniel O'Neill was aware that the Irish might even offer Ormond command of their army if he would lead it against the New Scots. In May Ormond was actually offered this command, it being hoped that this would not only persuade him to turn his own forces on the New Scots, but that it would put an end to the troublesome bickerings of Castlehaven and Antrim, for Ormond was the

2. Bagwell, *Stuarts*, II, 57; Tuchet, earl of Castlehaven, *Castlehaven's Review*, pp. 45-6; Gilbert, *Contemporary History*, I, 81.
3. Gilbert, *Contemporary History*, I, 572, 585; Gilbert, *Irish Confederation*, III, 3-7; Carte, *Ormond*, I, 496, III, 250-1.

only commander both were willing to serve under. But Ormond refused. Not only had he not the resources for a war on the Ulster Protestants, he knew any such action would lose him the support of virtually all Protestants throughout Ireland. As he wrote to Lord Digby early in July 'Here I do not think ten Protestants would follow me, but rather rise like one man against me, and adhere to the Scotts'. The most he would do was agree to advance his forces towards Ulster (if the Irish supplied them) to distract the Scots while the Irish attacked them.[4]

Robert Monro was naturally apprehensive at the preparations the Irish were making against him, though he vowed that if Antrim advanced against him he would capture him 'the third time to vindicate myself from the aspersion of the wicked'; not surprisingly some found it hard to believe that Antrim could have escaped twice without Monro's complicity.[5] Both the New Scots and British stressed the strength of the forces that Antrim and Castlehaven were reported to be raising against them.[6] But in many ways the Irish still seemed more scared of the Scots than the Scots were of them. Even the withdrawal of three New Scots regiments and Monro's difficulties with the British did not give the Irish much confidence. One of their troubles in 1644 was that they put all their hopes in Castlehaven's new army (if it was his, and not Antrim's, or even Ormond's), and this army was not ready to advance into Ulster until late July. In the interim no attempt was made to maintain pressure on Monro. Owen Roe O'Neill, either through lack of supplies (diverted to Castlehaven) or through indignation at not being given command of the new army himself, remained inactive. In March he withdrew most of his army from Ulster.[7] Thus in April Monro was able to cross the Bann into Armagh unopposed, and British forces from western Ulster under Sir Frederick Hamilton also moved south; it was said Monro had 8,000 men, Hamilton 2,000, and that they intended to march on Galway. Rumour

4.   Carte, *Ormond*, I, 496-7, III, 321-3; Gilbert, *Contemporary History*, I, 572; Gilbert, *Irish Confederation*, III, 91-2, 154, 158-9, 178-9, 197-8, 200-1, 325, 328; Lowe, 'Negotiations between Charles I and the Confederation of Kilkenny', pp. 235-6.
5.   H.M.C. 29: *Portland*, I, 172-3.
6.   S.R.O. PA.11/1, ff. 177-178v, 180-180v; S.R.O. PA.7/23/2/20. Baillie, *Letters*, II, 164.
7.   Hogan, *Warr of Ireland*, pp. 36-7.

spoke of 5,000 more Scots landing in Ulster, and the Irish renewed their appeals to Ormond for aid. No such dramatic advance by Monro materialised, but in mid-June Owen Roe wrote gloomily of how 'By the invencible power and force of the Scotts in the north I was driven with the few Creaghts and inhabitants of Ulster to repaire hether into the county of Lowth'.[8]

A major offensive by Monro did eventually come, at the end of June. He and the British commanders agreed that as many men as possible should try to bring Castlehaven's army to battle, with the intention of destroying it before it was fully assembled and trained. 10,000 footmen (with 2,000 more guarding the baggage train) and about 1,000 horse were brought together. Each man carried oatmeal sufficient for ten days, and ten days' more was carried in the baggage train. Lack of horses prevented more food being brought but even so Monro's forces were equipped to stay longer in the field than on most of his previous expeditions. He marched from Lisburn on 27 June and rendezvoused with other forces at Armagh on 30 June. He then marched without difficulty through Armagh, Monaghan and Cavan 'to the uttermost confines of Ulster'. Resistance by Irish forces then appeared, but it was swept aside, and Granard and Longford were captured. Castlehaven's army had been camped at Granard, but it retreated hastily as Monro approached. Intelligence reports said it was moving to unite with Owen Roe's army at Kells, so Monro turned east into Meath in pursuit. Panic among the Irish spread as far as Athlone. Owen Roe's creaghts were thrown into confusion; rumours said the Scots had reached Trim, less than thirty miles from Dublin. On 6 July the Irish supreme council issued a proclamation summoning all aged between eighteen and sixty to arms as the New Scots and their adherents were advancing to destroy the Irish nation. But the decisive battle that Monro sought never took place. Castlehaven and Owen Roe were at Portlester, not Kells, and Monro's food supplies were nearing exhaustion. Rather than risk his army any further he decided to withdraw north (after burning Kells and Navan, in addition to forty-seven castles in Longford and Westmeath) by way of Dundalk and Newry; thus the only time Monro ever marched

8.   Gilbert, *Irish Confederation*, III, 140-1, 154, 158-9; Carte, *Ormond*, III, 281-2; Gilbert, *Contemporary History*, I, 556.

through the Moyry Pass it was from south to north.[9]

This march with over ten thousand men was the largest scale campaign Monro ever undertook. It was also the longest, in terms of distance covered, and the most successful. The withdrawal of Owen Roe's Ulster army had enabled Monro to break out through the difficult country of Monaghan and Cavan into Leinster, penetrating into the heart of Ireland. His sudden appearance disorganised and demoralised the army that was being assembled against him in what the Irish had thought was a secure area. But, as so often before, Monro was prevented from exploiting a temporary success by failure to force the Irish to give battle, by lack of supplies and, probably, by orders from Scotland limiting his freedom of movement. Nonetheless the expedition was an impressive display of the power of the New Scots and British, in spite of their weaknesses and divisions. The motives that stirred Monro into such energetic action were mixed. It was sound strategy to try to disrupt Castlehaven's great army (which many of the Irish believed would be unbeatable) before it was ready to fight, rather than simply wait to be attacked. Monro must also have wanted to demonstrate the effectiveness of his army to its paymasters. Both the covenanters and the English parliament had only agreed to let the New Scots stay in Ireland with some reluctance, and they had made it clear that they expected some return, in the form of action against the Irish, for the resources they were diverting from the English civil war to Ulster. Finally, Monro must have wished to demonstrate his ability and energy to the British who were reluctant to accept him as their commander in chief, thus binding to him those who only obeyed him reluctantly by joint participation in a successful campaign.

From this last point of view the campaign was only partly successful. Sir Theophilus Jones and his men, for example, who only a few weeks before had refused to admit the New Scots to Lisburn, were forced to accompany Monro by threats that he would disarm them and cut off their supplies unless they obeyed him; Jones resolved that after the expedition he

9.   Gilbert, *Contemporary History*, I, 590, III, 10-11, 203, 204, 205-8; Gilbert, *Irish Confederation*, III, 211; Baillie, *Letters*, II, 232-3; Carte, *Ormond*, I, 495-6, III, 327, 337; Bagwell, *Stuarts*, II, 59-60; Tuchet, *Castlehaven's Review*, pp. 148-9; *A Full Relation of the Late Expedition of the Right Honourable, the Lord Monroe ...* (London, 1644), pp. 1-7; Carte MSS, 11, ff. 305, 396.

would abandon the service and leave Ulster.[10] On his return journey from Kells, Monro made further efforts to extend his control over the British. On 11 July he asked Seafoule Gibson, who commanded Ormond's garrison at Dundalk, for passage through the town. This was refused. The following day Monro repeated the performance at Newry, after drawing up his army before the town. Lieutenant Colonel Edmund Mathews, having been driven out of Belfast by Monro earlier in the year, was naturally suspicious, and he too refused. The New Scots made no secret of the fact that they believed Newry was rightly theirs as they had captured it from the rebels in 1642. Monro then asked simply for passage through Newry for his artillery, again without success (even though he tactfully sent English officers from the British forces with the request). At this point Monro is said (admittedly by hostile sources) to have resolved to take the town by storm, but in the end to have marched off uttering threats to return. Whether as a result of the confrontation at Newry or of longer standing resentment at Monro's conduct, the English among the British forces were said to have resolved not to accompany him on campaign again; though, as in the past when similar stories had circulated, such resolutions, if they were ever made, were not adhered to.

Thus Monro's successful expedition was soured at its close by renewed tension between him and the British. Whether he really intended to take possession of Dundalk and Newry is uncertain, but it is quite possible. Possession of the towns would have done much to secure the Moyry Pass route out of Ulster for his army; perhaps more important in the short term, it would have effectively blocked the route to his enemies. Ormond was still negotiating with the Irish, and might either join Castlehaven's attack on Ulster, or at least allow him to attack through the Pass. Yet in the end Monro refused to use force against the towns. This may simply have been for fear of alienating British opinion and driving Ormond into the hands of the Irish, but it may also indicate that all Monro had wanted was to make the garrisons recognise his authority by allowing him passage through them. Ormond rather oddly concluded that Monro had refrained from using force against his men to lull him into a false sense of security; Monro could

10. Carte MSS, 11, ff. 322, 336.

have done this much better by not making demands on the garrisons in the first place.[11]

In spite of the success of Monro's raid into Leinster, by late in July Castlehaven and Owen Roe O'Neill were ready to advance into Ulster. The Irish had managed to withdraw their forces in the face of Monro's advance with few losses, and Monro had not attempted any permanent occupation of the areas he had marched through; to have left garrisons to hold all the passes through bogs and river crossings that the Irish might have used would have drained the strength of his field army, and in any case it would have been impossible to keep them supplied. Castlehaven was therefore able to move his army into Ulster unmolested and reach a safe base at Charlemont before Monro could reorganise and provision his forces after their previous expedition.

On hearing of Castlehaven's advance Monro hastily began to gather his forces from their quarters. On 25 July he left Carrickfergus with New Scots forces and six days' supplies. He waited until 29 July in Kilwarlin Wood for Argyll's and Leven's regiments from Coleraine and North Antrim, but by the time they reached him his provisions were exhausted, preventing further advance. Parties were sent ahead to try to hold the crossing points on the Bann—it was now known that Castlehaven was camped at Tanderagee—while Monro turned his attention to procuring supplies. For seven days his army remained in the Kilwarlin area, living off the country people (though Monro admitted that they were extremely poor already). On 2 August the most important inhabitants of Down and Antrim were summoned to the army to agree on how quantities of food which Monro demanded should be raised from the two counties should be apportioned. Monro's aim was to provide himself with ten days' supplies, and in this he was successful; by 9 August he had supplies to last until the 22nd. While the food was being raised the army had occupied itself in preparing defences to delay the Irish if they crossed the Bann, and in trying to persuade the British of western Ulster to join it. The British ignored two orders from Monro, presumably fearing that if they joined him the Irish would fall on their quarters and homes, but after Monro sent for them a

11. Ibid. 11, ff. 431, 440, 464, 466; *A Full Relation of the Late Expedition*, pp. 7-8; Carte, *Ormond*, I, 496, III, 327.

third time they came, arriving on 11 August. They were not alone in fearing for the safety of their quarters in their absence; concern was raised by Irish boasts that they had friends within Monro's quarters who would help them. To thwart any Irish plot Monro ordered the removing of all remaining Irish and Catholics from Carrickfergus and Belfast. Two companies of Chichester's regiment which had remained in Belfast and included many Irish were disarmed.

The provisions and the Lagan forces arrived only just in time, for on 12 August Castlehaven's cavalry crossed the Bann and fell on some of Monro's men guarding a pass near Dromore. Seventy-two musketeers resisted the Irish but were driven back after thirty were killed and 'all the rest desperately wounded'. Further hard-fought skirmishes followed and in the end the Irish attack was halted. Monro was then able to advance his army over the Bann to Armagh, forcing the Irish back to Charlemont. Stalemate ensued. As Castlehaven put it 'neither of us being able to engage the other, we lay in a pretty good correspondence, and the small war we had was chiefly in cutting parties and convoys'. Monro's difficulties with the British and lack of supplies were paralleled on the Irish side. Castlehaven blamed Owen Roe O'Neill for obstructing his advance by refusing to co-operate; Owen Roe in reply accused Castlehaven of incompetence amounting to treachery. Many of Castlehaven's supplies had at first come through Ormond's garrisons of Drogheda, Dundalk and Newry. He had demanded virtual possession of Newry from Edmund Mathews (and cellarage for 'certaine wines'), but though Mathews refused this he allowed Castlehaven to obtain provisions from Newry and sent him intelligence of Monro's movements. Monro's advance to Armagh, however, cut off these supplies, and soon the lack of food among the Irish was acute.

Each army hung on stubbornly, neither strong enough to attack the other, each hoping to starve the other into retreat. On 1 September Monro and his officers discussed the possibility of withdrawing, but they decided unanimously to remain in the field, whatever misery this entailed, until the Irish were beaten or retreated—though the Lagan army was only persuaded to stay by offers of food and money from Monro. Next day the resolution of Monro was strengthened by the arrival of food to feed the army until 18 September, and soon after this more food arrived from Holland, 'whereof wee were glade for releefe of the poore countrey people'. Pressure on the Irish was maintained by sending out raiding parties to interfere with their supply convoys and fall on their patrols; on the night of 10 September, for example, a raiding party of cavalry was sent out, and to divert Irish attention from it a large number of trumpeters and drummers alarmed them by simulating the approach of a large army.

On 13 September, since it seemed possible that the stalemate might continue indefinitely, Monro began construction of a semi-permanent camp with houses and huts for his men. A second motive for this was 'to wearie the Enemy' by showing them that he was prepared to stay in the field for as long as necessary. It may well be that news of Monro's camp did indeed prove the last straw to Castlehaven. On 15 September intelligence reports, probably inspired by the Irish themselves, indicated that they were moving to intercept provisions being sent to Monro from Carrickfergus. In fact Castlehaven had withdrawn his army southwards in the night, rather than see it continue to waste away through sickness and desertion. Castlehaven camped at Clones, the move having shortened his supply routes and made them much less vulnerable to attack by Monro.

After waiting a few days for supplies Monro began to advance after Castlehaven, but he got no further than Tynan. There he was delayed for a week by bad weather rendering the rivers and bogs almost impassable. His men occupied themselves by scouring the countryside for food and fuel. But this work in the rain, after a long campaign in which food had always been scarce led to many of his men falling sick—most of the cavalry had already had to be sent back to its quarters. The soldiers' clothes were worn, most were without shoes or stockings. The majority even of the officers were living on 'Greddan meale [a coarse kind of oatmeal] and watter'. Nonetheless Monro and his officers resolved to remain in the field as long as the weather permitted, living off food plundered from the enemy. Not until 7 October, when it had become clear that Castlehaven had no intention of advancing again, did Monro and his army return across the Bann to their quarters.[12]

12. For Castlehaven's campaign see Carte, *Ormond*, I, 515-16, III, 337, Gilbert,

The New Scots in Ireland, 1644-1646

The honours of the 1644 campaign in Ulster undoubtedly went to Monro. In spite of the difficulties he had faced in the early part of the year, he had taken the initiative by attacking Castlehaven; and though Castlehaven had recovered quickly and followed him back into Ulster. Monro had successfully held him back and then forced him to retreat. Castlehaven's much vaunted army had got no further than Owen Roe O'Neill had got on his own the previous year. Castlehaven himself agrued that he had been successful in that he had prevented the other three provinces from being troubled by the Scots,[13] but this was only partly true—Monro had caused widespread panic in Leinster—and anyway the confederates had intended him to conquer Ulster, not just to contain the Scots. The great effort of the Irish had achieved nothing, partly through Monro's determination, partly through their own mistakes. The failure demoralised the confederates and intensified divisions among them, as Castlehaven and Owen Roe heaped recriminations on each other. Only one part of the 1644 plan for defeating the Scots had had any success at all—Antrim's invasion of Scotland. But the success was too long delayed to be of any help to Castlehaven. News of Montrose's first victory, Tippermuir, had probably not reached him by the time he retreated from Charlemont.

The failure of Castlehaven greatly enhanced the reputation of the New Scots as invincible champions of the Protestant cause in Ireland. Even in Cork the Protestants praised Monro for diverting the Irish from them; 'Were it not for the Scots in [the] North, which holds them hard to it, they would have been with us long since'. Many Protestants even outside Ulster were becoming convinced that Ormond and the king were not protecting Protestant interests in Ireland, and that Monro and the other allies of the English parliament in Ulster were more effective protectors. In July Lord Inchiquin and Protestant forces in Munster deserted Ormond and declared in favour of the English parliament, and it seems likely that among the

Contemporary History, I, 81-8, 203; Gilbert, *Irish Confederation*, III, 11-13, 230-1; Tuchet, *Castlehaven's Review*, pp. 49-53; *C.S.P.I. 1647-60* pp. 263-4; Young, *Old Belfast*, pp. 231-4; Hogan, *Warr of Ireland*, pp. 38-42; H.M.C. 63: *Egmont*, I, i, 238-9; Baillie, *Letters*, II, 232-3; Carte MSS, 12, ff. 3, 9, 48, 101, 120, 371, 446; Colles, *History of Ulster*, III, 69-70. Monro wrote a detailed account of the campaign but unfortunately only the sections dealing with the periods 25 July to 12 August and 1 to 21 September have survived, S.R.O. PA.7/23/2/26.
13. Tuchet, *Castlehaven's Review*, p. 53.

influences that persuaded them to do so was news of Monro's successes in Leinster.[14]

Ormond thus found himself becoming increasingly isolated. First most of the British of Ulster and now the Protestants of Munster defied him. In July he had concluded that his best interests lay in the continued enmity and balanced power of the Irish and the Scots,[15] so he could play them off against each other and neither would attack him. By the end of 1644 the enmity was still there, but the balance of power seemed to be swinging in favour of the Scots.

ii. Financial and Political Problems, 1644-1646

Like all the previous promises of the English parliament to the Scottish army in Ireland, those made in March and April 1644 were not kept in full. The £60,000 sterling was paid, but payment was not completed until well into 1645. The £4,000 sterling monthly promised was not paid at all. There were long delays over formally commissioning Robert Monro to command all parliament's forces in Ireland and George Monro to command the horse troops adjoined to the New Scots. Complaints to the English parliament were only considered after long delays, and even once considered little was usually done. In July 1644 the Scottish parliament appointed commissioners to reside with the army in Ulster, to form (in conjunction with English commissioners) a committee of both kingdoms to supervise the war there, as had been agreed in April. But, as the Scots complained in December, the English failed to appoint commissioners so the committee could not function. In October two of the Scots commissioners were ordered to go to Ireland to report on the state of the army. Whether they went or not is uncertain; if they did the army evidently did not trust them to represent its grievances adequately, for in December George Monro was in Edinburgh describing conditions in Ulster and warning that unless the army was speedily supplied it would have to disband.

The covenanters had in fact been doing their best to make up for the failure of the English to pay the army. In June 1644 the Scottish parliament had set up a committee to consider

14. H.M.C. 63: *Egmont*, I, i, 241; Bagwell, *Stuarts*, II, 59-61.
15. Carte, *Ormond*, III, 337.

the army's plight, and on 10 July, presumably as a result of its deliberations, a contract was signed for delivery of 10,000 bolls of meal to Monro's army by the end of August, and powers were granted to compel ship owners to carry it to Ireland. On 27 July orders were given for payment of £14,000 sterling to the army. Attempts were also made to supply the British forces. In August it was proposed that the earl of Lothian (who had returned from a mission to France) should go to Ireland to take up his post of lieutenant general, superseding Monro in command of both the New Scots and the British. The English agreed but in the event Lothian never went. It is probable that Monro and his officers protested at the idea of being commanded by one of the absentee officers they had long denounced, though they continued to demand that such officers be sent to take up their posts; on 2 January 1645 the committee of estates announced that all officers who were absent without valid reasons were to return to Ulster by 15 January or they would be replaced. The many soldiers who had fled to Scotland to escape continuing misery and starvation were to suffer death without mercy if they failed to return.[16]

Raising money in Scotland for the New Scots was becoming increasingly difficult. On 9 September 1644 Lord Balmerino wrote that some new source would have to be found quickly; 'without some such supply ... we may give over, for the borrowing of money is dried, and the excise [which Balmerino himself had taken a leading part in introducing] is like to be unfortunate first and last'. The scheme Balmerino had in mind was to obtain Dutch help in subduing the Irish rebels. The Dutch had been allowed to subscribe money in 1642 as adventurers, and attempts had been made to raise money in Holland for the Scottish army in England.[17] Balmerino now wrote to Sir Archibald Johnston of Wariston in London 'of what I told you before your last parting hence, for engaging the Hollanders with us in Ireland, whereof you have a fair ground from Generall Major Monro's letters sent you from

---

16. *A.P.S.* VI, i, 102, 123, 128, 142-3, 215, 222-3; Balfour, *Historical Works*, III, 181, 237; Meikle, *Correspondence*, pp. 40-1, 51, 55; McNeill, *Tanner Letters*, p. 177; *C.S.P.D. 1644-5*, pp. 200-1, 202, 230, 277, 333, 605; S.R.O. PA.11/3, ff. 26v-27, 71v, 75v, 79, 131-131v, 140v-141, 165.
17. Bottigheimer, *English Money and Irish Land*, p. 51; Stevenson, 'Financing of the cause of the covenants', *S.H.R.* LI, 103.

this committee; the town of Galway, and others, being in Inchiquin's hands, would be excellent invitations, as cautionary towns for them'.[18] The origins and details of the plan are obscure; though it may have been discussed in London nothing came of it, so the army continued to exist on the irregular shipments of money and food from England and Scotland, supplemented by what Ulster itself could provide.

The demands made by the army on the inhabitants of the province were increasingly severe. Monro was forced to act ruthlessly in levying contributions of food in order to remain in the field against Castlehaven, and the army's demands did not cease with the end of the campaign. In March 1646 Lord Claneboye's tenants complained that 1,500 New Scots were now, and 2,000 had been in the past, quartered on them.[19] Regular assessments were exacted in Belfast in food, money and services of boats and baggage horses for the garrison of about 400 men of Home's regiment, and similar assessments were raised elsewhere.[20] On 10 January 1645 a desperate petition to Scotland from Newtownards stated that 'The whole armie for these seaven weeks bypast, hes beene eating the meal out of our mowthes, and now they are fallen vpon that that should sowe the ground, which hes occasioned in many partes the giveing over of plowing'. If the seed grain was being eaten there was a serious danger of famine later in the year.[21]

That this petition did not exaggerate the seriousness of the situation was indicated by letters dispatched by the officers of the army the day before. George Monro was again commissioned to carry the army's appeals—to the English and Scottish parliaments, to Leven and Lothian, and to the general assembly of the church of Scotland. The letters contained the by now familiar denunciations of broken promises, threats that the

18. D. Dalrymple, Lord Hailes, ed. *Memorials and Letters relating to the History of Britain in the Reign of Charles the First* (Glasgow, 1766), pp. 154-5. The dating of the letter is by day and month only. Dalrymple suggested 1645 as the year but this cannot be right as the letter is dated from Edinburgh and by September 1645 the city had been abandoned by the covenanting regime because of an epidemic of plague. In spite of Balmerino's statement, Galway was not in fact in Inchiquin's hands.

19. *A.P.S.* VI, i, 376-7; Balfour, *Historical Works*, III, 210; S.R.O. PA.11/5, f. 112v.

20. R. M. Young, ed. *The Town Book of the Corporation of Belfast, 1613-1816* (Belfast, 1892), pp. 30-1, 34-7, 40, 41; Carte MSS, 13, f. 3.

21. N.L.S. Wodrow MSS, folio XXV, f. 52.

army would have to leave Ireland unless action was taken, and warnings of the evil consequences that would follow. The English parliament was told that the army was 'finding the Extremities soe pressing as we can no longer subsist without speedy Remedy to that Disease, which will putt this Kingdome totally from your Obedience, and strengthen the malignant Partie in both Kingdomes'. The Ayrshire committee of war was (it was hoped) to be stirred to action on the army's behalf by a warning that it would have to look to its own safety if the New Scots disbanded, as Irish invasion would probably follow. Also typical of earlier crises was the fact that Robert Monro was more willing to remain in Ireland than his officers. He signed the letters of 9 January along with them, but later in the month he wrote personally to the English parliament stressing that he would 'endeavour to contynue faithfull in the service to my Life's End; nothing will be able to divert me from the same (except Contempt, which I have not deserved)'.[22]

George Monro went first to the Scottish parliament. From it he got on 7 February a letter recommending him and the army's sufferings to the English parliament. The covenanters explained that they had hitherto tried to supply the army but that their other burdens (the war against Montrose) made it impossible for them to do so much in the future—though they did in fact sign a contract later in the month for the delivery of 10,734 bolls of oatmeal to Carrickfergus by 1 May.[23] George Monro got equally little satisfaction in London. The committee of both kingdoms agreed that £16,000 sterling of the £60,000 promised nearly a year before was still unpaid, and that the £4,000 sterling monthly had never been paid, so £44,000 of it was now payable, but offered little satisfaction. Monro and the Scots commissioners in London pressed the need for haste, but pressure of business led parliament to delay considering the matter; 'This makes George mutine feircly and tell his mind bot too freely'. On 21 March parliament proposed to pay the New Scots £6,000 sterling as part of their arrears, a tiny sum compared with the total due. By this time George Monro had left for Ireland, as a time limit had been put on his stay,

22. T.S.A.I. pp. 85-90; *L.J.* VII, 220; H.M.C. 5: *6th Report*, p. 48; Reid, *History of the Presbyterian Church*, I, 563-4; Peterkin, *Records of the Kirk*, p. 431.
23. Balfour, *Historical Works*, III, 261, 268; *L.J.* VII, 220; *C.S.P.D. 1644-5*, p. 292; *A.P.S.* VI, i, 331-2.

leaving the army's interests in the hands of the Scots commissioners. They protested that the money offered was inadequate, and listed broken promises and votes passed but not implemented whereby 'that army received nothing but the votes'.

The reactions of the army itself were similar. On hearing from George Monro that there was no hope of adequate payment many naturally favoured leaving Ireland. But in the end it was resolved to stay. The officers claimed that this decision was the result of realisation that their withdrawal would bring more danger and suffering to Scotland (by leaving her open to further Irish invasion) than to England, the country responsible for their plight. In fact the officers probably also calculated that once they left Ireland without permission and disbanded they would have even less hope of getting their arrears paid than if they hung on in Ireland.[24]

Just as in early 1644 the stay of the majority of the army in Ulster may have been facilitated by the removal of many of the officers most determined to leave (in the three regiments which returned to Scotland), so in 1645 the return of more officers to Scotland may have rid the army of some of the most disgruntled officers. In December 1644 or January 1645 Auchinbreck and all or most of his regiment left to help Argyll to resist Montrose. After the Campbells were routed at Inverlochy the Scottish parliament instructed Lothian (as lieutenant general of the New Scots) to order Robert Monro to send 1,000 men to Scotland, promising that replacements for them would be sent to Ulster; Monro's veteran soldiers, it was hoped, would be more effective against Montrose than the raw levies that would be sent to replace them. On 1 March the number of men to come from Ireland was raised to fourteen companies of 100 men, plus officers for two regiments. Ten days later, when the committee of estates instructed James MacDowall of Garthland and Sir William Cochrane of Cowdoun to go to Ireland to get the men the total had again risen, to 1,500 of the ablest and best armed men, and more if the army could spare them, together with whatever British forces could be persuaded to come to Scotland. To encourage

24. *C.S.P.D. 1644-5*, pp. 320, 333, 334, 336, 341, 348, 353, 357, 361; H.M.C. 29: *Portland*, I, 213, 215; Laing, *Correspondence*, I, 179; Meikle, *Correspondence*, pp. 63, 64; *C.J.* IV, 84, 86, 94, 120-1; *L.J.* VII, 282; McNeill, *Tanner Letters*, pp. 187-8; T.S.A.I. pp. 93-4.

the army to co-operate it was to be warned that failure to send the men would protract the war in Scotland and thus prevent supplies being sent to the army.[25]

By 4 April 1,400 men had reached Scotland with Sir William Cochrane, this evidently being all the army was willing to send. They were drawn equally from the New Scots regiments, though it was said they included both Irish and English recruited in Ireland. They were treated as a regiment in Scotland and Colonel Robert Home served as their commander; his lieutenant colonel, John Maxwell, took over the command of his New Scots regiment. It was promised that Scots levies would be sent to replace the men removed from Ireland but this was not done; all possible men were needed for service against Montrose. Robert Monro was voted a gold chain worth 2,000 merks for his co-operation in providing men for use against Montrose, but rumour said that only threats had persuaded him to agree to weaken his army.[26]

New demands were soon made on the army. After further victories by Montrose it was proposed in the Scottish parliament on 1 August 'that Generall Maior Monro be presently sent for wnto Irland, to be Generall of thir forces, and that he repair heir with all speed, and bring a 1000 musqueteirs with him; and that Sir William Cochrane be sent to Irland for him'. Monro was to bring the men to Scotland by 8 September and replace Lieutenant General William Baillie as commander in chief in Scotland. Before these orders could be carried out Baillie was again defeated, at Kilsyth, and Sir William Cochrane was joined in Ireland by the earls of Glencairn and Cassillis. The latter brought orders that Monro was to return to Scotland with his whole army.[27] Even though the move to Scotland involved promotion for him, Robert Monro (who had so often shown his preference for staying in Ireland) can hardly have welcomed the orders, and he must have been thankful for Montrose's defeat at Philiphaugh which rendered them obsolete.

By the time news of Philiphaugh arrived the army in Ireland had agreed that it was its duty to send 2,100 men, 'the most

25. Guthry, *Memoirs*, pp. 175, 183-4; *A.P.S.* VI, i, 357, 363-4; Balfour, *Historical Works*, III, 286, 287; S.R.O. PA.11/4, ff. 4-5, 11v-12.

26. S.R.O. PA.11/4, ff. 41v-43, 50; *C.S.P.I.*, *1647-60*, p. 634; T.S.A.I. pp. 91-4, 96; *A.P.S.* VI, i, 435; S.R.O. PA.7/3/144; Carte MSS, 14, ff. 297, 352, 384.

27. Balfour, *Historical Works*, III, 301; *A.P.S.* VI, i, 450-1; H.M.C. 10: *10th Report*, I, 55; S.R.O. PA.11/4, ff. 139v, 163.

considerable parte of our Army', to Scotland, but strict conditions were attached to the offer—though it may be that these were not decided on until after Philiphaugh, when the officers knew that their country's need for help was not so urgent as it had previously been. Before sending help the army insisted that it be sent a month's supplies; that it be assured that its rights would not be prejudiced by sending men out of Ireland without England's consent; that the absentee noble colonels resign 'so that the militia be not made ane monopolie contrare to the custome of all kingdomes' (many of the colonels had regiments in England or Scotland as well as in Ireland); and that 2,000 new recruits be sent to the army from Scotland. The committee of estates, still fearing Montrose would succeed in raising a new army, agreed to open negotiations with the army about these conditions. Instructions were issued on 7 November for Argyll and Sir William Cochrane to proceed to Ireland and promise the army, if it sent men to Argyllshire with all possible speed, fair treatment and one month's supplies. But the request that absentee colonels should resign was rejected. As Robert Monro was known to be reluctant to leave Ireland and George Monro had emerged as one of the most influential officers in the army, the latter was offered command of the men who came to Scotland and the rank of major general. The 2,100 men from Ireland were to form three foot regiments and a cavalry squadron of four troops. Blank commissions for the officers of the force were drawn up and entrusted to Argyll. In addition to the New Scots, Sir Frederick Hamilton was to be requested to bring his British regiment to Scotland.[28]

Before Argyll and Cowdoun could leave for Ireland, however, a letter arrived from Robert Monro announcing that the army was no longer willing to send men to Scotland. This sudden change of heart was the first fruit of the arrival in Ulster of commissioners from the English parliament to form part of a committee of both kingdoms—Arthur Annesley, Sir Robert King and Colonel William Beale. They arrived late in October, and the Scots had intended that Argyll and Cowdoun, along with Robert Monro, should join them to

---

28. S.R.O. PA.11/4, ff. 157v, 162-162v, 164-164v; T.S.A.I. pp. 95-8; Inveraray Vaults, Argyll Letters, II, nos. 33-41 (mentioned in H.M.C. 5: *6th Report*, p. 625). Confusingly some sources refer to 2,500 men rather than 2,100 to be brought from Ireland.

form the committee of both kingdoms. But on hearing of the attitude of the English commissioners Argyll and Cowdoun remained in Scotland.[29]

The decision to send commissioners to Ulster was far from indicating that at last the English parliament was going to take to heart the interests of the Scottish army in Ireland. On the contrary, it was in part a symptom of the increasing tension between parliament and the covenanters. Many parliamentarians in England were bitterly resentful of what they saw as Scottish interference in English affairs, and they were determined to exclude the Scots from any major part in a peace settlement there. To those with such views the victories of the royalist Montrose in Scotland seemed at times almost welcome, as they led to the weakening of the Scottish army in England and diverted the attention of the Scots to their own affairs. Parliament was now clearly gaining the upper hand in the English civil war, and many in it were resolved to give the Scots as little credit as possible for helping to bring about this victory. Already some saw the Scottish army in England as a potential enemy rather than as an ally. In such calculations the Scottish army in Ireland inevitably had a place. If it, or part of it, returned to Scotland it might enable the covenanters to mop up quickly the remaining royalist and Irish resistance, and then reinforce their army in England. This would be against parliament's interests. Its commissioners therefore persuaded the army not to send men to Scotland, doubtless by warning them that this would be a breach of the treaty if done without English consent, and would therefore lead to the army forfeiting its right to payment of arrears.

Though Monro's army might be regarded as a lesser potential danger to the English parliament in Ireland than in Scotland, it nonetheless was a danger. Parliament intended to turn to the conquest of Ireland once the king was defeated in England, and it did not wish the Scots to play a leading part in this. Scots pretensions in Ulster were therefore to be checked. A parliamentary and English interest was to be built up there independent of the Scottish interest; many in England had long wished to do this, but the declaration of Inchiquin in

---

29. S.R.O. PA.11/4, ff. 163, 170v, 171; Meikle, *Correspondence*, pp. 138-9; *C.J.* IV, 109; *L.J.* VII, 350, VIII, 192-3; *C.S.P.D. 1645-7*, p. 134; Bodleian Library, Rawlinson MSS, A.258, f. 1; Balfour, *Historical Works*, III, 332; Cox, *Hibernica Anglicana*, II, 160; Carte, *Ormond*, I, 537.

favour of parliament had diverted attention to Munster in late 1644 and early 1645.[30] One of the basic requirements for establishing such an English interest was possession of a major Ulster port. From the autumn of 1645 onwards the English parliament therefore repeatedly demanded that the New Scots give up Belfast. It was argued that they held, by the 1642 treaty, the two other ports convenient for landing supplies from England, Carrickfergus and Coleraine, so it was only reasonable that the English should have Belfast. This would give the British forces in eastern Ulster a safe base to retreat to in case of necessity, and a convenient magazine from which they could receive supplies from parliament.[31] In reply it could of course have been argued that Belfast could perform these functions while still in Scots hands. But the Scots were no longer trusted to exercise control of Belfast in parliament's interests, and supplying the British through the New Scots gave the latter too much power over the former. Parliament also wanted a port so it could, if necessary, land its own forces in Ulster safely even if the new Scots opposed them.

On 24 December 1645 the English commissioners formally ordered Colonel Robert Home (who had returned to Ireland) and the other Scots officers in Belfast to hand the town over to them. The officers refused to act without consulting Robert Monro, and he insisted on referring the matter to Leven and the Scottish parliament. A long and wordy controversy ensued. The English claimed the Scots had no right to Belfast. They replied that the treaty allowed them to garrison places taken from the rebels, and that Colonel Chichester had been in rebellion when driven out by Monro, as he had accepted the cessation and had obeyed the royalist Ormond. In any case, New Scots had been quartered in Belfast from their arrival in 1642 to early 1644. These arguments the English rejected, but Monro and his officers refused to submit, insisting that their army would have to leave Ireland if it lost Belfast. This was a point that the English were not ready to take up, for the safety of Ulster still depended on the New Scots; parliament was not yet able to replace them with its own troops.

Arguments between the English commissioners and the New Scots soon spread to other matters. Monro attempted to

30. Bottingheimer, *English Money and Irish Land*, pp. 90-2.
31. *C.S.P.I. 1633-47*, p. 417; *L.J.* VII, 697-8, VIII, 10, 11, 12, 14; *C.J.* IV, 353; Bodleian Library, Rawlinson MSS, A.258, ff. lv-2.

make up for the 1,400 men he had sent to Scotland by recruiting in Ulster; this was denounced as contrary to the treaty. Five horse troops had been raised in Ulster by New Scots officers (on advice from Scotland) to replace troops which had accepted the 1643 cessation. These were commanded by Auchinbreck, Robert and George Monro, Lieutenant Colonel William Cunningham and Lieutenant Colonel John Hamilton. Auchinbreck's had been disbanded after his death and the English now demanded that the other four disband. 'Oppression' of the inhabitants of Ulster by the New Scots was denounced; in future provisions were only to be raised with the consent of the English commissioners. Any renewal of attempts to send men to Scotland were to be resisted as 'destructive to the service'. Transporting horses or cattle to Scotland was forbidden.[32]

While the English commissioners in Ulster supervised and criticised Monro's army, parliament in London eroded the concessions formerly granted to it. In 1643-4 rather than abandon Ireland altogether parliament had agreed to Monro having command of all its forces there. This had been agreed (along with other points) by the 'treaty' at Edinburgh on 28 November 1643, which had been ratified by parliamentary ordinances of 9 March and 11 April 1644. But in December 1645 a grand committee of both houses resolved to abolish the united command, so Monro would no longer have power over the British. When the Scots commissioners protested that this was a breach of the November 1643 treaty they were told that it was not a treaty but an informal agreement; Monro's position as commander in chief in Ireland rested solely on resolutions of parliament which it could repeal without consulting the Scots. Parliament had never previously objected to the Scots calling the agreement a treaty, and on at least one occasion the house of commons itself had called it one,[33] so the indignation of the Scots commissioners at this disclaimer was justified; 'if these articles may be infringed, wee knowe not what a Treaty is, nor what wee may trust unto hereafter'. The quarrel between parliament and the Scots over

---

32. Bodleian Library, Rawlinson MSS, A.258, ff. 4v-5v; McNeill, *Tanner Letters*, pp. 105-6; *C.S.P.I. 1633-47*, pp. 393-4, 428, 441, 444, 446, 448, 460, 560-1; Balfour, *Historical Works*, III, 357; *A.P.S.* VI, i, 578; *L.J.* VIII, 180; Rushworth, *Historical Collections*, IV, i, 248; Hogan, *Warr of Ireland*, p. 186; T.S.A.I. p. 116.
33. *C.J.* III, 681.

peace proposals to be presented to the king was now bitter, and in the months that followed an additional element in it was the insistence of the Scots that the 'treaty' of November 1643 be mentioned in the propositions, and parliament's assertion that there was no such treaty, only some temporary concessions.[34] With this prolonged argument over his position in progress Monro's authority over the British naturally was weakened.

In February 1646 the Scottish parliament decided to try again to get military aid from Monro's army, and commissioned Argyll, Garthland and John Kennedy to cross to Ireland. An immediate difficulty was that no money was available to pay for transporting men from Ireland, but this problem was solved by agreeing to accept an immediate payment of 120,000 merks from the earl of Queensberry; a fine of 180,000 merks had been imposed on him for trying to join Montrose after Kilsyth, and the committee for moneys (on the recommendation of the committee of estates) now agreed to remit one-third of the fine provided the rest was paid promptly.[35]

It was later alleged that 'the marquis of Argyle was appointed to go into Ireland, and bring over the Scots army from thence; that being strengthened with that accession, their power might be so formidable to the English, as to make them, to eschew a national quarrel, deal more thankfully with them'.[36] This of course was exactly what the English parliament feared, but in reality it was at most a secondary motive. The real purpose of again trying to obtain men from Ireland under George Monro was to use them to clear Alasdair MacColla and his Irish and Highlanders from Argyllshire. This was why Argyll himself was taking such a prominent part in the negotiations; until the rebels were driven from his estates his power and reputation in Scotland would remain much reduced. That this was the real motive was made clear by a list of desires Argyll presented to the committee of estates on 14 March, asking for clarification of some of the instructions given to him about concessions to the New Scots. The points

34. Meikle, *Correspondence*, p. 147; H.M.C. 29: *Portland*, I, 326; *L.J.* VIII, 64-5, 217-18, 238; Rushworth, *Historical Collections*, IV, i, 256.
35. *A.P.S.* VI, i, 596, 756; S.R.O. PA.14/3, Register of the Committee for Moneys (South), 1646, pp. 40-2.
36. Guthry, *Memoirs*, p. 213.

included a request for definition of what powers he and George Monro were to have to negotiate with rebels in Argyllshire and Highland Perthshire.[37]

When Argyll, Garthland and Kennedy reached Ireland in mid-April they found that the New Scots were still in no mood to co-operate. The officers had just written to the Scots commissioners in London reiterating their grievances and complaining that 'we may by former proceeding easilie conjecture we will be suffered to stand and fall by ourselves'. If nothing was done Scotland's interest in Ireland would be lost and 'we with our sufferings utterlie forgot without any hope of recoverie or satisfaction'. Their needs were so well known that 'we need not insist at this time in repetition of particulars'. Argyll's request for 2,100 foot and 240 horse (as well as some British if possible) was, therefore, answered by a long list of demands by the army. Men must be sent to replace any that left. The earls of Crawford-Lindsay (the former earl of Lindsay) and Eglinton had undertaken to resign as colonels, and it was demanded that Glencairn and Argyll follow suit. The main stumbling block to agreement proved to be the question of the command of the army. George Monro was ready to lead men back to Scotland as a major general only on condition that he be subordinate only to the earl of Callander, David Leslie (both of whom were lieutenant generals) and Leven, and that he retain his rank of major general on his return to Ireland after the rebels in Scotland were defeated. To make this possible his uncle Robert Monro must be promoted to the rank of lieutenant general or general of the army in Ireland, following the resignation of Leven or Lothian.

Argyll and his colleagues urged that the best way for the army to create the good will in Scotland which would lead to its grievances being redressed was for it to send men to help Scotland willingly. If there was any delay Scotland might think the army disloyal, and the question of command was a formality which could be settled later. But the army refused to compromise. Garthland was sent to the committee of estates to settle the question of command, but the committee also proved stubborn. Probably neither Leven nor Lothian were willing to resign, and in any case as in the past the committee

37. S.R.O. PA.11/4, ff. 196v-199.

John Lindsay, earl of Crawford-Lindsay. Colonel of a regiment of the Scottish army in Ireland. Anonymous portrait 1663.

was doubtless unwilling to let the army dictate to it. In mid-May Argyll himself returned to Scotland, with another letter from the army complaining that its demands sent with Garthland had not been answered. This was the end of the episode. The committee abandoned the scheme for bringing men from Ireland. Argyll tried to use his own regiment in Ireland to reconquer Islay and Kintyre in May, but his men seem to have retreated hastily to Ireland in the face of superior enemy forces. The clearing of Argyllshire of rebels was therefore delayed for another year, and was then undertaken without help from Ireland.[38]

The New Scots were becoming increasingly isolated. By refusing to send men to Scotland they had offended the government of their native land, which had done much to supply them in previous years. They had insulted Argyll by replying to his personal plea for men to drive the rebels from his lands with a demand that he resign his post as a colonel in the army. In refusing to help Scotland they had of course pleased the English commissioners in Ulster, but on the other hand the commissioners were infuriated by their refusal to give up Belfast or to co-operate in other matters. In any case it was obvious that the English were determined to control strictly the activities of Monro's army. But after so many disappointments the army seems to have decided that it would achieve most for itself by insisting on remaining in Ireland and retaining the positions it held. For, in spite of earlier withdrawals to Scotland, the army was still a formidable force, and it probably counted on the fact that none of the factions in the political confusion of the three kingdoms would act in a way which would drive the New Scots into the hands of its enemies if this could be avoided. The estates of Scotland might deeply resent its disobedience, but feared that an open denunciation of such treachery might force it to declare for the English parliament, or even the king, for its own protection against the vengeance of the covenanters. The English commissioners in Ulster might be resolved to curtail its power,

38. T.S.A.I. pp. 98-9, 101-8; Meikle, *Correspondence*, p. 66; Guthry, *Memoirs*, p. 220. While in Ulster Argyll also had talks with British leaders, staying with Sir Robert Stewart at Culmore for two nights; and though he obtained no men for service in Argyllshire (except from his own regiment), he did manage to send 300 bolls of meal from Ulster to his garrisons, *Joint Print of Documents in causa His Grace ... the Duke of Argyll ... against Angus John Campbell of Dunstaffnage ...* (Edinburgh, 1911), pp. 176-7. See Stevenson, *Alasdair MacColla*, pp. 221-2.

but to treat it too harshly might provoke it into breaking with parliament altogether; it was known that the covenanters were secretly negotiating with the king, and the New Scots might join an alliance against their nominal paymasters. And in any case both the English and the Scots still needed the New Scots for the same reason that they had needed them in 1642; to prevent the Irish conquering Ulster.

The fast changing political scene in 1645-6 also brought about alterations in Monro's relations with Ormond and the British. After his seizure of Belfast in May 1644 and the general acceptance in Ulster of the solemn league and covenant, Monro's hold on the British had been strong. His successful resistance to Castlehaven had strengthened it further. In September 1644 some ministers in the Route of Antrim had set up a rival presbytery to that established by the New Scots in an attempt to free themselves from Scottish domination, but they failed to win much support and soon had to submit.[39] Monro's attempts in July to enter Dundalk and Newry temporarily increased suspicion of him among the British, but the only alternative to recognising his authority as the English parliament's commander in chief was to obey Ormond, who could not supply them and whose negotiations with the confederate Irish seemed to most a greater threat to English Protestant interests than domination by presbyterian Scots.

So strong was this feeling that late in 1644 some of the officers of Ormond's Drogheda garrison opened secret negotiations with Monro; fearing Ormond would betray them to the Irish, they resolved to hand over Drogheda to the Scots. Lady Moore, widow of a former governor of the town, played a leading part in the plot, taking wax impressions of keys to help the plotters seize control. Second thoughts and a lingering suspicion of the Scots led to modification of the plan. Monro was asked, instead of occupying the town, only to provide help (in return for half the property of papists, who were to be driven out of the town) until the English parliament sent troops to garrison it. Monro agreed to the plot, but had its execution delayed from 22 December 1644 to 22 January 1645, to allow him to complete his preparations.

39. Reid, *History of the Presbyterian Church*, I, 494-7; Adair, *True Narrative*, pp. 120-2.

On the latter date he was to march 2,500 men to Carrick-macross (County Monaghan) and bring a small force to Drogheda itself. A similar plot developed to betray Dundalk to Monro, and one of his officers held secret talks with sympathisers in Dublin. But the plots were thwarted by Major Seafoule Gibson, who learnt of the Drogheda plot and informed Ormond. The plotters were arrested and sent to Dublin.[40]

The plots thus failed, but their existence indicates the extent to which many British, even in Ormond's Leinster forces, were coming to regard Monro as the lesser of two evils. His authority was further strengthened in May 1645 when a large meeting of British officers in Antrim pledged themselves to obey him.[41]

Not surprisingly Monro's relations with Ormond continued to deteriorate. New Scots stole 140 cattle from Ormond's Greencastle garrison; Monro promised restitution but it was never made. In June and July 1645 Edmund Mathews was busy constructing fortifications near Greencastle to resist attack by Monro, while Monro in turn feared that the Greencastle and Newry garrisons intended to raid his quarters.[42] The king had apparently not realised (until the propositions of Uxbridge were presented to him by parliament late in 1644) that the English had appointed Monro commander in chief in Ireland. The royalists, partly for propaganda reasons, now expressed horror at parliament's action, asserting that 'in truth that whole Kingdom be thereby delivered into the hands' of the Scots, which was neither just, prudent or honourable. The Scots had 'wicked designs to gain an interest to themselves and their nation in the government of that Kingdom', and Ireland had been 'wholly given' to them by parliament. It was doubtless hoped that such allegations would stir up the Protestants of Ireland to resist the Scots through fear of their ambitions in Ireland. For good measure Ormond was informed that his estates in Ireland had been promised to the earl of Loudoun, the Scottish chancellor.[43]

40. Carte, *Ormond*, I, 524-7, III, 370; Gilbert, *Irish Confederation*, IV, 131-3. A report in Carte MSS, 13, f. 3 that Monro's forces were preparing for some sudden action early in December 1644 probably referred to his preparations to give support to the Drogheda plot.
41. Hill, *Montgomery Manuscripts*, pp. 162-4; Adair, *True Narrative*, p. 127; Gilbert, *Contemporary History*, I, 653-5.
42. Carte MSS, 14, ff. 572, 574, 15, ff. 57, 112, 222; Gilbert, *Irish Confederation*, IV, 287; Carte, *Ormond*, III, 414.
43. Carte, *Ormond*, II, 382, 383-4, 393-4; Gilbert, *Irish Confederation*, IV, 154;

In spite of this, however, Ormond was soon making advances to both the New Scots and the British in Ulster. His negotiations with the Irish for a peace between them and the king were getting nowhere. It was now obvious that the king had lost the English civil war and Ormond's bargaining position was therefore weak. But if he broke with the Irish he would need allies in order to resist them, and he believed he could find allies in Ulster. Many of the British had only declared for parliament through need of supplies from it to continue the war with the Irish, but parliament's promises of supplies had been badly kept. The meeting of British in Antrim in May 1645 which had promised to obey Monro had been mainly concerned with planning united action in demanding redress of grievances from parliament, and Ormond hoped to exploit this disillusionment. The New Scots, and indeed the covenanters as a whole, had similar grievances against parliament, which they found increasingly reluctant to supply Monro properly or to make a peace settlement in England acceptable to the Scots. The time therefore seemed ripe for trying to recreate a royalist party in Ulster. In this work Ormond's agent was Archdeacon Humphry Galbraith, 'a Scot by original, but well affected to Episcopacy and Monarchy, a man of very good sense and learning, great prudence and full as great resolution', as Thomas Carte described him. Galbraith was in close touch with many Ulster British officers, and also undertook to approach Robert Monro and some other New Scots officers who, it was thought, would be sympathetic; these included George Monro, Major Thomas Dalyell and Major George Gordon.

In October 1645 Galbraith travelled to Ulster to try to negotiate with the British and New Scots. Ormond proposed that the basis for the alliance should be the 1642 treaty; Monro would thus be subordinate to Ormond as lord lieutenant, and Ormond would also command the British; but he would appoint a commander in chief of the British who would be acceptable to Monro. No troops would be removed from Ireland without the consent of both Monro and Ormond, and Monro would send ammunition to Ormond's Leinster army to enable it to resist the Irish.

Gilbert, *Contemporary History*, I, 649-50; Gardiner, *Constitutional Documents*, pp. 278, 279; Dugdale, *A Short View of the Late Troubles*, pp. 838-41, 847, 851, 860, 948-51.

Robert Monro's first response to these proposals was favourable; he was trying to resist demands that he go to Scotland to oppose Montrose, and an agreement with Ormond would allow him to maintain that in refusing to go he was simply obeying the lord lieutenant according to the 1642 treaty. Moreover such an agreement would prevent Ormond co-operating with the Irish in sending aid to Montrose, and would thus help Scotland. But Galbraith's mission came too late to have any chance of success. Parliament, fearing the growing discontent of the British as well as the power of the New Scots, had dispatched its commissioners to Ulster, and they arrived there soon after Galbraith. They soon persuaded both Monro and the British that, as in 1644, they could not survive without supplies which only the English parliament could provide. Galbraith therefore had to report to Ormond that though the New Scots well knew that parliament intended to weaken them (in case the quarrel between England and Scotland came to a head), they still felt they could not afford to defy it. George Monro had shown himself especially favourable to agreement with Ormond but opinion in the army was against him and he insisted that his attitude be kept secret.[44]

The collapse of Galbraith's mission in Ulster forced Ormond back into negotiations with the Irish. The king, his armies in England defeated, had been demanding that he make a peace with them at all costs, but Ormond had delayed, reluctant to damage Protestant interests in Ireland by making concessions to the confederates. In March 1646 he signed a peace treaty with the Irish, though this remained a closely guarded secret for some months.[45] But at the same time that Charles was insisting that Ormond make an alliance with the Irish he was also working for an alliance with the Scots covenanters; he should have seen that the two policies were incompatible, but in his desperation he was clutching at straws. In Britain he expected the covenanters to co-operate with their hated enemy Montrose. In Ireland he sought the support of both the confederate Irish and their most consistent opponents, the New Scots. In January 1646 he was planning to establish with French help a fund to pay all the arrears of the New Scots

44. Carte, *Ormond*, I, 530-7, III, 432, 435-6; Cox, *Hibernica Anglicana*, II, 160-2; Gilbert, *Contemporary History*, I, 670-1.
45. Bagwell, *Stuarts*, II, 111-13; Carte, *Ormond*, I, 566.

and thus buy their support.[46] This particular plan got nowhere, but his general idea of reaching agreement with the covenanters succeeded—or almost did, for unfortunately the king and the covenanters never subsequently managed to agree on what the terms of their agreement were. In May 1646 Charles fled from Oxford and joined the Scottish army in England near Newark.

Meanwhile Ormond had, in April, opened negotiations with the three English commissioners in Ulster and the Scots who had recently joined them—Argyll, Garthland and John Kennedy—to form a committee of both kingdoms, of which Robert Monro was also a member. Ormond's intention was evidently to get some guarantee of protection for his Protestant forces; having made a secret treaty with the Irish he now feared for the fate of the British forces who remained loyal to him. In reply to his advances the Ulster committee insisted that before agreement could be reached he must undertake not to make a peace with the Irish, and must let New Scots and parliamentary forces reinforce Dublin and his other garrisons. In spite of the fact that he could not satisfy these conditions Ormond prepared to send commissioners to negotiate in Ulster, but in May the situation was abruptly changed by the news of the king's surrender to the Scottish army in England. On receiving the news Argyll hurried back to Scotland; he had failed to get Monro to agree to send troops to Scotland (except, it seems, from Argyll's own regiment) and in any case these might no longer be needed in the new circumstances created by the king's action.[47]

The reaction of the English parliament to the news that the king was now in the hands of the Scots was belief that the Scots had acted treacherously. The Scots commissioners in London denied that they had made any agreement with the king but news from Ireland soon arrived which seemed to prove the opposite. Whether in the belief that what he wrote was true or merely to encourage Ormond with good news, Charles had written to him stating that the Scottish army in England had agreed to fight for him, and that he hoped it would join with Montrose and English royalists. Ormond immediately sent a copy of the king's letter to Robert Monro, for the conclusions to be drawn from it seemed clear. If the

46. J. Bruce, ed. *Charles I in 1646* (Camden Society, 1856), p. 5; Fotheringham, *Correspondence*, I, 106.
47. Carte MSS, 17, ff. 40, 143, 146, 206, 214-15, 321, 337, 385.

covenanters in England had declared for the king, then surely the New Scots in Ireland thereby became the allies of Ormond, the king's representative. Ormond therefore proposed to open negotiations with Monro alone. Monro realised how much suspicion and hostility rumours of Ormond's action might cause between the English and the Scots in Ireland, and therefore hastily handed over Ormond's letter and the copy of the king's letter to the English commissioners.

Sir Robert King at once set off to present them to the English parliament. The Scots commissioners in London denounced the king's story when they heard of it as a 'most damnable Untruth', but publication of it intensified suspicion in parliament of the Scots, and of Robert Monro in particular; there was talk of impeaching him. This was most unfair, since it was he who had revealed the king's letter, and he would hardly have done so if he was really involved in some royalist plot against parliament. Argyll reached London in late June and delivered a spirited defence of Monro and his army before a grand committee of both houses. 'As for the Army in Ireland, I have been an Eye-witness to their Sufferings, and so may speak of it ... upon certain knowledge, That never men have suffered greater hardships, who might have been provided for: They have lived many times upon a few Beans measured out to them by number, and never had any other Drink but Water: And when they were in some better condition, they had but an Irish Peck of rough Oats for a whole week'. In the end no action was taken against Monro but it was obvious that the flight of the king to the Scots had increased the precariousness of his army's position in Ireland. If, as for a time seemed likely, war broke out between the covenanters and parliament, then the New Scots would have to choose between fighting for their countrymen (and thus abandoning hope of getting the English parliament to pay their arrears), and supporting parliament and betraying their country.[48]

iii.   The Campaigns of 1645 and 1646: Benburb

After the drama of 1644, with the thwarting of Castle-

---

48. Carte, *Ormond*, III, 455; Rushworth, *Historical Collections*, IV, i, 266-7, 272-4, 298-9; *L.J.* VII, 364-5, 365-6; *C.J.* 567; Gilbert, *Contemporary History* I, 675-6; Meikle, *Correspondence*, p. 192; Baillie, *Letters*, ii, 374-5; Whitelock, *Memorials of English Affairs*, II, 29, 30, 46.

haven's invasion of Ulster, the 1645 campaign proved an anti-climax. This was largely due to, in a word, Montrose; Monro was called on to send troops back to Scotland, and then to go there himself. Though some of these demands were resisted his army was weakened by the loss of perhaps 2,400 men, and with Montrose and the Irish victorious in Scotland behind his back he was naturally reluctant to undertake any ambitious projects in Ireland. Moreover even if he had wished to act vigorously, Montrose's successes hindered him from doing so by intensifying his usual supply problems. Scotland was concentrating her resources against Montrose and had little to spare for Ireland.

The lack of action in Ulster was, however, only in part the result of Monro's own decisions, for 'this year the Scottish and British Army had no Enemy to march against'.[49] Apart from Charlemont and a few tiny and remote garrisons, the Irish had virtually abandoned Ulster. Any forces that did venture into the province retired hurriedly on the merest rumour of a Scots advance. Monro thus had no enemy within easy reach of his headquarters at Carrickfergus; by the time he reached the borders of Ulster and began to approach large Irish forces his supplies were usually running out and his communication and supply lines were dangerously extended through difficult country. His movements early in the year are badly documented. Late in April Irish forces retreated into Cavan on a report that he was advancing, but the report seems to have been false. On 11 June and again early in July he was at Dundrum. In between the New Scots and British forces were said to be assembling, but they do not seem to have undertaken any expedition.[50]

In late May or June 1645 Sir Charles Coote landed in Ireland with a commission from the English parliament to be president of Connaught, and he asked for assistance from Monro. Since the previous December parliament had renewed its attempts to get the Ulster forces to send aid to the other provinces. A demand that 2,500 New Scots be sent into Connaught had been cancelled at the request of the Scots commissioners in London, but 2,000 Ulster British were ordered to be shipped to Munster (to help Inchiquin) and

49. Hogan, *Warr of Ireland*, p. 42.
50. Carte MSS, 14, f. 437, 15, ff. 57, 112, 222.

and 1,500 were told to march into Connaught. Nothing came of the Munster venture, and the Connaught one was much delayed. Monro was in no hurry to weaken his British forces unless he had to, and the British themselves had no wish to leave their native province. But Coote brought with him a new order from the committee of both kingdoms in London that he be given 1,500 British.[51] He at first ravaged County Galway and then moved north to besiege Sligo; for this task he demanded the help promised him from Ulster, and Monro reluctantly agreed to give it. Coote was able to assemble 4,500 men in County Tyrone, including many Old Scots, and on 8 July Sligo fell to his army. In spite of Irish reports to the contrary Monro had no direct part in this victory; Coote later complained that he had had much trouble in getting men from him, and that most of those sent were soon recalled to Ulster on news of Montrose's continued successes in Scotland. However, in mid-July the New Scots were reported to be on the march, and it may be that this was an expedition undertaken to prevent the Irish concentrating their forces against Coote.[52]

In late August Monro was again on the move, and a rather half-hearted attempt was made to besiege Charlemont. On 24 August he summoned Sir Phelim O'Neill to surrender Blackwatertown; on his refusal Monro marched on to Glaslough and Monaghan, according to one report venturing as far as Granard in County Longford. Fearing he was intending a major offensive the Irish again appealed to Ormond for help, but Monro soon retired; probably he had never intended to do more than alarm the Irish and plunder cattle and grain.[53]

In retrospect the inactivity in Ulster in 1645 can be seen as an interlude between major Irish efforts to break the deadlock which had existed since 1642. If anything, the balance of power in 1645 seemed to continue to move in favour of the Scots. Monro was able to march through the province at will, with only Charlemont held against him, and Coote's successes in Connaught distracted Irish attention from him.

The inspiration behind the new offensive attitude of the

51. *C.S.P.D. 1644-5*, pp. 200, 291, 294, 452, 487; Baillie, *Letters*, II, 264; Carte, *Ormond*, I, 535.
52. Bagwell, *Stuarts*, II, 95; Hogan, *Letters and Papers*, p. 190; Gilbert, *Irish Confederation*, IV, 353-6; Young, *Old Belfast*, p. 237; Aiazza, *Embassy*, pp. 51-3, 56; Carte MSS, 15, f. 278.
53. Carte MSS, 15, f. 497; Young, *Old Belfast*, p. 237; Hogan, *Warr of Ireland*, p. 43; Gilbert, *Irish Confederation*, V, 62, 64, 77.

Irish in Ulster in 1646 came from the newly arrived papal nuncio, Rinuccini. It was he who at last saw to it that Owen Roe O'Neill was adequately supplied and supported, and thus given a chance to put his military skills to effective use. Rinuccini resolved on his arrival in Ireland to give priority to defeating the Scots. 'Whether there be peace or no peace [with Ormond] ... at all events the war between this Kingdom, the Parliament and the Scots must go on. These last hold almost the whole of Ulster, and are only kept within that province by a few troops in garrison'.[54] One side of Rinuccini's determination to crush the New Scots was seen in his support for sending further aid to Montrose and Alasdair MacColla in Scotland; the other was his throwing his weight firmly behind Owen Roe O'Neill in the squabbles which divided the Irish confederates. Moreover Rinuccini had more than influence to offer; he had brought money and supplies from the continent, and in March 1646 he decided that the Ulster army should have first call on them, both because Ulster was almost entirely in enemy hands and because he judged that Owen Roe and his men were more 'Catholic' than the other Irish, which meant primarily that they were more willing than most of the Irish to support the extreme Catholic demands made by the nuncio in negotiations with the king.

The situation in Connaught also worried Rinuccini, but he calculated that if the Irish were successful in Ulster the Protestant forces in Connaught would retire. In March 1646 the supreme council ordered Owen Roe to advance into Ulster, and Ormond was persuaded to agree that, if the Irish sent him money, he would advance his forces up the coast towards Ulster to make the Scots fear that he intended to attack them. £2,000 sterling intended by Rinuccini for use in Connaught was therefore diverted to Ormond.[55]

Ormond's willingness to agree to co-operate with the Irish (though there is no evidence that he kept his promise to advance his forces) and their willingness to aid him followed from intelligence reports in February and March that Monro was preparing for a major offensive. Ormond wrote that 'the preparations of the Scots are very forward and greater than hitherto they have been, and I have certain intelligence their

54. Aiazza, *Embassy,* pp. 100-1.
55. Ibid. pp. 139-40, 148, 155, 159-60; Gilbert, *Contemporary History,* I, 666; Gilbert, *Irish Confederation,* V, 15, 17.

intent is towards this place [Dublin], where they expect to find more friends than enemyes'. Other reports indicated that the offensive would be against the Irish, with a rendezvous of the New Scots and British forces planned for near Athlone.[56] These reports were almost certainly false; apart from them there is no sign that Monro was planning any major action in February and March. It was very early in the year for a major expedition; the climate would make it very risky, and his cavalry and baggage horses usually needed the first of the spring grass to restore their strength before they could be used. His supply problems remained acute. Moreover the political situation militated against an offensive. His relations with the English commissioners in Ulster were strained, and he was involved in negotiations about sending 2,100 men (between a third and a half of the remaining New Scots) back to Scotland. In April when the English commissioners urged him to prepare to march against the Irish he expressed his eagerness to obey but complained that the extreme necessities of his army prevented it taking any effective action, and that he might be required at any moment to send men to Scotland.[57]

A month later, on 14 May, the New Scots officers at Carrickfergus wrote to the English commissioners at Belfast. Finding the season for advancing to the field approaching and their neighbours (the British) to be already engaging the enemy, they resolved if possible to advance 'for these ends of diversion' which Monro had (the letter states) discussed with the English the day before. But unless they were provided with half a month's means they would be unable to act. On 20 May the English commissioners duly authorised the payment of £550 sterling to Monro to enable his officers to take the field; similar payments were made to British officers.[58]

With this help Monro was able to march with 3,400 New Scots foot, eleven troops of horse and six field guns on 2 June. Monro subsequently explained the reason for the march; 'being extraordinarily scarce of Provisions, and hearing from all parts that the Irish had no considerable Army on foot, for Preservation of our Quarters [to prevent Irish infiltration], it was resolved by joynt advice to make the Fields with a Months Provision, for to purchase [plunder] Victuals or Cattle from

56. Gilbert, *Irish Confederation*, V, 14-15, 17, 261-2, 272.
57. T.S.A.I. pp. 99-101.
58. Ibid. pp. 108-9; *C.S.P.I. 1633-47*, pp. 522-3.

the Enemy'. George Monro was to march down the west side of Lough Neagh from Coleraine to join him. 'It was also condescended on by the English Commissioners and me, that the Laggan Forces should march into Connaught immediately, to keep the Enemy busied there, who were ordained to keep correspondency with us on all occasions'.[59] This account of his motives was written by Monro after his expedition had ended in disaster; but there seems no reason to question the truth of it, and it is supported in essence by the evidence of the letter of the New Scots officers of 14 May, as well as by Patrick Adair's assertion that Monro 'went to the fields for a prey, rather than expecting any encounter'.[60]

The point needs stressing, for it differs in two important respects from Irish accounts, which have generally been accepted. They claim that the Lagan army as well as George Monro were due to rendezvous with Robert Monro. The latter's account indicates that this was not so, though the Irish may well have believed that it was, since such conjunctions had taken place on several previous occasions. This belief that all the main Protestant forces in Ulster were joining together lent credibility to the second, much more important, Irish error—the belief that Robert Monro was in process of marching on Kilkenny, the confederate capital. Whether the Irish actually believed this before the battle of Benburb is uncertain; some sources state that they did,[61] but the only evidence the Irish ever cited to support the belief was papers actually captured at Benburb, on Lord Montgomery. These were said to have detailed a march on Kilkenny, and that this had been Monro's intention was said to have been confirmed by a confession by Montgomery.[62]

At first sight this does seem very strong evidence. But the indications that Monro did not intend to march on the confederate capital are even stronger. The fact that he did not plan to link up with the Lagan army; the fact that his agreement with the English commissioners was only for a limited expedition, a 'diversion'; and, finally, Monro's own explanation of his intentions and the complete lack of any evidence that a major undertaking by Monro was on foot until the Irish

59. Rushworth, *Historical Collections*, IV, i, 399.
60. Adair, *True Narrative*, p. 133.
61. E.g. Young, *Old Belfast*, p. 239; Gilbert, *Irish Confederation*, V, 25-6.
62. E.g. Aiazza, *Embassy*, p. 175; Gilbert, *Contemporary History*, I, 117.

published their accounts after the battle. This leaves the papers found on Lord Montgomery to be explained. It is, of course, conceivable that they were forgeries, but the most likely explanation seems to be that there was a plan for a march on Kilkenny among Montgomery's papers; but a plan drawn up as a military exercise, or as wishful thinking, something the Ulster forces would dearly have liked to implement, and even hoped one day to implement, rather than a plan that Monro's army was actually in course of executing. As to Montgomery's confession, it may not have existed, or he may have seen no harm in misleading the enemy who had captured him.

If this argument is accepted, it leads to a further question; did the Irish themselves really believe, after study of Montgomery's papers, that Monro had been marching on Kilkenny, or did they realise that the plan was not being implemented, but nonetheless exploit it for propaganda purposes? Whatever Monro's intentions had been, Owen Roe had won a major victory over him. But the significance of the victory would be very much greater if it was interpreted as having destroyed the most formidable opponents of the Irish just at the point of time when they were making a determined effort to destroy the Irish regime by capturing its capital.

The tendency to maximise the importance of a victory always exists. In this case it was greater than usual, for Benburb was not merely a victory for the confederate Irish; it was a victory for one party among them, the nuncio's party. The supreme council had negotiated the secret peace with Ormond; Rinuccini had declared his opposition to the peace for not giving sufficient concessions to the Catholic church. Now his most influential supporter among the Irish leaders had won a great victory, and Rinuccini and his party were determined to limit credit for the victory to themselves, thus emphasising that they were the true upholders of Ireland's interests. In these circumstances it was greatly to their advantage to be able to claim that they had saved Kilkenny from the Scots, while the supreme council treacherously made unnecessary concessions to Ormond. They may believed this to be true; even if they did not, its potential propaganda impact on the disputes among the Irish made the temptation to claim that it was true irresistible. One Irish account managed ingeniously to discredit Ormond, and thus those who

supported the treaty with him, by making him a party to
Monro's supposed march on Kilkenny. Ormond, it was asserted,
had sent Monro all the troops he could spare to help him on
his march, and planned to join him in triumph at Kilkenny.[63]
This fiction was more obviously untrue than that of Monro's
intention to seize Kilkenny, but it was not more untrue.

On 4 June Monro marched his army across the Bann, and
sent his own troop of horse under Lieutenant Daniel Monro
(probably his younger brother, who was later to settle in
Ireland) to 'scour the Fields', and to meet George Monro's
force from Coleraine to tell it to rendezvous at Glaslough the
next day. But near Armagh Daniel Monro's men captured an
Irishman who said that Owen Roe O'Neill's army, 5,000 foot
and twelve troops of horse, was at that moment marching
from Glaslough to Benburb. This was reported to Robert
Monro, and seems to have come as a complete surprize to
him; as he later wrote he had heard 'from all parts that the
Irish had no considerable Army on foot'. Owen Roe had only
entered Ulster a few days before and Monro's intelligence had
for once given him no warning of Irish movements. But if
Monro was ignorant of Owen Roe's movements until 4 June,
it seems quite possible that Owen Roe was equally unware of
Monro's. Much credit has been given to Owen Roe for the
strategic skill he showed in interposing his army between three
enemies before they could join together; but one of the three
(the Lagan army) had in fact no intention of joining the
others, and his appearance between the other two may well
have been more a matter of luck than of good judgement. For
far from having advanced in some unusual direction, to some
unusual point, in interposing himself between George and
Robert Monro, Owen Roe was simply doing what Irish forces
had often done before; marching down the Blackwater to the
Irish stronghold at Charlemont.

By the time Robert Monro heard that the Irish were in the
vicinity he had camped for the night, but on the news he
marched some miles further, to Hamilton's Bawn. There
Daniel Monro joined him, having been unable to get through
to George Monro. Early next morning the army advanced to
Armagh, which it reached by 4 a.m., Robert Monro 'thinking
the nearer our Army was to theirs, to hinder them from

63. Gilbert, *Contemporary History*, I, 117. See also Hogan, *Warr of Ireland*, p. 45.

MAP 4 QUARTERS OF FORCES IN ULSTER, MII

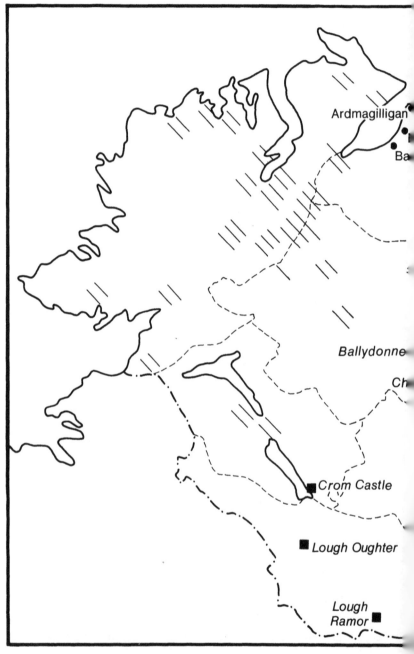

Ardmagilligan

Ba

Ballydonne

Ch

Crom Castle

Lough Oughter

Lough
Ramor

● Glenarm. Quarters of the New Scots. In addition to the places marked they quartered in 'all parts of the sea coast in the county of Antrim' and held 'other castles of Lecale' and two unidentified places; Cominge Ferry, on the Bann in County Antrim, and Little Belfast in County Down.

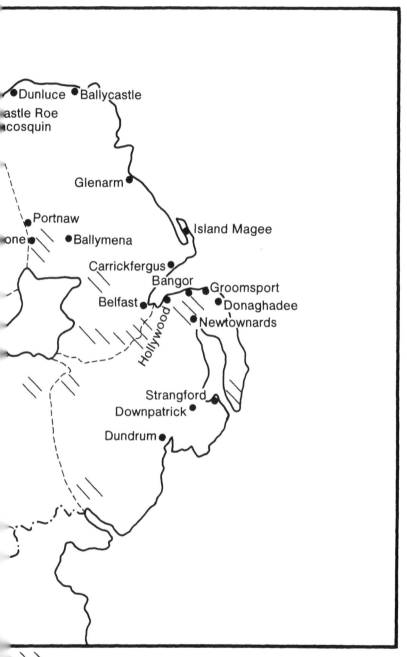

Dunluce ●Ballycastle
astle Roe
acosquin

Glenarm ●

●Portnaw
one● ●Ballymena

Island Magee

Carrickfergus●
Bangor
Belfast● ●Groomsport
Hollywood ●Donaghadee
●Newtownards

Strangford ●
Downpatrick ●

Dundrum ●

Quarters of the British Forces.

■ *Lough Ramor.* Irish garrisons in Ulster; the Irish also held the unidentified Phillipp O Relyes Castle in County Cavan. 'All these places are Islands (except Charlemont only) and not very considerable'.

sending any strength to fall upon Colonel [George] Monro, his way lying directly towards the Enemies Quarters'. Concern for his nephew made Robert Monro less cautious than he usually was.

Whether Owen Roe's interposition between the Protestant forces was the result of skill or of good fortune, he showed his ability as a general by immediately exploiting it. Retreating south or moving on to Charlemont would have brought him safety, but he now believed he could face his enemies in open battle, and indeed force Robert Monro to fight at a disadvantage by seeming to threaten his nephew. He therefore established himself in a strong position at Benburb, on the west bank of the Blackwater. Robert Monro reconnoitred the Irish position from the east bank and wisely decided that it would be impossible to cross the river safely in the face of Owen Roe's army. He therefore resolved to move south up the Blackwater and cross it by a ford near Caledon. This he did successfully. He may have hoped that Owen Roe would follow him up the river on the opposite bank, thus drawing the Irish out of their chosen position and away from George Monro. This did not happen, but by crossing the river to the same bank as the Irish Monro might at least distract them from falling on his nephew. It also meant that Monro's army was 'betwixt the Enemy and his Victuals' which he hoped might unnerve the Irish. But Owen Roe stood firm in his advantageous position, still counting on the fact that Robert Monro would advance to attack him out of concern for the forces from Coleraine. While this undoubtedly was one of the reasons that led Monro to decide to attack, it was not the main one; 'all our Army both Foot and Horse did earnestly covet fighting, which was impossible for me to gainstand, without being reproached of Cowardice'. This suggests that Monro himself may have had some doubts about the wisdom of attacking, but that the pressures on him to do so were strong. He had often been unfairly blamed for not being active enough against the Irish. Just a few weeks before his army had alienated Scotland by refusing to send men there, and the growing hostility of the English parliament was obvious. A victory in the field would greatly strengthen his position in negotiating with the two kingdoms; and, of course, the main object of his being in Ulster was to defeat the Irish. It seemed unthinkable to reject the offer of a pitched battle with their Ulster army when so often in the past he had been frustrated by their refusal to fight a major engagement.

Robert Monro therefore agreed to advance north down the Blackwater's west bank towards Benburb. Owen Roe had meanwhile acted to rid himself of his minor opponent before the major one attacked him; most of the Irish cavalry and some foot were sent to intercept George Monro and the Coleraine force. To give this detached force time to rejoin the main Irish army before battle commenced, parties were sent out up the Blackwater to delay Robert Monro's advance. Skirmishing with these Irish not only delayed Robert Monro's men; it also tired them. By the time they came in sight of the main Irish position it was about 6 p.m., and they had been on the march since well before 4 a.m., the time they had reached Armagh. From Hamilton's Bawn (Monro's camp site) to the battlefield by way of Caledon by the shortest possible route was a march of at least eighteen miles; and if (as seems likely) the army had marched some distance north out of Armagh, directly towards Benburb, before being diverted to the ford at Caledon, then it must have marched well over twenty miles. The eagerness to engage the enemy which his men displayed should not have influenced Monro into letting them attack, without resting after such a march, an enemy which had remained in the same position all day.

The two armies were probably about equal in strength. Owen Roe had about 5,000 foot and 500 horse (including the detached force sent against George Monro). Estimates of Monro's numbers varied. His own account mentions only 3,400 foot, but this seems to have been the number of New Scots he began his march with, before being joined by the British; a British officer estimated that he had about 5,000 foot of whom 3,000 were New Scots. The New Scots comprised the bulk of six regiments—Leven's, Monro's, Eglinton's, Glencairn's, Crawford-Lindsay's and Home's. The weakness of these regiments reflected losses through casualties, sickness and desertion, the men sent to Scotland with Colonel Home, and the men left in garrisons in Antrim and Down. One of the seven New Scots regiments was not represented at Benburb, Argyll's. Monro explained that this was because it had only just landed from Scotland; the regiment had returned to

Ireland at some point after the battle of Inverlochy in February 1645, but had now (as a result of Argyll's visit to Ulster) been used in an unsuccessful attempt to reconquer Islay and Kintyre from Alasdair MacColla. In addition to his 3,000 or 3,400 New Scots foot, Monro had about 2,000 British foot and perhaps seven or eight hundred horse, rather more than the Irish.

The battle opened with an attack by Monro, an attempt to drive back the Irish left wing from the Blackwater. The attack was repulsed, and at this moment the force which Owen Roe had sent against George Monro rejoined him; they had fallen on the men from Coleraine and scattered them near Dungannon. The appearance of more Irish, from a direction from which it must have been hoped George Monro himself would appear, was a blow to the morale of Robert Monro's army, already tired, its first attack just driven back.

After a pause, at about 8 p.m., a general Irish advance began. In the hard-fought conflict that followed the Irish gradually got the upper hand. Monro's left wing was forced back until his men were fighting with their backs to the river, unable to retreat. In the end part of the cavalry and Sir James Montgomery's regiment escaped, but the rest of the army was crushed with very heavy casualties. Of those who managed to flee many were drowned, others were cut down by the pursuing Irish as far as Caledon and Armagh. Monro himself escaped (after abandoning his wig, hat and cloak) but Lord Montgomery (who had commanded the cavalry) was captured and Lord Blayney (one of the British colonels) was killed. All Monro's guns and the entire baggage train of his army fell into Irish hands. So too did thirty-two colours and the main standard of the cavalry. Irish casualties were light, Monro's very heavy in proportion to the size of his army. Monro himself minimised them (as he minimised the size of his army), putting them at only five or six hundred. Irish claims ranged as high as 4,000 while a British estimate put losses at eighteen or nineteen hundred. The truth probably lies somewhere in between, in the range of two or three thousand. Thus of Monro's men between one in two and one in three died. The Irish victory could hardly have been more complete.[64]

64. For Benburb see Young, *Old Belfast*, pp. 239-42; Hogan, *Warr of Ireland*, pp. 44-52; Rushworth, *Historical Collections*, IV, i, 399-401; Adair, *True Narrative*, pp. 132-4; Gilbert, *Irish Confederation*, V, 25-9, 354; Gilbert, *Contemporary History*, I, 111-17, 676-86, III, 204-5; O'Connell and O'Ferrall, *Commentarius*

Robert Monro concluded sorrowfully that 'for ought I can understand, the Lord of Hosts had a controversie with us to rub shame in our faces ... till once we shall be humbled; for a greater confidence I never [did] see in any Army than amongst us'. Thus Monro himself realised that over-confidence had contributed to his downfall. Others agreed, but it was easier to see this in retrospect than at the time.[65] Past refusals by the Irish to fight had led to the belief that once they were brought to battle they were bound to be defeated; many had thought the only reason Owen Roe had stayed to fight was that his retreat had been cut off by Monro getting to the south of him.

It was anticipated that Owen Roe would follow up his spectacular victory at Benburb by an attempt to conquer Ulster. On 8 June, three days after the battle, Monro and the English commissioners wrote urgently to Ormond informing him, rather oddly, that their recent defeat made it a very good moment for him to declare war on the Irish. Two days later Monro, his nephew and the leaders of the Lagan army dispatched another letter to Ormond (carried by Humphry Galbraith) urging the need for unity against the Irish, though expressing confidence in their ability to resist them. Not surprisingly Ormond showed no inclination to ally himself to the defeated Scots and British, who thereupon roundly denounced him.[66]

News of Benburb reached the English parliament on 15 June, and immediate arrangements were made to send supplies to Ulster so that the expected Irish advance could be resisted.[67] But nothing happened. Owen Roe brought his army to Tanderagee as if preparing to cross the Bann and invade Down, but then retired and quartered his army in Westmeath and Longford.[68] Thus as early as 11 June Monro could report with relief that 'the enemy as yet (praised be God) hath not

Rinuccinianus, II, 238-48. There are two excellent accounts of the battle and the surviving evidence about it by G. A. Hayes-McCoy—in *The Irish at War* (Cork, 1964), pp. 47-58, and 'O'Mellan's Account of the Battle of Benburb 1646', in S. Pender, ed. *Feilscribhinn Torna: Essays and Studies presented to Professor Tadhg ua Donnchadha* (Cork, 1947), pp. 141-53.

65. Turner, *Memoirs*, p. 23; Rushworth, *Historical Collections*, IV, i, 400; Adair, *True Narrative*, pp. 133-4; Hogan, *Warr of Ireland*, p. 49.
66. Carte MSS, 17, ff. 363, 365, 367, 480, 490, 513-14, 522-3, 563, 565; Carte, *Ormond*, III, 479-81.
67. *C.J.* IV, 577; Bodleian Library, Rawlinson MSS, A.258, f. 10.
68. Gilbert, *Contemporary History*, III, 205-6; Gilbert, *Irish Confederation*, V, 32.

attempted to prosecute his Victory within our Quarters'.[69] Fear that Owen Roe would advance remained for many weeks. The officers of the New Scots begged both England and Scotland for help as they lacked men and arms and invasion was daily expected, while Robert Monro lamented 'the unparalelled sufferings of this army'.[70] On 3 July Sir James Montgomery wrote 'Truly I am afraid the weight of that blow is not yet found; the cloud never looked so black since this rebellion began, and if God (as hitherto he has) do not restrain the rebels from falling down amongst [us] until considerable supplies come from England, we are a lost people'.[71] A month later it was said 'if assistance do not come suddenly into the North, all the poor Protestants there will be ruined and destroyed'. But already the first shock of the defeat was wearing off; by early August Monro was reported to be back 'in the fields with a good number of men'.[72]

Still Owen Roe did not advance. He himself blamed lack of supplies,[73] but though some shortages doubtless existed in his army, he had after all just captured Monro's baggage train, which, according to Monro, should have still contained nearly a month's supplies, at least for the 3,000 or so New Scots, perhaps for his entire army. One of the influences restraining Owen Roe must have been the knowledge that even after Benburb he could expect determined and large-scale resistance if he attempted to conquer Ulster without further preparations. Benburb had been primarily a defeat of the New Scots, and even they could probably still muster several thousand men from those who had escaped from the battle field, those who had remained in garrisons, and Argyll's regiment. Moreover only about 2,500 perhaps 3,000 at most, of the British forces had been at Benburb. At the beginning of the year the strength of the British in Ulster had been put at just over 9,600 officers and men, horse and foot.[74] Thus only one third of the British forces at most were present at Benburb, and probably proportionately more of them than of the New Scots

69. Rushworth, *Historical Collections*, IV, i, 400.
70. T.S.A.I. pp. 110-17; R. K. Marshall, 'Calendar of the Correspondence in the Hamilton Archives at Lennoxlove' (Appendix to Ph.D. thesis, Edinburgh University, 1970), II, 288.
71. H.M.C. 63: *Egmont*, I, i, 296.
72. Ibid. I, i, 303.
73. Gilbert, *Irish Confederation*, VI, 7; Gilbert, *Contemporary History*, I, 690; Bagwell, *Stuarts*, II, 122.
74. *C.S.P.I. 1633-47*, p. 433.

had escaped.

However this in itself would hardly have deterred Owen Roe from making at least some attempt to follow up his victory. The real reason for his strange failure to take advantage of the best chance the Irish had ever had of subduing the Protestants of Ulster since the early weeks of the rebellion in 1641 were political, not military. Rinuccini's help had made the victory almost as much his as Owen Roe's; but it was Rinuccini who, through his influence over Owen Roe, made the victory almost meaningless. The struggle with the Protestants in Ulster had at first seemed to Rinuccini to deserve first priority, but his growing conviction that the peace which the supreme council had negotiated with Ormond would be fatal to the interests of both the Irish and the Catholic church led him to believe that destroying the peace must come before everything else. Though he won the support of the clergy he failed to achieve his ends by political means. On 30 July 1646 Ormond had the peace publicly proclaimed in Dublin; on 3 August the Irish followed suit at Kilkenny.

Rinuccini's reaction was to summon Owen Roe and his army south to support him; though there is no direct evidence for it, it seems likely that ever since Benburb Rinuccini had been preventing Owen Roe becoming too deeply involved in a campaign in Ulster so that he would be available to act quickly in support of the anti-peace party if he was needed. On the nuncio's orders Owen Roe marched on Kilkenny and camped near the town which, overawed by his army, then submitted to Rinuccini. The old supreme council was imprisoned and the Ormond Peace collapsed. Had not Owen Roe's own reputation, and that of his army, just been so greatly increased by Benburb it is doubtful if Rinuccini's *coup d'etat* could have succeeded. Thus Benburb proved 'a far greater disaster for the supreme council than for the protestants of the north'.[75] And though the *coup* was successful it inevitably greatly embittered the disputes among the confederate Irish, thus gravely weakening them.

The diversion of Owen Roe's army to Kilkenny meant that Benburb proved a far less serious defeat for the Ulster Protestants than it might have been. Just as political pressures had seriously hindered Robert Monro's freedom of action since

75. Beckett, *Making of Modern Ireland*, p. 98; Bagwell, *Stuarts*, II, 115, 122-9.

1642, so now political pressures prevented the Irish exploiting their victory. Even so, Benburb did have major consequences in Ulster. The majority of the New Scots had been defeated and scattered, while the British had suffered comparatively little—the Lagan army had escaped altogether. This altered the balance of the Protestant forces in Ulster. In 1642-3 the New Scots and the British had been roughly equal in strength, but since then the New Scots army had dwindled much faster than the British, through withdrawals to Scotland. Benburb carried the change further; the fact that the New Scots were no longer the dominant Protestant force in Ulster was plain. For this reason some English parliamentarians were not entirely sorry to hear of Benburb, just as in previous years Montrose's victories over the Scots had given them some satisfaction. Defeat in Ireland would force the Scots to limit their pretensions there. Only a day after the English parliament heard of the battle the Scots commissioners in London reported that the news 'makes many to thinke it unseasonable for us to contest the command of the forces in Ireland when wee have so few forces there'.[76] Scots demands that Monro be recognised as commander in chief in Ireland were no longer taken seriously. The high hopes held in 1642-3 that the New Scots would take the leading part in crushing the Irish rebellion had been slowly fading; now they were suddenly extinguished.

76. Meikle, *Correspondence*, p. 193.

CHAPTER SIX

The End of the New Scots

i. The Decline of the Army, 1646-1647

The Scottish army in Ireland continued to exist for more than two years after Benburb, but it undertook little action against the Irish. The Irish for their part made no attempt to advance into Ulster, so very little fighting took place. The strength of the army was only one third of what it once had been. A report to the English parliament in December 1646 put the strength of 'the Scotch army intermixt with the inhabitants' at 3,500 foot, while the British of Ulster could muster about 5,000 foot and seventeen troops of horse (with about fifty men in each). The following year it was said Robert Monro 'could draw into the field three or four thousand Foot, all Scotts or Scottish Irish ... and some two or three hundred Horse'.[1] The main preoccupation of the New Scots in these years lay not in the war with the Irish but in their deteriorating relations with the English parliament and their determination not to leave Ireland until their arrears were paid.

As has already been indicated, they got little sympathy from the English parliament after Benburb, since it was hoped that defeat would check their pretensions. There was an almost indecent haste about the zealous way the English followed up news of the battle by delivering further blows to the already battered New Scots. It was only a day after the news arrived that it was being used to reinforce arguments against Monro remaining commander in chief in Ireland. The

1. H.M.C. 29: *Portland*, I, 400; G. Leyburn, *The Memoirs of George Leyburn, being a journal of his agency for Prince Charles in Ireland, 1647* (Clarendon Historical Society, 1886), p. 11. Even allowing for the effects of Benburb the figure of *circa*, 5,850 British (horse and foot) in Ulster at the end of 1646 seems very low compared with the 9,624 British said to have been in arms in the province at the beginning of the year (*C.S.P.I. 1633-47*, p. 433). Either disease and desertion had led to massive wastage, or one set of figures (or both!) is wildly inaccurate.

day after this, 17 June, the committee of both houses for Irish affairs passed a new resolution demanding the surrender of Belfast; and on 18 June it ordered Sir Robert King to report on the state of the armies in Ulster and in particular on the origins of the men in the Scottish army. How many had really come from Scotland, and how many had been recruited (illegally, parliament claimed) in Ulster?[2]

At the end of the month the army sent Captain William Drummond to London to negotiate on its behalf. He was allowed to represent the army's grievances to the committee for Irish affairs but never received an answer. In March 1647 he was still awaiting a reply, and no supplies had reached the army from England since Benburb.[3] The committee was dominated by men hostile to the New Scots. Their old enemy Sir John Clotworthy was active in urging action against them over Belfast, and in August the lieutenant colonel of his regiment in Ulster submitted a petition complaining about the treatment of his horse troop by the New Scots.[4] In Ulster relations between the English commissioners and the New Scots grew increasingly strained. In August the committee in London sent orders to Monro to punish any of his officers who disobeyed the commissioners' orders, and to restrain his men from acting unjustly towards the inhabitants of Ulster.[5]

Of course from the point of view of getting sympathy from the English parliament, the New Scots could not have chosen a worse time to be defeated—less than a month after the king had fled to the Scottish army in England, while there were still fears that Robert Monro might be plotting with Ormond. Though in some respects Benburb was seen as a defeat inflicted on an ally and as a setback for English interests in Ireland, in others it seemed the defeat of a former ally who might soon be an enemy.

This conjunction of events, of the king's flight and Benburb, also proved a major disaster for Ormond. Benburb helped Rinuccini's party to overthrow the Ormond Peace; and the

2.   *C.S.P.I. 1633-47*, pp. 460, 461.
3.   T.S.A.I. pp. 110-17, 126, 137; Meikle, *Correspondence*, p. 203; A. F. Mitchell and J. Christie, eds. *The Records of the Commissions of the General Assemblies ... 1646-1652* (3 vols, S.H.S. 1892-1909), I, 577-8; McNeill, *Tanner Letters*, p. 230; *L.J.* VIII, 631-2.
4.   *C.S.P.I. 1633-47*, pp. 476, 495; Meikle, *Correspondence*, pp. 203, 207.
5.   *C.S.P.I. 1633-47*, p. 491; Bodleian Library, Rawlinson MSS, A.258, ff. 18-18v.

king had put himself in the hands of the covenanters who were hostile to any treaty with the Irish. Ormond had only negotiated the peace reluctantly, on the king's orders; now, at the end of June, Robert Monro and the English commissioners in Ulster sent him a declaration that the covenanters had forced the king to sign giving him express orders not to proceed with the treaty with the Irish rebels. Ormond evaded giving a direct answer, confusing the issue by asking for a safe conduct to send a messenger to the king (which Monro refused), for, as he wrote to the king on 29 July, he was in no state to resist the attack by the Irish which breaking off the treaty would expose him to.[6] He therefore proclaimed the peace in spite of the king's orders; by this time he knew that the king was being treated virtually as a prisoner and that his orders did not necessarily express his real desires.[7]

But Rinuccini's *coup d'etat* and denunciation of the peace in September made Ormond's determination to implement it in spite of the king's orders irrelevant. The peace had collapsed and an Irish attack on Dublin seemed imminent. Ormond believed there was no hope of resisting successfully. But to surrender Dublin to the Irish would infuriate parliament and the Scots against the captive king, so on 30 September he wrote to Monro and the English commissioners in Ulster asking for help. Not surprisingly they were suspicious of what he was trying to do, and in reply demanded that he give them Drogheda to garrison without specifying what help they would give. This Ormond refused to do, for he had also written direct to the English parliament and it showed itself willing to negotiate, eager to gain Dublin peacefully. On 16 October the committee for Irish affairs in London wrote to the commissioners in Ulster informing them that parliament was preparing to send troops to Dublin and urging them to do all they could to get the Protestant forces in Ulster to advance against the Irish, to prevent them attacking Dublin before troops could land there.[8]

However, though Ormond had opened negotiations with parliament as the most likely way to keep Dublin in Protestant hands, he would have preferred to hand the city over to the

6. Carte MSS, 17, ff. 563, 565, 18, ff. 43, 48, 60-1; Carte, *Ormond*, III, 479-82.
7. Bagwell, *Stuarts*, II, 115; H.M.C. 63: *Egmont*, I, i, 313-14.
8. Carte MSS, 19, ff. 52, 54, 115-16; Bodleian Library, Rawlinson MSS, A.258, f. 34v; Carte, *Ormond*, I, 588.

Scots; the king was still in Scots hands, and was still hoping to reach an agreement with them. To persuade the Scots to agree he could point out that if they failed to help him Dublin would fall to the Irish or parliament. 'If Dublin should fall, the full weight of the Irish Catholics would be pressed against them. If on the other hand Dublin had surrendered to parliament, their [the Scots] bargaining strength with Parliament would be seriously weakened'.[9] The New Scots should therefore occupy Dublin; the English parliament would then, for once, be forced to take their grievances seriously. Ormond sent appeals to the New Scots and to the British, for many of the latter had lingering royalist sympathies and now the Scots had possession of the king they would be more likely to work in co-operation with the Scots than with parliament. On 9 October a meeting of New Scots officers at Coleraine replied to Ormond's advances. George Monro was present but not his uncle; Robert Monro had never shown much taste for political intrigue. The officers probably met at Coleraine partly for security reasons, for a meeting there was less likely to come to the notice of the English commissioners at Belfast than one at Carrickfergus. It was also a convenient place for meeting with British officers, but in the event bad weather prevented them from attending. Or at least this was the excuse given to Ormond for the absence of the British, but it is notable that the New Scots seem to have made no attempt to bring the British into the plot later, which perhaps indicates they hoped to occupy Dublin without British help.

The officers cautiously expressed their willingness to negotiate with Ormond, as they had a common cause and a common enemy. The phrase was purposely vague; the common enemy to some might be the Irish alone, but to others it would include the English parliament as well. As in previous intrigues with Ormond, George Monro played a leading part, writing to him personally as well as signing the officers' letter.[10] The way having been cleared by these tentative approaches, Ormond on 24 October sent Captain William Cunningham to the New Scots with definite proposals. He admitted that his position was weak (the Irish having

9. J. Lowe, 'The Negotiations between Charles I and the Confederation of Kilkenny' (Ph.D. thesis, University of London, 1960), pp. 568-9.
10. Gilbert, *Irish Confederation*, VI, 28-9; T.S.A.I. p. 119; Carte MSS, 19, ff. 110, 179, 279.

taken some of his outposts) and asked that 1,000 foot and some horse be sent to help him. If these men remained together in one garrison the New Scots would be given command of it, but it they preferred some could be stationed in Drogheda and some in Dublin, though in this case they would be subordinate to Ormond's governors. They would be allowed free exercise of presbyterianism, and a church would be assigned to them. Ormond expressed his satisfaction at the affection of the New Scots to the public cause, but at heart he doubtless still considered them untrustworthy and mercenary; he promised them enough booty to recompense them for their trouble.[11]

Five days later Ormond sent Major Seafoule Gibson north with further inducements to persuade the New Scots to hasten to join him. Intelligence reports indicated that a major Irish offensive against him was imminent, and though the English parliament was preparing to send troops these might be insufficient to save Dublin. Gibson was also instructed to tell George Monro alone that Ormond feared that the troops parliament sent to 'help' him would seize Dublin from him. He was therefore willing to receive 500 New Scots into Dublin, but only on condition that they swore not to try to make changes in the civil, military and ecclesiastical government of the city. Room would be made for the New Scots by expelling members of Ormond's garrisons whom he suspected of favouring parliament.[12] The two messages carried by Gibson thus gave differing impressions of why New Scots were to be sent to Dublin. The message for the officers in general implied that the New Scots would be acting to help parliament's troops hold the city against the Irish, while the message to George Monro indicated that they would hold the city against parliament as well. Thus it seems that Ormond felt he could only discuss his true intentions with Monro. The rest of the New Scots were to be brought to Dublin under the impression that they were still acting as parliament's allies. Once they got there they would discover, too late, that they were to be used to resist parliament—and parliament would never believe that this had not been their intention all along. One immediate difficulty this interpretation raises is, if most of the New Scots

11. T.S.A.I. p. 120; Carte MSS, 19, ff. 279, 280-1; Gilbert, *Irish confederation*, VI, 29.
12. Gilbert, *Irish Confederation*, VI, 31-3; T.S.A.I. pp. 120-1; Carte MSS, 19, ff. 281-2; Carte, *Ormond*, I, 588-9.

officers thought they were acting in parliament's interests, what possible reason could there be for keeping the negotiations with Ormond secret from the English commissioners in Ulster? The answer probably lies in the fact that though the New Scots officers still regarded themselves as parliament's allies, they nonetheless had grievances against parliament, and they well knew that parliament, already demanding that they give up Belfast, would never consent to their occupying Dublin. Parliament was therefore to be presented with a *fait accompli* which would greatly strengthen the bargaining position of the New Scots.

However, the plotting of Ormond and George Monro failed. On 10 November the New Scots officers sent Gibson back to Ormond to tell him that they were too weak to send men to Dublin, and suggested that he deal with the British for aid instead. They admitted that they were so weak that they could only maintain themselves in Ulster with British help, so they could not act until Ormond got the British to agree.[13] Dublin was a tempting prize, but the risks of occupying it were too great. Some may have been suspicious of the motives of Ormond and George Monro, and in any case no matter how earnestly the New Scots might have claimed to have been acting in parliament's interests, its fury at such an unauthorised action by them might well have made the army's position in Ireland more difficult than ever. Ormond toyed with proposals to tempt all Scots in Ulster, Old and New, into supporting him by confirming them in possession of their lands in Ulster, granting them freedom of worship and getting the king to confer some honour and an estate on Robert Monro, but soon abandoned them.[14]

The failure of Ormond's negotiations with the New Scots left him with only the English parliament to turn to for help against the Irish. Five commissioners from the house of commons (including Sir John Clotworthy) arrived in Dublin on 12 November and negotiated with him, but in the end he refused to make the concessions they demanded in return for military aid without the king's permission. He was able to do this because the expected Irish attack on Dublin had not materialised; the Irish leaders were devoting more energy to

---

13. Carte, *Ormond*, I, 589; Gilbert, *Irish Confederation*, VI, 26-7, 33-5; Carte MSS, 19, ff. 283-4, 334, 338-9, 346; T.S.A.I. pp. 121-3.
14. Carte MSS, 20, ff. 234-5.

Carrickfergus Castle. Headquarters of the Scottish Army in Ireland, 1642-8.

internal disputes than to organising the attack.[15]

Ormond's unexpected refusal to surrender Dublin brough
new difficulties to the New Scots, for Clotworthy and th
other English commissioners shipped the men they ha
brought to occupy Dublin to Ulster instead. By 1 Decembe
the commissioners had reached Belfast and two English foo
regiments were landing at Bangor. The commissioners wrot
informing Robert Monro that parliament had ordered them t
quarter the regiments in Belfast. In reply he claimed that h
had not the power to order Colonel Home (who commande
the New Scots stationed in Belfast) to give up the town; onl
the earl of Leven could do this. The English would not accep
this evasion, and argued that all they wanted was shelter fo
their men; surely Monro would not let the English force
fighting in the same cause as he was, perish from exposure?
But Monro would not change his mind, Home was no more
co-operative, and an appeal to the Scottish parliament had no
effect. English claims that their troops would perish unless
they were given Belfast were countered by claims that the
New Scots would have to leave Ireland if they gave it up. In
the end a temporary agreement was reached whereby the
English were quartered in the Lecale, from which the New
Scots withdrew.

To both New Scots and the Scottish parliament Belfast
was as much a bargaining counter as a military necessity. A
meeting of officers at Carrickfergus on 22 December admitted
as much, resolving that the army would keep possession of it
as long as of its other garrisons. The officers also sent to the
English commissioners demanding that no English be mixed
with them in quarters (to prevent disputes) and threatening
that unless they were supplied equally with the English they
would hinder the service instead of advancing it. They also
enquired of the commissioners 'whether we had power to
treat with them for a final agreement for the Scottish Army
here, that they might be gone and comply with our desires
concerning the delivery of this [Belfast], as also the other
towns'. Almost simultaneously the Scottish parliament
resolved that the English should be asked either to supply the
New Scots effectively or to recall them and pay their arrears.
It was accepted that the usefulness of the Scottish army in

15. Bagwell, *Stuarts*, II, 132-9.

Ireland was over; it was only a fraction of its former strength and the English parliament had made it clear that its own troops, not Scots ones, would take the lead in conquering Ireland.[16]

In February 1647 the Scottish army in England withdrew to Scotland, leaving the king behind to fall into the hands of the English parliament since he had failed to make the concessions in religion that the covenanters had demanded. £200,000 sterling was paid to the army before it left, and payment of as much again was promised. This was less than the army had hoped for, but nonetheless it was still a very large sum, and it must have encouraged the Scottish government and the New Scots to hope that the English would prove equally willing to pay up in order to get rid of the Scottish army in Ireland. But there were at first disagreements about how best to put pressure on the English. The Scottish government believed that it would be best to reinforce the army in Ireland. This could easily be done for, with the withdrawal of the army from England it had far more troops at its disposal than it needed. It was therefore resolved to send back to Ireland the three New Scots regiments which had come to Scotland in 1644, and the 1,400 men who had come in 1645. Thus reinforced the New Scots would be in a better position to get good terms from the English than otherwise. As a first instalment Sinclair's and Lothian's regiments were ordered to proceed to Ireland; Lawers' would follow later, after being recruited. But the New Scots officers in Ireland protested at the order, on the grounds that they could only just maintain in their quarters the men already in Ulster; to send more would lead to starvation, since there was no sign of supplies being sent from outside.

The two regiments themselves were no more eager to cross to Ireland. Sinclair's, about 500 men in nine companies plus officers, 'women and bairnis', quartered in Peebles for two days (11-13 February) on their way to Portpatrick, but then 'efter a mutine' forced their officers to pay them. Most threw away their arms and deserted after terrorising and plundering

16. *C.S.P.I. 1633-47*, pp. 551-2, 553, 554-5, 558-62, 567-8, 569, 570, 571, 583, 584; G. Benn, *History of the Town of Belfast* (2 vols. Belfast, 1877-80), I, 114-16; *T.S.A.I.* pp. 124-7; *L.J.* VIII, 653, 656-62, IX, 99, 101-2; *C.J.* V, 74; *A.P.S.* VI,i, 624, 636, 642, 743-4; McNeill, *Tanner Letters*, p. 232; Fotheringham, *Correspondence*, II, 41, 64.

I

Peebles for several days. There was also confusion over whether the regiments were meant to leave for Ireland or wait to be recruited first; and Argyll and others were working to get the orders for the regiments to march to Ireland cancelled. When the remains of Sinclair's regiment reached Galloway Major James Turner was sent to Ulster to see what reception the regiment would get there from the New Scots officers, 'for that armie was then governed by a councell of officers, wherof the Major Generall was president'. He found that the coast was already being guarded against their landing, and that the officers were determined not to accept reinforcement. The reason given for this, lack of quarters, was genuine; Robert Monro wrote to Ormond asking that they be given quarters around Newry and Dundalk, but this was refused, while the officers suggested they be found quarters in the Lecale along with the recently arrived English forces. But Turner was right to think that this was not the only reason. The New Scots were expecting the English parliament to offer them a fixed sum in satisfaction of their arrears, and they did not want to have to share this with regiments which had not shared their sufferings of the previous three years.

The two regiments in Galloway were thus left in a difficult situation. The army in Ireland threatened to use force to prevent them landing, while early in April the committee of estates ordered Robert Monro to let them land and told the regiments to sail without Monro's consent, though he was supposed to be their commander. If they did not sail, they were to disband immediately or they would be treated as enemies of the kingdom and force used to disarm them. The conduct of Sinclair's men in Peebles had led to the regiments being regarded as a threat to law and order. Sinclair's regiment agreed to disband but Lothian's men were divided. Some wanted to go to Ireland, others to disband or to await orders from Lothian. In the end it seems that some 'went over' to Ireland, others remained in arms for a time and then dispersed.[17]

While the fate of the two regiments was being decided

17. *A.P.S.* VI, i, 675, 693, 704-5, 717, 723; T.S.A.I. pp. 127-8, 141; S.R.O. GD.2/53, petition of the Burgh of Peebles to Parliament; Laing, *Correspondence*, I, 204-5, 208-10, 213-14, 217-21; L. B. Taylor, ed. *Aberdeen Council Letters* (5 vols. Oxford and London, 1940-57), III, 96, 97; S.R.O. PA.11/5, ff. 9v, 10v-11, 11v, 12, 17; Turner, *Memoirs*, p. 44; Carte MSS, 20, ff. 439, 459-60.

negotiations with the English parliament over the army's arrears had been proceeding. In mid-February the army officers wrote to the Scottish parliament and to Arthur Annesley or Sir Robert King in London for advice. They desired reasonable satisfaction for their arrears and suggested that either the English send commissioners to negotiate with them in Ulster, or that some officers proceed to London for negotiations. The army claimed to be as discontented as the English parliament was about its lack of action against the Irish, and to win support for itself issued an emotional declaration protesting its loyalty and good service, though many men were trying to make it odious to the English parliament to prevent it reaping the just rewards of its labours. In five years' service the New Scots had never remained idle for as much as twenty days at a time when they had had enough food to enable them to go into the field. But food had always been so short that they had never been able to pursue the enemy satisfactorily. In five years they had only received five months' means; officers of good quality had gone for three or four days at a time without bread. In spite of this the army had driven the Irish from Ulster, but at Benburb 'when coming to push of pike they had no power to stand, but oppressed with weaknesse caused by famine dyed by the sword lyke withered reeds shaken by the wind for want of substance'. It was to be hoped the army would now receive the reward due for honest and loyal service.[18]

Such pleas had little effect on opinion in England. However, English commissioners in Edinburgh seemed prepared to begin genuine negotiations for satisfying the army. They offered either to send to Ulster for detailed accounts of what was due to the army, or to agree a general estimate, a round sum which would be paid to satisfy all claims (like the £400,000 sterling agreed on for the Scottish army in England).[19] But these suggestions were soon superseded by decisions taken in England. On 22 February 1647 the house of commons referred consideration of the treaty under which the Scottish army served in Ireland to the committee for Irish affairs. On 12 March the committee recommended that Scotland should be told that the English parliament would no longer pay the

18. T.S.A.I. pp. 127-33; Reid, *History of the Presbyterian Church*, II, 539-43.
19. Bodleian Library, Tanner MSS, 58.2, f. 729.

army, as it intended to carry on the war in Ireland with its own forces. The Commons accepted the committee's report and resolved that the army should be dismissed on one month's notice with fourteen days' pay, according to articles twelve and thirteen of the 1642 treaty. Its arrears would be paid later.[20]

The attitude of the Commons reflected the fact that, though the Scots had withdrawn from England and abandoned the king, relations between the two countries remained strained. Anti-Scots and anti-presbyterian feelings in the English parliament were still growing, and disagreement over the form of a peace settlement for England continued. In these circumstances the English were in no mood to offer to pay any large sums due in arrears to a Scottish army. They had been forced to pay up to rid themselves of the Scottish army in England because it had been in a strong bargaining position, occupying much of the north of England and having possession of the king. By contrast the New Scots, weak in numbers, occupying a corner of Ulster, represented no immediate or major threat to parliament's interests, and could therefore be treated with contempt. Few could have been so naive as to believe that, if the New Scots obeyed the order to withdraw without their arrears, they would ever be paid them.

Before they heard of the Commons' decision the New Scots officers had dispatched George Monro to London to negotiate with parliament about freeing the army from 'this miserable slaverie', equipped with receipts to show how much money was due to it and with detailed instructions as to how much to demand at first, and how far he should allow this to be beaten down if necessary.[21] News that the Commons had resolved to dismiss the army without payment of arrears was greeted with indignation both by the army and in Scotland. Argyll claimed that the army was owed nearly £800,000 sterling; this was doubtless an exaggeration, but the total certainly ran to some hundreds of thousands of pounds. However, Argyll and his supporters were in a difficult position. If they rejected the English resolution as insulting they would be playing into the hands of the Scots royalists and moderates who wanted to provoke war with the English on the king's

20. *C.J.* V, 95, 112, 113-14; *C.S.P.I. 1646-60*, pp. 736, 737; *L.J.* IX, 125.
21. *A.P.S.* VI, i, 764-5; *T.S.A.I.* pp. 137-40; *L.J.* IX, 274.

behalf. If on the other hand they supinely accepted the resolution they would be blamed for betraying the army's interests.

Similar difficulties troubled the other main political interest in Scotland, the duke of Hamilton's; for though he wanted to intervene in England to help the king he believed the time for this was not yet ripe. Thus neither party would support the claims of the New Scots fully, for fear that this would lead to war with England. In April George Monro passed through Edinburgh on his way to London. True to his reputation he was said to have spoken very violently, denouncing both the English parliament (for its resolution) and its Scottish counterpart (for failing to stand up for the army's interests). So disillusioned did he seem that the French agent in Edinburgh speculated that the New Scots might even join the Irish confederates![22] The Irish themselves may also have hoped to benefit from the anger of the New Scots, for in May Sir Phelim O'Neill wrote to Robert Monro, though the contents of his letter are not known.[23]

A breathing space in the controversy over the future of the New Scots was provided by the refusal of the house of lords for some months to agree to their dismissal, and in the interim the Scots commissioners in London, George Monro and Captain Drummond, tried time and again to get the Commons to act more reasonably.[24] But nothing was achieved, and in July the Lords accepted another resolution that undermined the position of the New Scots. It was agreed that Sir Charles Coote should command the Lagan army (with Sir Robert Stewart continuing to lead it under him) as well as the Connaught forces. The rest of the forces of Ulster, parliamentary and British, were to be commanded by Colonel George Monck.[25] Robert Monro's right to command the British was not specifically cancelled, it was simply ignored, and the British themselves were divided under different commanders. This last change made military sense, in that the Lagan army and the British of Antrim and Down had long operated as separate armies, but it was probably also a political

22. Fotheringham, *Correspondence*, II, 93, 120-1, 126, 127, 234.
23. S.R.O. PA.11/5, f. 32v.
24. *C.J.* V, 172; S.R.O. PA.11/5, ff. 27, 28v-29, 51, 61v; S.R.O. PA.12/2, minute of 8 July 1647; McNeill, *Tanner Letters*, p. 235; *L.J.* IX, 274.
25. *L.J.* IX, 336.

Owen Roe O'Neill. General of the Ulster army of the Irish confederates reproduced in Gilbert, *Contemporary History* from a Dutch portrait.

move, designed to make it more difficult for the British to act together as a party, perhaps in alliance with the New Scots.

A further sign of parliament's growing power in Ireland came at the end of July. Ormond at last surrendered Dublin. He had been coming under increasing Irish pressure. In February Monro, Coote and the Ulster British had been ordered to attack the Irish to divert them from Dublin, but if anything had been done in response to this order it had no long term effects, and in the end Ormond handed the city over to parliament to keep it out of Irish hands.[26] It was probably the news that Dublin was now safely in parliament's hands that at last persuaded the Lords that there was no longer any need to keep the New Scots in Ireland, especially since there appeared to be no sign that the Irish intended any attack on Ulster. Robert Monro had twice warned that attack was imminent. In March he had written that 10,000 Irish were marching to crush him before invading Scotland, but the comment of the French agent, Jean de Montereul, was probably justified; 'I fear this Scot is forging enemies in order to defeat them more easily, and that he excites this fear here in order to obtain more readily what he demands'.[27] This judgement could also be applied to Monro's warning in June that Owen Roe O'Neill (aided by Irish and Highlanders who had fled to Ireland as David Leslie's forces advanced in Argyllshire) intended to subdue Connaught, defeat the Lagan army and then fall on eastern Ulster; 'if they should prevaile Scotland cannot be in peace long', and the New Scots could not march against the Irish for lack of provisions.[28] The New Scots were trying desperately to prove how useful they were to Scotland, in that they protected the country from Irish invasion, in the hope that the Scottish government would not let the English treat them insultingly. But the Irish attacks on Ulster never materialised and on 24 August the Lords agreed that the New Scots should be dismissed. Orders to this effect were then sent to Scotland.[29]

Meanwhile the army's officers, meeting as a committee of

26. Bagwell, *Stuarts*, II, 140-4. *C.S.P.D. 1645-7*, pp. 523, 524-5; *C.S.P.I. 1647-60*, p. 730; H.M.C. 63: *Egmont*, I, ii, 367.
27. Fotheringham, *Correspondence*, II, 72.
28. S.R.O. PA.12/2, 14 June 1647, Monro to Argyll.
29. *L.J.* IX, 401, 404-5, 425; *C.J.* V, 285, 292, 294, 296-7; *C.S.P.I. 1647-60*, p. 764.

war on 11 and 27 August, were declaring their determination to stand together to obtain satisfaction. They decided to try to agree on a union with the British forces, and to try to improve morale and hold the army together by explaining the situation to the soldiers; many had resolved to desert since they had abandoned hope of getting paid and therefore saw no reason to continue serving in miserable conditions. The committee of estates was told that the army could be kept together by promises for only one or two months unless supplies were sent.[30]

The officers' pleas met with a sympathetic response in Edinburgh. The conduct of the English parliament, over payment of the army in Ireland and reaching agreement with the king, was leading to a royalist revival (led by Hamilton) which had the support of many moderate covenanters who believed that the English parliament was now a greater danger to the covenanters than the king was. On 27 September the committee of estates rejected the English demands that the New Scots leave Ireland according to articles twelve and thirteen of the treaty; it would only leave when the English fulfilled the other articles of the treaty, especially six and eleven, by paying all the money promised to the army. To enable the army to survive until this was done an extra half month's maintenance (a land tax) was imposed in Scotland for the use of the New Scots.[31] Hamilton's party which favoured renewed military intervention in England was now emerging as the dominant faction in Scotland, and the Scottish army in Ireland, so badly treated by the English, was coming to be seen by it as a major asset, too valuable to be withdrawn or allowed to disband for lack of food.

At some time in the course of the negotiations in 1647 a firm offer evidently had been made to the New Scots by the English for satisfaction of their arrears; exactly when it was made is not clear, but it seems that the English commissioners in Ireland were authorised to offer the army £150,000 sterling to start with, and if necessary to let the New Scots know that,

30. T.S.A.I. pp. 141-6; A. Mackenzie, *History of the Monros of Fowlis* (Inverness, 1898), pp. 262-3; Mitchell and Christie, *Records*, I, 323-4.
31. Fotheringham, *Correspondence*, II, 253-4, 299, 312-13; T.S.A.I. pp. 146, 148-9, 151-3; *L.J.* IX, 474-5, 640-1; McNeill, *Tanner Letters*, pp. 271-2; S.R.O. PA.11/5, ff. 92, 108v-109v, 137, 157, 193; *A.P.S.* VI, i, 66; Stevenson, 'Financing of the Cause of the Covenants', *S.H.R.* LI, 112-13.

provided they agreed in advance to accept it, £200,000 sterling would be offered. But, if the offer was made, it must have been rejected as inadequate, for nothing more was heard of it.[32]

ii. The Engagement, 1647-1648

There were two different ways in which the New Scots could be useful to Hamilton's party if it did undertake a war with England; by joining royalists in Ireland in opposing parliament's forces there, or by crossing to Scotland to take part in the invasion of England. At first the former alternative was favoured. At the end of August 1647 (just a month after Ormond had surrendered Dublin to parliament) Inchiquin's Scottish major general, Robert Sterling, and one of his servants, Thomas Marshall, wrote to Leven, Robert Monro, Johnston of Wariston and other leading Scots declaring their opposition to the proceedings of the new model army in England, which in June had seized the king and marched on London to overawe parliament in favour of the Independents. Sterling declared the willingness of Inchiquin's officers to up-hold the covenant and presbyterianism in opposition to parliament. This approach, hinting at the willingness of the Munster Protestants to ally themselves with Hamilton's party, was thwarted by Colonel Michael Jones, parliament's commander in Dublin; he intercepted the letters and sent them to London. Parliament then wrote to Inchiquin demanding that Sterling and Marshall be sent to England. If he refused 'or that army should stand on terms, we do conceive it will be understood a declaring of war against the Parliament'. It seems probable that Inchiquin knew of Sterling's and Marshall's actions—and parliament clearly suspected as much—but under this threat he sent them to London. After interrogation they were freed in February 1648 and given passes to travel to

32. The only evidence for this offer is R. Venables, *The Narrative of General Venables*, ed. C. H. Firth (Camden Society, 1900), pp. 2-3; Venables says Sir Robert King, who had been one of the commissioners, told him about it. The story is very plausible; the procedure of offering one sum but letting it be known that a higher offer would be made if an undertaking was given in advance that it would be accepted was exactly that which had been followed in negotiations with the Scottish army in England in 1646. King was one of the parliamentary commissioners to whom Ormond surrendered Dublin in July 1647, and it was probably at about that time that the offer to the New Scots was made. Carte, *Ormond*, II, 13 states that £200,000 sterling was due to the New Scots, but cites no source.

Scotland, it having evidently been decided that leniency was necessary to avoid antagonising Inchiquin's army.[33]

Hopes of an alliance with Inchiquin had disappeared for the moment, but the Scots were busy seeking other allies in Ireland. In October 1647 Ormond met the imprisoned king at Hampton Court, and Charles arranged a secret meeting between him and Scots commissioners who had been sent by Hamilton's party to negotiate with him, the earls of Loudoun, Lanark (Hamilton's brother) and Lauderdale. They met in a wood near Marlow and the Scots revealed that Hamilton intended to invade England to help the king. Ormond welcomed the idea and agreed to return to Ireland to create a royalist diversion there.[34] In the ever-changing political alignments of the time the refusal of the New Scots to garrison Dublin and Ormond's recent surrender of it to parliament became major miscalculations.

On 26 December the three Scots commissioners signed a secret treaty with the king which became known as the Engagement. Among its clauses was a stipulation that the king would see to it that the arrears of the Scottish army in Ireland would be paid 'out of the land of that kingdom or otherwise'.[35] It was, it seems, at first intended that the New Scots should help Ormond in Ireland, but difficulties arose because persuading the Scottish parliament to accept the decision to intervene in England took some months, so orders could not be sent to the army to co-operate with Ormond. In January 1648 Robert Monro therefore refused to grant passes to Ormond's agents,[36] and when in March Ormond wrote from France asking that (as had been agreed at the meeting near Marlow) the New Scots be sent orders to obey him, Loudoun, Lauderdale and Lanark had to reply that this could not be done as the Scottish parliament had not yet declared for the king, though they would advise the army to obey him. Ormond also asked that the New Scots be ordered to attack Owen Roe O'Neill to prevent him suppressing those of the

33. McNeill, *Tanner Letters*, pp. 259-65, 278-9, 281-2; H.M.C. 29: *Portland*, I, 433-5; *L.J.* IX, 445, 452, 513, 517, 647, 657, X, 45, 63, 64, 73; *C.J.* V, 307; H.M.C. 63: *Egmont*, I, ii, 467.
34. H.M.C. 36: *Ormond*, N.S. II, 354, 355; Cox, *Hibernia Anglicana*, II, 202; Carte, *Ormond*, II, 12; E. Hyde, earl of Clarendon, *The History of the Rebellion and Civil Wars in Ireland* (3rd ed. 1740), p. 80.
35. Gardiner, *Constitutional Documents of the Puritan Revolution*, p. 351.
36. Carte MSS, 22, f. 3.

Irish confederates who inclined to support the king, but again only advice, not orders, could be sent to Robert Monro.[37]

As Ormond's letter indicated, the Irish confederates were still being torn by internal feuds. In February 1648 Inchiquin opened negotiations with the Irish; in April he agreed on a truce with them and followed this up by declaring for the king, thus finally deserting parliament. But, as over the Ormond Peace of 1646, Rinuccini split the Irish by opposing the truce, fearing it would lead the Irish to betray the church's interests in favour of the king's. He therefore again appealed for help from Owen Roe O'Neill's Ulster army, and excommunicated all who accepted the truce. The New Scots did not, as Ormond had hoped, manage to stop Owen Roe from advancing south, and during the summer a half-hearted civil war was fought between Rinuccini and Owen Roe on the one hand and the Irish supreme council and Inchiquin on the other. Inchiquin sent an agent (Major William Paterson) to Scotland to appeal for help, and late in June the committee of estates agreed to accept him as an ally, promising to assist him 'to their power', to send agents to reside with him, and to include him in any peace treaties; but in the event nothing was done beyond ordering Robert Monro to keep correspondence with him.[38] Many in Scotland opposed alliance with Inchiquin since he had allied himself to Irish Catholics, and in any case all the resources of the Engagers were needed in Scotland; there was nothing to spare for Ireland.

Remarkably, though Rinuccini had spread dissension among the Irish by denouncing the truce with Inchiquin, he at the same time managed to justify to himself secret negotiations between Owen Roe O'Neill and the New Scots.[39] The origins and course of the negotiations are obscure, but they apparently began at the end of 1647. Rinuccini hoped that Monro's army bitterly resenting its treatment by the English parliament, would ally itself to Owen Roe, or at least make a truce

37. Carte, *Original Letters and Papers*, II, 353-4; H.M.C. 21: *Hamilton*, I, 120; Gardiner, *Hamilton Papers*, p. 214; Carte MSS, 22, f. 51; Carte, *Ormond*, II, 23.
38. Bottigheimer, *English Money and Irish Land*, p. 110; Bagwell, *Stuarts*, II, 164-71; H.M.C. 29: *Portland*, I, 469-70, 485-6; S.R.O. PA.11/6, ff. 45v-46v, 66v; Carte MSS, 22, ff. 222, 523; R. K. Marshall, 'Calendar of the Correspondence in the Hamilton Archives at Lennoxlove' (Appendix to Ph.D. thesis, Edinburgh University, 1970), II, 342, no. 2413.
39. P. J. Corish, 'Rinuccini's Censure of 27 May 1648', *Irish Theological Quarterly*, XVIII (1951), 324.

with him. This would allow the Ulster Irish forces (increasingly hated in the other provinces) to return to their homes 'and perhaps afterwards pass over to Scotland and carry the Catholic religion with them to that country. Certain it is that Ireland will never be at peace until the war be carried into the homes of others'.[40] This was a preposterous hope; the New Scots might be prepared to do many things to protect and advance their own interests, but it was inconceivable that they would agree to encourage an Irish Catholic invasion of Scotland. It may be that the New Scots made approaches for a truce with Owen Roe which would preserve the military *status quo* in Ulster in order to secure themselves from one enemy so they could concentrate their attention on forcing payment of arrears from the English. But if this was so the approaches failed, and when George Monck alleged that some New Scots were corresponding with the Irish this was indignantly denied.[41] The need for such a truce had been conveniently removed by Rinuccini himself, when he called Owen Roe south in his unsuccessful attempt to break the truce with Inchiquin.

The confused civil war among the Irish which followed on the Inchiquin truce, and the fact that Ormond did not even reach Ireland until the end of September (when he landed at Cork),[42] ment that no strong royalist interest emerged in Ireland to divert the English parliament's attention from the Scottish invasion of England. Moreover Hamilton and the Engagers met with much stronger opposition within Scotland than they had expected, from Argyll's party and the kirk. They therefore decided to abandon the plan for using the New Scots in Ireland and instead to bring many of them to Scotland to help in subduing resistance to the Engagement and in invading England.[43]

The first suggestions that New Scots be sent to Scotland to help the Engagers came in unofficial and secret approaches initiated by Lanark, who sent Lieutenant Colonel Borthwick to Ireland as his agent to 'by power of perswasion' get the New Scots to offer help. This was successfully done; on

40. Aiazza, *Embassy*, pp. 357, 360, 374; O'Connell and O'Ferrall, *Commentarius Rinuccinianus*, III, 73.
41. T.S.A.I. p. 153.
42. Bagwell, *Stuarts*, II, 171.
43. Carte MSS, 22, f. 312.

7 April the council of war at Carrickfergus wrote to the Scottish parliament that 'if it shall please God bussines betwixt both kingdomes draw to any publict ingagement we will be readie to our power to hazard our Interest with the parliament of the kingdom of Scotland for religion covenant king and countrie'—provided adequate supplies were sent for both those who returned to Scotland and those who remained in Ireland. In May the British leaders Lord Montgomery and Sir Robert Stewart joined the New Scots in offering to send men to help the Engagers in Scotland. But opposition to the Engagers as well as support for them was emerging in Ulster; from the first Argyll's regiment showed itself reluctant to support the army's offer to the Engagers.[44]

The Scottish parliament replied that it could not accept the offer of help since no resolution to intervene in England had yet been taken, but nonetheless the army was asked to prepare help in case it was needed. Early in May, after the raising of an Engager army in Scotland had begun, Lord Cochrane (as Sir William Cochrane of Cowdoun now was), Garthland and Alexander Crawford were commissioned to cross to Ireland to ask for troops from both the New Scots and the British, with promises that any peace treaty would include provision for complete settlement of the arrears of the New Scots. One month's pay would be given, half before the forces left Ireland, half after their arrival in Scotland.[45] English commissioners in Edinburgh, hearing of the mission to Ulster, hastily dispatched counter-appeals and promises for George Monck to present to the New Scots and British; the English parliament was willing to do something to satisfy their arrears, but if they betrayed parliament they would 'hazard their undoubted right to what is now due to them for their long and faithful services in Ireland'.[46] But such sudden expressions of good will and appreciation of the army's services came too late to be convincing.

44. T.S.A.I. p. 154; Burnet, *Hamilton*, 342; H.M.C. 21: *Hamilton*, II, 69-70 (the date suggested for this letter, 1644, is wrong; it should be about March 1648); Marshall, 'Calendar', II, 333, 334, 337, nos. 2404, 2405, 2320, 2399, 2332.
45. T.S.A.I. pp. 155-6, 159-62; Burnet, *Hamilton*, p. 349; *A.P.S.* VI, ii, 46, 67-8, 86-7; Guthry, *Memoirs*, p. 268; Reid, *History of the Presbyterian Church*, II, 344-5; S.R.O. PA.11/6, ff. 4v, 7v; Fotheringham, *Correspondence*, II, 487, 499. Lord Cochrane asked to be excused from going to Ireland, but without success, *A.P.S.* VI, ii, 91.
46. McNeill, *Tanner Letters*, pp. 202-3.

The army had in fact already made detailed plans for sending men to Scotland; 2,100 men were to go, 300 from each of the seven New Scots regiments, and the army stipulated that they must form a distinct command, subject only to the commander in chief, the Scottish parliament and their own officers. Recruits were to be sent to Ireland to replace New Scots who had previously left, and the 2,100 men were to be returned to Ireland later. Robert Monro was to remain behind in Ulster and to be appointed governor of the province. Though not stated at this point, the army was also resolved that George Monro should command the men sent to Scotland as major general, thus attaining the rank he had nearly reached in 1646. In reply both the committee of estates and parliament promised the army full satisfaction, and urged it to make haste in sending men as an English army was advancing against Scotland.[47] But the New Scots were no more willing to accept vague promises from Scotland than from England; they were determined to see at least some promises fulfilled before they acted.

This determination was made clear as soon as Cochrane, Garthland and Crawford landed in Ulster. They found Robert Monro very co-operative and most officers willing to support sending 2,100 New Scots to Scotland, and in addition some of them undertook to recruit 900 more footmen in Ulster. No British infantry units could be persuaded to leave Ulster, but it was hoped to provide 1,500 horsemen, raised mainly by George Monro, Sir Francis Hamilton and Sir Robert Stewart. But none of these men would sail from Ulster until they were paid specified sums; on this the officers were adamant. More than £11,000 sterling would have to be sent to Ulster. Moreover, Lord Cochrane and his colleagues soon found that their first report on the situation in Ulster had been too optimistic. On 16 June they had to report that Argyll's regiment absolutely refused to support the Engagement, and that though Glencairn's officers were willing to provide men the men themselves were showing reluctance. And though some British commanders had declared their willingness to help they had not the ability to carry out their promises. Nonetheless, it was still hoped that 3,000 foot and 1,200 horse would be

47. T.S.A.I. pp. 156-9, 164; S.R.O. PA.11/6, ff. 12, 12v-13, 14v; *A.P.S.* VI, ii, 103. 122-3.

ready to sail by 26 June.[48]

That Argyll's regiment should oppose the Engagement was natural, for Argyll was leading resistance to the Engagers in Scotland; but Glencairn was a strong supporter of the Engagement, though his regiment held out against it. In Eglinton's regiment the conflict was the other way round. Led by the earl's son, Colonel James Montgomery, the regiment agreed to join the Engagers, though his father wrote to him denouncing them: 'I sie no appearance thay have Godis direction in thair wayes, and thair is small appeirance they sall haue good success to their intentions'.[49] Such efforts of the opponents of the Engagement to turn the New Scots against it were however hindered by the interception and suppression of letters from Johnston of Wariston to the army urging rejection of it.[50]

The committee of estates at once accepted the terms proposed by the New Scots. By 21 June £8,000 sterling had been sent to Ireland and another £3,000 was being raised. George Monro was given power to dismiss any officers who refused to co-operate with him. Such men were to be regarded as enemies to religion, king and kingdom, and reduced by force if necessary. Orders were given to collect boats ready to go to Ireland to bring over the men—though a proclamation forbade any men to go to Ireland without permission, to prevent anti-Engagers fleeing the country to avoid being recruited into the Engagers' army.[51]

On 27 June the New Scots officers at Carrickfergus formally declared that Glencairn's regiment was no longer part of the army, being an enemy to its undertakings; its officers had first agreed to help the Engagers but then 'resyled'. Individual officers and men who joined the rest of the army would however be excepted from this denunciation. Argyll's regiment presented a different problem, for it was said that its refusal to help the Engagers was against the wills of most of the

---

48. S.R.O. PA.12/2, letters of 10 and 16 June 1648; Fotheringham, *Correspondence*, II, 519; see also Marshall, 'Calendar', II, 336, 339, 340, nos. 2324, 2335, 2338.
49. Fraser, *Memorials of the Montgomeries*, I, 286; H.M.C. 10: *10th Report*, I, 56-7.
50. C. H. Firth, ed. 'Narratives illustrating the Duke of Hamilton's expedition to England in 1648', *S.H.S. Miscellany*, II (1904), 294.
51. S.R.O. PA.11/6, ff. 28, 29-29v, 34-34v, 128; S.R.O. PA.16/3/12; Steele, *Proclamations*, II, 335, 342.

officers and men, but that they were afraid of oppression by their superiors. They were therefore offered the protection of the rest of the army if they became Engagers.[52] This action was effective; by 29 June it could be reported that the regiment had agreed to supply men—though only after Lieutenant Colonel Sir Dugald Campbell of Auchinbreck and Major William Campbell had been cashiered by George Monro and replaced by two of the regiment's captains, Duncan Campbell of Inverliver and Alexander MacAulay respectively.[53] Only Glencairn's regiment remained obstinate, though its lieutenant colonel, William Cunningham, was doing all he could to persuade it to change its mind. Thirty-six companies of foot, good experienced soldiers and well led, had by this time been paid and were ready to sail. Money had also been distributed to provide 1,100 horse, and negotiations for more men were continuing. Those who were ready would sail to Kirkcudbright early in July on their way to join Hamilton's army which was assembling on the western Borders.[54]

Bringing men to Scotland took longer than expected, through shortage of ships, but they had probably all landed by the end of July, for by that time Lord Cochrane and the other commissioners were back in Edinburgh, and they had been ordered to remain in Ireland until all the men had left.[55] As well as being hindered by shortage of ships, the transport of the men was complicated by ships of the English parliament which tried to intercept the forces crossing to Scotland; it was said they captured 300 men and sent them back to Ireland. In addition a frigate owned by Argyll was active, doubtless being mainly concerned with preventing men of his own regiment helping the Engagers.[56]

How many men George Monro managed in the end to bring to Scotland is uncertain. Royalist propaganda put the

52. T.S.A.I. p. 165.
53. S.R.O. PA.11/6, ff. 126-7. In 1663 Archibald Stewart of Ballintoy claimed the credit for having persuaded 500 of Argyll's men to join the Engagers under the command of Alexander MacAulay, who was Stewart's son in law, Hill, 'Stewarts of Ballintoy', *U.J.A.* N.S. VII (1901), 17.
54. S.R.O. PA.12/2, letters of 29 June and 6 July 1648; S.R.O. PA.11/6, ff. 73-73v; Marshall, 'Calendar', II, 344, no. 2416.
55. S.R.O. PA.11/6, ff. 73-73v, 92-92v, 103v.
56. *C.S.P.D. 1648-9*, p. 201; Rushworth, *Historical Collections*, IV, ii, 1202; S.R.O. PA.11/6, f. 100v; Fotheringham, *Correspondence*, II, 530; Burnet, *Hamilton*, p. 357; Reid, *History of the Presbyterian Church*, II, 73; *C.J.* VI, 645; Marshall, 'Calendar', II, 345, no. 2353.

total as high as 4,000 men. Henry Guthry thought there were 2,000 foot and 1,000 horse. Cromwell heard that the total was 1,500 foot and 1,200 horse, Montereul that it was 2,400 men. But perhaps the most accurate estimate was the lowest; James Turner was adjutant general to Hamilton's army and he reported that George Monro had not more than 1,500 foot and 400 horse.[57] The latter were, it seems, divided into twelve troops.[58]

Hamilton invaded England on 8 July, before the men from Ireland had joined his army, and advanced slowly south. At the beginning of August George Monro arrived at Kendal to ask for his orders. Hamilton wished him to bring his men to join the main army, but was deterred from doing so by disputes among his senior officers, sparked off by Monro. Monro claimed that his commission made him directly dependent on Hamilton, and he therefore refused to obey orders from the two lieutenant generals, the earl of Callander (a man almost as touchy as Monro himself, especially where precedence was concerned) and William Baillie. A further complication was that the committee of estates had, on Hamilton's advice, commissioned Crawford–Lindsay (who had remained in Scotland) to command the forces from Ireland, stating that he was to be subordinate to both Hamilton and Callander, and Monro to him. Hamilton weakly sought to solve the problem by separating the main parties to it. Instead of ordering George Monro to march his men south he ordered him to remain in Scotland to guard an artillery train that was supposed to be being assembled.[59]

Thus 'For all practical purposes Monro might as well have remained in Ireland'.[60] At considerable expense the Engagers had brought men from Ireland to help them, but when they faced Cromwell at Preston on 17 August Monro's forces were many miles away. At the battle of Preston and in the days that followed Hamilton's army was completely destroyed. On news of this the anti-Engagers in Scotland, who were becoming known as the kirk party, raised forces, marched on

57. *Joyfull Newes from the Kings Majesty* ... (1648), p. 5; Guthry, *Memoirs*, p. 279; Abbott, *Writings and Speeches of Oliver Cromwell*, I, 634; Fotheringham, *Correspondence*, II, 530, 531; Turner, *Memoirs*, pp. 242-3.
58. *A.P.S.* VII, appendix, pp. 12, 97.
59. S.R.O. PA.11/6, f. 40v; Burnet, *Hamilton*, pp. 357-8; Guthry, *Memoirs*, p. 283.
60. Gardiner, *Civil War*, IV, 181.

Edinburgh and set up a new regime.

George Monro and his men had proved useless to the Engagers in helping them towards victory, but they proved very useful to them in defeat. Since Monro had not been involved in the disaster at Preston he was able to fall back and join forces with the earl of Lanark and the few other Engagers in arms in Scotland, thus providing them with an army. Even with his help the Engagers could not resist the new kirk party regime (which had Cromwell's backing), but it did at least allow them to negotiate for terms instead of surrendering unconditionally. Early in September Monro and Lanark marched north and occupied Stirling, enabling them to threaten to retire into the Highland and begin a civil war unless generous terms were granted to them.

One of their main demands was that the forces from Ireland should be given a month's pay 'and that boates and shipps presently be provided for our transportation into Ireland'. But when at the end of September a treaty was signed nothing was said about this; the Engagers undertook to disband all their forces on being promised that their lives and estates would not be forfeited. Monro opposed accepting these terms, but found little support; even among those who had come with him from Ireland only Thomas Dalyell and James Galbraith were willing to stand by him. He attempted to march west to take ship for Ireland to 'try what fortune they could make there'. But on the march the 'people of the West Countrey fell upon those who were returning to Ireland, plundered, abused and dispersed them in their way betwixt Glasgow and Air'. The final blow came when it was learnt that they would find no refuge in Ulster, as in their absence the remaining New Scots had been dispersed by parliament's forces. George Monro disbanded his men and fled to Holland.[61]

By sending troops to help the Engagers the New Scots had made war on the English parliament. It was therefore to be expected that parliament would take advantage of the opportunity presented by the removal of most of the New Scots to rid itself of those who remained. Parliament had at first tried to prevent George Monro leaving Ireland, but once he had gone orders were sent to prevent him or his men

61. Turner, *Memoirs*, p. 69; Burnet, *Hamilton*, pp. 368-9, 371, 375; Guthry, *Memoirs*, pp. 284, 288-90, 295-6; H.M.C. 55: *Various Collections*, V, 147; Birch, *State Papers*, I, 104; S.R.O. PA.11/7, f. 16.

returning, and George Monck was instructed to encourage Argyll's and Glencairn's regiments, and any other Scots who opposed the Engagement, by giving them supplies; Glencairn's men were to be given 600 suits of clothes. In addition Monck was to do all he could to obtain possession of Belfast.[62]

In September Monck decided he could do more than this. The absence of Owen Roe O'Neill in the south meant that he had little to fear from the Irish, and news of Preston must have greatly strengthened parliament's prestige in Ulster. Monck believed he could attack the New Scots without fear that the British would come to their aid, and he must have feared that George Monro, still in arms in Scotland, would return to Ireland and reinforce the New Scots unless he acted quickly. In taking action against Robert Monro, Monck was helped by some of the New Scots themselves. As the result of its refusal to support the Engagement Glencairn's regiment had been deprived of some of its quarters; this and hostility to the Engagers led some of its officers to hold secret talks with Monck. The result was a plot to seize Carrickfergus in which Major William Knox, Captain Bryce Cochrane and Sir Robert Adair of Kinhilt (as captain of one of the horse troops attached to the New Scots) took leading parts. According to one account Glencairn's regiment was still helping to guard Carrickfergus and early in the morning of 16 September Bryce Cochrane, captain of the night watch, opened the north gate to Adair and his men; by another account the men of Glencairn's regiment overpowered the guards and opened the gate. The garrison surrendered without a fight, partly perhaps because they were reluctant to resist fellow Scots who had recently been their comrades. Robert Monro was ignominiously captured in 'bed with his ladye' and dispatched to London as a prisoner. On news of the fall of Carrickfergus the New Scots in Belfast surrendered, and when Monck advanced against Coleraine it too capitulated.[63]

Thus tamely the Scottish army in Ireland ceased to exist.

62. *C.S.P.I. 1647-60*, pp. 24, 27, 784, 785; *C.S.P.D. 1648-9*, p. 260; Young, *Old Belfast*, pp. 67-8; *C.J.* VI, 645.
63. Adair, *Narrative*, pp. 149-52; Hogan, *War of Ireland*, pp. 65-6; H.M.C. 6: *7th Report*, pp. 52-3; Shuckburgh, *Two Biographies*, p. 174; *A Letter concerning Colonel Monks surprising the Town and Castle of Carrickfergus and Belfast ...* (London, 1648); Rushworth, *Historical Collections*, IV, ii, 1277, 1282, 1284; *C.J.* VI, 4, 37, 41, 43; Guthry, *Memoirs*, p. 296; Reid, *History of the Presbyterian Church*, II, 75-8.

Monck had suppressed the once formidable New Scots so easily that there were rumours that Robert Monro had betrayed his own army to Monck for money,[64] but there is no need to search for such far fetched explanations. The New Scots were demoralised by disputes among themselves about the Engagement and had been much weakened by George Monro's departure with something like half their men. After news of the battle of Preston arrived they must have been near despair. Most of them had staked their hopes on the Engagement, and now that it had failed it was obvious that the English parliament would not pay their arrears. The final blow was the betrayal of Carrickfergus by Glencairn's men. Resistance seemed pointless. The army no longer had any powerful allies to support it, for the new kirk party regime in Scotland was hostile to it (because of its support for the Engagement), and many of the British of Ulster had come to see the New Scots as oppressors rather than saviours. Only Lord Montgomery and Sir James Montgomery showed any tendency to resist Monck's dispersal of the army; they demanded to know why he had attacked the New Scots, and they refused to join him on his march to Coleraine.[65] The rest of the British, even those who had supported the Engagement, kept quiet, fearing Monck would act against them too.

Such fears were justified, for though the New Scots had been dealt with so easily, parliament's hold on Ulster was still fragile, reflecting the demoralisation of its opponents rather than the strength of support for it or the strength of its own forces. Monck was instructed to garrison Carrickfergus with Englishmen and the other Ulster ports with men of undoubted loyalty, and an inquiry was begun to discover which of the British commanders had co-operated in sending men to help the Engagers in Scotland. On 4 October he was ordered by Sir Charles Coote to arrest such men—but gradually, to prevent resistance developing. News that Ormond had landed in Cork increased fears about the reliability of the British, for he might provide a focus for a royalist revival. Cromwell was urged to

---

64. Benn, *History of Belfast*, I, 123; Carte, *Ormond*, II, 44. There is no evidence for the allegation in T. Gumble, *The Life of General Monck, Duke of Albemarle* (London, 1671), p. 27 that Monck seized Monro because Monro was planning to seize him.
65. Hill, *Montgomery Manuscripts*, pp. 173-5, 181; Reid, *History of the Presbyterian Church*, II, 78-9.

send five or six hundred English troops to Ulster, since most of the Ulster British were of Scots origin and only obeyed parliament out of fear, and on 4 November instructions were dispatched from London to Coote and Monck to arrest Lord Montgomery, Sir James Montgomery, Sir Robert Stewart, the officers of Sir William Stewart's regiment and Colonel Audley Mervyn (all but the last Old Scots) for fear that they declare for the king.[66]

Monck and Coote had af first tried to conciliate the Scots—Monck attended a presbytery meeting at Lisburn, protesting his good will, to disarm suspicion—but soon turned to suppressing them. He called a council of war of the British forces nominally under his command at Lisburn. Lord Montgomery and the earl of Clanbrassil (the former Lord Claneboye) were too suspicious to attend, prudently sending representatives; Sir James Montgomery appeared and was promptly arrested. In the west Sir Robert Stewart and Audley Mervyn were captured by Coote by similar trickery. The prisoners were sent to England; Stewart escaped from custody in February 1649 and fled to Holland, while Montgomery and Mervyn were allowed to return to Ireland in May after swearing to live peaceably.[67]

Thus, by the end of 1648, the New Scots had been dispersed, the Old Scots forced into resentful submission with some of their leaders removed.

iii. The Aftermath, 1648-1650

The kirk party regime in Scotland was at first reliant on Cromwell's support. Even after the Engagers disbanded the new regime could not afford to offend him and the English parliament, even though the hated Independents now held power in England. An uneasy alliance therefore emerged between the revolutionary regimes in the two kingdoms. In some ways the kirk party doubtless regretted the loss of the Scottish army in Ireland, since the loss of a foothold in Ulster weakened Scotland's bargaining position in negotiations with England and left the country open to attack from Ireland.

66. *C.S.P.D. 1648-9*, pp. 268, 298, 311, 318; *C.S.P.I. 1647-60*, pp. 30, 31, 785.
67. Hill, *Montgomery Manuscripts*, pp. 182, 186; *C.S.P.D. 1649-50*, pp. 101, 103, 119, 123, 526, 572; Carte, *Ormond*, II, 59-60; Gilbert, *Irish Confederation*, VII, 224-5; Adair, *Narrative*, p. 152.

But as most of the New Scots had supported the Engagement the kirk party was obliged to approve Monck's action against them. Sir Robert Adair came to Scotland to explain his conduct in helping Monck, and by giving its approbation to his action the committee of estates tacitly approved the suppression of the New Scots.[68] But it was still hoped to save something from the debacle. On 3 November Major James Wallace was dispatched to Ulster to contact former New Scots who had 'continued honest' by opposing the Engagers. He was to get them to authorise representatives to negotiate on their behalf with the English parliament for payment of their arrears. At the same time a message was sent to England asking for pay for such 'honest' men and inquiring what was to be done with the New Scots still in Ireland. Finally, the committee of estates ordered the compilation of an inventory of the artillery and ammunition in Ulster which belonged to Scotland.[69] Thus the kirk party still hoped to get some arrears paid, to salvage some equipment from Ulster, and perhaps even that the English would continue to employ some New Scots. Such hopes were vain; England simply ignored all inquiries.

What had happened to the New Scots officers and men after Monck seized Carrickfergus, Belfast and Coleraine? Some no doubt fled to Scotland, but the majority seem to have remained in Ireland. Many continued for some time in arms, evidently still exacting food from the inhabitants of their quarters as in the past. This was particularly true of those who had opposed the Engagement; they presented no immediate threat to parliament's interests and Monck doubtless feared that any harsh action against them might endanger parliament's fragile hold in Ulster. Thus though the Scottish army in Ireland no longer existed no attempt was made to expel those who had served in it from Ulster. In December 1648 seventeen officers of Argyll's regiment who were, as they put it, free from the late unlawful Engagement, signed a commission at Dunluce for a commissioner from them to consult with the marquis of Argyll and the kirk party in Scotland about appointing representatives to join with those of other regiments in seeking payment of arrears by England.[70] In June

68. S.R.O. PA.11/7, f. 57.
69. Ibid. f. 75; S.R.O. PA.12/2, report of subcommittee approved on 2 November 1648; *A.P.S.* VI, ii, 149, 696.
70. Argyll MSS, Inveraray Vaults, V, 19 (copy in Argyll Transcripts, XII, 201).

1649 Bryce Cochrane was serving as captain of Carrickfergus Castle, presumably with some of the men of Glencairn's regiment serving under him, though the town did have an English governor.[71] Another example of a former New Scot being employed by the English parliament was Patrick Bruce, a captain in Home's regiment who had been cashiered for refusing the Engagement in 1648 but served under Monck as a lieutenant colonel in 1649.[72] Probably some whole companies of New Scots soldiers as well as many individuals were taken into parliamentary pay, provided they had opposed the Engagement.

This leniency towards the New Scots was wise in that it prevented them being driven into desperate resistance to parliament, but Monck must have realised from the first that, as with many of the British, they had submitted because there seemed no option, and felt no real loyalty to parliament—as events proved, for most of them soon rejected parliament's authority in Ulster. In December 1648 the province had seemed completely subdued, but two events in January 1649 completely changed the situation; the execution of the king, and the signing of a new peace between Ormond and the Irish confederates.

The execution of Charles I was generally condemned in Ulster, both by those with royalist sympathies and by extreme presbyterians who looked to the kirk party in Scotland for leadership. On hearing of the execution the kirk party immediately denounced it (and the subsequent abolition of monarchy in England and Ireland), and proclaimed Charles II king of England and Ireland as well as of Scotland. This abruptly broke the alliance between the kirk party and what was now the commonwealth of England. Covenanters and royalists now had in common detestation of the English regime, and the possibility of an alliance between them was greatly increased.

The other event of January 1649 which changed the political situation in Ireland brought the royalists very different allies. The Irish confederates, weakened by internal disputes and fearful of the growing power of the English parliament, concluded the Second Ormond Peace, whereby their

71. S.R.O. PA.7/23/2/64/1; Carte MSS, 25, ff. 25-6.
72. *C.S.P.I. 1647-60*, p. 634.

confederation was dissolved. Rinuccini denounced the peace but was unable to force its revocation; he therefore left Ireland in February. News of the peace gave the royalist-inclined British of Ulster hope that with their new Irish allies they would be able to successfully challenge parliament's power, while the news of the king's execution made them determined to reject the regime that had committed such an act.

On 15 February the presbytery in Ulster, imitating the kirk party in Scotland, denounced the English sectaries at length and ordered the renewal of the solemn league and covenant. The presbytery claimed also to oppose malignant royalists, but it clearly now saw the English commonwealth as the most serious threat to its interests. This proved very influential in turning many of the common people of Ulster, especially Scots, against the English regime, thus providing the British commanders with the men with which to undertake a rising against parliament. The fact that, for most of its leaders, it was a royalist rising, was at first carefully concealed to avoid offending the many presbyterians among the soldiers. By the end of March much of the Lagan army had risen against parliament and was besieging Sir Charles Coote in Londonderry. The king was proclaimed but the revolt was in its early stages a presbyterian one, led by Sir Alexander Stewart (son of the late Sir William Stewart); but royalists flocked to join him and gradually turned the rising into a royalist one, whereupon Stewart withdrew from the siege. In Antrim and Down on the other hand the leaders of resistance to parliament were from the first secret royalists, Lord Montgomery and the earl of Clanbrassil, though they renewed the covenant and led a rising ostensibly concerned with upholding it. Montgomery was chosen commander in chief of the British, and proclaimed Charles II; this was acceptable to presbyterians, for the kirk party had done the same in Scotland. But whereas the presbyterians would only admit the king to power once he had made concessions demanded by the kirk party, Montgomery was secretly determined to use the forces he raised (partly by false pretences) to help the king whether or not he made concessions.

As royalist and presbyterian reaction to the execution of the king grew, Monck's power in Ulster collapsed. The British regiments nominally under his command refused to obey him.

Montgomery seized Belfast, appointing as governor a New Scot, Lieutenant Colonel James Wallace, a man acceptable to presbyterians as he was committed to the kirk party. Monck lamented from Lisburn on 29 March 'Things are come to such a height now in these quarters that I cannot expect any better but that all the Scots will shake off their dependence upon the kingdom of England ... I cannot see how I, with these few English here that adhere to the Parliament, can hold this place'. It was said that 'Ther is non in thes pairts, except Papists, that have not taken the Covenant, even all the Englishe under Monck's command'. Monck was soon forced to abandon Lisburn and retire to Dundalk. Even once there his position was so weak that on 8 May he was forced to make a cessation or truce with the only possible ally available, Owen Roe O'Neill. Owen Roe for his part was prepared to accept this odd alliance because his position was just as isolated as Monck's; for he had remained loyal to Rinuccini and denounced the Ormond Peace, refusing to accept any alliance with royalists. In desperate need of supplies, he had informed Monck in March that he was willing to make a cessation. The two men had in common opposition to the royalists, though one was the most implacable of the native Irish Catholic leaders, the other the servant of the violently anti-Catholic and anti-Irish English parliament. By the terms of the cessation in May Monck and Owen Roe bound themselves not to make any peace with the royalists, and to assist each other if attacked. When parliament, several months later, heard of the cessation it denounced it, but by that time it had served its purpose by temporarily providing Monck with an ally.[73]

The 'royalist' risings in Ulster had taken place independently of Ormond and the new king; but they had meanwhile been making their own plans to regain Ulster. On fleeing from Scotland George Monro had joined Charles II (then still prince of Wales) in exile at the Hague. On 18 December 1648 Charles signed a letter for him to present to Ormond, recommending him as someone trustworthy who might be of use in the north

73. Cox, *Hibernia Anglicana*, II, Charles II, p. 15; Hill, *Montgomery Manuscripts*, pp. 177-81; H.M.C. 36: *Ormonde*, II, 90, 91; Adair, *Narrative*, pp. 153-64; Carte, *Ormond*, II, 67; Gilbert, *Contemporary History*, II, ix-x, xii, 216-19, 221-2, 227-8, 440; Reid, *History of the Presbyterian Church*, II, 101-10, 545-8; Colles, *History of Ulster*, III, 124-6; *The Declaration of the British in the North of Ireland ...* (1649).

of Ireland. Monro, however, did not leave for Ireland until late in February 1649, perhaps because he was dissatisfied with the vagueness of the king's letter. By the time he sailed he had got Charles to grant him a commission to be commander in chief of the Scottish army in the north of Ireland, though the commission was entrusted to Ormond to suppress or issue as he thought best. Ormond apparently agreed to issue the king's commission, but he also issued one of his own to Monro (who was also knighted, either by the king or Ormond). Ormond's commission, dated 7 March, appointed Monro commander in chief of all forces, horse and foot, to be employed on an expedition to the north of Ireland, in immediate subordination to the marquis of Clanricarde, who was the nominal commander of the expedition.[74] It is not certain that when he issued this commission Ormond already knew of the king's; probably he did, his own commission being intended to add to the king's by giving Monro authority over men to be sent to Ulster as well as over Scots already there.

Judging by his commission from the king Sir George Monro's task was to revive the New Scots army and join with the Old Scots in subduing Ulster for the king. It was also hoped that he would be able to spread the war to Scotland; he later described this as being the main reason for his return to Ireland. He brought from the Hague a letter from Montrose to Ormond asking for help, and Ormond still had some contacts with Lanark and Lauderdale, the Engager leaders.[75] But in the event neither Monro nor Ormond were ever to be in a position to help the king's Scottish supporters, who wasted much of their time and energy in personal feuds; Montrose and the Engager leaders despised and distrusted each other.

Ormond's plan for an expedition to Ulster was conceived before the risings there against parliament, but it soon turned into an attempt to help and extend these risings. On 14 May he instructed Monro to march to Roscommon and there consult with Clanricarde about reducing Sligo and other places in Connaught still held by parliament's supporters. He was

74. Gilbert, *Irish Confederation*, VII, 261, 354; Gilbert, *Contemporary History*, I, 294, II, 40; H.M.C. 70: *Pepys*, p. 242; Carte MSS, 23, ff. 186, 400; Carte, *Original Letters and Papers*, II, 368.
75. Wishart, *Memoirs of Montrose*, p. 245; Carte MSS, 22, ff. 455-6, 26, f. 339; Gilbert, *Irish Confederation*, VII, 232-3.

also to discover what the situation in western Ulster was and, if not delayed in Connaught, march to help in the siege of Londonderry. He was to get in touch with Lord Montgomery and other British leaders; but he was not to reveal to Montgomery and his followers his commission from the king unless, after consulting with Humphry Galbraith, he thought this adviseable. The difficulty was that Ormond had learnt that the British of Antrim and Down had chosen Montgomery to be their commander in chief, and he had applied to Ormond for a commission to regularise his position. This Ormond had granted, making Montgomery chief commander in the field in Ulster, though Monro already had a commission from the king to command the Scots in Ulster. Ormond was now trying to prevent a quarrel between the two commanders by concealing Monro's commission, though he did concede that Monro should command the Lagan army, which presumably meant Montgomery's command was to be limited to Antrim and Down.[76]

When Charles II at the Hague heard of Montgomery's rising he added further to the confusion by signing a commission to him to be commander in chief of all forces in Ulster under Ormond. This he entrusted to Sir Robert Stewart, who was returning to Ulster, with orders not to deliver it until Ormond had sorted out some demarcation between Montgomery and Monro, unless such a delay would endanger the king's service. Charles justified his action by arguing that though he had granted a similar commission to Monro this had been done because he thought only the former New Scots in Ulster would rise on his behalf; now many of the British, who had never been commanded by Sir George Monro, had also risen, so it was necessary to appoint a British commander.[77] The argument made sense, but such a confusion of commissions was bound to lead to trouble.

Quite apart from worries about who was to command in Ulster, Ormond had doubts about the strength of the royalist position there, for the presbyterians were still 'the great rulers of that country'. 'I confess, I understand not perfectly the submission of that province, that fatal ingredient of the

76. Carte MSS, 23, ff. 699, 708; Gilbert, *Contemporary History*, I, 757-9.
77. Carte MSS, 24, ff. 706, 709-10; Hill, *Montgomery Manuscripts*, p. 181n; O. Ogle, W. H. Bliss and W. D. Macray, eds. *Calendar of Clarendon State Papers* (3 vols. Oxford, 1869-76), II, 11; *C.S.P.D. 1649-50*, p. 140.

Covenant having still some mixture in it'. The British leaders might serve the king, but most of the rank and file fought for the covenant. Lord Montgomery wished for a royal commission, but hoped at first to keep it secret, for to reveal it would turn his army against him unless the king reached an agreement with the kirk party in Scotland, since it was to the kirk party that his men looked for guidance.[78] Sir George Monro was ordered to play down the second Ormond Peace in Ulster, and not insist on acceptance of it, for fear of offending presbyterian consciences unhappy at dealings with the Catholic Irish.[79]

The force Ormond assigned to Sir George Monro was, he claimed, composed of English, Scots and Irish. In fact Irish Catholics predominated, together with some 'redshanks' (Catholic MacDonnells and their Ulster allies, and perhaps some Catholic Highlanders). They included a regiment commanded by Colonel MacDonnell (Antrim's brother). After helping Clanricarde to reduce Sligo, Monro advanced into Ulster. A garrison was placed in Enniskillen and aid was then given to the Lagan forces besieging Londonderry. The arrival of Monro and the presence of Sir Robert Stewart and Colonel Audley Mervyn (who both arrived late in May) finally turned the siege from a presbyterian to a royalist one, but Monro did not stay long before Londonderry. Impatient to recover what the New Scots had lost the previous year, he moved on and seized Coleraine before turning south through Antrim. Here he came into conflict with Lord Montgomery, for Montgomery tried to assert authority over Monro by publishing his commission from the king. Monro demanded entry to Belfast but this was refused, and for good measure Montgomery dismissed his own governor of the town, James Wallace. As Wallace was a New Scot it may have been feared that he would favour Monro, but it is more likely that Montgomery got rid of him since he was a supporter of the kirk party and therefore could no longer be trusted to obey Montgomery, whose royalism was increasingly open.

Though refusing Monro entry to Belfast, Montgomery offered him Carrickfergus in return for his help in capturing the town, which was still holding out for parliament under

78. Carte, *Original Letters and Papers*, II, 381, 391.
79. Carte MSS, 24, f. 699.

Monck's governor, Major Edmond Ellis, and his captain of the castle, Bryce Cochrane, formerly of Glencairn's regiment. Under their protection the presbytery met in the town and issued violent denunciations of Montgomery and Monro. The garrison of Carrickfergus sent desperate appeals for help to the kirk party in Scotland. This placed the Scots regime in a difficult position. Ellis and Cochrane were holding Carrickfergus for the English commonwealth, which the Scots refused to recognise and with which they were in bitter dispute over the covenant and the execution of the king. Yet those who were besieging Carrickfergus were royalists, even more hostile to the kirk party. If the royalists, in league with the Irish, subdued all Ulster this might lead to a royalist-Irish invasion of Scotland. The Scottish parliament therefore decided to help the Carrickfergus garrison; on 2 July orders were given to send it five or six hundred bolls of meal.

This resolution came too late, however. The garrison repulsed an attack on 28 June, but surrendered on terms on 4 July. The officers of the garrison were to be free to leave Ireland if they wished, the new royalist garrison was to be composed of 'recall Protestants', not Catholics, and Scotland's right to much artillery in the town was accepted. In furtherance of this last condition two Scots (Sir Robert Adair of Kinhilt being one) were dispatched to Ulster, but there is no evidence that the guns were ever returned to Scotland. Monro commissioned Thomas Dalyell, a fellow New Scot, to command Carrickfergus under him, and granted him the right to levy customs duties to support his garrison; this led to new disputes with Montgomery, who claimed the right to all customs duties in Ulster.

The royalists now controlled all Ulster except Londonderry, and after Carrickfergus fell many of what Ormond called 'Independent Presbyterians (for so they now distinguish the worst of them)' fled to Scotland. These were men who, like some of the adherents of the kirk party in Scotland, found the king's cause even more obnoxious than that of the English Independents. But the royalist triumph was fragile. Montgomery's open admission that he was fighting for the king in alliance with Irish Catholics led his own army and the Lagan forces to dwindle away fast. Many of their men insisted, like the kirk party, on the distinction between recognising Charles as king, in defiance of the English parliament's abolition of monarchy, and actually fighting for him, which would not be legitimate until he signed the covenants and submitted to presbyterianism.

Thus, though the Scottish army in Ireland no longer existed, the presbyterian missionary work that had been carried out under its protection now bore fruit and prevented the royalists holding on to their gains in Ulster. Some ministers had always been hostile to Montgomery's rising, and their numbers grew rather than declined as the risings against parliament prospered and their royalism became more clear cut. The fall of Carrick-fergus deprived the presbytery of a safe base to revile the royalists from, but it continued to defy Montgomery, issuing from Bangor on 7 July a declaration denouncing him for preferring the king's cause to that of religion, and forbidding anyone to obey him. Men began to desert from the royalist army in large numbers. Montgomery and Clanbrassil took their depleted forces to Dundalk but were repulsed by parliament's troops from Dublin. The demoralised Lagan forces before Londonderry were scattered by Owen Roe O'Neill, who now intervened to help Sir Charles Coote, just as he had previously helped Monck. Montgomery's forces were soon too weak for any offensive action, and an attempt by Monro (on Ormond's orders) to renew the siege of Londonderry failed. Rather absurdly Monro appealed to the Irish ancestry of the Monros in trying to persuade Owen Roe O'Neill not to oppose him; 'By my owen extraction I have some interest in the Irish Nation'. The point was hardly a convincing one, but his argument that Owen Roe in co-operating with the English parliament was helping the natural enemies of the Irish people who would reduce them to slavery was valid. Owen Roe refused to listen, and continued to help parliament. But just as the royalist forces in Ulster were collapsing through internal divisions brought about by the unnatural alliance between presbyterians, royalists and Irish, so were parliament's forces. Many of Monck's men at Dundalk deserted in disgust at his alliance with Owen Roe, and after Owen Roe's forces were scattered in a skirmish Monck was forced to abandon the town to a royalist force under Inchiquin.

This did nothing to revive the fortunes of the royalists, however; their Ulster forces had disintegrated, and some weeks before (on 2 August) Ormond's main army had been completely routed at Rathmines, just outside Dublin.[80] Thus the royalist attempts to subdue parliament's outposts in Ireland before its long-expected attempt to reconquer the country began failed. On 15 August Oliver Cromwell landed in Dublin, and moving north, he stormed Drogheda (11 September). Owen Roe had at last agreed to co-operate with Ormond, but he was already ill, and died on 6 November. Dundalk was abandoned by the royalists, and though Cromwell and most of his army returned to Dublin, news of the Drogheda massacre left few in Ulster willing to continue to resist when he sent Colonel Robert Venables north to join Sir Charles Coote. Carlingford, Newry and Belfast hastily surrendered to him; in Belfast it was said '800 Scots were afterwards turned out of the town, whither they had brought their wives and children to plant themselves there'.[81] Coote advanced from Londonderry and drove Monro from Coleraine, while Venables' approach from the south forced Monro to burn and abandon Lisburn and Antrim. In Carrickerfgus Thomas Dalyell resisted, but on 2 November he undertook to surrender to Coote and Venables on 13 December if he was not relieved by then. If he did surrender, the members of the garrison would be allowed to retain their arms, houses and baggage, and they and their families would be free to remain without persecution or to leave, as they wished. Before they surrendered the countryside would supply them with six weeks' pay for soldiers, one month's for officers.[82]

These terms seem remarkably generous; but it seems likely that they were carefully calculated, in the hope that they

80. For the confused campaign in Ulster in 1649 (up to July) see Hogan, *Warr of Ireland*, pp. 77-9; Adair, *Narrative*, pp. 165, 167-73; Carte, *Ormond*, II, 70-1, 77; Carte, *Original Letters and Papers*, II, 381, 384; Carte MSS, 25, ff. 1, 23, 24, 25-31, 73, 83-4, 219, 258, 373, 454, 456, 457, 465; Gilbert, *Contemporary History*, I, xi, 440-6, 704-5, 758, II, 40-1, 203-4, 229-30, 244-5, 446-7; S.R.O. PA.7/23/2/64/1-4; S.R.O. PA.11/8, ff. 94, 95; *A.P.S.* VI, ii, 459, 732; H. Cary, ed. *Memorials of the Great Civil War* (2 vols. London, 1842), II, 153; H.M.C. 8: *9th Report*, II, 236; Cox, *Hibernia Anglicana*, II, Charles II, p. 15; Hill, *Montgomery Manuscripts* pp. 186-90; Abbott, *Writings and Speeches of Oliver Cromwell*, II, 54, 78, 98, 102, 114-15, 131; Bagwell, *Stuarts*, II, 179-86; Reid, *History of the Presbyterian Church*, II, 111-34.
81. Gilbert, *Contemporary History*, III, 159.
82. Bagwell, *Stuarts*, II, 190-7; Gilbert, *Contemporary History*, II, 267-8, 329, 465; Carte MSS, 25, f. 581; Venables, *Narrative*, pp. 2-3; S. McSkimin, *The History and Antiquities of the County of the Town of Carrickfergus* (new ed. Belfast, 1909), pp. 58-9; Adair, *Narrative*, pp. 174-7; Reid, *History of the Presbyterian Church*, II, 136-9.

might tempt the remaining forces in Ulster into attempting the relief of Carrickfergus, thus giving Coote and Venables a chance to bring them to battle, instead of having to pursue them to remote parts of the province. Whether or not this was what was intended, it was what happened. Sir George Monro had retreated to Enniskillen, but when he heard of Carrickfergus' plight he determined to go to its relief. First he tried to shake parliament's hold on eastern Ulster; on 12 November he captured Strabane House, which had been held against him in defiance of the Catholic dowager Lady Strabane's wishes. Monro was by this time being helped by Sir Phelim O'Neill, and they next marched to Charlemont, where Lady Strabane at last married Sir Phelim 'after long courting between them by letters'. The object of Monro's offensive in eastern Ulster had been to persuade Sir Charles Coote to march back there north of Lough Neagh, while Monro advanced round the south of the lough from Charlemont with the remaining forces of Lord Montgomery and Clanbrassil to attack Venables. But this attempt to divide parliament's forces failed; on 26 November Venables, Coote and Sir Theophilus Jones assembled their combined forces (about 1,500 foot and 1,200 horse) at Lisburn to bar the way of the royalists advancing northwards to relieve Carrickfergus.

Monro marched his men through Maccartan's Wood to Comber and then Newtownards, trying to raise men from the Scots settlers in Down, but the activities of the presbyterian ministers prevented any but a few gentlemen joining him. The royalists tried to force a passage across the Lagan near Lisburn, with about 2,000 foot and 800 horse, hoping to evade parliament's forces and relieve Carrickfergus without a fight. But at Lisnestrain parliament's army fell on his rearguard. Monro believed they were simply trying to halt his army until lack of provisions destroyed it, and therefore tried to continue his march while the rearguard held off the attackers. This proved a disastrous miscalculation; a major attack on his army developed, but his men were not drawn up ready to meet it, and his attempt to continue his march must have seemed to his men to be an inglorious retreat. Colonel Alexander Mac-Donnell's regiment was ordered to charge the enemy; a few officers obeyed but the rest of the regiment fled. So did troops of horse ordered to charge, and in their flight they disordered the remaining infantry and 'a panick feare possessed all the rest'. Only Lieutenant Colonel John Hamilton (formerly of Lindsay's regiment) and fifty horse were willing to fight, and the rest of the army soon fled in panic, men being cut down by the pursuing enemy for eight or ten miles, nearly 1,000 being killed. Hamilton was captured but Monro and Lord Montgomery escaped, retreating with the few men they could gather together to Charlemont and then Enniskillen. Monro concluded that he had been defeated because God had taken the hearts of his men; Humphry Galbraith (who was present at the battle) could only suggest that a divine hand had spread panic. A week later Carrickfergus surrendered, Venables becoming its new governor.[83]

After this defeat Monro decided that the situation in Ulster was hopeless; the only chance of redeeming it was to transfer the war to Britain. This was what had brought him back to Ulster, but it now seemed impossible, and in any case the invasion of Scotland by Montrose which he had hoped to assist had not materialised. He therefore applied to Ormond for permission to retire to France.[84] This was evidently not granted, for Monro was still in charge of the Enniskillen garrison early in 1650. But the appointment of Emer Mac-Mahon, the Catholic bishop of Clogher, to be general of the Irish army in Ulster, and thus his commander, proved unacceptable to Monro. Ormond himself had no liking for the new general but by the terms of his agreement with Owen Roe O'Neill the Irish nobles and gentry of Ulster had had the right to elect Owen Roe's successor. Some had favoured Antrim's candidacy, one of the arguments in favour of it being that he would be more acceptable to Monro and the Ulster Scots, but MacMahon was elected.

On 18 April Monro informed him that he was forced to open negotiations with the enemy for the safety of the Protestants under his command. The bishop rightly took this

83.. Reid, *History of the Presbyterian Church*, II, 139-40, 151-60; Bagwell, *Stuarts*, II, 209; Hogan, *Warr of Ireland*, pp. 97-104; Carte MSS, 26, ff. 41, 43, 201, 337, 339, 341, 343; H.M.C. 31: *13th Report*, IV, 387; Hill, *Montgomery Manuscripts*, pp. 191-4; Carte, *Original Letters and Papers*, II, 418, 421-2; Gilbert, *Contemporary History*, II, 335-7; Turner, *Memoirs*, pp. 322-4; *Two Letters from William Basil, Attorney General of Ireland ... of a victory obtained by the Parliament's forces on the plain of Lisnegarvy* (London, 1649), pp. 1-6.
84. Carte MSS, 26, f. 339; though Monro evidently did not know it, forces sent by Montrose had in fact landed in Orkney. Montrose joined them in the spring of 1650 and landed on the mainland, but was promptly defeated and executed.

K

to be a reaction to his appointment as general, and assured
Monro that 'if your countrymen, by [be] generally jealous
for it, or if it staggers or hinders them a jott from his Majesties
service, I begg that you will intimate soe much unto me, and
I doe promise if that may be any way satisfactorie, that I will
resign my place', and he accused Monro of seeking to join an
enemy which hated the Scots nation and would reduce the
Scots in Ireland to slavery. Monro was not convinced, and
though he denied he was making trouble on religious grounds
this doubtless lay at the heart of his discontent. Though not
the most scrupulous of men he had after all come to Ireland
in 1642 to crush the Catholic Irish, and now he was being
asked to accept a Catholic Irish bishop as general. But the
other motives which he told MacMahon about were also
genuine influences on his conduct. There seemed to be no
hope of success and supplies were running out. Through divisions among the royalists and the Irish, Cromwell's army had
been able to conquer most of Ireland without any major battle
being fought. He therefore thought it his duty to get from
the enemy the best terms he could for the men under his
command. As MacMahon put it, Monro 'went from one to
another of Scotts and sowed a world of sedition and muteny
amongst them', finally (at about the end of April) surrendering
Enniskillen and some minor garrisons to Sir Charles Coote
(who was advancing to attack him) 'for £500, and other
trivial things'. the bishop-general issued a proclamation
denouncing attempts to sow discord between Irish and Scots,
promising that he would make no distinction between men of
the two nations and warning that the English would not let
Scots inhabit the parts of Ulster opposite Scotland. But few if
any Scots Protestants responded to an appeal from such a
source, and within a few weeks of issuing it the bishop was
captured by Coote and executed. In August Charlemont fell
to Coote and Venables, and parliament's conquest of Ulster
was complete.[85]

The Scottish government had taken no direct part in the
Ulster campaigns of 1649-50, but their outcome was nonetheless of great significance to it. As the resolution (passed too

85. Bagwell, *Stuarts*, II, 227-31; Carte MSS, 27, ff. 333, 339; Gilbert, *Contemporary History*, II, lii, 390-3, 418-20, III, 147; Hogan, *Warr of Ireland*, pp. 113-16;
Colles, *History of Ulster*, III, 130-5; Reid, *History of the Presbyterian Church*, II,
145-51.

late to be implemented) to help the parliamentary garrison in Carrickfergus in July 1649 had indicated, the question of who controlled Ulster was regarded as of considerable importance by the kirk party. Moreover, events in Ireland had had a strong influence on the kirk party's negotiations with the exiled Charles II. To the young king and his advisers early in 1649 two alternative courses of action had seemed open as ways of regaining his thrones; action through Scotland, or through Ireland. Montrose favoured the Irish venture, though the other Scots nobles around the king opposed it; and the second Ormond Peace, Ormond's early successes, and the royalist risings in Ulster for a time made restoration through Ireland seem possible. Charles negotiated with commissioners sent by the kirk party but, having Ireland to turn to as an alternative to Scotland, would not make the concessions they demanded. The negotiations broke down and Charles made his way to Jersey, intending to go to Ireland. But in Jersey he heard that Ormond had been defeated at Rathmines, and news of Cromwell's victories soon followed.

In February 1650 Charles finally abandoned all hope of using Ireland as a stepping stone to England, and turned back to Scotland instead. In negotiations at Breda he reached agreement with the kirk party, undertaking to sign the covenants and surrender almost all royal power. He landed in Scotland in June, and among the further concessions forced from him there was the signing in August of a declaration which disowned the second Ormond Peace since he was convinced of the 'exceeding great sinfulness and unlawfulnes of that treaty and peace made with the bloody Irish rebels'. Subsequently he managed to send a secret message to Ormond explaining that 'what concerns Ireland [in the declaration] is no ways binding, for I can do nothing in the affairs of that kingdom without the advice of my council there; nor hath that kingdom any dependence upon this, so that what I have done is nothing'. But such private assurances could not compensate for the fact that the king had publicly denounced the peace with the Irish which he had formerly approved; and in any case the position of the royalists in Ireland was already hopeless. In December 1650 Ormond sailed for France.[86]

86. Bagwell, *Stuarts*, II, 186-7, 239-44; S. R. Gardiner, ed. *Letters and Papers illustrating the relations between Charles the Second and Scotland in 1650* (S.H.S. 1894), p. 143.

For Scotland the most obvious result of the confused fighting in Ulster in 1649-50 was that it brought many refugees to the country. The first of these were, on the whole, welcome, for they consisted mainly of officers and soldiers who had resisted the royalist take-over in Ulster in March to July 1649. As they had fled from Ireland rather than submit to the royalists, they could be trusted to resist royalists in Scotland. Consequently they provided ideal recruits for the kirk party's army at an opportune moment, for the purging of men suspected of royalist or Engager sympathies was being carried out. In June 'well affected officers and souldiers as have fled out of Ireland' were ordered to be recruited into the army, and on 6 August orders were given to form some such officers and soldiers from Ireland into four foot companies, which were not to exceed 500 men.[87] A subcommittee of the committee of estates was established to choose officers for the companies; among its members were two former colonels of the Scottish army in Ireland, Argyll and Lothian, and Sir Robert Adair of Kinhilt, himself a refugee; Sir George Monro and his men had plundered his house and lands in Ulster, forcing his wife and family to flee to Scotland. On 10 August, presumably on the recommendation of the subcommittee, the committee of estates established six companies, totalling 396 men, and forty horsemen (plus officers) out of the refugees. The foot were to be commanded by Lieutenant Colonel James Wallace and Major Bryce Cochrane, and most of the other officers and men were probably also New Scots, though there were some Old Scots among them, including Sir Alexander Stewart (who was to be killed at the battle of Dunbar).[88] Four days later orders were given to distribute £100 sterling among the officers of the 400 foot (as the 396 men were usually referred to) and the forty horse, and among forty-seven other officers from Ireland who were not being employed—many of whom were probably Old Scots. A month later more permanent provision for the unemployed officers was provided by orders to disband one trooper in every twenty-five in the cavalry and one footman in twenty in the infantry throughout the Scottish army; the pay thus saved was to be given to the officers though, if the army preferred, the money could be provided by pay cuts

87. *A.P.S.* VI, ii, 447, 535, 538.
88. S.R.O. PA.11/8, ff. 101, 102v-105; G. E. Cokayne, *Complete Peerage* (14 vols, London, 1910-59), IX, 349.

instead of by the reductions in strength. By this time the total of unemployed officers from Ireland had risen to ninety-seven. Early in October Lieutenant Colonel Sir Dugald Campbell of Auchinbreck, Major William Campbell and twelve other officers formerly of Argyll's New Scots regiment were added to this list of 'reformer' officers from Ireland who were receiving allowances; it was said they had refused to join the Engagers and had now fled from Ireland rather than comply with the royalists, many leaving behind their wives, children and property. In November the former surgeon general of the New Scots, Andrew Brown, was also granted an allowance.[89]

The 400 foot and forty horse from Ireland were mustered at Leith on 1 September. At first they were employed from month to month, but in June 1650 the employment of the foot was made permanent. Charles II had just arrived in Scotland and the Scottish parliament ordered that 'the Irish companyes' should form a lifeguard of foot for him. Later Lord Lorne, Argyll's eldest son, was appointed commander of the lifeguard.[90] It is a notable tribute to the loyalty of these refugees from Ireland to the kirk party that they should have been chosen to form a lifeguard, for they were intended to protect the king from his friends rather than from his enemies, to prevent him from falling into hands hostile to the kirk party. Lorne was chosen to command them as Argyll was one of the few great nobles the kirk party had any faith in. It needs to be stressed that there is no evidence whatever of any continuity between the new lifeguard and Argyll's regiment of the Scottish army in Ireland, for it has been claimed that the guard was formed from 'Irish companies descended from the Argyll regiment of 1642'. In fact so far as is known the 'Irish companies' levied in August 1649 contained no officers or men of that regiment. Many of the regiment's officers had been given allowances but they had not been employed. It is possible that a few served in the lifeguard; it would be natural for Lorne to show favour to men who had served his father, but there is no evidence to this effect.[91]

The refugees who came from Ireland up to about July or

89. S.R.O. PA.11/8, ff. 108v, 113-113v, 160-1, 169v-170, 188v-189, 192.
90. Ibid. ff. 108v-109, 197v-199; S.R.O. PA.11/9, ff. 17-18, 30-30v; A.P.S. VI, ii, 572, 578, 593, 597, 600, 605, 633, 637, 650, 651; Stevenson, 'Financing the Cause of the Covenants', S.H.R. LI, 120; H.M.C. 3: 4th Report, p. 491.
91. Maurice, History of the Scots Guards, I, 11-12, 22; Stevenson, 'The Myth of the Founding of the Scots Guards in 1642', S.H.R. LVI, 114-18.

August 1649 were mainly welcomed by the kirk party; but the royalist triumph in Ulster which forced them to flee to Scotland was not. It placed a province just a short sea crossing away from Scotland in the hands of the Scottish regime's enemies. Sir Robert Adair and others were employed to restrain all persons, armed or not, from crossing to Ireland[92] since it was feared that Scottish royalists would gather in Ulster and attempt some action against Scotland; at the end of September there was a rumour that Charles II himself was at Carrickfergus.[93] But the flow of royalists from Scotland to Ireland was soon reversed by the advance of Robert Venables into Ulster on behalf of the English parliament. On 16 October the committee of estates approved the action of the committee of war of Renfrewshire in arresting malignant and disaffected persons who had landed from Ireland. Forces sent by Montrose had recently occupied Orkney and it was now feared that royalists from Ireland would try to join them.

The most prominent of the new wave of refugees was Sir James Montgomery, who had wisely fled from Ulster as Venables advanced, for he had broken his oath (not to act against the commonwealth) by encouraging the royalism of his nephew, Lord Montgomery. Officers among the earlier 'kirk party' refugees whom Sir James had helped to drive from Ireland gave in a supplication to the committee of estates denouncing him as a leading betrayer of the cause of God there. Eglinton, his kinsman, intervened on his behalf but the committee ordered that he be banished from Scotland, on pain of £20,000 Scots or death (at his own option!) if he returned or failed to leave by 1 January 1650. Sir James duly left for Holland, but he returned to Scotland late in 1650 when the power of the kirk party was crumbling in the face of a royalist revival. His banishment was revoked but he evidently failed to find employment in the army for early in 1651 he left again for Holland, only to be fatally wounded in an encounter with Dutch pirates on the voyage.[94] Lieutenant Colonel George Keith who had commanded Belfast for Lord Montgomery after James Wallace was expelled was also

92. S.R.O. PA.11/8, ff. 107-107v, 109.
93. Ibid. f. 169v.
94. Ibid. ff. 175, 176v, 180-180v, 190v, 191v, 192v, 196-196v; Hill, *Montgomery Manuscripts*, pp. 333-5, 337-8, 343-5; *A.P.S.* VI, ii, 622; Adair, *Narrative*, pp. 175-6.

banished from Scotland on pain of death.[95] Like Sir James Montgomery, Keith was (it seems) an Old Scot, but there were doubtless also New Scots among the royalist refugees of late 1649.

Certainly there were some New Scots among the refugees who reached Scotland nearly a year later, late in 1650. Though Thomas Dalyell surrendered Carrickfergus in December 1649 he was still in Ireland in August 1650, but shortly afterwards he was back in Scotland. His banishment was ordered but on appeal he was allowed to stay, and took part in the 1651 invasion of England with the rank of major general. Less lucky was his former commander, Sir George Monro, who came to Scotland after giving up Enniskillen to Coote; in spite of the growing royalism of the Scottish regime his banishment was enforced after he took part in an attempted royalist *coup d'etat*, and he sailed to exile in Holland for the second time.[96] But by late in 1650, with the exception of men like Monro whose conduct made them particularly obnoxious, all refugees from Ireland were welcome. All men possible were wanted to resist the English invasion, and men fleeing English rule in Ulster were usually ready to fight the English in Scotland. Especially welcome must have been those Scots who in February 1651 seized an English ship at Londonderry and brought it to Bute, complete with a large cargo of cloth, clothes, 700 red coats (presumably uniforms), 250 carbines, 500 muskets and ammunition.[97] In May 1651 eleven Scots landed 'at the back of Kintyre' from Ulster with passes from the English granted as they had surrendered on terms; some had been in Enniskillen when Monro had surrendered it a year before. They said they had come to help fight the English and were therefore sent to join the army.[98]

By this time, however, there was little of their native land left free of English domination; all Scotland south of the Forth was in English hands, and by the end of the year the

95. S.R.O. PA.11/9, ff. 3v-4.
96. H.M.C. 8: *9th Report*, II, 169; *A.P.S.* VI, ii, 580, 638; Balfour, *Historical Works*, III, 169, IV, 297; S.R.O. PA.11/10, ff. 6v-7. According to Sir E. Walker, *Historical Discourses* (London, 1705), p. 182 it was at first proposed to execute Monro and Dalyell on their return to Scotland.
97. Balfour, *Historical Works*, IV, 250-1.
98. S.R.O. GD.40/portfolio V/26-36. Hazlett, 'Recruitment and Organisation of the Scottish Army in Ulster', in Cronne, Moody and Quinn, *Essays in British and Irish History*, p. 129 conjectures that these men were New Scots, but there is no evidence for this.

rest of the Lowlands had been subdued. Cromwell's 1649 invasion of Ireland had been followed in 1650 by invasion of Scotland. That the new English commonwealth would turn on Scotland as soon as the Irish had been dealt with had long been obvious. The kirk party had been in the difficult situation of approving the Cromwellian conquest of Ireland (since it had crushed the hated and feared Catholic Irish and royalists who might have tried to intervene in Scotland), but fearing what would happen once that conquest was completed. The regime was therefore, disconcerted by the ease and speed of Cromwell's success, for it must have been hoped that the English would be bogged down in Ireland for some years, and therefore be unable to attack Scotland. The quick conquest of Ulster was particularly unwelcome, since it meant that Scotland could again be threatened with English invasion from the province. Hopes of restoring the Scottish domination of Ulster now disappeared. According to one report this was deeply resented in Scotland; 'The better sorts of the Scots have most villainous intents towards us and often say they will revenge all their late losses and affronts receued from England. The loss of Ulster they digest worst of all'.[99]

The conquest of Ireland opened the way for the English to the conquest of Scotland. It also made the conquest of Scotland more necessary for them, for the loss of Ireland drove the king into the hands of the kirk party, and the threat to England from an alliance of the kirk party and the Scottish royalists was much greater than the threat of the two separately.

When Cromwell led his army into Scotland in July 1650 the fact that Ireland had already been largely subdued gave him two advantages. He had no need to fear that the Ulster Scots would send help to their native country, and he could supplement invasion from England with an attack from Ulster, as Charles I had hoped to do in 1639 and 1640. Such a landing from Ulster was part of Cromwell's plan of campaign. On 28 August the lord deputy of Ireland, Henry Ireton, wrote to him favouring landings between Lochryan and the Clyde (and especially the seizure of Ayr or Irvine) rather than at Kirkcudbright, these being the alternatives Cromwell had suggested to him. Ireton was making preliminary preparations for such an

99. H.M.C. 51: *Leyborne-Popham*, pp. 58-9.

undertaking, though he could not carry it out until men, money and provisions were sent to him from England. But (again as in 1639 and 1640) a great show of preparations for an immediate invasion was to be made in Ulster, to alarm the Scots. Ships were to be sent to make small scale raids on Scotland, but they were only to operate north of the Clyde, so the Scots would think the invasion would come there.[100]

Cromwell's victory at Dunbar (3 September) put most of Scotland south of the Forth in his hands, and resistance in the western Lowlands collapsed after the battle of Hamilton in December. These successes made an invasion from Ulster unnecessary, though the idea was revived in August 1651 when the Scots undertook a despairing invasion of England which was halted at the battle of Worcester.[101] And just as, in 1650-1 as well as in 1639-40, invasion of Scotland from Ireland was considered, so in both periods the English feared the opposite; in September 1651 there were rumours in Ireland that 2,000 Scots soldiers had assembled at Portpatrick ready to invade Ireland,[102] but this soon proved to be a false alarm.

iv.   Scotland and Ireland in the 1650s

From the first the English commonwealth showed deep suspicion of, and hostility to, the Ulster Scots. Scotland had tried to replace English rule in Ulster with Scots domination. Many Ulster Scots had fought against parliament. Even after they were subdued it was obvious that many remained at heart loyal to the king, to presbyterianism and the covenants, and to their native country (in varying proportions), rather than to the republican commonwealth, to Independency and to England. The English were determined on drastic action to solve the Irish problem once and for all, and though the main problem was obviously that of Catholicism and the native Irish, action was also planned to curb the power of the Scots.

Like Monck before him, Venables at first took no action against presbyterians in Ulster, even against ministers who prayed for the king. But once parliament's power was firmly

---

100.   J. Nickolls, ed. *Original Letters and Papers of State, addressed to Oliver Cromwell* (London, 1743), p. 15.
101.   R. Dunlop, ed. *Ireland under the Commonwealth* (2 vols. Manchester, 1913), I, 18n, 26.
102.   Ibid. I, 43, 52.

established persecution began. In 1650 ministers were given the alternatives of undertaking not to speak against the government or returning to Scotland. Stipends were confiscated, and some ministers were imprisoned for a time. The following year many were deported to Scotland, and persecution of ministers continued until 1653, when it was planned to include some ministers in a forced transplantation to other parts of Ireland.[103]

Schemes for solving the Ulster Scot problem by transportation had been under consideration for some time. As soon as the council of state in London had heard of the routing of the royalists at Lisnestrain by Venables and Coote in December 1649 it had ordered its Irish subcommittee to consider the planting of parts of Ulster and the disposal of the Scots; this was to be done quickly so that the victory could be 'improved', or followed up to best advantage.[104] Nothing resulted from this rather vague order, perhaps because once Scotland as well as Ireland was conquered there seemed less urgency about trying to disperse the Ulster Scots, for they could no longer appeal for help to, or be stirred up to cause trouble from, Scotland. Trade and all other contact between Scotland and Ireland had been forbidden in April 1649 on news of the royalist risings in Ulster, and restrictions had remained during the conquest of the two countries, but in May 1652 it was thought safe to remove all prohibitions and encourage trade.[105] When in August 1652 an act for settling Ireland was passed it was thought sufficient to exempt from pardon only a few individual Ulster Scots—Lord Montgomery, Sir James Montgomery (who in fact was already dead), Sir Robert Stewart, and the New Scot Sir George Monro.[106] Two months later it was laid down that no Scots officer who had fought against parliament should be allowed to live in Ulster unless he took an oath of loyalty,[107] but there is no sign that any action was taken to implement this order.

However, the authorities were stirred into action in February 1653 by news that Highlanders who had not submitted to the commonwealth were corresponding with

---

103. Adair, *Narrative*, pp. 177-203; Reid, *History of the Presbyterian Church*, II, 141-2, 160-84.
104. *C.S.P.D. 1649-50*, p. 458.
105. Ibid. pp. 93, 94; Dunlop, *Ireland under the Commonwealth*, I, 135.
106. Gilbert, *Contemporary History*, II, 342.
107. Dunlop, *Ireland under the Commonwealth*, II, 293.

royalists in the north of Ireland, trying to get men and supplies from them and to stir up trouble. Catholic Irish were said to be crossing to the Western Isles. Venables was therefore instructed to find out what meetings Ulster Scots (especially New Scots) were holding, and to ban contact with Scotland; he was also informed that the removal of all officers who had served against parliament from Ulster was being considered.

Venables and parliament's other commissioners in Ulster acted promptly. By 9 April they could report that their spies (including one in the Highlands) were doing all they could to find out what was going on; but it was impossible to cut off all correspondence with Scotland while Scots were allowed to live along the coasts of Ulster. They had decided that it was necessary to transport 'all popular Scots' who could not be trusted to other parts of Ireland; this would be doubly advantageous, for the Scots hated the Irish and so, if planted among them would help keep them in subjection, while removing the Scots from Ulster would help to cut them off from Scotland and thus in time anglicise them.

The idea was welcomed in Dublin, and orders were given for the transplantation of the most dangerous popular Scots to Counties Kilkenny, Tipperary and Waterford, provided this could be done without causing any disturbances in Ulster. On 23 May a proclamation duly ordered the transportation of about 260 Scots from Antrim and Down (the area in closest contact with Scotland) including Lord Montgomery, Clanbrassil and other prominent Old Scots as well as lesser men; 'popular' in this context meant the most influential Scots of all ranks, 'the special persons whether for estates or parts, not principled their way, both ministers and others'. They were to be given full compensation in their new homes for the land and other property they had to leave behind, and Sir Robert Adair and others were sent to Tipperary to begin preparations for the move.[108]

But in the end nothing happened. These were months of political confusion in England, with the dissolution of the long parliament, the meeting of the little or nominated parlia-

108. Ibid. I, cxxxv-cxxxvi, II, 326, 329-31, 333-4, 338-9, 342-3, 346-50, 351-4, 360-1, 370; *C.S.P.D. 1652-3*, pp. 190, 194; Young, *Old Belfast*, pp. 78-83; Bagwell, *Stuarts*, II, 341-2; Benn, *History of Belfast*, I, 705-7; Reid, *History of the Presbyterian Church*, II, 187-91; III, 552-5; Adair, *Narrative*, pp. 197-202; F. D. Dow, *Cromwellian Scotland* (Edinburgh, 1979), p. 80.

ment and the establishment of Cromwell as lord protector. The Ulster transplantation scheme was quietly shelved, and in August Lord Montgomery and other Ulster Scots were in London petitioning against its revival.[109] The danger of collusion between Ulster Scots and Highlanders seemed to have receded, and many increasingly favoured trying to conciliate enemies of the regime, including the Ulster Scots. One sign of this, perhaps, was the release of Robert Monro from the Tower of London, where he had lain since 1648, in August 1653. He was virtually destitute, and on his release was given £10 sterling to help him return to Scotland. Cromwell also ordered that the estates which Monro claimed through his wife, the dowager Lady Montgomery, be restored, but resistance in Ireland delayed this. When Cromwell renewed his orders the commissioners for governing Ireland obtained from George Monck a certificate stating that Monro had always refused to obey parliament's orders; but in the end the lands were restored.[110]

The hostility to Robert Monro in Ireland was probably in part at least inspired by the fact that a royalist rebellion had broken out in the Highlands, and that one of its leaders was his nephew Sir George Monro. This naturally renewed fears about the loyalty of the Ulster Scots; Lord Montgomery had been restored to his estates but was now summoned to reside in Dublin so that he could not stir up trouble in the north. But by and large the Highland rebellion did not provoke panic measures against the Ulster Scots; indeed it was felt safe to transport troops from Ireland to Scotland, as well as to send a 'great quantity of Provision' from Dublin to Inverlochy for the use of the forces operating against the rebels, and the rebellion collapsed before it could have any serious repercussions in Ireland.[111]

Nonetheless it is surprising that the scheme for transporting Ulster Scots was not revived during the Highland rebellion, for it was still being considered. In February 1656 the council of state of Ireland ordered that all Scots inhabitants of Ulster

109. Ogle, Bliss and Macray, *Calendar of Clarendon State Papers*, II, 240.
110. *C.S.P.S. 1650*, pp. 289, 382, 597, *1651-2*, pp. 12, 96, *1652-3*, p. 128, *1653-4*, pp. 114, 116; Young, *Old Belfast*, pp. 98-100; Birch, *State Papers*, II, 427.
111. Hill, *Montgomery Manuscripts*, p. 201; Abbott, *Writings and Speeches of Oliver Cromwell*, III, 238, 506n; *C.S.P.D. 1654*, p. 77; Bodleian Library, Rawlinson MSS, A.328, ff. 144-5; Dunlop, *Ireland under the Commonwealth*, II, 468; Birch, *State Papers*, IV, 374; Dow, *Cromwellian Scotland*, p. 118.

who had ever been in arms against the state, had not received pardons, and were not freeholders should leave and settle elsewhere in Ireland by 27 September 1657. All Scots, without exception, who had settled in Ulster since 24 June 1650 were to leave and no Scots were to settle there in future. The following month Cromwell endorsed the scheme and extended it to include County Louth.[112] Like its predecessor this plan was never put into operation, but it is of interest in that, though it is still a plan to transport Scots, it is in some ways a reversal of the 1653 scheme. It had then been the most influential Scots, including many landowners, who were to be transported; now in 1656 it was the common people, those who were not freeholders, who were to leave. The earlier idealistic hope that the mass of the Scots settlers would become loyal to the commonwealth (once the evil influence of a relatively small number of royalist and presbyterian individuals had been removed) had disappeared. The protectorate regime was becoming increasingly conservative in outlook and increasingly sought, as in England and Scotland, the support of those who had traditionally had power—landowners and clergy—in spite of the fact that many of them had previously been hostile to it. Such men with something to lose could be won over to support the regime, it was hoped, while distrust of the masses as volatile and uncontrollable grew. But in the end, yet again, nothing was done; it proved less trouble in the short run to leave the Scots in Ulster, both landlords and the common people, than to move them.

Fear and suspicion of them continued, however. It was said in parliament in 1656 that the Ulster Scots could raise 40,000 fighting men (who could easily cross to Scotland and cause trouble there) and that they persisted in keeping 'up an interest distinct in garb and all formalities' from the English. In June 1657 Colonel Thomas Cooper (who was in command at Carrickfergus) warned that even those of English origin in the town 'have too much a Scotch spirit', being contaminated by the Scots. He urged that only Scots ministers of known loyalty should be allowed in the main Ulster ports, and suggested that all Scots inhabitants should be expelled from them, at least for some years, as 'ther is more dainger to be

112. *C.S.P.I. 1647-60*, pp. 825, 826, 853; Dunlop, *Ireland under the Commonwealth*, II, 581; Dow, *Cromwellian Scotland*, pp. 190-1.

expected from that interest, then the Ireish in Ulster'.[113]

But in spite of such warnings moderation prevailed. In 1654 landowners like Lord Montgomery and Clanbrassil were finally restored to their estates, and in the same year efforts began to win over presbyterian ministers in Ulster instead of trying to force them into submission. It was realised that they might remain hostile to the regime at heart, but offers of financial support and the futility of continuing resistance gradually brought many of them at least to accept the regime and not work actively against it. Some difficulties were caused by the spread to Ulster, by ministers deported in 1650-1 who later returned, of the divisions which had split presbyterianism in Scotland into two factions; the resolutioner majority, which supported both Charles II and the covenants, and the remonstrant (or protester) minority which virtually disowned the cause of a malignant king and stood for religion and the covenants alone. In Ulster as in Scotland the commonwealth at first hoped to be able to reach agreement with the protesters, believing that since they disowned the king they would look with favour on the commonwealth. But while some protesters responded favourably to government advances, many regarded both commonwealth and king with equal hostility. Their unwillingness to tolerate any form of Protestantism except their own made the regime turn increasingly to the resolutioners. The commitment of the latter to the king prevented any real alliance being made, but their increasing readiness (since there seemed no alternative) to live peaceably under the regime so long as they were not persecuted led the government to show them favour. Thus the government in the end tolerated both factions in Ulster without winning the whole-hearted support of either. In these conditions presbyterianism thrived. The faction disputes in Ulster were not nearly so bitter and demoralising as in Scotland, for most ministers proved willing to support a resolution that the Scottish conflict should not be allowed to divide the church in Ulster, perhaps realising that since their religion was a minority one in Ireland they could not afford the luxury of such feuds. In 1653 it was estimated that there were twenty-four presbyterian ministers in Ulster; a few years later there were nearly eighty. The

---

113. Reid, *History of the Presbyterian Church*, II, 214n, 223n, 226, 227; Birch, *State Papers*, IV, 447, VI, 349; T. Burton, *Diary*, ed. J. T. Rutt (4 vols. London, 1828), I, 4.

original presbytery set up by the New Scots subdivided into four separate meetings or committees, virtually separate presbyteries, which occasionally met together in a 'general presbytery' or synod; the four were Down, Antrim, the Route and Lagan, the last named indicating the spread of presbyterian organisation from its original stronghold in Antrim and Down to western Ulster.[114]

Both presbyterianism in Ulster and the position of Scots as the dominant element in the Ulster plantation thus survived Cromwellian rule. Charles I and Strafford, the confederate Irish, and the commonwealth and protectorate regimes had all wished to oust them, but all had failed.

114. Adair, *Narrative*, pp. 204-15, 217-18, 220-1, 222-3; Reid, *History of the Presbyterian Church*, II, 193-238; Barnard, *Cromwellian Ireland. English Government and Reform in Ireland, 1649-1660* (Oxford, 1975), pp. 122-6, 145-6. Barnard, pp. 123, 124, rather oddly sees the remonstrants or protestors as 'comparatively moderate', the resolutioners as 'intransigent'. He also refers to resolutioners in Ulster early in 1649; in fact the resolutioner-protester split did not occur in Scotland until late in 1650!

George Monck, duke of Albemarle. Parliamentary commander in Ulster 1647-9.
Portrait from studio of Sir Peter Lely.

CHAPTER SEVEN

The Relations of Scotland and Ireland

The early and mid-seventeenth century was an age of transition in relations between Scotland and Ireland. Before 1600 the most significant contacts between inhabitants of the two kingdoms were those of the Gaelic Irish with Gaelic High-landers; and contacts between the two governments were mainly concerned with the consequences of these links between their most unruly subjects. The relative success of James VI's efforts to bring order to the Western Highlands and Isles in the first two decades of the century, and the submission of the Ulster Irish to the English in 1603 (and the flight of the earls and plantation which followed) gravely weakened the connections between the two parts of Gaeldom. But they remained strong enough to be revived in the 1640s so success-fully that many Highlanders came to Ireland to fight for the confederates; and an Irish army under Alasdair MacColla fought in Scotland in alliance with some of the Highland clans. These links, however, did not survive the conquest of the native Irish and the 'royalist' (or, more accurately, anti-Campbell) clans. Never again was there to be extensive military and political co-operation between the two parts of the disintegrating Gaelic world, though cultural links lingered on for a few generations. Alasdair MacColla thus has, in retrospect, a symbolic significance as the last major figure who was equally at home in Ireland and the Highlands. After the middle of the century the Irish problem and the Highland problem were completely separate; the governments concerned could deal with them in isolation, without the former complication of having to take account of their inter-relationship. Not until the late nineteenth century, when Irish agitation for land reform was to help to stir up similar agitation in the Highlands, were events in one section of the Gaelic world again to have major effects in the other.

Thus the period *circa* 1600 to 1660 removed one problem that had long worried governments in Dublin and Edinburgh, that of co-operation between Scots and Irish Gaels. But in the same period another major problem of joint concern emerged, largely as the result of a government policy intended to help to solve the previous problem—the encouragement of Lowland Scots as well as English colonisation of Ulster.

The native Irish were naturally hostile to the Lowland Scots presence in Ulster from the start, and within little more than a generation of the Ulster plantation the London and Dublin governments were also—for very different reasons from the Irish—showing increasing hostility. The religious sympathies of many Ulster Scots were complicating the position of the already weak established church of Ireland, and in the growing quarrel between king and covenanters indications of sympathy for the latter among the Ulster Scots contributed greatly to the fact that Ireland was unable to give significant help to the king in the Bishops' Wars. Charles I's and Strafford's plans to destroy the Ulster Scots as a distinct community, consciously Scottish in outlook and loyalties, failed as a consequence of their larger failure to subdue Scotland. Cromwell, on the other hand, failed to uproot the Scottish plantation for precisely the opposite reason—because he had succeeded in subduing Scotland. Once Scotland had been conquered the Ulster Scots no longer seemed a major danger to English interests in Ireland, so the plans for dispersing them were not implemented.

Between these two threats to the Ulster Scots, that of Charles I in the late 1630s and that of Cromwell in the 1650s, came the most dangerous threat of all, the attempt of the native Irish to undo the plantation. The failure of the Irish attempt to overrun all Ulster in the early days of the rising was the result of their own inefficiency and of the speed with which the English and Scottish settlers organised resistance. It seems unlikely, however, that this resistance could have been successfully maintained if large scale help had not arrived from Scotland in the form of the New Scots army. Without this reinforcement the increased political and military efficiency of the Irish after mid-1642, following from the establishment of the confederate government and the arrival of Owen Roe O'Neill, might well have led to the collapse of British resistance in Ulster. The presence of Owen Roe O'Neill may have prevented the New Scots and their allies crushing the Irish rebellion in 1642; but equally the presence of the New Scots probably prevented O'Neill from conquering Ulster. Had he done that, it seems unlikely that the other main centre of Protestant resistance to the Irish, Dublin, could have held out for long. All Ireland might well have fallen into the hands of the confederates, with consequences for the future of the British Isles as a whole which are incalculable.

With the help of the New Scots, raised, transported and (in the event) largely supplied by the covenanting regime in Scotland, the Scots (and English) Protestant plantation in Ulster survived the greatest and most prolonged threat it ever had to face. After 1660 the Lowland Scots presence in Ulster was accepted by the English. It might complicate the social, religious and political problems of Ireland, but the events of the 1640s had shown how firmly established the plantation was, and how tenaciously the Ulster Scots would fight for survival if threatened. Events had also shown that Scotland was ready to intervene if necessary to protect 'her' Ulster plantation; it might be recognised that Ireland was an English dependency, but the Scots blood of many of the planters, and Ulster's proximity to Scotland, led Scotland to claim a right to some say in Ulster affairs. Moreover, increasingly the English had no wish to threaten the Ulster Scots. As the politics of England and Scotland gradually became more closely linked, culminating in the parliamentary union of 1707, fears that a Scots presence in Ulster would prove a threat to English domination of Ireland declined.

If, as has been argued above, the Scottish army in Ireland played a central part in ensuring the survival of the English and Scottish plantation in Ulster, why did that army find so few advocates among contemporaries, and why has it found so few among later historians? Even those with whom the army fought in alliance tended to denigrate it. The usual charges made against the army were that it failed completely to do the military service required of it, and that it oppressed the British of Ulster whom it had been sent to protect. Clarendon is typical in stressing Scottish ambitions in Ireland and claiming that the New Scots 'did in truth, at our charge, as much oppress the English that were there as the rebels could

have done'.[1] Robert Blair confirmed that the British themselves held this view; many of them 'complained that they
thought the oppression and insolence of the Scots army that
came over for their aid, was worse nor the rebellion'.[2] As to
the military prowess of the New Scots the judgement that
'litle or nothing worth the mentioning was ever done or
attempted by them'[3] has been generally accepted—as is
indicated by the modern conclusions that after clearing Antrim
and Down the New Scots were 'to all intents and purposes
useless', being 'as an agressive force ... an almost complete
failure.'[4]

It is easy to see why it was that so many contemporaries,
representing a wide range of political and religious outlooks,
disliked the Scottish army in Ireland. The king had originally
agreed to the army crossing to Ireland, and its last action was
to support the Engagement which was intended to help him,
but royalists in general denounced it because it had opposed
the king in the intervening period. English parliamentarians
denounced the army as ineffective, oppressive and dis-
obedient in order to warrant breaking promises made to it,
ignoring treaty obligations, and generally neglecting it; and
once this mistreatment had driven the army to take action
against parliament (by supporting the Engagement), parliamentarians could refuse to pay its arrears by denouncing its
treachery with indignant self-righteousness. Most of the
British of Ulster, who had originally been very glad to see the
arrival of a Scottish army to help them, soon came to take the
protection which the New Scots provided them with for
granted. They complained of the cost of supporting the army
(which the failure of the English parliament to provide pay
and supplies burdened them with), and claimed that it was
British forces, not the New Scots, who deserved most credit
for holding back the Irish rebels. And when the royalist-
parliamentarian split spread to Ulster, whichever side the
British took they were given added reasons for carping about
the New Scots.

1. Hyde, *History of the Rebellion*, I, 438.
2. Blair, *Life*, p. 166.
3. Shuckburgh, *Two Biographies of William Bedell*, p. 174.
4. H. Hazlett, 'History of the Military Forces operating in Ireland, 1641-9'
(Ph.D. thesis, Queen's University, Belfast, 1938), II, 220; Hazlett, 'The Recruitment and Organisation of the Scottish Army in Ireland', *Essays in British and Irish
History*, ed. Cronne, Moody and Quinn, p. 130.

One might have expected that at least the covenanters in Scotland would have tried to uphold the reputation of their army in Ireland; and it is true that many leading covenanters, in negotiations with the English, did stand up for the army's interests and rights. But their arguments were ignored at the time and the covenanting movement was soon defeated. Its later apologists did not concern themselves with such a peripheral issue as the reputation of the long vanished army in Ireland. Even before the covenanters were crushed by English invasion, the spread of civil war to England and to Scotland had diverted the covenanters' attention from Ireland. The New Scots became the least important of the Scots armies, with the lowest priority for pay and supplies. In addition, the covenanters became disillusioned with the New Scots since they provoked invasion of Scotland from Ireland instead of preventing it; and the fact that many of them joined the Engagers led the kirk party regime to disown them.

Rather surprisingly, the frustration and bitterness felt by many of the New Scots officers at the way they were treated did not provoke any into writing and publishing any defence of the army and its conduct. The only officer who wrote of his experiences in Ireland was James Turner. But not only did he leave Ireland in 1644 and thereafter show little interest in the army, he wrote his memoirs after he had become a royalist, and was therefore more concerned with trying to explain away his service with the New Scots and disassociating himself from them than with telling of their grievances or difficulties.

There is one important exception to the general denigrating or ignoring of the New Scots by contemporary writers. Patrick Adair came from Scotland to Ireland in the 1640s and became minister of Cairncastle, County Antrim. Later he wrote a history of the presbyterian church in Ireland, and in this he included a spirited defence of the New Scots. 'Many in England and Ireland have taken liberty to represent this army as having done little service in the country, and not worth the pay they had from England. But all representations of that kind, coming from emulous, envious pens and tongues, ought not to be received ... It is ... certain they did many considerable services against the rebels in Ulster, so that they became a terror to them; and most of them laid down their arms, and came in and sat down under their mercy. The truth is, this army was irritated for want of the pay promised them; matters then falling into confusion in England, and the Parliament not being able to support so many armies at home and in divers places of Ireland, they were much neglected, being strangers, and quartering upon the Scotch in Ulster ... Upon this, they were not only disabled from Service, but were forced to take free quarters off the country, in doing which they restrained the officers to a small maintenance, and the common soldiers to a pitiful allowance which was not sufficient for their comfortable subsistence. Yet, their coming over upon a wasted country, where the people had generally little or nothing left to themselves ... became intolerable to the people, and they were reflected on as oppressors—yea, as doing nothing but lying in their quarters and oppressing the country ... And yet they themselves were discouraged, and the soldiers just starved ... So that as the country was weary of them, so they were as weary of the country. And indeed in the end, though they had spent much blood, besides travel and misery in the service of Ireland, the remainder of them were badly requited, being forced out of Carrickfergus and Coleraine by Colonel Monck—then under the parliament of England—and disbanded, without satisfying their arrears ...'.

Adair's support for the New Scots was partly due to his belief that they had been divine agents; 'It is certain God made that army instrumental for bringing church government, according to His own institution, to Ireland—especially to the Northern parts of it—and for spreading the covenants'.[5] The fact that the army had thus established presbyterianism in Ulster, creating the first presbytery there, clearly biased Adair in its favour. But nonetheless most of his arguments are sound. The army did have considerable achievements to its credit, and would have had more had it been adequately paid and supplied. It was lack of money and food which forced it to act oppressively, extorting them from the unfortunate British. And, as Adair argued, the fear the Irish showed of the New Scots is an impressive testimony to their effectiveness. For four years, up to their defeat at Benburb, they were the strongest opponents the Irish confederates had to face. Even if the British forces on their own (without the help of the New Scots) had proved able to continue to hold the parts of Ulster

5.   Adair, *True Narrative*, pp. 88-90.

still in their hands early in 1642, their position would have been precarious and they would have had to remain on the defensive, presenting no real threat to the confederate hold on other parts of Ireland. The arrival of the New Scots diverted Irish attention from what had been (and, arguably, should have continued to be) their main objective, gaining possession of Dublin. Their prime objective came to be preventing the Scots from advancing out of Ulster, and they tended to panic at minor expeditions by Monro, fearing that they were attempts to invade other provinces. Such fears helped to drive them into negotiations with Ormond; and it was noticeable that the more threatening the movements of the New Scots seemed, the more urgent their negotiations became and the more concessions they were willing to grant Ormond in order to buy his help against them.[6] The decision to send Irish help to Montrose in Scotland and the way in which the Irish concentrated their resources on the campaigns in Ulster in 1644 and 1646 reflect the way in which the New Scots at times seemed to dominate the military situation.

It was not only the Irish who by their actions testified to the significance of the presence of the New Scots in Ireland; the English parliament did so as well. It might constantly complain at the lack of action by the New Scots, but the eagerness with which it made promises of better pay and supply for the future whenever there seemed a possibility of the army having to leave Ulster indicated that it did not really believe the army was entirely useless. Even the fact that for a time in 1643 parliament favoured transferring the army to England shows that it was believed to be an effective fighting force. That it was the most formidable army in parliament's pay in Ireland was recognised when it was agreed that Major General Robert Monro should command all the forces in Ireland. This was only agreed by parliament reluctantly, for it was worried and angered by the way in which the New Scots obeyed orders from Scotland rather than from England; but the fact that in these circumstances parliament nonetheless made Monro commander in chief was an admission of the importance of his army. Its autonomy might be resented, but

6. Gilbert, *Irish Confederation*, II, xcix-c, 163, 362, III, 178-97, 200-1, IV, 154-5, V, 62, 77; J. Lowe, 'Negotiations between Charles I and the confederation of Kilkenny' (Ph.D. thesis, University of London, 1969), pp. 97-8, 235-6; J. Lowe, 'Charles I and the confederation of Kilkenny'; *I.H.S.* XIV (1964), pp. 10-11.

the army was needed. For a time only the existence of the New Scots gave parliament a foothold in Ireland. It seems likely that the great majority of the leaders of the British in Ulster would have declared for the king in 1643-4 had it not been for the presence of the New Scots. It was pressure from them (and to a lesser extent from the common soldiers in the British regiments) which forced most of the British to accept the solemn league and covenant and reject the cessation. And would Inchiquin (in spite of his personal grievances) have declared in favour of parliament in 1644 if the New Scots had not been entrenched in Ulster? Those in the English parliament who favoured abandoning Ireland until the civil war in England was won might well have prevailed if the New Scots had not proved reluctant to leave Ireland.[7]

Thus the New Scots had a military importance which extended far beyond the areas of Antrim and Down in which they were quartered. Indeed, their military importance extended beyond Ireland, for the possibility that they might be summoned to intervene in England or Scotland was almost constantly present. But it is true that it was often the existence of the army, its potential, rather than its actions, which gave it such importance; and the very fact that its importance extended beyond Ireland made a major contribution to its failure to play a more decisive part in the war in Ireland. It was too important to be risked too far in what at times seemed from Edinburgh to be a campaign of secondary importance in Ulster.

Thus the army's perennial lack of money, food, clothes, arms, ammunition and all other necessities of war was not the only reason for the limited nature of its military successes. It undoubtedly did, on some occasions, show a lack of enterprise and aggressive spirit, or rather a willingness to take to the offensive up to a certain point after which it failed to follow up and exploit successes already gained; and part of the explanation for such restraint undoubtedly lay in orders from the regime in Scotland. Little direct evidence for this has survived, but there seems no doubt that such orders existed; a good reason for keeping them secret lay in the fact that they contravened the treaty with England under which the army served in Ireland. The terms of the orders may have changed

---

7. Bottigheimer, *English Money and Irish Land*, pp. 87-8.

from time to time, but in general it seems that Monro was instructed to confine his activities (except for small-scale raids and foraging parties) to Ulster, and only to venture out of the province in force (as in June 1644) if this was regarded as absolutely necessary for the defence of Ulster from invasion.

It seems likely that, in addition, Monro was required to keep his headquarters in Carrickfergus and to quarter the majority of his men in Antrim and north Down, only a short sea crossing from Scotland, so the army would be available promptly for service in Britain if it was needed. It is true that there were other reasons for keeping the army based in north east Ulster. The treaty had agreed that the New Scots should garrison Coleraine and Carrickfergus, and they, along with Belfast, were the most convenient ports at which to land supplies for the army. North Down and parts of Antrim were also well cultivated areas, with many Scots settlers, which had largely escaped devastation in the early stages of the Irish rebellion; they could therefore provide the army with more supplies than other areas. But as early as May 1642 Monro had complained that Carrickfergus and quarters around it were inconveniently far from the areas where fighting was taking place; he had therefore recommended that a large part of the army be permanently stationed in south Down. This would have made it much easier for Monro to have responded promptly to Irish advances and to stamp out infiltration by small parties of rebels. Above all, with a permanent camp in south Down Monro might have been able to besiege Charlemont effectively, supplying the army through Carlingford Lough and Newry. Having proposed such a move of the army's quarters it is hard to see why Monro did nothing to implement it in the years that followed unless orders prevented him from acting, for almost every expedition he made emphasised how useful such a move would have been. Thus it is hardly fair to blame Monro for the failure of the New Scots to break out of Ulster and reproach him for laziness and incompetence.[8] Lack of supplies and restrictive orders from his superiors greatly curtailed his freedom of action.

Nonetheless, more limited criticisms of Monro as a commander probably are justified. It would not be surprising

8.   J. Lowe, 'Some Aspects of the Wars in Ireland', *Irish Sword*, IV (1959-60), 85-6.

if, like many of his officers, he became frustrated and demoralised by the abject poverty to which his army was often reduced, and embittered by the neglect of his 'forgotten army' by its employers, English and Scottish. Such a mood may well have, on occasion, led to opportunities for inflicting damage on the enemy being lost. In particular, Monro may be criticised for his failure to show more determination in attacking Charlemont (though in 1643 it might well have fallen to him had the cessation not forced him to withdraw). The number of occasions on which he approached Charlemont suggests that he did regard it, the last major Irish stronghold in Ulster, as of significance. But on most of these expeditions once he found it was impossible to surprise and overrun the fort immediately he either moved off or attempted a loose blockade rather than a close siege. Lack of supplies was the usual reason for this, but on some occasions the Irish garrison was small and an immediate assault might well have been worth risking.

However, it is possible that historians have over-estimated the importance of Charlemont. Monro may have regarded its continuance in Irish hands as a nuisance that he would have liked to remove, but not have seen its capture as his first priority. To say that the retention of the fort by the Irish nullified Monro's other successes is a gross exaggeration.[9] Its normal garrison was too small to constitute a major threat to Monro and the British, and, though it provided a secure base for Irish armies advancing into Ulster to march towards, this proved of little real advantage to them. Indeed it could be argued that possession of Charlemont proved a snare to the Irish, leading them to devote much energy to supplying it and to adopt defensive tactics. Since the fort was available as a base they tended to hasten armies advancing into Ulster straight to it, and thereafter to show reluctance to venture far from it. They might have been better advised to have marched directly towards the Protestant held areas of Ulster instead of wasting time and supplies at Charlemont. For once an Irish army reached Charlemont it usually began to experience supply problems, since its communications and supply routes from the south were vulnerable to attack by Monro and the

9.   Hayes-McCoy, 'O'Mellan's Account of the Battle of Benburb', *Feilscríbhinn Torna*, ed. Pender, pp. 142-3.

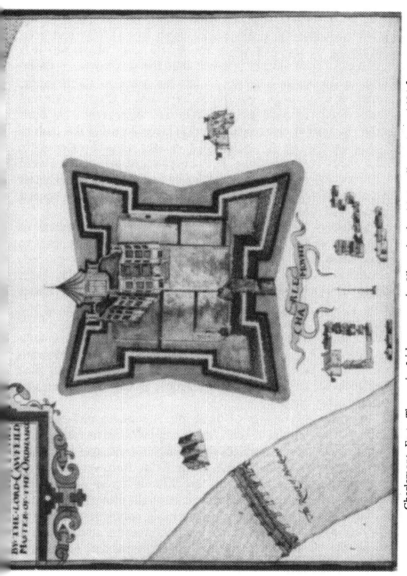

Charlemont Fort. The main Irish outpost in Ulster in the 1640s. Illustration c.1624 from map in British Library MS Add. 24,200, ff. 38v-39.

British. Shortage of supplies forced the Irish back on the defensive and then into retreat without having achieved anything.

It is of course true that Charlemont played a part in the great Irish victory at Benburb; Owen Roe O'Neill had been advancing to the fort when the battle took place. But it is significant that Monro believed that the way to force Owen Roe to do battle was not to bar his route to Charlemont, which is what might have been expected if Charlemont had really been regarded as of paramount importance by both sides. Instead Monro calculated that he could bring the Irish to battle by cutting off their supply routes, thus threatening to trap them in Charlemont. In the event such manoeuvres were unnecessary, as Owen Roe was eager to fight, but nonetheless Monro's thinking is interesting; Charlemont might be turned into a trap for the Irish rather than a haven.

If Robert Monro's generalship was usually uninspired, so was that of his Irish enemies. Sir Phelim O'Neill appears to have despaired of victory when the New Scots landed. Castlehaven was more competent than has usually been allowed, but little can be said positively in his favour. Owen Roe O'Neill showed great talent and energy in organising and inspiring his men, and his generalship at Benburb was of a high order. But apart from the 1646 campaign he showed little enterprise, largely because all too often he subordinated military action to personal considerations, like his quarrel with Castlehaven, or to political ambitions, as was seen especially clearly after Benburb.

Basically the failings of both the New Scots and the Irish sprang from similar causes. Both armies were nearly always short of equipment and food, leading to prolonged inactivity punctuated by short periods in the field. Both were hindered when taking the offensive by the difficult terrain of southern Ulster. And, perhaps most important of all, though the armies of Monro and Owen Roe were ostensibly concerned only with the campaign in Ulster, their political masters always had in mind the possibility that they might be needed elsewhere. Monro was weakened by the withdrawal of men to oppose Montrose in 1645; Owen Roe's army was used to overthrow the confederate supreme council in 1646. Both generals had to spend as much time looking over their shoulders at events elsewhere as in concentrating their attention on the enemy.

In military terms the sending of a Scottish army to Ireland had been comparatively successful, even if the New Scots had failed to live up to the high expectations of their English and Scottish employers. The army also had other, non-military, effects on the future history of Ireland. Under its patronage presbyterianism became so firmly rooted in Ulster that it proved impossible to eradicate it, in spite of intermittent official hostility in the generations that followed; and presbyterianism was to be the main agency which preserved the Ulster Scots as a separate interest in Ireland, binding them together more strongly then vague ties of blood and a common Scottish origin. The New Scots also added physically to the Scots plantation, for many of them settled in Ulster, replacing men who had fled or been killed by the rebels. Already by the time of the dispersal of the army in 1648 the distinction between Old and New Scots was no longer clear cut. Old Scots has been recruited into the army; New Scots had married local women or had brought their families from Scotland and settled into the community. Early in 1645 one of Ormond's officers in Lisburn hoped that the New Scots would soon return to Scotland to fight Montrose; but he feared that if they did they would carry all the local girls with them![10] Robert Monro married the widow of Lord Montgomery of the Ards. His nephew George (after the death of his first wife, Robert's daughter Anne, in 1647) married a daughter of Sir Frederick Hamilton in 1649.[11] In the same year Lieutenant Colonel James Wallace married a daughter of Mr Edmondstone of Ballycarry (five miles from Carrickfergus).[12] Captain (later Major) Alexander MacAulay of Argyll's regiment married a daughter of the royalist Archibald Stewart of Ballintoy. Even less appropriate were the marriages of at least two officers to Catholics. Captain George Gordon married the earl of Antrim's sister [13] and Major James Turner married Mary White, a girl of good family whom he met in Newry while garrisoned there—though because of her religion the

---

10. Carte MSS, 14, f. 299.
11. *D.N.B.* under George Monro; H. Monroe, *Foulis Castle and the Monroes of Lower Iveagh* (London, 1929), p. 24.
12. *D.N.B.* under James Wallace.
13. Hill, 'Stewarts of Ballintoy', *U.J.A.* N.S. VII, 17; Hill, *Montgomery Manuscripts*, pp. 76-7n.

marriage did not take place until after he left Ireland in 1644.[14] Of these six officers who are known to have married in Ulster only one settled there permanently; the 'honest, kind Major general [Robert] Monro', given to melancholia, died on his wife's estates in County Down in about 1680. His son Andrew was killed at the siege of Limerick in 1690, while his younger brother Daniel was granted lands in County Down in the 1660s and founded a landed family there.[15]

It is impossible to know how many New Scots, officers and men, settled in Ulster, but their numbers must have been considerable. Moreover, in the mid-1640s many Scots crossed to Ulster to escape civil war—and, doubtless, the high taxation and military service demanded by the covenanters. According to Patrick Adair after Montrose's victory at Kilsyth in 1645 'many families fled from Scotland to Ireland for shelter'. The persons of quality among them soon returned home but 'many of the more common sort of people staid in the country and added to the new plantation here'.[16]

Again, Adair says that 'in the year 1646, and thereafter, the new plantation in Down and Antrim did increase'.[17] It is, incidently, an indication that the 'oppression' of the New Scots, so often complained of, cannot have been so extreme as was sometimes suggested that many men evidently found life in Antrim and Down under their control preferable to life in Scotland.

One of the most interesting aspects of the history of the Scottish army in Ireland is the way in which its officers at times seem almost to regard themselves as, and to act as, an autonomous political unit rather than merely as an army obeying orders.

Internally the army came to be largely controlled by the council of officers. According to James Turner, writing of 1647, 'that armie was then governed by a councell of officers, wherof the Major Generall was president'.[18] The council consisted of all senior officers and representatives of the junior officers of each regiment. It probably existed from the army's first arrival in Ireland, and it quickly attained con-

14. Turner, *Memoirs*, p. 34.
15. Hill, *Montgomery Manuscripts*, p. 213; Monroe, *Foulis Castle*, pp. 19-26.
16. Adair, *True Narrative*, p. 127.
17. Ibid. p. 135.
18. Turner, *Memoirs*, p. 44.

siderable power; it was far from simply a rubber stamp for the decisions of Robert Monro as president. As early as the autumn of 1642 the officers were well enough organised, and had a strong enough sense of common interest (and common grievances), to bind themselves together by an oath of mutual assurance and to defy effectively their commander in chief, Leven. Officers sent to represent the army's interests in England and Scotland usually had their commissions and instructions signed by members of the council as well as by Monro, who on occasion (probably on more than evidence survives for) had to modify or change his plans to satisfy the council of officers. Early in 1644 the officers were prepared to remain bound by oath to act together even if they withdrew to Scotland; and the decision to withdraw had been taken in defiance of Monro's wishes. In 1648 it was the officers rather than Monro who took the initiative in deciding to support the Engagement.

Externally as well as internally the capacity of the army for joint action (in non-military spheres) is striking. It negotiates with the English and Scottish governments about its future, bargaining with them rather than receiving orders from them. Sometimes its decisions to stay or to leave Ireland seemed determined by a policy of doing the opposite of what it was ordered to do. In 1643-4 it first insisted on staying in Ireland, then tried to insist on leaving. In 1646 it refused to send men back to Scotland. It refused to hand over Belfast to parliament.

Yet, in the end, on really vital issues the army never carried out its threats to defy its masters—or at least not until 1648, when it had to choose which of its masters, English and Scottish, to serve, and chose the latter by supporting the Engagement. Thus three questions need to be answered about the army's behaviour. Why did the army adopt such a belligerent attitude towards its masters? Why did its masters let it get away with such insubordination? And why did the army not carry its successful insubordination further than it did?

The army's belligerence is easy to account for. It did not arise from the army adopting any political or religious ideology which conflicted with that of its masters (as was the case with the new model army in England), but from the much more mundane matter of breach of contract. The army was not paid or supplied as promised in the 1642 treaty, and consequently suffered considerable privations. Any army so neglected by its paymasters would have shown resentment and acted to try to ensure that its just claims were met, that arrears were paid. But the ways in which the army tried to obtain justice doubtless owed much to the fact that many of its officers were former mercenaries, used to bargaining with their employers and to standing up for their rights by banding together. To the true mercenary loyalty was only due when the pay agreed on was provided. Often implicit in the negotiations with England and Scotland was a threat that loyal service could not be expected indefinitely if promises about pay were broken. The peak of the influence of mercenary attitudes in the army was perhaps reached early in 1644 when the army resolved to move to Scotland and remain in arms there until payment of arrears had been exacted; it was at this time that the officers of the Newry garrison were evidently ready to sell it to the highest bidder. This was to be the closest that the New Scots approached to the phenomenon many of its officers must have met with in the Thirty Years War of 'armies more or less independent of political rule', ready to conclude treaties with states as if they themselves were states.[19]

Special circumstances inclined or forced the army's masters to turn a blind eye to such conduct. The ambiguity of the 1642 treaty as to from whom precisely the commander of the New Scots was to receive his orders strengthened the army's position. So did the fact that the English parliament was its theoretical paymaster but that for much of the time in practice the Scottish government was more efficient in providing supplies. For most of the army's career parliament and the Scots were allies, but nonetheless their attitudes to events in England and Ireland differed significantly—and increasingly. Neither wished, by any firm reaction to the insubordination of the New Scots, to drive them into the hands of the other. The New Scots could thus play off these rivals for their loyalty against each other. Moreover, though the army might be neglected through necessity, its value was recognised. Except in late 1643 and early 1644, when transferring the army to England was considered, both the Scottish regime and the English parliament were anxious that it should

19. D. H. Pennington, *Seventeenth Century Europe* (London, 1970), p. 236.

remain in Ulster to preserve a Protestant and parliamentarian foothold there and to prevent large-scale Irish intervention in England or Scotland. Harsh denunciations by the army of the way it was being treated were tolerated in Edinburgh and London because (at least up to 1646) the only alternatives were to disband the army or, by trying to discipline it, provoke it into mutiny, and Ulster would then probably have fallen into the hands of the Irish or the king.

If the bargaining position of the New Scots was so strong, why did they gain so little for themselves? The obvious answer is that, in the end, they chose to support the Engagement instead of the English parliament, and thus committed themselves to a cause which was to be defeated. But why did they support the Engagement? Why had they not, long before, sold themselves like true mercenaries to the highest bidder once it became clear that they were not going to be paid properly? No doubt support for the Engagement was influenced strongly by belief that this was the course of action most likely to lead to payment of arrears. But in a wider context New Scots acceptance of the Engagement can be seen as the last of many indications the army had given through its actions that it felt a loyalty to Scotland. Even though it was infuriated sometimes by the way the Scottish government treated it, and therefore at times failed to obey orders from Scotland, it recognised that that government had the strongest claim to its services and loyalty.

It could be argued that this loyalty to Scotland was consistent with a mercenary interpretation of the army's motives and conduct; the Scots government had proved to be a marginally better paymaster than the English parliament, and promised to see that the army's arrears were paid (an undertaking to this effect being included in the Engagement). But this argument, that loyalty to Scotland was based solely on hopes of payment, only makes sense in the later years of the army's career, whereas from the very first it has shown a clear preference for obeying orders from Edinburgh rather than from London. In 1642 and 1643 the New Scots refused to send forces out of Ulster as the English ordered; instead they served the interests of Scotland's security by refusing to advance into the heart of Ireland. The army sent troops back to Scotland to oppose Montrose in 1645 without consulting

L

the English who were their employers. If the New Scots had little choice but to serve Scotland rather than the English parliament in the 1648 war, it was because from their first arrival in Ireland they had served Scotland's interests rather than England's when the two conflicted. This had contributed greatly to the growing hostility of the English to the army, and to their reluctance to pay it or its arrears. Had the New Scots been purely mercenary in their outlook, they would surely have at first shown themselves more ready to obey and satisfy their English employers.

Many of the smaller states of seventeenth century Europe were ready to raise and hire out regiments or whole armies to serve greater powers in their wars in return for pay; and the Scots, in offering to provide an army to be sent to Ireland if the English would agree to pay it were doubtless influenced by such examples. But nonetheless the army the covenanters sent to Ireland could not be a purely mercenary one, for the war it was hired to fight in was one which directly effected Scotland's interests. The state to which Scotland hired the army was not a completely foreign power but one to which Scotland was already linked by the union of the crowns. Had the transaction been simply a mercenary one, Scotland would have withdrawn the New Scots once it became clear that the English could not pay them. But instead Scotland undertook the burden of partially supporting the army herself. Even before this, the Scottish government had assumed a right to a predominant voice in the direction of the army, and the army had accepted this right. It frequently grumbled, it sometimes disobeyed, but fundamentally it saw itself fighting for Scotland and for the covenanters. This is, it seems, the main reason why though its grievances on occasion drove it to political intrigue, in the end it always drew back from treachery. An important influence here was the character of Robert Monro. He refused, whenever possible, to step beyond his role of military commander. Sometimes he could not stop his bitter and frustrated officers from defying orders from Edinburgh or from intriguing with Ormond, but he was consistent in his disapproval. His control over the army was inevitably weakened by the success of the officers in defying Leven in 1642, but he always tried to influence the officers in favour of avoiding extreme action. Royalist attempts to buy him and his army were ignored, and he insisted that the officers, in their debates on whether to stay in Ireland or to leave, consider the interests of the Ulster Protestants they had come to protect and of their own native country, not just their own grievances. Had it been George Monro, a quick tempered and unscrupulous intriguer, and not his uncle who was effective commander of the army its career might have been very different, its conduct more mercenary.

The New Scots army provided a training for many officers who were later to achieve high rank. 'Some who were then but majors to regiments and captains of companies, became thereafter generals and lieutenant-generals in foreign kingdoms'.[20] Robert Monro's military career was over, but his nephew Sir George landed in the Highlands early in 1654 with John Middleton, who was to take over leadership of a royalist rising against the English conquerors. Monro had the rank of lieutenant general, and with him were two fellow New Scots, Thomas Dalyell of the Binns and William Drummond. Both had also been with him in Scotland in 1648 supporting the Engagement, and in Ulster in 1649, and both had fought in the king's army at the battle of Worcester in 1651. They now had been promoted to the rank of major general. The Highland rising proved a failure, divisions among the royalists being intensified by Monro's tactlessness and bad temper. He denounced the earl of Glencairn's Highland troops as thieves and robbers, which led to a duel between the two men in which Monro was wounded.

After the Restoration of the monarchy in 1660 Monro was at one point suspected of having covenanting sympathies, being briefly imprisoned during the 1666 rebellion against the regime, but was soon regarded as sufficiently loyal to be made a privy councillor (1674) and to be employed in the army with the rank of major general (1674-7, 1688). He also served as a member of the Scottish parliament on a number of occasions. In the 1688-9 revolution, however, he deserted the Stewart cause, and was appointed to command a militia force raised to protect the revolution from the Jacobites. It was said that in this, his final command, he 'affected nastiness, brutality and fanaticism'. He died in 1693 and can have been lamented by few.[21]

20. Adair, *True Narrative*, pp. 88-9.
21. J. Gwynne, *Military Memoirs of the Great Civil War ... and an account of the*

On the failure of the 1653-4 Highland rising Thomas Dalyell and William Drummond continued their careers together by taking service in the Russian army, the former becoming a general, the latter a lieutenant general. In 1665 they returned to Scotland at the request of Charles II and the following year Dalyell was appointed commander in chief of the forces in Scotland, with Drummond as his lieutenant general. Under their command there must have been many of their former New Scots colleagues. Among them was Sir James Turner, serving in the Scots guards after being knighted at the Restoration, and William Borthwick, who had become lieutenant colonel of the same regiment in 1662. The four New Scots took part in trying to suppress the religious dissidents, conventiclers or covenanters, in the south west. In the 1666 Pentland Rising Sir James Turner was captured by the rebels, whose military commander was an old colleague of his, James Wallace, who had remained loyal to the covenants. The rebels were soon routed by Dalyell at Rullion Green, and Wallace escaped to Holland where he died in 1678. Dalyell and Drummond were subsequently active in policing the south west and earned themselves evil reputations in presbyterian mythology, as Turner had already done. Dalyell was noted for his cruelty and intemperance, Drummond as a harsh disciplinarian, characteristics some blamed on their service with the barbarous Russians. Turner, 'naturally fierce, but very mad when he was drunk, and that was very often', was not employed after the 1666 rising as his conduct was thought to have played a part in provoking it. However, this forced retirement allowed him time to concentrate on his literary ambitions. While serving with the Scots army in Ireland at Newry in 1643 he had begun a treatise on 'Buchanan Revised' refuting the subversive political theories of George Buchanan, and since then had produced essays on a wide range of topics—religious controversy, history, and political theory. These papers he gathered together and revised in retirement, publishing those on military topics as *Pallas Armata. Essays on the Art of War* (Edinburgh, 1683). When James VII and II came to the throne Turner was granted a pension, but he died

earl of Glencairn's expedition, ed. Sir W. Scott (Edinburgh, 1822), pp. 163n, 167-8, 175-9; *D.N.B.* under George Monro; *R.P.C.S. 1673-6*, pp. 266, 267, 268, 498-9, *1676-7*, pp. 14, 15, 229, *1686-9*, p. xxvi, *1689*, pp. 567, 605-6; C. Dalton, *The Scots Army, 1661-1688* (Edinburgh and London, 1909), part 1, pp. 35-42.

shortly afterwards. His literary ambitions had to some extent been shared by one of his old New Scots colleagues, for William Drummond wrote a substantial family history, *The Genealogy of the most noble and ancient house of Drummond* (Edinburgh, 1831). Drummond died in 1688, two years after being created Viscount Strathallan. As Thomas Dalyell had died in 1685 this left Sir George Monro as the only leading officer of the Scottish army in Ireland to survive long enough to witness the century's second revolutionary upheaval in Britain, the 'Glorious Revolution' of 1688-9. By that time the career of the Scottish Army in Ireland in the 1640s had largely been forgotten.[22]

The effects of the army's years in Ulster remained, however. The Irish confederates had been prevented from conquering Ulster. The Scots-dominated Ulster plantation had survived. And presbyterianism had been firmly established in Ulster. These were all, obviously, of immense importance in the development of Ireland in the centuries ahead. It is not too much to say that the part played by the Ulster Scots in the Bishops' Wars, the career of the New Scots in Ulster, and the revival (and subsequent swift collapse) of links between the Highlands and Gaelic Ireland, all combine to make Scottish-Irish relations in the mid-seventeenth century of greater importance in the history of Britain as a whole than they had been at any time since the Bruce invasion of the early fourteenth century, and than they were to be at any time up to the present day.

---

22. *D.N.B.* under Dalyell, Drummond, Turner and Wallace; Turner, *Memoirs*, pp. xii-xvi, 145-89; Adair, *True Narrative*, pp. 155n, 168n; Maurice, *History of the Scots Guards*, I, 18, 20, 22, 26-30, 46; Dalton, *The Scots Army*, part I, pp. 17-28. Another New Scot to gain notoriety in the restoration period was the famous Major Thomas Weir (captain lieutenant in Home's regiment, 1642-3), executed for bestiality and incest in 1670, D. Stevenson, 'Major Weir: A Justified sinner?' *Scottish Studies*, XVI (1972), 161-73. More reputable was the fame gained by Dr Robert Cunningham, who had been one of the physicians attached to the New Scots army. He fought for Charles II at Worcester in 1651 and subsequently became the king's physician in Scotland. Cunningham was created a baronet in 1673 and died the following year, 'a worthy man, very usefull in his tyme', G. E. Cokayne, *Complete Baronetage* (6 vols. Exeter, 1900-9), IV, 295.

Ballygalley Castle, County Antrim. A symbol of the Scottish presence in Northern Ireland: an early seventeenth century tower house, Scottish in design but built in Ulster.

APPENDIX ONE

Summary of the Treaty for sending a Scottish Army to Ireland, 1642

Articles of the Treaty concerning the reducing of Ireland to the obedience of the king and the crown of England, agreed upon by the commissioners of Scotland (authorised by the king and the parliament of that kingdom) and the commissioners of England (authorised by the king and the parliament of that kingdom). Assented to by the English parliament 7 July 1642 and ratified by the Scottish parliament 21 July 1644.[1]

1. The Scottish commissioners, out of a sense of duty to the king and affection for England, and being willing to contribute to the speedy relief of the distressed parts of Ireland which lie nearest to Scotland, have offered 10,000 men for that service. They have declared that Scotland shall pay the cost of levying and transporting these men.
2. Scotland shall send with her army 6,000 muskets and 4,000 pikes, with cannon and ammunition. England shall send to Scotland at once 4,000 muskets and 2,000 pikes. The residue of the 10,000 arms, and 10,000 swords and belts, shall be sent to Scotland by 1 August next. England shall also send to Scotland as many cannon as Scotland sends to Ireland. At the end of the war these arms shall be returned to England, after Scotland has received satisfaction out of them for any arms lost in Ireland. England shall send to the Scottish army in Ireland six demi-cannon of twenty four pound ball.
3. Two ships of war shall be sent by England to Lochryan, Lamlash, Portpatrick or Ayr to guard the army while it is crossing to Ireland. They shall then attend at Irish ports to

---

1. *A.P.S.* VI, i, 189-92.

to serve the Scottish army and keep the sea passages to Scotland open. They shall receive orders from the chief commanders of the Scottish army, according to instructions from the Admiralty.

4. England shall levy and equip ten troops of horse (sixty men to a troop, plus officers) with a commissary general, a sergeant major and a quartermaster over them. They shall join and remain with the Scottish army and obey the orders of its commanders. England shall advance £1,200 sterling to levy a troop of 100 horse plus officers in Scotland to be a guard for the general of the Scottish army.

5. The Scottish officers and soldiers shall be paid at English rates, according to a list agreed upon, and have wagon allowances according to the list [printed in Appendix Two].

6. The towns and castles of Carrickfergus and Coleraine shall be put into the hands of the Scots army for magazines and garrisons. They shall remain in Scots hands until the war ends or the Scots army is discharged. The commissioners of Scotland promise on the public faith of Scotland to restore these towns and castles to any having commission from the king and English parliament. The commissioners of England promise on the public faith of England that all payments due to the Scottish army under this treaty shall be made, and that when the army is discharged it shall be disbanded by regiments and no less proportion.

7. England shall provide Carrickfergus and Coleraine with victuals necessary for the army according to a list agreed on, to be sold to the Scots army at agreed prices. England will also provide in these towns, according to a list to be agreed on, carts and wagons for use of the army; and also gunsmiths, carpenters and one or two engineers, and hand mills to serve the soldiers on marches.

8. England shall advance £2,000 sterling to be used by the general of the Scottish army for fortifications, intelligence, etc. Not more than £2,000 sterling *per annum* shall be allowed for such purposes without special warrant of the English parliament. £2,000 sterling shall be advanced to provide 1,000 horses for carrying the artillery, baggage and victual of the army, and for dragoons on occasion.

9. The inhabitants of places in Ireland occupied by the

Scottish army shall receive orders from the Scottish officers, sell victual to them, and rise and concur with them if ordered to do so.

10.   The 10,000 men from Scotland shall go as an army under their own general and officers. The province of Ulster is appointed for them 'wherin they shall first prosecute the warr' as they think most expedient. The commanders of the army shall have power to give conditions to towns, castles and persons who surrender, provided no toleration of the popish religion be granted and no conditions be made concerning rebel lands. Places recovered from the rebels by the Scottish army shall be at the disposal of its commanders. The Scottish army shall, if ordered, join with the lord lieutenant of Ireland and 'receive in a frie and honourable way instructions from him' or his deputy or other governors of Ireland. The Scottish general alone shall give orders to the officers of his army, and the army shall not be mixed with other forces in quartering or marching. Forces may be detached from the Scottish army, but shall be ordered out by their own general on the lord lieutenant prescribing the number, which shall not exceed one quarter of the foot or of the horse appointed to join with them. The whole Scottish army may be called out of Ulster by the lord lieutenant or other governors of Ireland if he or they think fit, even if the rebels are not totally suppressed in Ulster.

11.   The Scottish army shall be entertained by England for three months from 20 June 1642 and from then until discharged. They shall have a month's pay advanced to them when they are first mustered in Ireland, and shall be paid monthly thereafter. A muster master shall be appointed by the muster master general of England to make frequent musters of the army.

12.   The Scottish army shall receive its discharge from the king and the English parliament, or persons authorised by them. It shall have a month's warning before disbanding; this is to be given to the privy council or chancellor of Scotland. When dismissed the common soldiers shall be allowed fourteen days' pay to carry them home.

13.   At any time after the three months now agreed upon expires, notice may be given that the English parliament

shall not pay the Scottish army after one month more, and it shall not be obliged to do so.

APPENDIX TWO

The Establishment and Pay of the Scottish Army in Ireland, 1642

The list of officers and soldiers of the army, and their pay and wagon allowances, referred to in the fifth article of the treaty, is not appended to the printed versions of the treaty, but a copy survives in T.S.A.I. pp. 7-8. A transcript of this list follows; in spite of its title it is concerned only with the officers of the army. Pay is given in sterling.

The List of officers and soldiers of the Scotts army agreed upon by the Commissioners for both kingdoms wherunto the article of the Irishe Treaty is relative and which is holdin as a parte of that treaty.

The officers of the staffe and there intertainement

	per diem	per mensem
To the Generall of the Scotts army	£10	£300
To the Generall Leiutenant	£5	£150
To the Generall of the artiliarie	£3	£90
To the Sergeant major Generall	£2	£60
To quartermaster Generall	£1	£30
To the Generall adjutant	12/-	£18
To the procurator fiscall	10/-	£15
To the clerke of the Counsell of warre	6/8	£10
To the cariage master Generall and his mates	6/-	£9
To 2 ministers for the staffe at 6/8 a peece	13/4	£20
To 2 phisitianes for the staffe at 5/- a peece	10/-	£15

The Establishment and Pay of the Scottish Army in Ireland, 1642

	per diem	per mensem
To 2 Chirurgians for the staffe at 4/-	8/-	£12
To 4 Chirurgianes mates at 2/-	8/-	£12
To 2 apothecaries at 2/6 a peece is	5/-	£7:10:0
To provost marishell General at 5/-	5/-	£7:10:0

The List of waggons allowed to officers of the staffe

	per diem	per mensem
To the Generall 15 waggons at 4/8	£3:10:0	£150
To leiutenant Generall sex	£1:8:0	£42
To sergeant major Generall 3	14/-	£21
To quartermaster Generall 1	4/8	£7
To provost marishell Generall 2	9/4	£14
To cariage master Generall 1	4/8	£7
To procurator fiscall 1	4/8	£7
Two ministers 1	4/8	£7
To 1 [sic] phisitian 1	4/8	£7
To Chirurgian and apothecarie 1	4/8	£7
Generall of artaliarie 4	18/8	£28

[in margin] The Generall officers have likewise there allowance as collonells and captains for waggons

The officers of a Regiment of foott with there entertainement per diem to be payed to the officers of ten Regiments

	per diem	per mensem
To the Collonell	£1:4:0	£36
To the Leiutenant Collonell	12/-	£18
To the sergeant major	8/-	£12
To the Regiment minister	4/-	£6
To provost marishell	4/-	£6
To the Chirurgian	4/-	£6
To 2 Chirurgians mates at 2/-	4/-	£6
To the quartermaster	4/-	£6
To waggon master	3/-	£4:10:0
To Regiments Scriver	2/6	£3:15:0

The Establishment and Pay of the Scottish Army in Ireland, 1642

The officers of the Collonells company and there entertainement per diem

To the Captaine	12/-	£18
To the Leiutenant	4/-	£6
To the Ensigne	3/-	£4:10:0
To 3 sergents at 1/4	4/-	£6
To 3 Corporalls at 1/-	3/-	£4:10:0
To a Captaine at armes	1/-	£1:10:0
To a scriver	1/-	£1:10:0
To a drumber major	1/4	£2
To 2 drumbers at 1/- a peece	2/-	£3

The like number of officers and the same entertainement is allowed to the Rest of the Companys of the Regiment excepting one sergent and a drumber major

Item there is allowed in each Regiment

	per diem	per mensem
To the Collonell 2 waggons at 4/8 per diem	9/4	£14
To the Leiutenant Collenell one	4/8	£7
To sergeant major	4/8	£7
To each two captains one which is 5 in all	£1:3:4	£35
To every minister and Chirurgiane one	4/8	£7
The leiutenant of the Collonells company 1	4/8	£7

[in margin] The Collonell, Leiutenant Collonell, and major have their allowances as Captaines

The List of the officers of the Traine and there entertainement

To the lieutenant Collonell of the artaliary	£1:4:0	£36
To the major or Comptroller	8/-	£12
To sex Gentlemen of the artaliarie	£1:4:0	£36
To 4 Cannoneers	8/-	£12
To 60 mattrossers	£3	£90

The Establishment and Pay of the Scottish Army in Ireland, 1642

To one waggon master	4/-	£6
To one Commissarie	5/-	£7:10:0
To 4 clerks at 2/- a peece	8/-	£12
To 4 Conductors 2/6	10/-	£15
To a quartermaster	4/-	£6
To a proviant master	4/-	£6
To a minister	4/-	£6
To a chirurgian	4/-	£6
To Leiutenant Collonell for 2 wagons	9/4	£14
To the major [for one wagon]	4/8	£7

Though this is apparently the full list that was appended to the treaty, it is incomplete and inadequate in several respects. It omits the 10,000 foot soldiers, and contains no mention of how many regiments and companies the army was to be divided into—without which it is impossible to know how many of the various regimental and company officers listed above there were supposed to be. The list also fails to detail the lifeguards of horse and of foot, and the pioneers, and its version of the establishment of the artillery train differs from that contained in the army accounts (see below).

These defects can mostly be remedied by reference to the draft accounts of the army up to 1 February 1643, contained in Cambridge University Library, MS Ee.iii.39(D), referred to below as 'the accounts' and by use of the muster rolls (for which see Appendix Three below).

The accounts show that the pay of the 10,000 common soldiers was 8d sterling a day, £1 a month—the same as that of the Scottish army in England in 1644-7 and of the new model army.[2] The muster rolls and the accounts show that the army was divided into ten regiments of ten companies of 100 men (plus officers) each—nominally; in practice there was a good deal of variation. Similarly the establishment of officers

2.   C. S. Terry, ed. *Papers relating to the army of the Solemn League and Covenant, 1643-7* (2 vols. S.H.S. 1917), I, lxxxv-lxxxvi; C. H. Firth, *Cromwell's Army* (London, 1962), p. 184. The pay rate of £1 a month is the same as the rate of 18/8 a month on the list printed in H. Hazlett, 'The Recruitment and Organisation of the Scottish Army in Ulster, 1642-9', in *Essays in British and Irish History*, ed. Cronne, Moody and Quinn, p. 115, as the former is calculated on a thirty day month, the latter on a twenty eight day month. The pay rates for officers of the army listed loc. cit. are much higher than were finally agreed on in the list appended to the treaty.

sometimes varied slightly from that laid down in the above list (see Appendix Three below).

The fourth article of the treaty specified that the lifeguard of horse was to contain 100 troopers, and the muster rolls show it had twelve officers (captain, lieutenant, cornet, quartermaster, three corporals, two trumpeters, a kettle-drummer, a saddler and a smith), with twenty three horses and four wagons. The accounts are confused as to their pay; the total monthly pay of the officers was either £4:6:6 or £4:16:6 sterling, and the troopers received either 2/- or 2/6 sterling a day.

The lifeguard of foot appears from the musters to have had the same complement of officers, eleven in all, as the companies commanded by colonels in the ten regiments of foot; this differs slightly from the establishment laid down in the list appended to the treaty. Its nominal strength was evidently the usual 100 men of an infantry company, and its officers and men were paid at the same rates as those of the ten regiments; indeed, as the accounts indicate, the lifeguard of foot was sometimes regarded as constituting the tenth company of Leven's regiment, though it was commanded by Colonel Home.

The establishment of the train of artillery shown in the accounts differs in several ways from that shown on the list printed above. The accounts, probably correctly, replace the proviant master with a provost marshall, and they give the total daily pay of the four clerks as 4/-, not 8/-. A more serious divergence is that the accounts include forty gunners at 1/6 each a day (instead of four cannoneers at 2/- a day) and four matrossers (assistant gunners) instead of sixty. The proportions of gunners to matrossers appears very odd in both the list and the accounts, and it seems likely that both are wrong; a draft list of the train's establishment mentions forty cannoners and sixty matrossers,[3] and these are probably the correct figures.

Included with the artillery train in the accounts are the following pioneers.[4]

	per day	per month
Captain of pioneers	4/-	£6

---

3. Ibid. p. 132.
4. For a draft list of pioneers see ibid. p. 133.

The Establishment and Pay of the Scottish Army in Ireland, 1642

	per day	per month
Lieutenant	2/-	£3
Stall or tent master	4/-	£6
Two master engineers (6/8 each)	13/4	£20
Two assistants (3/- each)	6/-	£9
Two petardiers (4/- each)	8/-	£12
Two assistants (1/6 each)	3/-	£4:10:0
Six workmasters (1/- each)	6/-	£9
Six carpenters (1/11 each)	11/6	£17:5:0
Two coopers (2/- each)	4/-	£2
Four smiths (1/9 each)	7/-	£10:10:0

The ordinary pioneers were not brought from Scotland but hired in Ireland; the accounts include an item for 120 Irish pioneers employed for three weeks at 8d each a day.

A final addition to the establishment of the army provided by the accounts concerns the general staff; the provost marshal commanded twelve horse guards, who were paid 2/- each a day.[5]

5. See also *C.J.* II, 494.

APPENDIX THREE

The Muster Rolls of the Scottish Army in Ireland, 1642

Two almost complete sets of muster rolls of the Scottish army in Ireland in 1642 have survived in the Public Record Office in London—two rolls for each of the ten foot regiments, and two each of the general's lifeguards of horse and of foot. The rolls (together with those of many of the British forces in Ulster) are in SP.28/120, Commonwealth Exchequer Papers, except two which have found there way into State Papers, Domestic; the second muster of Argyll's regiment is at SP.16/492/58 (see *C.S.P.D. 1641-3*, 407) and the first muster of the foot lifeguard is at SP.16/539/1/105 (see *C.S.P.D. 1625-49*, 643).

Hew Kennedy mustered the army as it landed in Ulster. The artillery train being 'dispersed in several places' was not mustered, but Kennedy had its officers and men listed and sent this list off with the muster rolls; but it does not appear to have survived.[6]

Thomas Clayton, who conducted the second muster, was evidently an Englishman, and was appointed by the muster master general of England in accordance with article eleven of the treaty. He mustered the great majority of the army on 9 to 14 September 1642; the exceptions were Sinclair's (mustered 28 September) and Argyll's (16 to 18 November) regiments, and a few men of Lindsay's (5 November) and Lothian's (10 November). His musters of the ten regiments and the lifeguards produce a total of 1,136 officers and 10,157 men, figures which agree closely with Kennedy's (1,131 officers and 10,144 men). Clayton apparently did muster the artillery train, for the army accounts (referred to in Appendix Two) refer to it being mustered on 26 September, when it

6. McNeill, *Tanner Letters*, pp. 162-3; S.R.O. PA.14/1, f. 45v; *L.J.* VI, 289.

consisted of ninety six officers and artificers (including pioneers), but the muster roll itself has been lost.

Clayton's musters at times provide more information than Kennedy's. He states where the musters took place; though he usually only does this for one or two companies of each regiment, it seems likely that the other companies were in the same vicinity—in many cases they must have been since the whole regiment was mustered on the same day. Clayton also marks officers and men who were sick, though he probably was not consistent about this—it seems highly unlikely that Argyll's regiment really had no sick men at all. Finally, he gives the numbers of wagon horses each company possessed; these have been omitted from the summary printed below since their numbers are consistent throughout the army—a colonel's company has ten, those of lieutenant colonels and majors have six each, and all other companies have two each, while the foot and horse lifeguards have ten and four respectively, making a total of 358 for the whole army. This distribution of wagons to the companies does not seem compatible with the wagon allowances laid down in the list appended to the treaty (see Appendix Two).

The structure of the army emerges clearly from the muster rolls. Each regiment has a staff of twelve officers—colonel, lieutenant colonel, major, minister, surgeon and two mates, quarter master, provost marshal, wagon master, drum major, and the regimental clerk, secretary or scrivener. This corresponds with the list appended to the treaty except that there are no sergeant majors in the muster rolls, a drum major being added to the staff instead.

The ten regiments were supposed to consist each of ten companies of 100 men plus officers; in fact Leven's and Lothian's had only nine companies and Monro's had fourteen. Three companies in each regiment were usually led by the senior officers, colonel, lieutenant colonel and major, while captains led the rest, but again this was not always the case; neither Leven nor Lothian had companies of their own, nor did the major of Glencairn's regiment. Each company normally had ten officers—captain, lieutenant, ensign, two sergeants, two drummers and three corporals. A colonel's own company also had a third sergeant, and its lieutenant was known as a captain lieutenant. This differs from the list appended to the treaty in omitting a captain of arms and a scrivener from each company's establishment, and a drum major from each colonel's company—though as noted above the latter were listed with the regimental staff. There are some exceptions to the usual establishment; several colonels' companies lacked third sergeants, while Clayton's muster of Home's regiment includes four drummers in his own company and a clerk in his lieutenant colonel's. Lawers' regiment at first included third serjeants in five of its companies (and Eglinton's in one), but though Kennedy accepted this Clayton evidently refused to, for in his musters the extra sergeants (all but the one in Lawers' own company) are 'demoted' to common soldiers.

The following is a summary of the two musters, the order of regiments being that indicated by numbers on the muster rolls. The names of officers are taken from Kennedy's rolls; in the very few cases where those given by Clayton are different they are added in brackets. The numbers of officers given as the total for regimental staff exclude staff officers who were also captains of companies (normally the colonel, lieutenant colonel and major) to avoid counting them twice. For the same reason Colonel Home has been omitted from the total of officers of the foot lifeguard since he is counted along with his regiment. Several colonels who were not present in Ireland in 1642 have also been omitted from the figures given, though they are not always marked as absent—the earls of Lothian, Glencairn and Lindsay, and the marquis of Argyll. Leven and Eglinton have been omitted from Kennedy's muster but included in Clayton's since they had reached Ireland by then. Thus so far as is possible the totals given represent officers and men who were actually in Ireland at the time of the musters. The figures given in brackets after many of Clayton's totals indicate the numbers marked as sick.

The Earl of Leven's Regiment

	Offs.	Kennedy Men	Date	Offs.	Clayton Men	Date	Place
Col. Leven							
L. C. George Monro	10	102	20 May	10	100(6)	9 Sept.	Carrickfergus
Maj. John Home	10	90	2 June	10	102(6)	9 Sept.	
Capts.							
William Carmichael	10	110	14 May	10	92(4)	"	
William McClellan	10	110	16 May-2 June	10	105	"	
Robert Blair	10	110	17 May	10	97	"	
James Blair	10	97	19 May	10	100(11)	"	
George Gordon	10	100	3 June	10	94(7)	"	
Robert Melville	10	91	20 June	10	94(14)	"	
John Leslie	10	90	20 June-15 July	10	98	"	
Staff	5						
TOTAL	95	900		10	882(48)	"	Carrickfergus
	100						

328

| Col. Lothian | Kennedy | | | Clayton | | | Place |
	Offs.	Men	Date	Offs.	Men	Date	
L. C. Walter Scot	10	96	3 Aug.	10	91(4)	9 Sept.	Carrickfergus
Maj. James Riddell	10	97	2 July-24 Aug.	10	97(4)	"	
Capts.							
Sir John Murray	10	93	4 July-10 Aug.	10	91	"	
Sir James Lockhart	10	95	18 July-3 Sept.	10	94(6)	"	
Alexander Lindsay	10	90	1 Aug.	10	88(6)	"	
Gideon Murray	10	98	2 Aug.	10	97(4)	"	
Sir Walter Riddell	10	56	23 July	10	86(3)	"	
Alexander Drummond	10	73	23 July-3 Nov.	10	67(2)	9 Sept.-10 Nov.	
William Kerr	10	100	3 Aug.	10	92(5)	9 Sept.	
Staff	9			9		"	
TOTAL	99	798		99	803(34)		

Major General Robert Monro's Regiment

	Offs.	Kennedy Men 96	Date 7 Apr.	Offs.	Clayton Men 99(8)	Date 9 Sept.	Place Carrickfergus
Col. Robert Monro	10	96	7 Apr.	10	99(8)	9 Sept.	Carrickfergus
L. C. Hew Fraser	10	108	,,	10	105(2)	,,	
Maj. George Barclay	10	90	,,	10	98(6)	,,	
Capts.							
Charles Arnot	10	109	,,	10	105(6)	,,	
Thomas Dalyell	10	108	,,	10	116(8)	,,	
Sir William Blair (James Lidderdail)	10	94	,,	10	93(5)	,,	
William Drummond	10	99	,,	10	98(4)	,,	
James Wallace	10	121	,,	10	118(5)	,,	
Andrew Bryden	10	90	,,	10	96(3)	,,	
John Leslie	10	100	,,	10	97(5)	,,	
Robert Forbes	10	97	,,	10	96	,,	

330

	Offs.	Men	Date	Offs.	Men	Date	Place
Andrew Leslie	10	100	"	10	96(10)	"	
Robert Wauchope	10	84	"	10	87	"	
Staff	9[7]			9		7 Sept.	Carrickfergus
TOTAL	149	1405		149	1411(78)		

The Earl of Glencairn's Regiment

	Offs.	Kennedy Men	Date	Offs.	Clayton Men	Date	Place
Col Glencairn	10	90	20 May	9	85	9 Sept.	Carrickfergus
L. C. William Cunningham	10	103	16 May–2 June	10	110(7)	"	
Maj. Alexander Barclay							
Capts.							
John Houston	10	93	20 May	10	88	"	
William Cunningham	10	101	23 May	10(1)	95(12)	"	

7. The muster of staff in this roll is by Clayton, though the rest of it is by Kennedy.

The Earl of Glencairn's Regiment (contd)

	Kennedy			Clayton			Place
	Offs.	Men	Date	Offs.	Men	Date	
Alexander Cunningham	10	102	20-26 May	10	104(9)	9 Sept.	
Robert Cunningham	9[8]	82[8]	20 May-2 Aug.	10	74(12)	,,	
Malcolm Crawford	10	95	20 May-1 Aug.	10	97	,,	
John Crawford	10	74	27 May-6 July	10	73(15)	,,	
William Knox	10	88	30 May	10	73(19)	,,	
Bryce Cochrane	10	81	23 May-4 June	10	80	,,	
Staff	10			10		,,	Carrickfergus
TOTAL	109	909		109(1)	879(74)		

8. The total given on the roll is 10 officers, but only nine are named; as elsewhere (see notes below) the usual total of 10 was evidently automatically put down by mistake. The number of soldiers in this company's muster is also confused; the total is given as 82 but 101 names are listed. Probably some should have been deleted (as has been done in some other rolls) but were overlooked.

Co. Eglinton	Kennedy			Clayton			
	Offs.	Men	Date	Offs.	Men	Date	Place
Co. Eglinton	10	100	23 May	10	100(10)	13 Sept.	Bangor
L. C. Colin Pitscottie	10	99	26 May-5 June	10	100(4)	13 Sept.	
Maj. Andrew Bell	10	100	23 May	10(1)	99(5)	10 Sept.	
Capts.							
James McCombie (James Montgomery)	11	100	"	10	96(6)	13 Sept.	
Bryce Blair (James Brice)	10	97	"	10	99	10 Sept.	
George Boyd	10	97	"	10	95(12)	13 Sept.	
Alexander Moore	10	100	23 May-28 June	10	99(5)	"	
William Birsbane	10	105	4-28 June	10	83(6)	"	
Robert Montgomery	10	105	23 May-14 June	10	86(9)	"	
John Hamilton	10	103	28 May-28 June	10	96(4)	"	
Staff	9			9		"	
TOTAL	110	1006		109(1)	953(61)		Bangor

The Earl of Lindsay's Regiment

	Kennedy			Clayton			
	Offs.	Men	Date	Offs.	Men	Date	Place
Col. Lindsay	9	60	20 June	9	91(20)	13 Sept.-5 Nov.	Bangor
L. C. John Hamilton	10	97	20 May-10 July	10	97(12)	13 Sept.	
Major William Borthwick	10	84	5 June-1 July	10(2)	78(6)	,,	
Capts.							
Robert Hamilton	10	100	13 May	10(1)	94(2)	,,	
Claud Hamilton	10	97	,,	10(2)	97(12)	16 Sept.	
Alexander Adair	10	100	24 May-6 June	10	98(5)	13 Sept.	
William Morton	10	92	5 June-1 July	10(1)	94(6)	,,	
Mungo Murray	10	42	13 June	10(1)	91(6)	,,	
Thomas Borthwick	10	84	16 June	10(1)	83(14)	,,	
Robert Drummond	10	100	16-20 June⁹	10(1)	99(10)	,,	
Staff	9			9		,,	
TOTAL	108	906		108(9)	922(93)		Bangor

9. According to the roll part of the company was mustered 16 June, the rest on 20 May; presumably the latter is a mistake for June

334

	Offs.	Men	Date	Offs.[10]	Men	Date	Place
Col. Lawers	11	127	10 Apr.	11	129(16)	10 Sept.	Temple Patrick
L. C. Andrew Mylne	10	100	1 May	10	107	"	
Maj. Colin Campbell	10	66	18 Apr.	10	85	"	
Capts.							
Archibald Campbell	11	108	"	10	106(6)	"	
John Drummond	11	102	"	10	96(6)	"	
William Bruce	11	108	"	10	105(5)	"	
James Lennox	10	100	"	10	100(8)	"	
Henry Gibson	11	115	"	10	103(17)	"	
John Moncrieff	10	108	"	10	93(6)	"	
William Hamilton	10	84	18 Apr.-22 May	10	100(14)	"	
Staff	9			9			
TOTAL	114	1018		110	1024(78)		Temple Patrick

10. The roll gives the total as 10 though 11 officers are named.

Robert Home of the Heugh's Regiment

		Kennedy			Clayton		
	Offs.	Men	Date	Offs.	Men	Date	Place
Col. Robert Home	10	144	7 Apr.	12[11]	132(9)	9 Sept.	Carrickfergus
L. C. John Maxwell	10	88	14 June	11[12]	84(4)	,,	
Maj. William Cochrane	10	81	7 Apr.	10	84	,,	
Capts.							
Sir Charles Arnot	10	107	7-20 Apr.	10	101(8)	,,	
George M'Gill	10	86	7 Apr.	10	86(5)	,,	
Robert Hepburne	10	117	,,	10	114(5)	,,	
Robert Kennedy	10	115	,,	10	110(12)	,,	
James Durham	10	87	,,	10	94(3)	,,	
Michael Elphinstone	10	79	,,	10	83(8)	,,	
Samuel Stewart	10	78	24 June-1 Aug.	10	92(5)	,,	
Staff	8			9		,,	
TOTAL	108	982		112	980(59)		Carrickfergus

11. The roll gives the total as 10 though 12 officers are named.

336

| | Kennedy | | | Clayton | | | |
	Offs.	Men	Date	Offs.	Men	Date	Place
Col. Sinclair	10	104	7 Apr.	10	106	28 Sept.	Newry
L. C. Henry Sinclair	10	120	"	10	122	"	
Maj. James Turner	10	114	"	10	109(15)	"	
Capts. William Innes	10	108	"	10	109	"	
Patrick Sinclair	10	112	28 Apr.-23 May	10	102	"	
David Seatoun	10	100	29 Apr.-15 June	10	91(10)	"	
John Rouche	10	104	4-26 May	10	102	"	
David Chirnside	10	98	20 May-14 June	10	98(5)	"	
Alexander Bannerman	10	100	4 June	10	96(10)	"	
Patrick (Peter) Leslie, General Adjutant.	10	81	4 May-15 June	10	97(4)	"	
Staff	9			9			
TOTAL	109	1041		109	1032(44)	"	Newry

The Marquis of Argyll's Regiment

	Offs.	Kennedy Men	Date	Offs.	Clayton Men	Date	Place
	9	99	1 May	10	104	17 Nov.	Ballintoy
Col. Argyll							
L. C. Sir Duncan Campbell of Auchinbreck	10	116	"	10	117	16 Nov.	Dunluce
Maj. William Campbell	10	101	"	10	111	17 Nov.	Ballycastle
Capts.							
Duncan Campbell of Dunans	10	96	"	10	98	16 Nov.	Dunluce
Duncan Campbell of Inverliver	10	99	"	10	106	16 Nov.	Dunluce
John Campbell	10	95	"	10	104	17 Nov.	Ballycastle
Colin Campbell	10	98	"	10	100	16 Nov.	Dunluce
Mathew Campbell	10	94	"	10	101	18 Nov.	Ballymoney
Alexander Macaulay	10	99	"	10	108	17 Nov.	Ballycastle
—— McClellane (McKleane)	10	94	"	10	99	18 Nov.	Ballymoney
Staff	9			9		16 Nov.	Dunluce
TOTAL	108	991		109	1048		

	Kennedy			Clayton			
	Offs.	Men	Date	Offs.	Men	Date	Place
Capt. Col. Robert Home	10[13]	107	25-28 June	10[13]	122(8)	14 Sept.	Donaghadee
Lifeguard of Horse							
Capt. Maj. James Balledine	12	81	1 July	12	101(11)	10 Sept.	Carrickfergus
TOTAL FOR ARMY	1,131	10,144		1,136(11)	10,157(588)		

13. Excluding Colonel Home, who has been counted with his regiment.

BIBLIOGRAPHY

Sources: Manuscript

Bodleian Library, Oxford

Carte MSS, vols. 1-29, Correspondence of James, 1st Duke of Ormond, 1633-51
Rawlinson MSS, A.258, Copies of letters and orders of the committee for the affairs of Ireland, September 1645-September 1648
Tanner MSS, 58 and 62

British Library, Department of Manuscripts

Add MSS 23, 112, Register of the Secretary of State of Scotland, 1635-40

Cambridge University Library

MS Ee.111.39(D), The pay of the Scottish army in Ireland, 1642

Inveraray Castle, Argyllshire

Argyll Letters, II
Argyll Transcripts, XII
Boxes V.19 and V.39

National Library of Scotland

MS Adv.33.4.8, Transactions of the Scotts army in Ireland from 1643 to Junii 1649 (cited as T.S.A.I.)
Wodrow MSS, Folio volumes XXV, LXV, LXVI and LXVII
MS 3368, Scottish historical letters and documents

National Museum of Antiquities of Scotland

MCR 40, The Black Book of Clanranald

Public Record Office, London

SP.16/492/58, Muster roll of the marquis of Argyll's regiment in Ireland, 1642
SP.16/539/1/105, Muster roll of the Scots life guard in Ireland, 1642
SP.28/120, Muster rolls of Scottish army in Ireland and other British forces there, 1642-3
SP.28/139/13, 14, Accounts of John Davies, commissary of victuals in Ulster
SP.46/106, ff. 90-128, Orders, receipts etc. for the Scottish army in Ireland, 1643-7

Scottish Record Office

PA.7/2-5, Supplementary Parliamentary Papers, 1606-48
PA.7/23/1-2, Additional Parliamentary Papers
PA.11/1-9, Registers of the Committee of Estates, 1643-50
PA.12/1-5, Warrants of the Committee of Estates, 1640-50
PA.13/2, Proceedings of the Scots Commissioners for concluding the articles of the Treaty, 1641-2
PA.13/3, Register of Letters to and from the Scots Commissioners in London, 1642, 1644-5
PA.14/1, Register of the Committee for Common Burdens, 1641-5
PA.14/2, Proceedings of the Scots Commissioners for conserving the articles of the Treaty, 1642-3
PA.14/3, Register of the Committee for Moneys (South), 1646
PA.16/1, Papers relating to burdens, losses, etc. 1640-58

PA.16/3, Army Papers, 1640-54.
GD.2/53, Petition by Burgh of Peebles to Parliament for payment of quarters and
plundering by Lord Sinclair's Regiment, 1647 (British Records Association
MSS)
GD.40, Portfolio V, Letters 1651-6 (Lothian Papers)
GD.112/39, Mounted Letters (Breadalbane Muniments)
GD.112/40/2, Letters, 1636-59 (Breadalbane Muniments)
GD.112/43/1, State Papers, 1545-1690 (Breadalbane Muniments)
GD.188/21/3/1-13, Letters of John Leslie, Bishop of Raphoe, and Robert Leslie
(Guthrie of Guthrie MSS)

Sources: General Printed

Abbot, W. C., ed. *The Writings and Speeches of Oliver Cromwell* (4 vols. Cam-
bridge, Mass. 1937-47)
The Acts of the Parliaments of Scotland, vols. V-VI (1870-2)
Adair, P., *A True Narrative of the rise and progress of the Presbyterian Church in
Ireland*, ed. W. D. Killen (Belfast, 1866)
Aiazza, G., ed. *The Embassy in Ireland of Monsignor G. B. Rinuccini* (Dublin,
1873)
Baillie, Robert, *Letters and Journals* (3 vols. Bannatyne Club, 1841-2)
Balfour, Sir James, *Historical Works* (4 vols. Edinburgh, 1824-5)
Birch, T., ed. *A Collection of State Papers of John Thurloe*, vol. I (London, 1742)
Bray, W., ed. *Diary and Correspondence of John Evelyn ... to which is subjoined
the Private Correspondence between King Charles I and Sir Edward Nicholas*
(London, n.d.)
Bruce, J., ed. *Charles I in 1646* (Camden Society, 1856)
Burton, T., *Diary*, ed. J. T. Rutt (4 vols. London, 1828)
Calendar of State Papers, Domestic, Charles I, vols. XII-XXII, 1637-49 (London,
1869-97)
Calendar of State Papers, Domestic, Commonwealth, vols. I-II, 1649-50 (London,
1875-6)
Calendar of State Papers Relating to Ireland, Charles I and Commonwealth,
vols. II-III, 1633-60 (London, 1901-3)
Carte, T., ed. *A Collection of Original Letters and Papers* (2 vols. London, 1739)
Cary, H., ed. *Memorials of the Great Civil War* (2 vols. London, 1842)
Cuningham, T., *The Journal of Thomas Cuningham of Campvere, 1640-54* (S.H.S.
1928)
Dalrymple, D., Lord Hailes, ed. *Memorials and Letters relating to the History of
Britain in the Reign of Charles the First* (Glasgow, 1766)
D'Ewes, Sir S., *Journal*, ed. W. H. Coates (New Haven, 1942)
Dugdale, W., *A Short View of the Late Trouble* (Oxford, 1681)
Dunlop, R., ed. *Ireland under the Commonwealth* (2 vols. Manchester, 1913)
Firth, C. H., and Rait, R. S., eds. *Acts and Ordinances of the Interregnum* (3 vols.
London, 1911)
Fotheringham, J. G., ed. *The Diplomatic Correspondence of Jean de Montereul*
(2 vols. S.H.S. 1898-9)
Fraser, Sir W., ed. *The Melvilles Earls of Melville, and the Leslies Earls of Leven*
(3 vols. Edinburgh, 1890)
Fraser, Sir W., ed. *Memorials of the Montgomeries, Earls of Eglinton* (2 vols.
Edinburgh, 1859)
Fraser, Sir W., ed. *The Sutherland Book* (3 vols. Edinburgh, 1893)
Gardiner, S. R., ed. *Constitutional Documents of the Puritan Revolution* (3rd
edn. Oxford, 1906)

M

Bibliography

Gardiner, S. R., ed. *Hamilton Papers* (Camden Society, 1880)

Giblin, C., ed. *The Irish Franciscan Mission to Scotland, 1619-1646* (Dublin, 1964)

Gilbert, J. T., ed. *A Contemporary History of Affairs in Ireland* (3 vols. in 6, Dublin, 1879-80)

Gilbert, J. T., ed. *History of the Irish Confederation and the War in Ireland* (7 vols. Dublin, 1882-91)

Gordon, J., *History of Scots Affairs, 1637-41* (3 vols. Spalding Club, 1841)

Gordon, P., *A Short Abridgement of Britane's Distemper* (Spalding Club, 1844)

Gordon, Sir R. and G., *A Genealogical History of the Earldom of Sutherland* (Edinburgh, 1813)

Guthry, H., *Memoirs* (2nd edn. Glasgow, 1748)

Hamilton, Sir J., Lord Claneboye, *The Hamilton Manuscripts*, ed. T. K. Lowry (Belfast, 1867)

Hickson, M. A., ed. *Ireland in the Seventeenth Century, or the Irish Massacres of 1641-2* (2 vols. London, 1884)

Historical Manuscripts Commission:

   HMC 5: *6th Report* (House of Lords), (1877)

   HMC 6: *7th Report* (house of Lords), (1879)

   HMC 8: *9th Report*, II (Dalyell of the Binns; Traquair), (1884)

   HMC 10: *10th Report*, I (Eglinton; Keir), (1885)

   HMC 13: *10th Report*, IV (Stewart), (1885)

   HMC 21: *Hamilton*, I, II (1887, 1932)

   HMC 23: *Cowper*, II (1888)

   HMC 29: *Portland*, I (1891)

   HMC 31: *13th Report* (Loder-Symonds), (1892)

   HMC 36: *Ormonde*, I, II, and N.S. II (1895, 1899, 1903)

   HMC 45: *Buccleuch*, I (1899)

   HMC 53: *Montagu* (1900)

   HMC 55: *Various Collections*, V (1909)

   HMC 63: *Egmont*, I, i, ii (1905)

   HMC 65: *Franciscan MSS* (1906)

   HMC 70: *Pepys MSS* (1911)

   HMC 78: *Hastings*, IV (1947)

Hogan, E., ed. *The History of the Warr of Ireland ... By a British Officer of the Regiment of Sir John Clotworthy* (Dublin, 1873)

Hogan, J., ed. *Letters and Papers relating to the Irish Rebellion between 1642 and 1646* (I.M.C. 1936)

Hogan, J., ed. 'Rawlinson Manuscripts, Class A.110', *Analecta Hibernica*, 4 (I.M.C. 1932), 1-98

Innes, C., ed. *The Book of the Thanes of Cawdor* (Spalding Club, 1859)

Innes, C., ed. *The Black Book of Taymouth* (Bannatyne Club, 1855)

Journals of the House of Commons, II-VI (London, 1803)

Journals of the House of Lords, IV-X (London, n.d.)

[Joy, H.], *Historical Collections relative to the Town of Belfast* (Belfast, 1817)

Knowler, W., ed. *The Earl of Strafford's Letters and Dispatches* (2 vols. London, 1739)

Laing, D., ed. *Correspondence of Sir Robert Kerr, First Earl of Ancrum, and his son William, Third Earl of Lothian* (2 vols. Edinburgh, 1875)

Laud, W., Works (7 vols. Oxford, 1847-60)

Leyburn, G., *The Memoirs ... being a Journal of his Agency for Prince Charles in Ireland, 1647* (London, 1886)

Livingstone, J., 'Life', in *Select Biographies*, ed. W. K. Tweedie (2 vols. Wodrow Society, 1847), I, 129-97

Bibliography

Macbain, A., and Kennedy, J., eds. *Reliquiae Celticae. Texts, Papers and Studies in Gaelic Literature and Philology left by the late Rev. Alexander Cameron* (2 vols. Inverness, 1892-4)

McCrie, T., ed. *The Life of Mr Robert Blair* (Wodrow Society, 1848)

McInnes, C. T., ed. *Calendar of Writs of Munro of Foulis* (S.R.S. 1940)

McNeill, C., ed. *The Tanner Letters* (I.M.C. 1943)

Macphail, J. R. N., ed. *Papers from the Collection of Sir William Fraser* (S.H.S. 1924)

Mactavish, D. C., ed. *Minutes of the Synod of Argyll* (2 vols. S.H.S. 1943)

Marshall, R. K., ed. 'Calendar of the Correspondence in the Hamilton Archives at Lennoxlove' (6 vols. Appendix to Ph.D. thesis, Edinburgh University, 1970, and part of National Register of Archives (Scotland) survey no. 332, Hamilton Muniments)

Marwick, J. D., ed. *Extracts from the Records of the Burgh of Glasgow, 1573-1642* and *1630-1662* (S.B.R.S. 1876, 1881)

Meikle, H. W., ed. *Correspondence of the Scots Commissioners in London, 1644-1646* (Roxburghe Club, 1917)

Mitchell, A. F., and Christie, J., eds. *Records of the Commissioners of the General Assemblies of the Church of Scotland, 1646-1652* (3 vols. S.H.S. 1892-1909)

Monro, R., *Monro his Expedition with the worthy Scots Regiment (called Mac-Keyes Regiment)* (London, 1637)

Monro, R., *The Scotch Military Discipline Learned from the Valiant Swede* (London, 1644)

Moody, T. W., and Simms, J. G., eds. *The Bishopric of Derry and the Irish Society of London, 1602-1705*, I (I.M.C. 1968)

Nalson, J., ed. *An Impartial Collection of the Great Affairs, of State* (2 vols. London, 1682-3)

Napier, M., ed. *Memorials of Montrose and his Times* (2 vols. Maitland Club, 1848-50)

Nickolls, J., ed. *Original Letters and Papers of State* (London, 1743)

O'Connell, D., and O'Ferrall, B., *Commentarius Rinuccinianus* (6 vols. I.M.C. 1932-49)

Ogle, O., Bliss, W. H., and Macray, W. D., eds. *Calendar of the Clarendon State Papers*, I, II (Oxford, 1869-72)

O'Mellan, T., 'A Narrative of the Wars of 1641' in *Historical Notices of Old Belfast*, ed. R. M. Young (Belfast, 1896), pp. 199-247. The Irish text is printed in *Analecta Hibernica*, 3 (1931), 1-61

Peterkin, A., ed. *Records of the Kirk of Scotland* (Edinburgh, 1838)

Pinkerton, W., ed. 'Proceedings of the Scottish and English Forces in the North of Ireland, A.D. 1642', *U.J.A.* VIII (1860), 77-87

Register of the Great Seal of Scotland. Registrum Magna Sigilli Regum Scotorum, IX (Edinburgh, 1897)

Register of the Privy Council of Scotland, 2nd series, VI-VIII (Edinburgh, 1905-8)

Rushworth, J., ed. *Historical Collections* (8 vols. London, 1659-1701)

Scrope, R., and Monkhouse, T., eds. *State Papers collected by Edward, Earl of Clarendon* (3 vols. Oxford, 1767-86)

Shuckburgh, E. S., ed. *Two Biographies of William Bedell, Bishop of Kilmore* (Cambridge, 1902)

Spalding, J., *Memorialls of the Trubles in Scotland and in England* (2 vols. Spalding Club, 1850-1)

Steele, R., ed. *A Bibliography of Royal Proclamations of the Tudor and Stuart Sovereigns* (2 vols. Oxford, 1910)

Terry, C. S., ed. *Papers relating to the Army of the Solemn League and Covenant* (2 vols. S.H.S. 1917)

Bibliography

Tuchet, James, Earl of Castlehaven, *The Earl of Castlehaven's Review, or his Memoirs of his Engagement and Carriage in the Irish Wars* (Dublin, 1815)

Turner, J., *Memoirs of his own Life and Times* (Bannatyne Club, 1829)

Venables, R., *The Narrative of General Venables* (Camden Society, 1900)

Walker, E., *Historical Discourses* (London, 1705)

Whitaker, T. D., ed. *The Life and Original Correspondence of Sir George Radcliffe* (London, 1810)

Whitelock, B., *Memorials of the English Affairs* (4 vols. Oxford, 1853)

Wishart, G., *The Memoirs of James Marquis of Montrose*, ed. A. D. Murdoch and H. F. M. Simpson (London, 1893)

Young, R. M., ed. *Historical Notices of Old Belfast* (Belfast, 1896)

Young, R. M., ed. *The Town Book of the Corporation of Belfast* (Belfast, 1892)

Sources: Contemporary Pamphlets

A Bloody Fights in Ireland, and a Great Victory obtained by Sir Charles Coote ... (London, 1649)

The Declaration of the British in the North of Ireland ... (1649)

A Declaration of the Presbytery at Bangor in Ireland, July 7 1649 (1649)

A Full Relation of the Late Expedition of the Right Honourable, the Lord Monroe, Major-generall of all the Protestant Forces in the Province of Ulster ... (London, 1644)

A Glorious Victory obtained by the Scots against the Rebels in Ireland ... (London, 1641/2)

Good Newes from the Scottish Army in Ireland ... (London, 1642)

[Howel, J.] , *Mercurius Hibernicus: or a Discourse of the late Insurrection in Ireland* (Bristol, 1644)

Joyfull Newes from the Kings Majesty ... (1648)

A Late and True Relation from Ireland ... With the entrance of some English and Scottish Forces into the North Parts of Ireland ... (London, 1641)

A Letter concerning Colonel Monks surprising the Town and Castle of Carrickfergus and Belfast, in Ireland; and his taking General Major Monro prisoner (London, 1648)

A Letter of Great Consequence; sent by the Honorable, Robert Lord Monro, out of the Kingdom of Ireland ... (London, 1643)

More Happy Newes from Ireland of a Battell fought betwixt the Scottish Volunteers against the Irish Rebels ... (London, 1641)

[Newark, D.] , *A True Relation of the last great Battell fought in Ireland betwixt the Scots and the Irish* ... (London, 1642)

Newrobe, R., *Delightfull Newes to all Loyall Subjects* ... (London, 1642)

Orders from the High Court of Parliament ... As also, a Relation of 4,000 Redshanks that are sent over into Ireland with Generall Lesley ... (London, 1641)

Pike, R., *A True Relation of the Proceedings of the Scots and English Forces in the North of Ireland* ... (London, 1642)

A Polt [sic] Discovered in Ireland and prevented without the shedding of Blood ... (London, 1644)

A True and Exact Relation of Divers Principal Acions of a late Expedition, undertaken in the North of Ireland ... (London, 1642)

A True Relation of the Proceedings of the Scottish Armie now in Ireland by Three Letters ... (London, 1642)

Two Letters from Sir Charles Coote ... relating to the redition of the Towne and Castle of Carrickfergus ... (London, 1650)

Two Letters from William Basil, Attorney General of Ireland, ... of a Victory obtained by the Parliament's Forces on the Plain of Lisnegarvy (London, 1649)

Bibliography

Secondary Works

Aldis, H. G., *A List of Books printed in Scotland before 1700* (revised edn. Edinburgh, 1970)

Bagwell, R., *Ireland under the Stuarts* (3 vols. London, 1909)

Barkley, J. M., 'Some Scottish Bishops and Ministers in the Irish Church, 1605-35' in *Reformation and Revolution*, ed. D. Shaw (Edinburgh, 1967), pp. 141-59

Barnard, T. C., *Cromwellian Ireland. English Government and Reform in Ireland, 1649-1660* (Oxford, 1975)

Beckett, J. C., 'The Confederation of Kilkenny reviewed', *Historical Studies*, II (1959), 29-41

Beckett, J. C., 'Irish-Scottish Relations in the Seventeenth Century' in *Confrontations: Studies in Irish History* (London, 1972), pp. 26-46

Beckett, J. C., *The Making of Modern Ireland* (London, 1966)

Benn, G., *History of the Town of Belfast* (2 vols. Belfast, 1877-80)

Black, R., 'Colla Ciotach', *Transactions of the Gaelic Society of Inverness*, XLVII (1972-4), 201-43.

Bottigheimer, K. S., 'Civil War in Ireland: The Reality in Munster', *Emory University Quarterly*, XXII (1966), 46-54.

Bottigheimer, K. S., *English Money and Irish Land. The 'Adventurers' in the Cromwellian Settlement of Ireland* (Oxford, 1971)

Buchan, J., *Montrose* (London, 1931)

Burnet, G., *The Memoires of the Lives and Actions of James and William Dukes of Hamilton* (London, 1677)

Carte, T., *The LIfe of James Duke of Ormond* (3 vols. London, 1735-6)

Casway, J. I., 'Owen Roe O'Neill's return to Ireland in 1642: The Diplomatic Background', *Studia Hibernica*, IX (1969), 48-64

Clarke, A., 'The Earl of Antrim and the First Bishops' War', *Irish Sword*, VI (1963-4), 108-15

Clarke, A., 'Ireland and the General Crisis', *Past and Present*, no. 48 (1970), 79-99

Clarke, A., *The Old English in Ireland, 1625-42* (London, 1966)

Cokayne, G. E., *Complete Peerage* (revised edn. 14 vols. London, 1910-59)

Colles, R., *The History of Ulster* (4 vols. London, n.d.)

Coonan, T., *The Irish Catholic Confederacy and the Puritan Revolution* (Dublin, 1954)

Cooper, J. P., 'The Fortune of Thomas Wentworth, Earl of Strafford', *Economic History Review*, 2nd series, XI (1958-9), 227-48

Corry, S. R. Lowry-, Earl of Belmore, 'James Spottiswoode, Bishop of Clogher (1621-1644)', *U.J.A.*, 2nd series, Special Volume (1903), 83-133

Cowan, E. J., *Montrose. For Covenant and King* (London, 1977)

Cox, R., *Hibernia Anglicana* (2 vols. London, 1689-90)

Cregan, D. F., 'The Confederation of Kilkenny' in *The Irish Parliamentary Tradition*, ed. B. Farrell (Dublin, 1973), pp. 102-15

Cregan, D. F., 'The Confederation of Kilkenny; its Organisation, Personnel and History' (Ph.D. thesis, National University of Ireland, 1947)

Cregan, D. F., 'Daniel O'Neill, a royalist agent in Ireland, 1644-50', *I.H.S.* II (1940-1), 398-414

Davies, G., *Bibliography of British History, Stuart Period* (2nd edn. Oxford, 1970)

Dictionary of National Biography, ed. Stephen, L., and Lee, S. (63 vols. London, 1885-1900)

Dow, F. D., *Cromwellian Scotland, 1651-1660* (Edinburgh, 1979)

Dunlop, R., 'The Forged Commission of 1641', *English Historical Review*, II (1887), 527-33

Bibliography

Edwards, R. D., *An Atlas of Irish History* (London, 1973)

Fairley, J. A., 'Lord Sinclair, Covenanter and Royalist', *Transactions of the Buchan Field Club*, VIII (1904-5), 129-84

Fitzpatrick, T., 'Sir Phelim's Commission', *New Irish Review*, XXI (1904), 333-48

Fitzpatrick, T., *The Bloody Bridge and other papers relating to the Insurrection of 1641* (Dublin, 1903)

Fitzpatrick, T., 'The Ulster Civil War, 1641', *U.J.A.* N.S. XIII (1907), 133-42, 155-9, XIV (1908), 168-77, XV (1909), 7-13, 61-4

Gardiner, S. R., *History of the Great Civil War* (4 vols. London, 1893-4)

Gardiner, S. R., *History of the Commonwealth and Protectorate* (4 vols. London, 1903)

Gardiner, S. R., *History of England* (10 vols. London, 1883-4)

Giblin, C., 'The Franciscan Mission to Scotland, 1619-1647', *Proceedings of the Irish Catholic Historical Committee* (Dublin, 1957), 15-24

Gumble, T., *The Life of General Monck, Duke of Albermarle* (London, 1671)

Hamilton, Lord E. W., *The Irish Rebellion of 1641* (London, 1920)

Hamilton, C. L., 'Scotland, Ireland and the English Civil War', *Albion*, VII (Appalachian State University, 1975), 120-30

Hayes, R. J., *Manuscript Sources for the History of Irish Civilisation* (11 vols. Boston, 1965)

Hazlett, H., 'The Financing of the British Armies in Ireland, 1641-9', *I.H.S.* I (1938-9), 21-41

Hazeltt, H., 'A History of the Military Forces operating in Ireland, 1641-9' (Ph.D. thesis, Queen's University, Belfast, 1938)

Hazlett, H., 'The Recruitment and Organisation of the Scottish Army in Ulster, 1642-9' in *Essays in British and Irish History in honour of James Eadie Todd*, ed. H. A. Cronne, T. W. Moody and D. B. Quinn (London, 1949), 107-33

Hill, G., *An Historical Account of the Macdonnells of Antrim* (Belfast, 1873)

Hill, G., 'The Stewarts of Ballintoy: with notices of other families in the district in the seventeenth century', *U.J.A.* N.S. VI (1900), 17-23, 78-89, 142-61, 218-23, VII (1901), 9-17

Hyde, E., Earl of Clarendon, *History of the Rebellion and Civil Wars in England*, ed. W. D. Macray (6 vols. Oxford, 1888)

Hyde, E., Earl of Clarendon, *History of the Rebellion and Civil Wars in Ireland* (3rd edn. London, 1740)

Jope, E. M., 'Scottish Influences in the North of Ireland: Castles with Scottish Features', *U.J.A.* 3rd series, XIV (1951), 31-47

Kearney, H. F., *Strafford in Ireland, 1633-41. A Study of Absolutism* (Manchester, 1959)

Lewis, S., *Topographical Dictionary of Ireland* (2 vols. London, 1850)

Lindley, K. J., 'The Impact of the 1641 Rebellion upon England and Wales, 1641-5', *I.H.S.* XVIII (1972-3), 143-76

Loder, J. de V., *Colonsay and Oronsay in the Isles of Argyll* (Edinburgh, 1935)

Love, W. D., 'Civil War in Ireland: Appearances in Three Centuries of Historical Writing', *Emory University Quarterly*, XXII (1966), 57-72

Lowe, J., 'The Glamorgan Mission', *Studia Hibernica*, 4 (1964), 155-96

Lowe, J., 'Charles I and the Confederation of Kilkenny, 1643-9', *I.H.S.* XIV (1964), 1-19

Lowe, J., 'The Earl of Antrim and Irish Aid to Montrose in 1644', *Irish Sword*, IV (1959-60), 191-8

Lowe, J., 'The Negotiations between Charles I and the Confederation of Kilkenny, 1642-9' (Ph.D. thesis, University of London, 1960)

Lowe, J., 'Some Aspects of the Wars in Ireland', *Irish Sword*, IV (1959-60), 81-7

MacCormack, J. R., 'The Irish Adventurers and the English Civil War', *I.H.S.* X (1956-7), 21-58

Bibliography

McCoy, G. A. Hayes-, 'The Battle of Benburb' in *The Irish at War* (Cork, 1964), 47-58

McCoy, G. A. Hayes-, 'Gaelic Society in Ireland in the late Sixteenth Century', *Historical Studies*, IV (1963), 45-61

McCoy, G. A. Hayes-, *Irish Battles: a Military History of Ireland* (London, 1969)

McCoy, G. A. Hayes-, 'O'Mellan's Account of the Battle of Benburn, 1646' in *Feilscríbhinn Torna: Essays and Studies presented to Professor Tadhg ua Donnchadha*, ed. S. Power (Cork, 1947)

McCoy, G. A. Hayes-, *Scots Mercenary Forces in Ireland, 1565-1603* (Dublin, 1937)

McCoy, G. A. Hayes-, 'Strategy and Tactics in Irish Warfare, 1593-1601', *I.H.S.* II (1940-1), 255-79

McCracken, E., *The Irish Woods since Tudor Times. Distribution and Exploitation* (Newton Abbot, 1971)

MacCurtain, M., *Tudor and Stuart Ireland* (Dublin and London, 1972)

Macdonald, A. J. and A. M., *The Clan Donald* (3 vols. Inverness, 1896-1904)

McKechnie, H., *The Lamont Clan* (Edinburgh, 1938)

Mackenzie, A., *History of the Macdonalds and Lords of the Isles* (Inverness, 1881)

Mackenzie, A., *History of the Monros of Foulis* (Inverness, 1898)

McKerral, A., *Kintyre in the Seventeenth Century* (Edinburgh, 1948)

McKerral, A., 'West Highland Mercenaries in Ireland', *S.H.R.* XXX (1951), 1-14

McSkimin, S., *The History and Antiquities of the County of the Town of Carrickfergus* (new edn. Belfast, 1909)

Marshall, J. J., *History of Charlemont and Mountjoy Forts* (Dungannon, 1921)

Mathew, D., *Scotland under Charles I* (London, 1955)

Maurice, Sir F. B., *The History of the Scots Guards* (2 vols. London, 1934)

Maxwell, M. Perceval-, 'The adoption of the Solemn League and Covenant by the Scots in Ulster', *Scotia. American-Canadian Journal of Scottish Studies*, II (1978), 3-18.

Maxwell, M. Perceval-, 'Strafford, the Ulster-Scots and the Covenanters', *I.H.S.* XVIII (1972-3), 524-51.

Maxwell, M. Perceval-, 'The Ulster Rising of 1631 and the depositions', *I.H.S.* XXI (1978-9), 144-67.

Maxwell, M. Perceval-, *The Scottish Migration to Ulster in the Reign of James I* (London, 1973)

Monroe, H., *Foulis Castle and the Monroes of Lower Iveagh* (London, 1929)

Moody, T. W., *The Londonderry Plantation, 1609-41* (Belfast, 1939)

Moody, T. W., 'The Treatment of the Native Population under the scheme for the Plantation of Ulster', *I.H.S.* I (1938-9), 59-63

Moody, T. W., Martin, F. X., and Byrne, F. J., eds. *A New History of Ireland, III: Early Modern Ireland, 1534-1691* (Oxford, 1976)

O'Connell, J. J., *The Irish Wars: a Military History of Ireland* (Dublin, c. 1920)

O'Danachair, C., 'Montrose's Irish Regiments', *Irish Sword*, IV (1959-60), 61-7

O'Domhnaill, S., 'Warfare in Sixteenth Century Ireland', *I.H.S.* V (1946-7), 29-54

O Mordha, P., 'The Battle of Clones, 1643', *Clogher Record*, IV, no. 3 (1962), 148-54

Paul, Sir J. B., *The Scots Peerage* (9 vols. Edinburgh, 1904-14)

Prendergast, J. P., *The Cromwellian Settlement of Ireland* (3rd edn. Dublin, 1922)

Prendergast, J. P., 'The Ulster Creaghts', *Journal of the Royal Society of Antiquaries of Ireland*, III (1855), 420-30

Read, J. M., 'Atrocity Propaganda and the Irish Rebellion', *Public Opinion Quarterly*, II (1938), 229-44

Scott, H., ed. *Fasti Ecclesiae Scoticanae* (9 vols. Edinburgh, 1915-50)

Bibliography

Stevenson, D., *Alasdair MacColla and the Highland Problem in the Seventeenth Century* (Edinburgh, 1980)

Stevenson, D., 'Conventicles in the Kirk, 1619-37: The Emergence of a Radical Party', *Records of the Scottish Church History Society*, XVIII (1972-4), 99-114

Stevenson, D., 'The Deposition of Ministers in the Church of Scotland under the Covenanters, 1638-51', *Church History*, 44 (1975), 321-35

Stevenson, D., 'The Desertion of the Irish by Coll Keitach's Sons, 1642', *I.H.S.* XXI (1978-9), 75-84

Stevenson, D., 'The Financing of the Cause of the Covenants, 1638-51', *S.H.R.* LI (1972), 89-123

Stevenson, D., 'The Irish Franciscan Mission to Scotland and the Irish Rebellion of 1641', *Innes Review*, XXX (1979), 54-61

Stevenson, D., 'The King's Scottish Revenues and the Covenanters, 1625-1651', *Historical Journal*, XVII (1974), 17-41

Stevenson, D., 'The Massacre at Dunaverty, 1647', *Scottish Studies*, XIX (1975), 27-37

Stevenson, D., 'The Myth of the Founding of the Scots Guards in 1642'. *S.H.R.* LVI (1977), 114-18

Stevenson, D., 'The Radical Party in the Kirk, 1637-45', *Journal of Ecclesiastical History*, XXV (1974), 135-65

Stevenson, D., *Revolution and Counter-Revolution in Scotland* (London, 1977)

Stevenson, D., *The Scottish Revolution, 1637-44. The Triumph of the Covenanters* (Newton Abbot, 1973)

Terry, C. S., *The Life and Campaigns of Alexander Leslie, First Earl of Leven* (London, 1899)

Warner, F., *The History of the Rebellion and Civil War in Ireland* (2 vols. London, 1768)

Wedgwood, C. V., *The King's Peace, 1637-41* (London, 1955)

Wedgwood, C. V., *The King's War, 1641-7* (London, 1958)

Wedgwood, C. V., *Thomas Wentworth, First Earl of Strafford, 1593-1641. A Revaluation* (London, 1961)

INDEX

References to illustrations are italicised. 'NS' stands for New Scots or New Scot, i.e., the Scottish Army in Ireland or its officers and men. All NS officers are identified as such, and their regiment and rank in the army is given.

Aberdeen, 31, 67-8, 75, 141, 156; battle of, 174, 177
Aboyne, Lord, *see* Gordon, James
Adair, Captain Alexander (NS: Lindsay's), 334
Adair, Archibald, Bishop of Killala, 20-1
Adair, Patrick, 76, 225, 306
defence of NS, 297-8
Adair of Kinhilt, Sir Robert, 21, 263, 266, 273, 280, 282, 287
horse troop of, 74, 151, 263
Adventurers' Act, 60-1
Alexander, Jean, Lady Montgomery, 288
Alford, battle of, 174, 179
Ancrum, earl of, *see* Ker, Robert
Anderson, David (NS clerk of council of war), 70
Annesley, Arthur, 1st earl of Anglesey (1661-86), 207, 247
Antrim, 275
Antrim, County, 5, 8-9, 13-14, 39, 301, 306
Glens of, 4, 112, 115
presbytery of, 291
Route of, 112, 215; (1639), 18-19, 22, 33; (1641), 41, 95, 98-9; (1642), 104, 110-12, 114-15, 117-19, 296; (1644), 153, 162, 173; (1645), 182, 197, 216-17; (1646), 231; (1647), 249; (1649), 268, 271-2; (1650s), 287
Antrim, earls and marquis of, *see* MacDonnell, Randal
Archer, Patrick, 172
Ardnamurchan, 33
Argyll (Argyllshire)
links with Ireland, 1
raid on (1643-4), 166
and 1644-7 war in Scotland, 168, 175, 177-9, 182, 184-7, 207, 211-12, 251
see also Highlands *and* Bishops' Wars
Argyll, earls and marquis of, *see* Campbell, Archibald
Argyll's regiment (NS)
musters of, 325-6, 338
raised, 62-3, 70, 72, 75-7; (1642), 110-11, 114-15, 126; (1644), 155, 179, 197; (1645), 179-80, 207; (1646), 214, 219, 231-2, 234; (1648), 257-60, 263, 266; (1649), 281

Armagh, 95, 108, 117, 131, 138, 194, 198, 227, 231
Armagh, County, 10, 127, 193-4
Arnot, Captain Charles (NS: Monro's), 330
Arnot, Captain Sir Charles (NS: Home's), 77, 336
Arran, 26, 31, 69
Athlone, 194
Atholl, 174
Auldearn, battle of, 174, 178
Ayr, 32, 37, 53-4, 69, 262, 284, 315
Ayrshire, 8, 204

Baillie, Lieutenant General William, 206, 261
Balfour, Sir William, 70, 74, 159
Ballahack, 172
Balledine, James, *see* Bannatyne
Ballintoy, 338
Ballycastle, 101, 114, 338
Ballygalley Castle, *314*
Ballymena, 101
Ballymoney, 101, 338
Ballyshannon, 127
Balmerino, Lord, *see* Elphinstone, James
Bangor, 12, 244, 274, 333-4
Bann, River, 121
Lower, 101, 111-12, 115, 123
Upper, 117, 192, 197-9, 227, 232
Bannatyne (Balledine), Major James (NS: Lifeguard of Horse), 78, 339
Bannerman, Captain Alexander (NS: Sinclair's), 337
Barclay, Major Alexander (NS: Glencairn's), 331
Barclay, Major George (NS: Monro's), 330
Barry, David, 1st earl of Barrymore (1628-42), 32
Beale, William, 207
Beg, Lough, 112
Belfast, 301
NS dispute with English parliament over, 209, 214, 238, 242, 244
NS seize, 161-3, 191, 196, 215; (1644), 150, 154, 160-3, 198, 203; (1646), 224, 238, 242, 244; (1648), 263, 266; (1649), 269, 272, 275, 282
Bell, Major Andrew (NS: Eglinton's), 333
Benburb, battle of, 110, 224-33, 247,

349

Index

Index

Index